essential
ASIAN

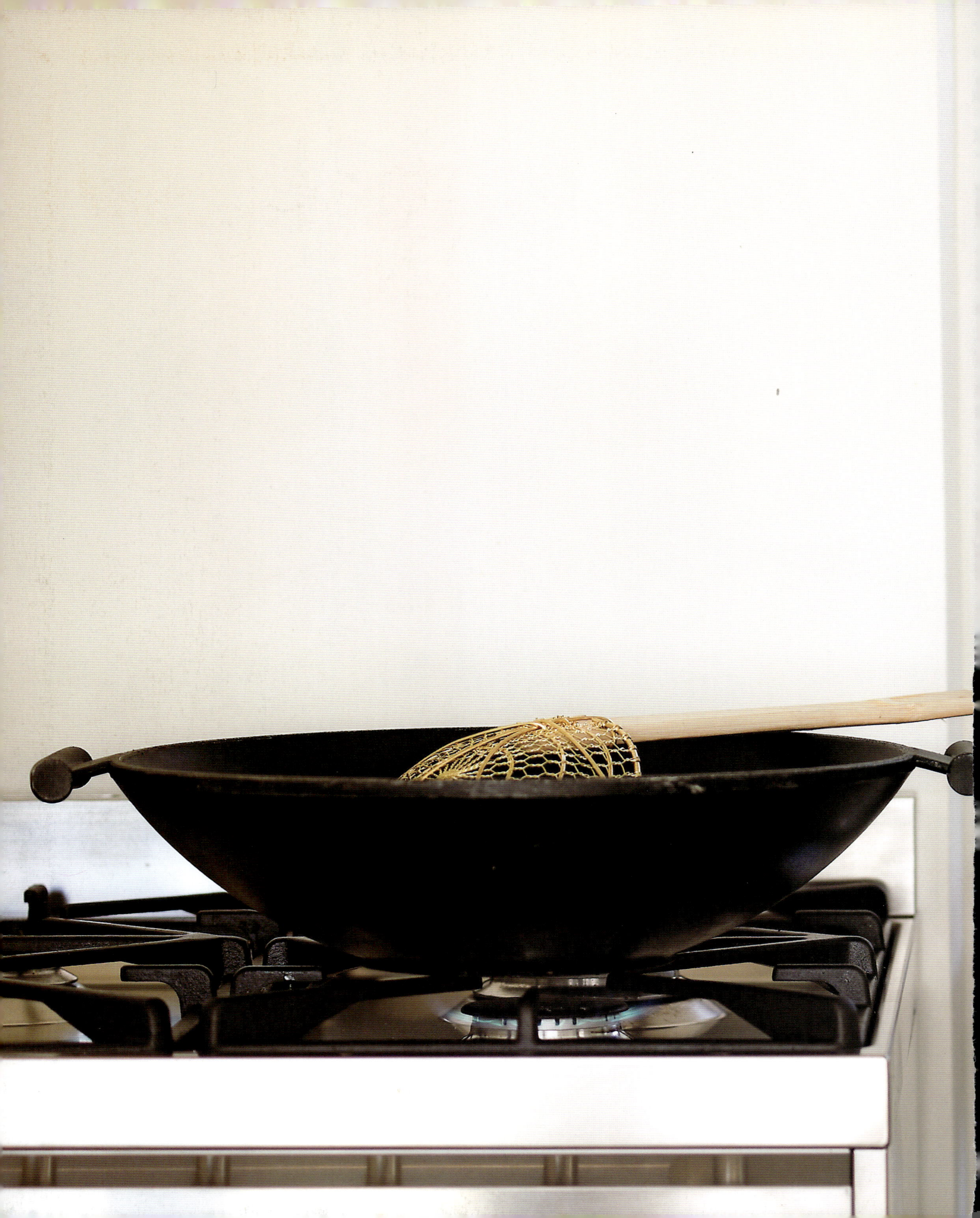

# essential ASIAN

bay books

This edition published in 2012 by Bay Books, an imprint of Murdoch Books Pty Limited
First published in 2011 by Murdoch Books Pty Limited

Murdoch Books Australia
Pier 8/9
23 Hickson Road
Millers Point NSW 2000
Phone: +61 (0) 2 8220 2000
Fax: +61 (0) 2 8220 2558
www.murdochbooks.com.au


Publisher: Kylie Walker
Project Editor: Melody Lord
Food Editor: Anneka Manning
Editor: Katri Hilden
Concept Design: Vivien Sung
Designer: Susanne Geppert

Photographers: Jared Fowler, Julie Renouf
Stylist: Cherise Koch
Food preparation: Alan Wilson

Text copyright © Murdoch Books Pty Limited
Based on The essential Asian cookbook, first published by Murdoch Books in 1996
Recipes developed in the Murdoch Books Test Kitchen
Design copyright © Murdoch Books Pty Limited

All rights reserved. No part of this publication may be reproduced, stored in a retrieval system or transmitted in any form or by any means, electronic, mechanical, photocopying, recording or otherwise, without the prior written permission of the publisher.

ISBN: 978-1-74266-699-0

Printed by 1010 Printing International Limited, China

IMPORTANT: Those who might be at risk from the effects of salmonella poisoning (the elderly, pregnant women, young children and those suffering from immune deficiency diseases) should consult their doctor with any concerns about eating raw eggs.

CONVERSION GUIDE: Cooking times may vary depending on the oven you are using. For fan-forced ovens, as a general rule, set the oven temperature to 20oC (35oF) lower than indicated in the recipe. We have used 20 ml (4 teaspoon) tablespoon measures. If you are using a 15 ml (3 teaspoon) tablespoon add an extra teaspoon for each tablespoon specified. We have used 60 g (Grade 3) eggs in all recipes.

# unique asia

Although it's been around for thousands of years, Asian food is suddenly the smart new food. Restaurant chefs from Vancouver to London are introducing Asian ingredients and cooking techniques into their repertoire, suburban greengrocers and supermarkets are stocking fresh coriander and lemongrass, and no wonder ... Asian food is fresh and colourful, full of flavour, and never boring or bland. With its emphasis on grains and vegetables, it is also healthy, cheap and often quick to prepare. Yet it's dangerous to generalise. Asian food is as multifaceted and diverse as European food. While neighbours share some common ingredients and cooking styles, Asian countries have developed cuisines that are uniquely their own. Sampling the food of each is truly an adventure. Selamat makan.

# contents

your asian kitchen ........... 8
   useful preparation techniques .. 11
   asian pantry ................... 12
china ....................... 20
indonesia ................... 44
singapore & malaysia ........ 66
the philippines ............. 86
thailand .................... 98
laos & cambodia ............ 126
vietnam .................... 136
korea ...................... 158
japan ...................... 170
india & pakistan ........... 192
burma ...................... 218
sri lanka .................. 228
desserts ................... 238
index ...................... 248

### special features

yum cha .................... 34
satays & kebabs ............ 52
finger food ................ 72
rice ....................... 94
curry pastes & powders .... 114
dipping sauces ............ 148
pickles & chutneys ........ 162
teas ...................... 180
raitas & relishes ......... 202
breads .................... 210

prawn laksa (page 77)

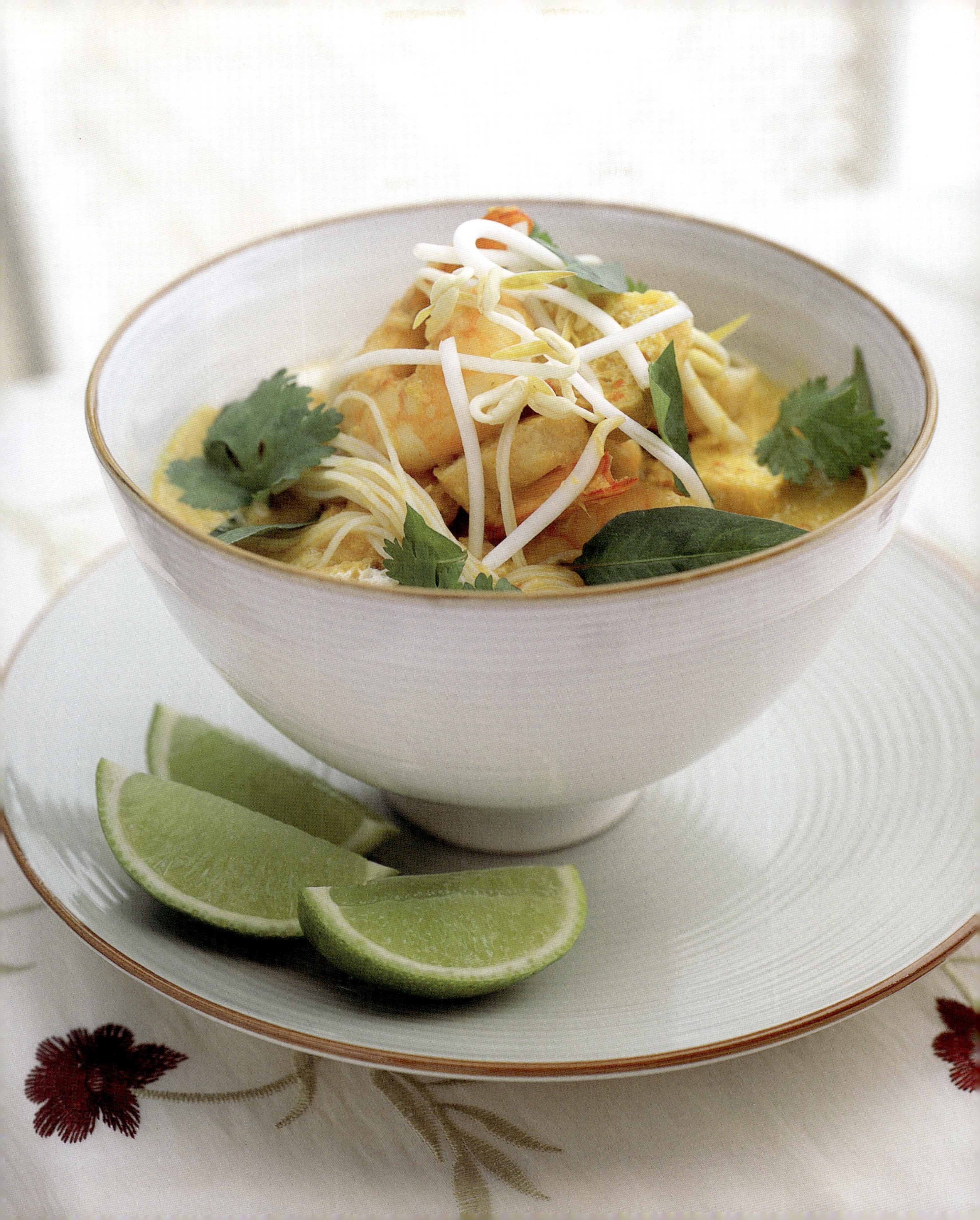

essential asian

# your asian kitchen

Although the countries of Asia are spread over nearly half the globe, the various Asian cuisines have many things in common. Spices and herbs are used extensively, rice is a staple, and many ingredients, such as noodles, soy sauce and tofu, have crossed borders from one country to another and continue to do so. Stir-frying, deep-frying and steaming are techniques used in most Asian countries and there is one utensil, the wok, that is found, in various forms and with different names, throughout Asia.

## the wok
No-one contemplating cooking a range of Asian dishes should be without a wok. With its large surface area and high sides it is ideal for stir-frying, and for deep-frying it requires less oil than a straight-sided pan. A wok is also ideal for steaming. Its sloping sides allow bamboo and metal steamers to fit firmly in place.

There are many types of woks available today. They vary in size, shape and the materials from which they are made. The traditional wok has a round base and is made from rolled steel. Woks are also made from stainless steel, cast iron and aluminium, and some have non-stick surfaces. A wok with a flat base is the best one to use on an electric stove because it will sit more directly and securely on the heating element, allowing a more even conduction of heat. Round-based woks work best on gas stoves; however a wok trivet may be necessary to provide stability. Choose a trivet which is open because this allows sufficient air to flow through, thus providing optimum heat. Gas stoves are ideal for wok cooking as the heat is delivered instantly and can be more easily controlled than it can with electric stoves.

## seasoning and cleaning a wok
Rolled steel woks — the standard inexpensive ones available from Chinese and Asian stores — are coated with a thin film of lacquer to stop them rusting while they are being shipped and stored before being sold. This film has to be removed before the wok can be used. The best way to do this is to place the wok on the stove top, fill it with cold water and add 2 tablespoons of bicarbonate of soda. Bring the water to the boil and boil rapidly for 15 minutes. Drain, scrub off the varnish with a plastic scourer, and repeat the process if any lacquer remains. Then rinse and dry the wok.

The wok is now ready to be seasoned. This is done to create a smooth surface which stops the food sticking to it or discolouring. Place the wok over low heat. Have a small bowl of oil, preferably peanut oil, nearby and scrunch a paper towel into a wad. When the wok is hot, wipe it with the wadded paper that has been dipped into the oil. Repeat the process with fresh paper until it comes away clean and without any trace of colour.

A seasoned wok should not be scrubbed. To wash a wok after cooking, use hot water and a sponge, or soak the wok in warm water and detergent if food is stuck to it. Dry it well after washing by heating it gently over low heat, and rubbing it all over with an oiled paper towel. Store the wok in a dry, well-ventilated place. Long periods in a dark, warm, airless cupboard can cause the oil coating to turn rancid. Using the wok frequently is the best way to prevent it from rusting.

## essentials for grinding
No Asian kitchen would be without some sort of grinding apparatus, usually a mortar and pestle. Ground spices quickly lose their flavour and aroma, so it is best to grind small amounts of whole spices when needed. While it is generally considered that a mortar and pestle gives the best results, an electric coffee grinder is ideal for this task: the motor, designed for hard beans, is strong enough to take the strain of grinding spices, the blades are low down and the bowl is appropriately small in size. If you cannot set aside a coffee grinder just for spices, grind a little rice to remove coffee flavours, and again after spices have been processed to remove their aromas.

Pounding the ingredients using a mortar and pestle is the best way to make curry and spice pastes, but if the paste is wet enough, a blender or food processor can be used.

## your asian kitchen

### essentials for cutting
Sharp, good-quality knives are essential as so much Asian cooking involves cutting up raw ingredients. For most jobs, a Western chef's knife is the easiest to handle. A medium-weight cleaver is useful when chopping a chicken Chinese-style. If preferred, a heavy-bladed chef's knife can be used. However, once you are used to the feel of it, a cleaver can be a very versatile instrument.

### steaming tips
Food that is steamed is cooked by the moist heat given off by steadily boiling water. To get the best results:
- Fill your wok or saucepan about one-third full with water. Place the steamer over the water to check that it is the correct level before you bring the water to the boil. It is important that you have enough, but not too much water, in your wok or pan. If there is too much water, it will boil up into the food and if you have too little water, it will quickly boil dry during cooking.
- When the water is boiling, arrange the food in the steamer and place it carefully in the wok.
- Cover the wok and maintain the heat so the water boils rapidly, allowing the steam to circulate evenly around the food.
- When lifting the lid on a wok while steaming is in progress, always lift it up and away from you like a shield so the skin on your wrist is not exposed to a blast of scalding steam.

Bamboo steamers placed over water in a wok are ideal for steaming dishes such as won tons and fish parcels.

Whole fish can be steamed on a serving plate placed on a wire rack in a wok.

### stir-frying tips
Stir-frying involves cooking small pieces of food over medium to high heat for a short period of time. To get the best results:
- Prepare all the ingredients before you start to cook. The meat is often cut into even, paper-thin slices, fast-cooking vegetables are evenly sliced or cut into small pieces, and slower-cooking vegetables are cut thinly or blanched before being added to the stir-fry. Once the slicing and cutting is done, all the ingredients for the sauce should be measured out. If rice or noodles are part of the dish, these should be ready to be added as well.
- Heat the wok before adding the oil.
- Heat the oil before adding the food. This ensures that the cooking time will be short and that the ingredients, especially meat, will be seared instantly, sealing in the juices and the flavour.
- Toss and turn food carefully while it cooks. Keeping it moving constantly ensures even cooking and prevents burning. Stir-fried vegetables should be crisp and meat tender and succulent.

### deep-frying tips
It is important to make sure that the wok or pan you are using for deep-frying is stable and secure on the stovetop, and you should never leave the kitchen while the oil is heating as it can quickly overheat and ignite. To get the best results:
- Add the oil, never filling the pan or wok more than half full, and heat over high heat. When the oil is the required temperature for deep-frying (180°C/350°F), it will start to move and a 3 cm (1¼ inch) cube of bread lowered into it will brown in just 15 seconds. Lower the heat to medium if that is all that is needed to maintain the right temperature.
- Carefully add the food to the oil with tongs and move small pieces around, gently turning them to ensure even cooking.
- When ready, carefully lift out the food with tongs, a wire mesh strainer or a slotted spoon and drain on a tray of paper towels.
- If you are frying in batches, keep the cooked food warm in a 180°C (350°F/Gas 4) oven.
- When frying food in batches, make sure you reheat the oil to the required temperature after each batch. Use a slotted spoon to remove any small fragments of food left in the oil as these will burn.

### curry pastes
In Thai and Indian markets, mounds of colourful curry pastes, made fresh each day, await the home cook. Red (from fresh or dried red chillies), yellow (turmeric) and green (fresh green chillies and fresh green herbs), they come in a range of strengths and blends. Ready-made curry pastes are available in jars and cans, but making your own will give you the best results. Make a batch of each of your favourite pastes and store them in the refrigerator. This will save time when you are preparing a meal. Fresh paste will keep for up to three weeks in an airtight container in the refrigerator. Alternatively, place tablespoons of paste in an ice cube tray, cover and freeze. When the paste is frozen, release the cubes into a freezer bag, and store in the freezer until required. Allow the cubes to defrost for 30 minutes

at room temperature before using them. Frozen paste will keep for up to four months.

## spices and blends

It is best to grind small amounts of whole spices when needed as ground spices quickly lose their flavour and aroma. Dry-roasting whole spices brings out the flavour and makes them easier to grind. You can dry-roast each spice individually or, if doing small quantities, together. Heat a clean, dry, heavy-based frying pan over low heat. Add the spices, stir constantly until aromatic and lightly browned, then turn onto a plate to cool. Ground spices can also be dry-roasted to make them more aromatic, but they will burn quickly and so need the very lowest heat. While freshly prepared spices produce the best results, it may often be convenient to prepare a quantity of spice blends (see page 114) such as Garam masala or Ceylon curry powder. These will last well if stored in airtight glass jars away from sunlight and heat.

## basic stocks

A number of recipes in this book include stock in the ingredients. The list of ingredients in a basic stock recipe can be modified to produce beef, chicken or seafood stock by varying the type of carcasses, bones or trimmings used and by following the cooking instructions for the type of stock. For chicken stock use chicken necks, feet or wings; for seafood stock, use fish heads or prawn heads and shells or lobster shells; and for beef stock, use bones, oxtail or shanks. Stock can be stored in the refrigerator for up to a week and in the freezer for up to six months.

1 kg (2 lb 4 oz) carcasses, bones or trimmings with fat removed
1 carrot, roughly chopped
3 red Asian shallots or 3 spring onions (scallions), roughly chopped
2 litres (70 fl oz/8 cups) cold water
5 cm (2 inch) piece fresh ginger, sliced
5 black peppercorns
2 garlic cloves, sliced

BEEF STOCK

1. Bake the beef bones in a baking dish, at 230°C (450°F/Gas 8) for 40 minutes, adding the carrots and shallots to the dish halfway through the cooking time.
2. Deglaze the baking dish with a little of the water and transfer the contents to a stockpot or large saucepan, with the remaining ingredients, including the remaining water, and bring to the boil. Remove any scum that has risen to the surface of the liquid.
3. Reduce the heat and simmer gently for 3 hours (or longer if you prefer a more concentrated stock). Occasionally remove any scum that rises to the top during simmering.
4. Strain the stock through a fine sieve, pressing the solids to extract all the liquid and then allow to cool. Remove any fat from the surface.

CHICKEN STOCK

1. Place the carcass or bones in a stockpot or large saucepan with the remaining ingredients and bring to the boil. Remove any scum that has risen to the surface of the liquid.
2. Reduce the heat and simmer for 1 hour. Occasionally remove any scum that rises to the top during simmering.
3. Strain the stock through a fine sieve and allow to cool. Remove any fat from the surface.

FISH STOCK

1. Cut the bones and fish trimmings into pieces, discard the eyes and gills. Soak the bones and trimmings in cold salted water for about 10 minutes to remove any blood. Break up prawn or lobster shells.
2. Place bones, trimmings or shells in a stockpot or large saucepan with the water and other ingredients and bring to the boil.
3. Simmer 20 minutes, skimming off the surface scum as it rises.
4. Strain the stock through a fine sieve and allow to cool.

VEGETABLE STOCK

For vegetable stock, increase the number of red Asian shallots to eight and use two extra carrots.

1. Put the chopped vegetables in a stockpot or large saucepan with the water and remaining ingredients. Bring to the boil and simmer for up to 1 hour.
2. Strain the stock through a fine sieve, pressing the vegetables with a ladle to extract all the liquid. Set aside to cool.

---

**Our star rating:**

When we test recipes, we rate them for ease of preparation. The following cookery ratings are used in this book:

✻   A single star indicates a recipe that is simple and generally quick to make, perfect for beginners.

✻✻   Two stars indicate the need for a little more care or a little more time.

✻✻✻   Three stars indicate special dishes that need more investment in time, care and patience, but the results are worth it. Even beginners can make these dishes as long as the recipe is followed carefully.

your asian kitchen

# useful preparation techniques

### chopping a chicken or duck, chinese-style

When cutting the chicken, bring the cleaver or knife down sharply in one clean stroke. With a dense bone mass, you may need to lift the blade with the food attached to it and bring it down sharply on the board again until the food is cleanly cut.

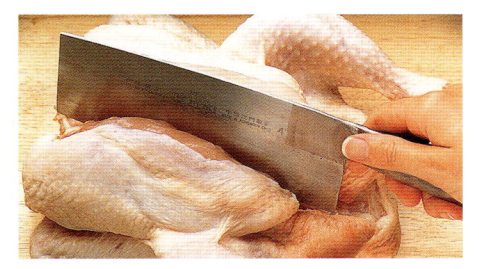

Cut the chicken in half by cutting along the breast bone, continuing down through the backbone.

Remove the wings, drumsticks and thighs. If you don't have a cleaver, use a heavy-bladed chef's knife.

Chop each large segment, such as the breasts or legs, into two or three pieces. The pieces must be a manageable size for handling with chopsticks.

### preparing meat

Many Asian dishes call for the meat to be very thinly sliced. If the meat is partially frozen, this makes it firmer and much easier to slice.

Trim all the fat and sinew from the meat and cut it across the grain.

### peeling prawns

Don't throw prawn heads and shells away but reserve them for use in stocks. They can be stored in the freezer for up to six months.

To peel prawns, break off the head then snap the shell away from the underbody. Depending on the recipe, either leave the tail intact or remove it by gently squeezing it off the body.

Cut down the back of the prawn with a sharp knife, then gently remove the vein.

### handling chillies

Take great care when chopping or seeding chillies. Capsaicin, the pungent substance that gives chillies their hot taste, can cause severe skin irritation and remains active even in dried chillies. Wear disposable rubber gloves and handle the chilli, especially the membrane and seeds, as little as possible. Don't touch your eyes or any other sensitive part of your body. Immediately after preparing chillies, dispose of the gloves, wash your hands, the board and utensils. If you like a hot flavour, leave the seeds and membrane (the hottest parts) in, but for a milder flavour, remove them.

To seed a chilli, use a sharp knife to cut off the stalk, slit open the chilli lengthways and scrape out the central membrane and seeds.

### preparing fresh herbs and spices

A number of herbs and spices are used time and time again in Asian recipes. The way they are prepared depends on the dish. Some common methods are shown here. Many fresh herbs are essential in Asian cooking. Wrap any leftover herbs in a damp paper towel and refrigerate them in a sealed plastic bag in the vegetable crisper for up to a week.

essential asian

# asian pantry

Today many of the herbs, spices, vegetables and other items needed to create authentic Asian dishes are readily available, often in local supermarkets. The more unusual ingredients can be found in Asian food stores.

## asian greens

*Bok choy* (pak choy), also known as Chinese chard and Chinese white cabbage, has fleshy white stems and leaf ribs and green flat leaves. It has a slightly mustardy taste. Separate the leaves and wash well. The stems can be sliced thinly and eaten raw. Look for firm stems and unblemished leaves. A smaller type is baby bok choy or Shanghai bok choy.

*Chinese broccoli* (gai larn), also known as Chinese kale, has smooth, round stems sprouting large dark green leaves and small, white flowers. The juicy stems, trimmed of most of their leaves, are the piece of the plant which is most commonly eaten. Chinese broccoli has a similar flavour to Western broccoli, but without the large flower heads.

*Chinese cabbage* (wong bok), also known as celery cabbage and napa cabbage, has a long shape and closely packed broad, pale green leaves with wide white stems. It has a delicate mustard-like flavour. This is the vegetable which is always used in cabbage rolls and Kimchi.

*Choy sum*, also known as Chinese flowering cabbage, is slimmer than bok choy and has smooth green leaves and pale green stems with clusters of tiny yellow flowers on the tips of the inner shoots. The leaves and flowers cook quickly and have a light, sweet mustard flavour; the stems are crunchy and juicy.

## bamboo shoots

Crunchy in texture and with a subtle, refreshing taste, these are the edible young shoots of certain types of bamboo. Spring bamboo shoots are pale, fibrous and chunky; winter shoots are thinner with a finer texture and more pronounced flavour. Fresh bamboo shoots are hard to get and, if not already prepared, must be peeled then parboiled to remove toxic hydrocyanic acid — boil whole or in chunks for five minutes or more until they no longer taste bitter. Tinned and bottled bamboo shoots are the ones most often used.

## banana leaves

The large flexible leaves of the banana plant are used throughout Asia to wrap foods for steaming or baking. They keep the food moist and impart a mild flavour. Remove the thick central stalk, rinse the leaves well and blanch in boiling water to soften. Foil can be used instead.

## basil

Three varieties of basil are used in Asian cooking, all of which are very aromatic. If any are unavailable, substitute fresh sweet basil or fresh coriander in cooked dishes and fresh mint in salads.

*Thai basil* (bai horapha) has slightly serrated green leaves on purple stems. It has a sweet anise flavour and is used in stir-fries, red and green curries, shredded in salads and as a garnish for soups.

*Lemon basil* (bai manglaek) has small green leaves with a lemony scent and peppery flavour. It is usually sprinkled over salads or used in soups. Its seeds (luk manglak) are used in desserts and drinks.

*Purple or holy basil* (bai kaphrao) has narrow, dark, purple-reddish tinged leaves with a pungent, clove-like taste. It is added to stir-fries and strong-flavoured curries.

## your asian kitchen

### black beans

One of the most popular flavours in the cooking of southern China, black beans are dried soy beans that have been cooked and fermented with salt and spices. They are soft with a sharp, salty taste. Wash before use and lightly crush or chop to release the aroma. Black beans are available in tins or packets; once opened, refrigerate in an airtight container.

### black fungus

Also known as cloud ear, this tree fungus has little flavour of its own, but is valued for its crunchy texture. It is most commonly available in its dried form, which looks like wrinkled black paper. Before use, soak in warm water for 15–30 minutes, until the fungus swells to about five times its size.

### candlenuts

These hard, waxy, cream-coloured nuts are similar in shape to macadamia nuts, but have a drier texture. Roasted, then ground, they are used to thicken and enrich curries and sauces. They should be stored in the freezer to prevent them becoming rancid. Candlenuts should not be eaten raw as the oil is thought to be toxic. They are quite safe once cooked.

### cardamom

This very aromatic spice of Indian origin is available as whole pods, whole seeds or ground. The pale green oval pods, each up to 1.5 cm (⅝ inch) long, are tightly packed with sweetly fragrant brown or black seeds. When using whole pods, lightly bruise them before adding them to the dish.

### chinese barbecued pork

Also known as char siu, these are strips of pork fillet which have been marinated in five spice powder, soy sauce, sugar and red colouring (usually from annatto seeds) then barbecued over charcoal.

### chillies, dried

*Chilli flakes* are dried red chillies that have been crushed, usually with the seeds (leaving in the seeds increases the hotness). Store in a cool, dark place in an airtight container.

*Common dried red chillies* will vary in size and degree of heat, depending on which type has been dried (it is not usually specified). Soak in hot water until soft, then drain well before adding to dishes. If preferred, remove the seeds before soaking to reduce the fieriness. The tiny chillies are very hot.

*Chilli powder* is made by finely grinding dried red chillies and can vary in hotness from mild to fiery. Chilli flakes can be substituted, but not Mexican chilli powder, which is mixed with cumin.

### chillies, fresh

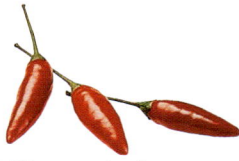

*Bird's eye chillies* are the hottest chillies of all. Measuring from 1–3 cm (½–1¼ inches) long, they are available fresh, dried or pickled in brine.

*Small red chillies*, approximately 5 cm (2 inches long) and also very hot, are the chillies used to make chilli powder and chilli flakes.

*Medium chillies*, 10–15 cm (4–6 inches) long, are the most commonly used in Indonesian and Malaysian cooking. Long thin chillies, these are hot but not overpowering.

*Large red and green chillies*, 15–20 cm (6–8 inches) long, are thicker than medium chillies. The ripened ones are very hot.

essential asian

### coconut cream and milk

*Coconut cream*, also known as thick coconut milk, is extracted from the flesh of fresh coconuts and has a thick, almost spreadable consistency. It is very rich.

*Coconut milk* is extracted from fresh coconut flesh after the cream has been pressed out and has a much thinner consistency. Once opened, the milk or cream does not keep, so freeze any that is left over. (Coconut milk is not the clear, watery liquid found in the centre of fresh coconuts — this is coconut water or coconut juice.)

### coriander (cilantro)

Also known as cilantro and Chinese parsley, all parts of this aromatic plant — seeds, leaves, stem and root — can be eaten. The leaves add an earthy, peppery flavour to curries, and are used in salads and as a garnish, and the stems and roots are ground for curry pastes. Dried coriander is not a suitable substitute.

### crisp fried garlic and onion

These are very thin slices of garlic cloves and onions or red Asian shallots that have been deep-fried until they are crisp. They are used as a crunchy, flavoursome garnish, and can be added to peanut sauce. Available in packets or they can be prepared at home.

### cumin

These small, pale brown, aromatic seeds have a warm, earthy flavour. In its ground form cumin is an essential component of curry pastes and many other spice mixes. Black cumin is smaller and darker than common cumin and sweeter in taste.

### curry leaves

These small, shiny, pointed leaves from a tree native to Asia have a spicy aroma and are used in southern India, Sri Lanka and Malaysia to impart a distinctive flavour to curries and vegetable dishes. Use as you would bay leaves, and remove before serving. Bay leaves are not a substitute.

### daikon

Much used in Japanese and Chinese cooking, this carrot-shaped white radish can be up to 30 cm (12 inches) long, depending on the variety, and has a similar taste and texture to ordinary radish. It is added to stewed dishes, grated and mixed with finely chopped chillies as a relish, pickled in a solution of soy sauce, or thinly sliced as a garnish. The leaves can also be eaten raw in a salad or sautéed.

### dashi

Made from dried kelp (kombu) and dried fish (bonito), this is the basic stock used in Japanese cooking. It is available as granules or a powder which are dissolved in hot water to make up the stock (page 174).

### eggplant (aubergine)

Native to Asia, eggplants come in a variety of shapes, sizes and colours. Tiny *pea eggplants* are small, fat, green balls which grow in clusters, and can be bitter in flavour. They are used whole in Thai curries or raw in salads.
*Slender eggplants*, also called baby and Japanese eggplants, are used in Indian curries and vegetarian cooking, where they readily absorb the flavours; the common eggplant used in Western cooking can be substituted.

### fenugreek

An important ingredient in Indian cooking, the dried seeds from this plant of the pea family are small, oblong and orange-brown. They are usually gently dry-fried, then ground and added to a curry paste; in Sri Lanka a few seeds are often used whole in seafood curries. Use sparingly, as the flavour can be bitter. Pungently flavoured fenugreek leaves are cooked in vegetable dishes or ground as part of a tandoori marinade.

### fish sauce

This thin, clear, brown, salty sauce with its characteristic 'fishy' smell and pungent flavour is an important ingredient in Thai, Vietnamese, Laotian and Cambodian cooking. It is made from prawns (shrimp) or small fish that have been fermented in the sun. Its strong flavour diminishes when cooked with other ingredients. It is also used as a base for dipping sauces. There is no substitute.

## your asian kitchen

### five-spice
This fragrant, ready-mixed ground spice blend is used extensively in Chinese cooking. It contains star anise, sichuan peppercorns, fennel, cloves and cinnamon. Use sparingly, as it can overpower lesser flavours.

### flours
*Asian rice flour* is ground from medium-grain rice. It has a fine, light texture and is used in noodles, pastries and sweets, and gives a crunch to fried foods if used in a batter or as a coating.

*Atta flour*, also known as chapatti flour, is a finely milled, low-gluten, soft-textured, wholemeal wheat flour used for making Indian flatbreads, especially parathas and chapattis. Plain wholemeal (whole-wheat) flour can be used instead — sift first and discard the bran — but may result in heavier, coarser bread.

*Besan* is a pale yellow, finely milled flour made from dried chickpeas. Used in Indian cooking to make batters, doughs, dumplings and pastries, it has a slightly nutty aroma and taste.

### galangal
This root is similar in appearance to its close relative, ginger, but it is a pinkish colour and has a distinct peppery flavour. Use fresh galangal if possible. When handling take care not to get the juice on your clothes or hands, as it stains. Dried galangal, sold in slices, must be soaked in hot water before use. It can also be bought sliced and bottled in brine. Galangal powder is also known as Laos powder.

### garam masala
This is a mixture of ground spices which usually includes cinnamon, black pepper, coriander, cumin, cardamom, cloves and mace or nutmeg, although it can sometimes be made with mostly hot spices or with just the more aromatic spices. Commercially made mixtures are available, but garam masala is best freshly made (page 114).

### garlic
Garlic is used in large quantities in all Asian cooking except Japanese. Asian varieties are often smaller and more potent than those used in Western cooking. The pungent flavour is released when a clove is cut; crushing releases maximum flavour. The strength diminishes with cooking. Pickled garlic is used as a garnish and relish.

### garlic chives
Also known as Chinese chives, these thick, flat, garlic-scented chives, stronger in flavour than the slender variety used in Western cooking, are particularly prized when topped with the plump, edible flowerbud.

### ginger
This spicy-tasting root, used fresh, is an indispensable ingredient in every Asian cuisine. Look for firm, unwrinkled roots and store them wrapped in foil in the refrigerator. The brown skin is usually peeled off before use. Ground ginger cannot be substituted for fresh.

### golden mountain sauce
This thin, salty, spicy sauce made from soy beans is used as a flavouring in Thai cooking. It is available from Asian food stores.

### hoisin sauce
From China, this thick, red-brown sauce is made from soy beans, garlic, sugar and spices and has a biting, sweet-spicy flavour. It is used in cooking and as a dipping sauce, usually with meat and poultry dishes.

### kaffir lime (makrut) leaves
Native to Southeast Asia, this variety of lime tree has fragrant double-lobed green leaves and bears a dark green, knobbly fruit. The leaves and fruit zest are added to curries and other dishes to give a citrus tang (the fruit is not very juicy and is seldom used). Remove the coarse central vein from the leaves and tear or shred; pare or grate zest from limes. Leaves and limes are available fresh from Asian food stores; leftover fresh leaves can be frozen in airtight plastic bags. Also available are dried leaves and dried zest; these must be soaked in water before use. Fresh young lemon leaves and strips of zest from a standard lime can be substituted, but the flavour will not be quite the same.

### kecap manis
Also known as sweet soy sauce, this thick, dark sauce is used in Indonesian cooking as a seasoning and condiment, particularly with satays. A substitute can be made by gently simmering 250 ml (9 fl oz/1 cup) dark soy sauce with 6 tablespoons treacle and 3 tablespoons soft brown sugar until the sugar has dissolved.

### lemongrass
This long, grass-like herb has a citrus aroma and taste. Trim the base, remove the tough outer layers and finely slice, chop or pound the white interior. For pastes and salads, use the tender, white portion just above the root. The whole stem, trimmed, washed thoroughly and bruised with the back of a knife, can be added to simmering curries and soups (remove before serving). Dried lemon grass is rather flavourless so it is better to use lemon zest, although this will not duplicate the flavour of lemongrass.

### miso
A staple of the Japanese diet, this is a protein-rich, thick, fermented paste made from soy beans and other ingredients, including wheat, rice or barley. It has a pungent, wine-like taste. Varieties include

red, brown, light brown, yellow and white, each having a distinctive flavour and varying in texture from smooth to chunky. Lighter coloured miso is usually milder and sweeter. .

## mushrooms

*Dried Chinese mushrooms*, also called Chinese black mushrooms, grow on fallen trees. Their distinctive woody, smoky taste is intensified by the drying process, and they are rarely eaten fresh.

*Shiitake mushrooms* are closely related to the Chinese black mushroom and are the most commonly used mushrooms in Japan. They have a rich smoky flavour, are grown on the bark of a type of oak tree, and are used fresh and dried. The fresh mushroom has a fleshy, golden-brown cap and a woody stem.

*Straw mushrooms* are named for their growing environment — straw — and are cultivated throughout Asia. They have globe-shaped caps, no stems and a musty flavour. They are available in tins; drain and rinse before use.

## noodles

*Dried mung bean vermicelli*, also known as cellophane or glass noodles, are wiry, threadlike, translucent noodles made from mung beans. They are tough and difficult to break, and need to be soaked in warm water and cut into shorter lengths for boiling or adding to stir-fries. Small bundles of unsoaked noodles can be deep-fried for use as a garnish.

*Dried rice stick noodles* are short, translucent flat noodles made from rice. They need to be soaked in hot water until soft, then cooked briefly in boiling water until just tender. They are then ready for use in stir-fries, soups and salads.

*Dried rice vermicelli* are thin translucent noodles. They need to be soaked in hot water until tender, then drained thoroughly before being used in stir-fries and soups. Small bundles of unsoaked noodles quickly deep-fried until they expand can be used as a garnish.

*Dried soba (buckwheat) noodles*, a speciality of northern Japan, these are beige-coloured noodles made from a mixture of buckwheat and wheat flours; some are lightly flavoured with green tea or beetroot. They are cooked in simmering water, then rinsed in cold water to cool before use. The noodles are served either hot in a broth or cold in a salad with a dipping sauce.

*Fresh egg noodles* are made from egg and wheat flour and are pale yellow. Before use they need to be shaken apart and cooked in boiling water until tender and then drained well. In addition to their traditional use in chow mein, Chinese stir-fries and short soups, they are now used in recipes from many other parts of Asia. Fresh egg noodles are sold in a range of widths. The noodles are dusted lightly with flour before packing to stop them sticking together. Store in the refrigerator.

*Fresh rice noodles* are made from a thin dough of rice flour. This is steamed, giving it a firm, jellylike texture, then lightly oiled and packaged ready for use — the pearly white noodles need only to be rinsed in hot water to loosen and separate, then drained. They come in thick or thin varieties, or in a sheet that can be cut to the desired width. Rice noodles are used in stir-fries or added to simmered dishes near the end of cooking. Store in the refrigerator.

*Harusame noodles* are very fine, white, almost translucent Japanese noodles. They are made from mung bean flour and are very similar to dried mung bean vermicelli — use in the same way.

*Hokkien noodles*, also known as Fukkien and Singapore noodles, are thick, yellow, rubbery-textured noodles made from wheat flour. They are packaged cooked and lightly oiled and need no preparation before use — simply stir-fry or add to soups or salads. Store them in the refrigerator.

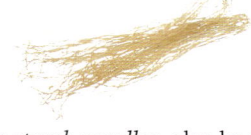

*Potato starch noodles*, also known as Korean vermicelli, are long, fine, green-brown, translucent dried noodles. Cook in rapidly boiling water for about 5 minutes or until plump and gelatinous; overcooking will cause them to break down and become gluggy.

*Shanghai noodles* are white noodles made from wheat flour and water, similar to the somen noodles of Japan. They can be thick or thin. Cook in boiling water before use. Fresh noodles are dusted lightly with flour before packing to stop them sticking together. Store in the refrigerator. Dried wheat flour noodles are also available.

*Shirataki noodles* are a basic ingredient in the Japanese dish sukiyaki. Thin, translucent and jellylike, they are made from the starchy root of a plant known in Japan as devil's tongue. They have a crunchy texture, but little flavour. They are available fresh or dried. Store the fresh noodles in the refrigerator.

*Somen noodles* are fine, white, dried wheat flour noodles used in Japanese cooking. Before use cook in boiling water for 1 to 2 minutes, then rinse in cold water.

*Udon noodles* are white, wheat flour noodles used in Japanese cooking. They may be round or flat. Cook in boiling water or miso soup before use. Udon noodles are used in Japanese soups and simmered dishes, or can be braised and served with a sauce.

## nori

This is the most common form of dried seaweed used in Japanese and Korean cooking. It comes in paper-thin sheets, plain or roasted. Before use it can be toasted lightly over a naked flame to freshen and produce a nutty flavour. Keep in an airtight container at room temperature or in the freezer.

## okra

Also known as ladies' finger, this vegetable of African origin is a narrow, five-sided seed pod, pointed at one end and containing small white seeds; it has a gelatinous quality when it is cooked. It is much used in Indian cooking where it is added to curries and stir-fries, stuffed with spices and deep-fried, or pickled. It is available fresh in summer, and it is also sold frozen, dried and in tins.

## oyster sauce

This is a thick, smooth, deep brown sauce with a rich, salty, slightly sweet flavour. Although it is made from oysters and soy sauce, it does not have a fishy taste.

## palm sugar (jaggery)

Made from the boiled-down sap of several kinds of palm tree, including the palmyra palm and the sugar palm of India, palm sugar ranges in colour from pale golden to deep brown. It is sold in block form or in jars. Palm sugar is thick, crumbly or solid and can be melted or grated before adding to sauces or dressings. Soft brown sugar can be substituted.

## pawpaw, green

Green pawpaw is an underripe pawpaw. It is commonly used in Asian salads and some soups, or as a snack with sugar and chilli. To shred green pawpaw, peel and slice finely. It is sometimes lightly blanched before shredding.

## plum sauce

This sweet-sour, jam-like sauce is used in Chinese cooking and as a dip with fried meats and snacks. It is made from plums, garlic, ginger, sugar, vinegar and spices.

## rice vinegar

This clear, pale yellow, mild and sweet-tasting vinegar is made from fermented rice. Diluted white wine vinegar or cider vinegar can be substituted.

## rice wine

*Mirin* is a golden-coloured, sweetened rice wine. In Japanese cooking it is added to salad dressings and marinades, mixed with soy sauce to make teriyaki sauce, or used as a seasoning in long-simmered dishes. Sweet sherry can be substituted.

*Sake* is a clear-coloured Japanese liquor made from fermented rice. In cooking it is combined with soy sauce and sugar to make rich-tasting sauces, added to water for steaming or simmering, or used as a tenderiser. It should be used within a year of manufacture and, once a bottle is opened, the sake begins to lose flavour.

*Shaoxing rice wine*, also known as Chinese rice wine, is amber-coloured with a rich, sweetish taste. It adds flavour and aroma to a variety of Chinese dishes and is also used in marinades and sauces. Dry sherry can be substituted, but grape wines are not suitable.

## saffron powder and threads

Made from the dried, thread-like stigmas of the saffron crocus, this costly spice adds a vivid yellow colour and subtle flavour to food. It is available as bright orange threads (sealed in small glass jars or tiny plastic packets) or ground into powder (the powder is often adulterated and of inferior quality).

Saffron threads are usually soaked in a little warm water before use to release the colour into the water. The threads and liquid are then both added to the dish to give the characteristic saffron colouring.

## sambal oelek

This is a hot paste made from fresh red chillies mashed and mixed with salt and vinegar. It is used as a relish in Indonesian and Malaysian cooking, and can be used as a substitute for fresh chillies in most recipes. Covered, it will keep for months in the refrigerator. Available ready-made or see recipe on page 114.

## sesame oil

This dark amber, very aromatic oil is pressed from toasted white sesame seeds and has a strong, rich, nutty flavour. It is used as a flavouring in Chinese, Korean and Japanese dishes. It is not used for frying. Store in a cool dark place, but not in the refrigerator where it will turn cloudy. Cold-pressed sesame oil, pressed from the raw seed, has little flavour and cannot be used as a substitute.

## sesame seeds

The tiny, oval, oil-rich seeds of an annual herb, sesame seeds are used throughout Asia for their flavour and their high protein content.

*Black sesame seeds* have a more earthy taste. They are used in sesame and seaweed sprinkle, a Japanese condiment, and in some Chinese desserts.

*Japanese sesame seeds* are plumper and have a nuttier flavour than other sesame seeds.

*White sesame seeds* are most common. Toasted and crushed, they are an essential ingredient in Japanese and Korean dressings, dipping sauces and marinades. Whole seeds are used as a garnish for many dishes and breads, and pressed seeds are made into a variety of pastes.

## shallots, red asian

Small reddish-purple onions, these grow in bulbs, like garlic, and are sold in segments that look like large cloves of garlic. They have a concentrated flavour and are easy to slice and grind. If unavailable, substitute French shallots (eschalots) or brown or red onions.

## shrimp paste

Also known as blachan, this type of shrimp paste, used in the cooking of Thailand, Malaysia and Indonesia, is made from prawns or shrimps that have been dried, salted and pounded. Sold in blocks, it has a very pungent odour and when opened should be wrapped in plastic, sealed in an airtight container and stored in the refrigerator or freezer (this is to reduce the smell as the paste itself does not require refrigeration). Use sparingly; always roast or fry before adding to a dish.

*Bagoong*, also known as shrimp sauce, is a soft, thick paste made from shrimps or prawns that have been salted and fermented in earthenware pots. It has a strong odour and taste, and is used in cooking and as a condiment, particularly in the Philippines.

## snake beans

Also called long beans and yard-long beans, this legume grows wild in tropical Africa, where it probably originated. Growing to 38 cm (15 inches) and longer, with a crunchy texture and similar taste to green beans, it comes in two varieties: pale green with slightly fibrous flesh, and darker green with firmer flesh. Use as fresh as possible; snip off the ends and cut into bite-sized lengths. Stringless green beans can be substituted.

## soy sauce

Soy sauce is made from fermented soy beans, roasted grain (usually wheat, but sometimes barley or rice) and salt. Dark-coloured with a rich, salty flavour, it is widely used in Asian cooking, and is essential for flavour and colour in many dishes.

*Light soy sauce* is thinner, lighter in flavour, but saltier and pale golden in colour. It is suitable for soups, seafood, vegetable dishes and dipping sauces.

*Japanese soy sauce*, also known as shoshoyu, is less salty and much lighter and sweeter than standard soy sauce, but not thick, like kecap manis. It is used in cooking and as a condiment. Because it is naturally brewed, it must be refrigerated after opening.

## spring onions (scallions)

Also called green onions, these are immature onions which are pulled before the bulb has started to form and sold in bunches with the roots intact. Discard the roots and base of the stem, and wash stem leaves well before use. Spring onions add colour and a mild onion flavour and they need little, if any, cooking.

## star anise

The dried, star-shaped seed pod of a tree native to China, star anise adds a distinctive aniseed taste to long-simmered meat and poultry dishes and is one of the components of five spice powder. Available whole or ground.

## your asian kitchen

### tamarind

The tropical tamarind tree bears fruit in pods like large, brown beans. The fruit is tart-tasting and has fibrous flesh and a flat stone at the centre. An essential flavour in many Asian dishes, tamarind is available in bottles as tamarind concentrate (also known as tamarind purée), a rich brown, ready-to-use liquid, and as blocks of compressed pulp that has to be soaked, kneaded and seeded (page 101).

### tofu

Also called bean curd, tofu is a processed extract of soy beans. It is an excellent source of protein, and is available fresh or deep-fried.

*Fresh tofu* comes in two forms: a soft, white variety, also known as silken tofu, which is cut into cubes and used in Japanese dishes; and a firmer variety which is cut into cubes, wedges or slices and deep-fried. Both are available in blocks sealed in plastic; once opened, store in the refrigerator in water that is changed daily and use within a few days. Fresh tofu has little flavour when uncooked, but absorbs other flavours.

*Tofu pouches,* also known as inari, are deep-fried, thin slices of tofu, crisp on the outside and dry on the inside, that can be cut open to form bags. In Japan inari are stuffed with vegetables or vinegar-seasoned rice; they can also be added whole or shredded to soups and other dishes.

*Tofu puffs* are cubes of tofu that have been deep-fried until they are puffed and golden. They can be cooked in their own right with a strongly flavoured sauce, used in vegetarian cooking and braised dishes, added to salads or used as garnish for soups, or cut open and filled.

### turmeric

This is a bitter-tasting spice which comes from the root of a plant related to ginger. It is used for its intense, bright yellow-orange colour and, dried and ground, it is the main ingredient in many curry powders. The fresh root is used in the same way as fresh ginger root — peel away the skin and finely slice, chop or grate the flesh. Store in a plastic bag in the refrigerator.

### vietnamese mint

Also called laksa leaf and Cambodian mint, this trailing herb with narrow, pointed, pungent-tasting leaves does not belong to the mint family, despite its common name. It has a flavour resembling coriander but slightly sharper, and is eaten raw in salads, or as an accompaniment to most Vietnamese dishes.

### wasabi paste

Also known as Japanese horseradish, this is a pungent paste made from the knobbly green root of the wasabi, a plant native to Japan. It is used as a condiment with seafoods and is extremely hot, so use it sparingly.

### water chestnuts

These white-fleshed roots of a variety of water grass are prized for their semi-sweet taste and crisp texture, which is retained when cooked. They are used throughout China and Southeast Asia in both savoury and sweet dishes. Available tinned and sometimes fresh; cut off the woody base, peel away the papery skin, and cover in water to stop discolouring.

### watercress

Watercress was introduced into Asia by the British. Its peppery flavour is added to soups and steamed vegetables in Chinese cooking, and it is used in salads in Thailand, Laos and Vietnam and as a garnish in Japan.

### wrappers

These are thin pieces of dough used to wrap bite-sized savoury fillings. They are available fresh and frozen; defrost before use. When filling, work with one at a time and keep the others covered with a damp cloth to prevent them from drying out.

*Dried rice paper wrappers* are paper-thin, round, square or triangular, and are made from a dough of rice flour, water and salt. Soak them in water before use so they soften and become pliable.

*Gow gee wrappers* are round and made from a wheat flour and water dough.

*Spring roll wrappers* are square or round, and made from a wheat flour and egg dough.

*Won ton wrappers* are thin squares of a wheat flour and egg dough.

# china

Chinese cuisine uses the freshest meats and vegetables in an endless variety of ways to create dishes in perfect balance. The Cantonese cooking of the south makes use of the abundant fresh ingredients, steamed or stir-fried over high heat and flavoured with just a little soy sauce, ginger or spring onion. Peking cuisine struggles with the harsher climate and geography of the north, but the result is wonderfully warming hotpots, dumplings and the famous Peking duck. Sichuan food is flavoured with vibrant chillies and spices, while ingredients in Shanghai are braised slowly to create rich meat and fish dishes.

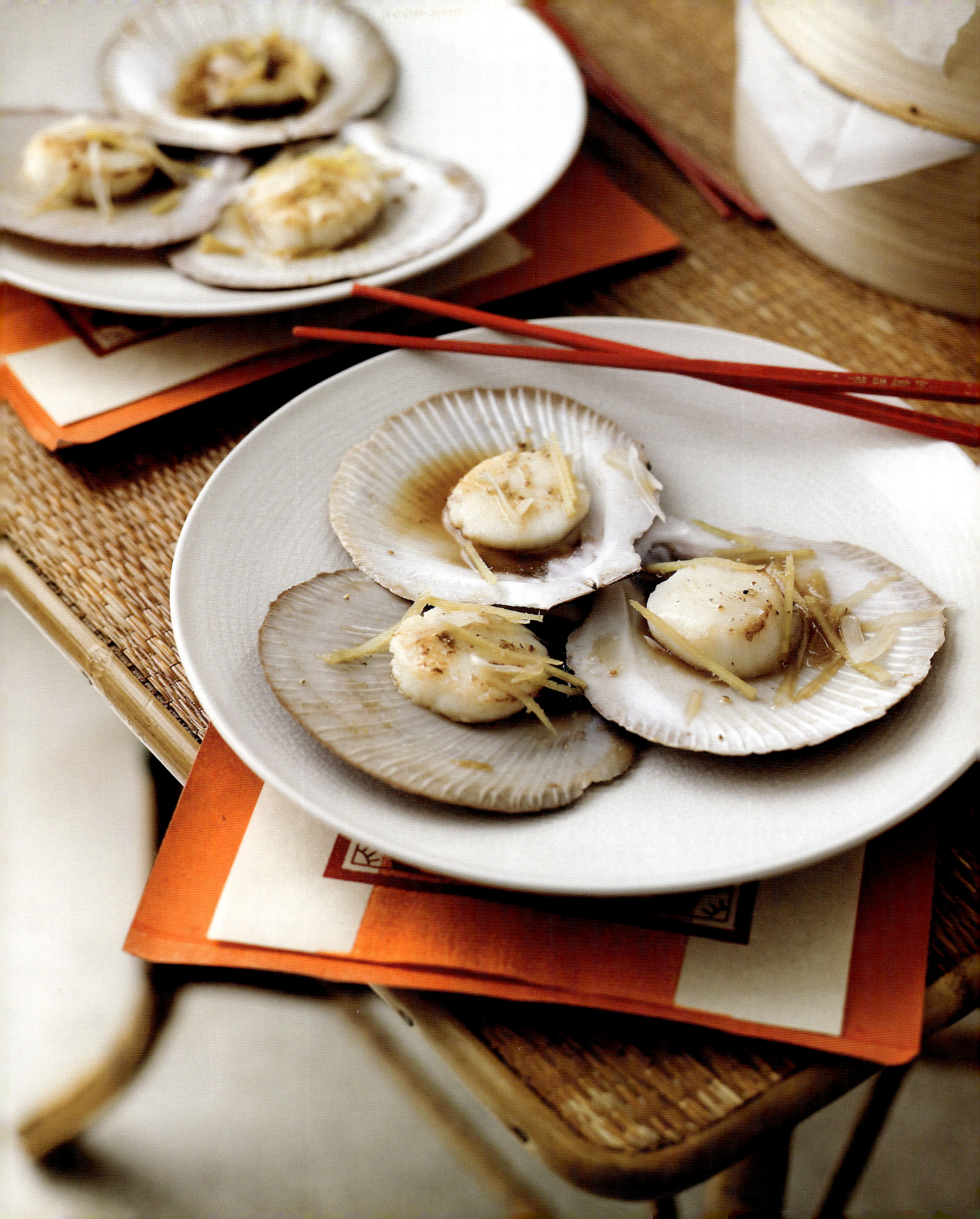

## prawn omelette with oyster sauce

✻ ✻ ✻

Preparation time: 30 minutes
Cooking time: 25 minutes
Serves 4

2 dried Chinese mushrooms
400 g (14 oz) raw prawns (shrimp)
3 tablespoons oil
5 cm (2 inch) piece fresh ginger, finely grated
125 g (4½ oz/½ cup) drained, tinned bamboo shoots, roughly chopped
6 spring onions (scallions), chopped
5 eggs
½ teaspoon ground white pepper
3 tablespoons oyster sauce
2 tablespoons soy sauce
2 tablespoons shaoxing rice wine (Chinese rice wine)
2 teaspoons cornflour (cornstarch)
spring onion (scallions), thinly sliced, extra, to garnish

**1** Soak the mushrooms in hot water for 20 minutes. Drain, then squeeze to remove any excess liquid. Discard the stems and chop the caps finely.
**2** Meanwhile, peel the prawns and gently pull out the vein from each prawn back, starting at the head end. Roughly chop the prawn meat.
**3** Heat 1 tablespoon of the oil in a wok and stir-fry the ginger and prawn meat over very high heat for 2 minutes; transfer to a plate. Add the bamboo shoots, spring onion and mushroom and stir-fry for 1 minute. Transfer to a plate and wipe the wok clean with paper towels.
**4** Whisk the eggs, 2 tablespoons of water and ½ teaspoon of salt and pepper in a bowl until foamy. Add the remaining oil to the wok, swirling it around to coat the base and side. Heat the wok until it is extremely hot and the oil is slightly smoking. Give the egg mixture a quick whisk again and immediately pour it into the very hot wok, swirling the wok a little so that the egg mixture coats the side to about 5 mm (¼ inch) thickness. Cook for 2–3 minutes, swirling the wok to form an even omelette, until the mixture is just cooked through. Transfer carefully to a board.
**5** Use a slotted spoon to drain away any juices from the prawn and bamboo shoot mixture and spoon down one side of the omelette. Roll up the omelette to enclose the filling. Cut into portions and place on a serving platter.
**6** Add the oyster sauce, soy sauce and rice wine to the wok. Mix the cornflour and 1 tablespoon of water and add to the wok, stirring constantly until the sauce boils and thickens slightly. Spoon over the omelette, garnish with spring onion and serve.

Finely slice the soaked mushrooms. (Everything should be ready before you begin cooking.)

Swirl the wok so the egg mixture coats the sides. (Make sure the wok is extremely hot before adding the egg as the heat produces the traditionally lacy appearance of the omelette.)

Divide the omelette into 4 or 5 sections with a spatula, and turn each section over to cook the other side.

china

# cantonese lemon chicken

✹ ✹

Preparation time: **15 minutes**
Cooking time: **25 minutes**
Serves **4**

500 g (1 lb 2 oz) boneless, skinless chicken breasts
1 egg yolk, lightly beaten
2 teaspoons soy sauce
2 teaspoons dry sherry
3 teaspoons cornflour (cornstarch)
60 g (2¼ oz/½ cup) cornflour (cornstarch), extra
2½ tablespoons plain (all-purpose) flour
oil, for deep-frying
4 spring onions (scallions), thinly sliced, to garnish

LEMON SAUCE
80 ml (2½ fl oz/⅓ cup) lemon juice
2 tablespoons sugar
1 tablespoon dry sherry
2 teaspoons cornflour (cornstarch)

**1** Cut the chicken into long strips, about 1 cm (½ inch) wide, and then set aside. Combine the egg, 1 tablespoon water, soy sauce, sherry and cornflour in a small bowl and mix until smooth. Pour the egg mixture over the chicken, mixing well, and set aside for 10 minutes.
**2** Sift the extra cornflour and plain flour together onto a plate. Roll each piece of chicken in the flour, coating each piece evenly, and shake off the excess. Place the chicken in a single layer on a plate.
**3** Fill a wok one-third full of oil and heat to 180°C (350°F), or until a cube of bread dropped into the oil browns in 15 seconds. Carefully lower the chicken pieces into the oil, in batches, and cook for 2 minutes, or until golden brown. Remove the chicken with a slotted spoon and drain on paper towels. Repeat with the remaining chicken. Set aside while preparing the sauce. Reserve the oil in the wok.
**4** To make the lemon sauce, combine 2 tablespoons water, the lemon juice, sugar and sherry in a small saucepan. Bring to the boil over medium heat, stirring until the sugar has dissolved. Mix the cornflour and 1 tablespoon water and add to the lemon juice mixture, stirring constantly until the sauce boils and thickens. Set aside.
**5** Just before serving, reheat the oil in the wok to very hot, add all the chicken pieces and deep-fry for 2 minutes, or until very crisp and a rich golden brown. Remove the chicken with a slotted spoon and drain well on paper towels. Pile the chicken onto a serving plate, drizzle over the sauce, sprinkle with the spring onion and serve immediately.

NOTE: The first deep-frying of the chicken pieces can be done several hours in advance.

## shaoxing rice wine

China's best known rice wine is shaoxing, from Chekiang (Zhejiang) province in the northeast of the country, where for more than 2000 years it has been made from a mixture of glutinous rice, millet, yeast and local spring water. In China it is known as 'carved flower', for the pattern on the urns in which it is stored, and also as 'daughter's wine', because traditionally some is put away at the birth of a daughter to be drunk at her wedding. Shaoxing is aged for at least 10 years and sometimes as long as 100 years. As a drink to accompany food it should be served warm in small cups without handles.

## dried mandarin and tangerine peel

The dried fruit of these closely related Asian fruit trees is used in Chinese cooking to add a rich, fruity flavour. The peel is added dried to long-simmered dishes; otherwise it is either soaked in warm water to soften, or very finely chopped. It is available in packets from Asian food stores, or the peel of the fresh fruit can be slowly dried until hard in a very slow oven or in the sun.

## beef with mandarin

❋

Preparation time: 30 minutes
Cooking time: 5 minutes
Serves 4

2 teaspoons soy sauce
2 teaspoons dry sherry
1 teaspoon chopped fresh ginger
1 teaspoon sesame oil
350 g (12 oz) rib eye steak, thinly sliced
1 tablespoon peanut oil
¼ teaspoon ground white pepper
2 teaspoons finely chopped dried mandarin or tangerine peel
2 teaspoons soy sauce, extra
1½ teaspoons caster (superfine) sugar
1½ teaspoons cornflour (cornstarch)
80 ml (2½ fl oz/⅓ cup) beef stock
steamed rice, to serve

1  Combine the soy sauce, sherry, ginger and sesame oil in a bowl. Add the beef and stir to coat in the marinade. Set aside for 15 minutes.

2  Heat the peanut oil in a wok, swirling gently to coat the base and side. Add the beef and stir-fry over high heat for 2 thinly sliced minutes, or until the beef changes colour. Add the white pepper, peel, extra soy sauce and sugar and stir-fry briefly.

3  Mix the cornflour and a little of the stock and add to the wok. Add the remaining stock and stir until the sauce boils and thickens. Serve with steamed rice.

# china

## chicken and sweet corn soup

❋

Preparation time: 30 minutes
Cooking time: 10 minutes
Serves 4

200 g (7 oz) boneless, skinless chicken breast
2 egg whites
750 ml (26 fl oz/3 cups) chicken stock
250 g (9 oz/1 cup) creamed corn
1 tablespoon cornflour (cornstarch)
2 teaspoons soy sauce
2 spring onions (scallions), thinly sliced, to garnish

**1** Wash the chicken under cold water and pat dry with paper towels. Place the chicken in a food processor and process until finely chopped. Add 1 teaspoon salt.
**2** Lightly beat the egg whites in a small bowl until foamy. Fold the egg whites into the chopped chicken.
**3** Bring the stock to the boil and add the creamed corn. Mix the cornflour in 1 tablespoon water and add to the soup, stirring until the mixture thickens.
**4** Reduce the heat and add the chicken mixture, breaking it up with a whisk. Allow to heat through, without boiling, for about 3 minutes. Season to taste with soy sauce. Serve immediately, sprinkled with the spring onion.

## won ton soup

❋ ❋

Preparation time: 40 minutes
Cooking time: 5 minutes
Serves 4–6

4 dried Chinese mushrooms
250 g (9 oz) raw prawns (shrimp)
250 g (9 oz) minced (ground) pork
1 tablespoon soy sauce
1 teaspoon sesame oil
2 spring onions (scallions), finely chopped
1 teaspoon finely grated fresh ginger
2 tablespoons tinned drained, chopped water chestnuts
250 g (9 oz) won ton wrappers
cornflour (cornstarch), to dust
1.5 litres (52 fl oz/6 cups) chicken or beef stock
4 spring onions (scallions), extra, thinly sliced, to garnish

**1** Soak the mushrooms in hot water for 20 minutes. Drain, then squeeze to remove any excess liquid. Discard the stems and chop the caps finely. Meanwhile, peel the prawns and gently pull out the dark vein from each prawn back, starting at the head end. Finely chop the prawn meat and mix in a bowl with the mushrooms, pork, soy sauce, sesame oil, chopped spring onion, ginger and water chestnuts.
**2** Cover the won ton wrappers with a damp tea towel (dish towel) to prevent them drying out. Taking one wrapper at a time, place a heaped teaspoon of mixture on the centre. Moisten the edges with water, fold in half diagonally, seal, and then bring the two opposite points together and seal again. Place on a tray dusted with the cornflour. Cook the won tons in a saucepan of rapidly boiling water for 4–5 minutes or until the filling is cooked.
**3** In a separate saucepan bring the stock to the boil. Remove the won tons with a slotted spoon and place in serving bowls. Scatter the sliced spring onion over the top. Ladle the stock over the won tons.

won ton soup

## fried and steamed scallops with ginger

✳ ✳

Preparation time: 10 minutes
Cooking time: 10 minutes
Serves 4 as an entrée

12 scallops on the half shell
¼ teaspoon ground white pepper
2 tablespoons soy sauce
2 tablespoons dry sherry
2 tablespoons oil
8 cm (3¼ inch) piece fresh ginger, shredded
1 spring onion (scallion), white part only, sliced into long shreds

**1** Sprinkle the scallops with the white pepper. Mix together the soy sauce and sherry in a bowl.
**2** Heat the oil in a large, heavy-based frying pan until very hot. Carefully add several shells, scallop-side down, and cook for 30 seconds to sear. Turn face-up and place in a shallow dish. Repeat with the remaining scallops.
**3** Sprinkle the scallops with the sherry and soy mixture and scatter a few shreds of ginger and spring onion over each of them.
**4** Fill a wok about one-third full with water and bring to a simmer. Put a steamer lined with baking paper in the wok and place six scallops on it. Cover the steamer tightly and steam the scallops for 1 minute. If they aren't cooked, they may need about 30 seconds more. Remove and set aside to keep warm. Repeat with the remaining scallops. Serve immediately.

*fried and steamed scallops with ginger*

## crystal prawns

✳ ✳

Preparation time: 15 minutes + 30 minutes marinating time
Cooking time: 10 minutes
Serves 4

750 g (1 lb 10 oz) raw prawns (shrimp)
2 spring onions (scallions), roughly chopped
1 tablespoon cornflour (cornstarch)
1 egg white, lightly beaten
125 g (4½ oz) sugar snap peas or snow peas (mangetout)
1 small red capsicum (pepper)
1 tablespoon oyster sauce
2 teaspoons dry sherry
1 teaspoon cornflour (cornstarch), extra
1 teaspoon sesame oil
oil, for deep-frying
½ teaspoon crushed garlic
½ teaspoon finely grated fresh ginger

**1** Peel the prawns and gently pull out the dark vein from each prawn back, starting at the head end. Place the prawn shells, heads and the spring onion in a saucepan with enough water to cover them. Bring the water to the boil; simmer, uncovered, for 15 minutes. Strain the liquid into a bowl, discarding the shells. Reserve 125 ml (4 fl oz/½ cup) of the prawn stock. Place the prawns in a glass bowl. Add 1 teaspoon salt and stir briskly for a minute. Rinse under cold, running water. Repeat the

# china

procedure twice, using ½ teaspoon salt each time. Rinse the prawns thoroughly the final time. Pat dry with paper towels.

**2** Combine the cornflour and egg white in a bowl, add the prawns and place in the refrigerator, covered, for 30 minutes.

**3** Wash and string the sugar snap peas. Cut the capsicum into thin strips. Combine the reserved prawn liquid, oyster sauce, sherry, extra cornflour and sesame oil in a small bowl. Heat the oil in a wok over medium-high heat until hot, and deep-fry the prawns in batches for 1–2 minutes or until lightly golden. Carefully remove from the oil with tongs or a slotted spoon. Drain on paper towels and keep warm.

**4** Carefully pour off all but 2 tablespoons of the oil (if you are keeping it to re-use, only use it for seafood, as the prawn flavour will have permeated). Add the garlic and ginger to the wok and stir-fry for 30 seconds. Add the peas and capsicum and stir-fry over high heat for 2 minutes. Add the combined sauce ingredients and cook, stirring, until the sauce boils and thickens. Add the prawns and stir to combine. Serve immediately.

## crispy fried crab

✿ ✿ ✿

Preparation time: 30 minutes + 2 hours freezing + overnight marinating time
Cooking time: 15 minutes
Serves 4 as an entrée

1 kg (2 lb 4 oz) live mud crab
1 egg, lightly beaten
1 red chilli, thinly sliced
½ teaspoon crushed garlic
¼ teaspoon ground white pepper
oil, for deep-frying

SEASONING MIX
4 tablespoons plain (all-purpose) flour
4 tablespoons rice flour
3 teaspoons caster (superfine) sugar
1 teaspoon ground white pepper

**1** Place the crab in the freezer for 2 hours or until it is absolutely immobile and dead (this is the most humane way to kill crab or lobster).

**2** Scrub the crab clean of any mossy bits. Pull back the apron from the underbelly and snap off. Twist off the legs and claws. Pull the body apart and remove the feathery gills and internal organs. Using a cleaver, chop the body into four pieces. Crack the claws with a good hit with the back of the cleaver.

**3** Combine the egg with the chilli, garlic, ½ teaspoon salt and the white pepper in a large bowl. Put the crab pieces in the mixture; cover and refrigerate overnight.

**4** To make the seasoning mix, sift all the seasoning ingredients together on a large plate. Dip all the crab segments in the seasoning and dust off any excess.

**5** Heat the oil in a wok and deep-fry the claws for 7–8 minutes, the body portions for 3–4 minutes and the legs for 2 minutes. Drain on paper towels and serve.

NOTE: Eat the crab with your fingers. This dish should be served on its own, without rice.

*crispy fried crab*

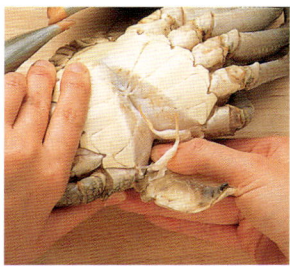

Pull back the apron from the underbelly and snap it off. Pull the body apart.

Remove the feathery gills and internal organs.

Use the back of the cleaver to crack the claws, or you may break the blade.

essential asian

## stir-fried beef and snow peas

✳

Preparation time: 15 minutes
Cooking time: 5 minutes
Serves 4

400 g (14 oz) rump steak, thinly sliced
2 tablespoons soy sauce
½ teaspoon grated fresh ginger
2 tablespoons peanut oil
200 g (7 oz) snow peas (mangetout), topped and tailed
1½ teaspoons cornflour (cornstarch)
125 ml (4 fl oz/½ cup) beef stock
1 teaspoon soy sauce, extra
¼ teaspoon sesame oil
steamed rice, to serve

1  Place the beef in a bowl. Mix the soy sauce and ginger and stir through the beef to coat it.
2  Heat the peanut oil in a wok or heavy-based frying pan, swirling gently to coat the base and side. Add the beef and snow peas and stir-fry over high heat for 2 minutes, or until the beef changes colour.
3  Mix the cornflour in a little of the stock and add to the wok with the remaining stock, extra soy sauce and the sesame oil. Stir until the sauce boils and thickens. Serve with steamed rice.

NOTE: If time allows, place the beef in the freezer for 30 minutes before slicing. This will firm it and make slicing it finely much easier.

chilli spare ribs

## chilli spare ribs

✳ ✳

Preparation time: 20 minutes
Cooking time: 1 hour
Serves 4

750 g (1 lb 10 oz) pork spare ribs
1 tablespoon peanut oil
2 teaspoons finely chopped garlic
60 ml (2 fl oz/¼ cup) dry sherry
1 tablespoon chilli bean paste or sambal oelek
500 ml (17 fl oz/2 cups) water
2 teaspoons hoisin sauce
3 teaspoons caster (superfine) sugar
1 tablespoon soy sauce, preferably dark

1  Place the pork in a large saucepan with enough water to cover. Bring to the boil, reduce the heat, simmer for 5 minutes; drain well.
2  Place all the remaining ingredients and the pork in a wok or deep, heavy-based saucepan. Cover and simmer for 45 minutes. Drain, reserving 250 ml (9 fl oz/1 cup) of liquid. Heat a clean wok or heavy-based frying pan and sear the pork pieces to brown them.
3  Add the reserved cooking liquid and cook over medium heat until it forms a glazed coating for the pork.
4  Chop the pork into 3 cm (1¼ inch) pieces and pour the sauce over them.

# china

## noodles with prawns and pork

✳

Preparation time: 20 minutes
Cooking time: 10 minutes
Serves 4

10 raw large prawns (shrimp)
200 g (7 oz) Chinese barbecued pork (char siu)
500 g (1 lb 2 oz) shanghai noodles
60 ml (2 fl oz/¼ cup) peanut oil
2 teaspoons finely chopped garlic
1 tablespoon black bean sauce
1 tablespoon soy sauce
1 tablespoon white vinegar
60 ml (2 fl oz/¼ cup) chicken stock
1 stalk celery, cut into fine strips
1 carrot, cut into thin matchsticks
125 g (4½ oz) bean sprouts, trimmed
3 spring onions (scallions), finely shredded

**1** Peel the prawns and gently pull out the dark vein from each prawn back, starting at the head end. Cut the pork evenly into thin slices.
**2** Cook the noodles in a large saucepan of rapidly boiling water until just tender. Drain and set aside.
**3** Heat the oil in a wok or heavy-based frying pan, swirling gently to coat the base and side. Add the garlic and cook, stirring, until pale gold. Add the prawns and pork, and stir for 3 minutes, or until the prawns are pink. Add the black bean sauce, soy sauce, vinegar and stock. Stir-fry over high heat until the mixture is heated through and the sauce is absorbed.
**4** Add the celery and carrot and cook for 1 minute. Serve the noodles topped with the stir-fry and sprinkled with the bean sprouts and spring onions.

**NOTE:** Barbecued pork can be bought ready-cooked from speciality Chinese stores. If you enjoy a little 'fire' in your food, add a garnish of chopped chillies or a splash of chilli oil at the end of cooking.

## chilli bean paste

A thick, red-brown sauce made from soy beans, dried red chilli, garlic and spices, chilli bean paste has a hot, nutty, salty taste and is much used in the fiery dishes of Sichuan and Hunan in central western China. Available in jars from Asian food stores and some supermarkets. Sambal oelek has a different flavour but can be used as a substitute.

essential asian

## stir-fried prawns with leeks

Preparation time: 15 minutes
Cooking time: 5 minutes
Serves 6

800 g (1 lb 12 oz) raw king prawns (shrimp)
2 young leeks, white parts only
1 red chilli
3 cm (1¼ inch) piece fresh ginger
3 tablespoons oil
2 teaspoons light soy sauce
1 tablespoon mirin
80 ml (2½ fl oz/⅓ cup) chicken stock
1 teaspoon cornflour (cornstarch)
steamed rice, to serve

1  Peel the prawns and gently pull out the dark vein from each prawn back, starting at the head end.
2  Rinse the leeks well. Cut them first into 4 cm (1½ inch) lengths and then lengthways into fine shreds. Slit open the chilli, remove and discard the seeds and cut the flesh into fine shreds. Cut the ginger into fine shreds.
3  Heat a little of the oil in a wok over high heat and stir-fry the prawns in batches until just pink; remove from the wok. Add the remaining oil and stir-fry the leek, chilli and ginger over high heat for 40 seconds, then push to one side of the wok. Return the prawns to the wok and stir-fry for 1½ minutes, or until just cooked through.
4  Add the soy sauce and mirin to the wok. Mix the chicken stock and cornflour and pour in. Cook on high heat, stirring, until thickened. Serve immediately with steamed rice.

stir-fried prawns with leeks

## chinese fried rice

Preparation time: 15 minutes
Cooking time: 10 minutes
Serves 4

2 eggs, lightly beaten
1 onion
4 spring onions (scallions)
250 g (9 oz) piece ham
2 tablespoons peanut oil
2 teaspoons lard (optional)
270 g (9½ oz/1⅓ cups) long-grain rice, cooked and cooled (see Note)
40 g (1½ oz/¼ cup) frozen peas
2 tablespoons soy sauce
250 g (9 oz) cooked small prawns (shrimp), peeled

1  Season the eggs with salt and pepper.
2  Cut the onion into 8 wedges. Cut the spring onions diagonally into short lengths. Cut the ham into very thin strips.
3  Heat 1 tablespoon oil in a wok or large frying pan and add the egg, pulling the set egg towards the centre and tilting the wok to let the unset egg run to the edges. When the egg is almost set, break it up into large pieces so it resembles scrambled egg. Transfer to a plate and set aside.
4  Heat the remaining oil and lard, if using, in the wok, swirling to coat the base and side. Add the onion and stir-fry over high heat until it starts to turn translucent. Add the ham and stir-fry for 1 minute. Add the rice and peas and stir-fry for 3 minutes until the rice is heated through. Add the egg, soy sauce, spring onion and prawns. Heat through and serve immediately.

NOTE: If possible, cook the rice a day ahead and refrigerate it overnight. This makes the grains separate and means the fried rice is not gluggy.

# china

## soy sauce

Soy sauce, indispensable in the cooking of eastern Asia, has a long history. A mixture of brine and fermented soy beans was being made in China more than 3000 years ago. Known as shih, its original function was probably as a preservative for vegetables during the winter months. Over the centuries, techniques were developed for adding grain meal to the fermenting mash, ageing it and then straining off and bottling the liquid; by 1500 years ago, a sauce fairly similar to the modern version was being used. The darker sauce of the north is aged longer and is tinted and flavoured with molasses. The Japanese learned sauce-making skills from China about a thousand years ago and introduced their own refinements; Japanese soy sauce is lighter and less salty as it contains more wheat. In Indonesia, palm sugar, garlic, star anise and thickeners were added to produce kecap manis.

## clay pot chicken and vegetables

Preparation time: 20 minutes + 30 minutes marinating time
Cooking time: 35 minutes
Serves 4

500 g (1 lb 2 oz) boneless, skinless chicken thighs
1 tablespoon soy sauce
1 tablespoon dry sherry
6 dried Chinese mushrooms
2 tablespoons peanut oil
2 small leeks, white part only, sliced
5 cm (2 inch) piece ginger, finely grated
125 ml (4 fl oz/½ cup) chicken stock
1 teaspoon sesame oil
250 g (9 oz) orange sweet potato, halved lengthwise and sliced
3 teaspoons cornflour (cornstarch)
steamed rice, to serve

1  Cut the chicken into small pieces. Put it in a bowl with the soy sauce and sherry, cover and marinate for 30 minutes in the refrigerator.
2  Meanwhile, soak the mushrooms in hot water for 20 minutes. Drain, then squeeze to remove any excess liquid. Discard the stems and chop the caps finely.
3  Drain the chicken, reserving the marinade. Heat half the peanut oil in a wok, swirling gently to coat the base and side. Add half the chicken pieces and stir-fry briefly until seared on all sides. Transfer the chicken to a flameproof clay pot or casserole dish. Stir-fry the remaining chicken and add it to the clay pot. Heat the remaining oil in the wok. Add the leek and ginger and stir-fry for 1 minute. Add the mushroom, reserved marinade, stock and sesame oil and cook for 2 minutes. Transfer to the clay pot with the sweet potato and cook, covered, on top of the stove over very low heat for 20 minutes or until the sweet potato is tender.
4  Mix the cornflour and 1 tablespoon water and add it to the pot. Cook, stirring over high heat, until the mixture boils and thickens. Serve the chicken and vegetables at once with the steamed rice.

NOTE: Like all stews, this is best cooked 1–2 days ahead and stored, covered, in the refrigerator to allow the flavours to mature. It can also be frozen, but omit the sweet potato. Steam or boil the potato separately and stir it through the reheated stew.

Remove the seeds from the cucumber and slice into matchsticks. Slice the spring onion sections and place in iced water to form brushes.

Roll the dough balls into circles. Lightly brush one circle with sesame oil and place another circle on top.

When cool enough to handle, peel the two halves of the double pancake apart.

# peking duck with mandarin pancakes

✺ ✺ ✺

Preparation time: 1 hour + 30 minutes standing time
Cooking time: 1 hour 15 minutes
Serves 6

1.7 kg (3 lb 12 oz) whole duck
3 litres (105 fl oz/12 cups) boiling water
1 tablespoon honey
12 spring onions (scallions)
1 Lebanese (short) cucumber
2 tablespoons hoisin sauce

MANDARIN PANCAKES
310 g (11 oz/2½ cups) plain (all-purpose) flour
2 teaspoons caster (superfine) sugar
250 ml (9 fl oz/1 cup) boiling water
1 tablespoon sesame oil

**1** Remove the neck and any large pieces of fat from inside the duck carcass. Hold the duck over the sink and very carefully and slowly pour the boiling water over it, rotating the duck so the water scalds all the skin. Drain well.
**2** Put the duck on a rack in an ovenproof dish. Mix the honey and 125 ml (4 fl oz/½ cup) hot water and brush two coats of this glaze all over the duck. Dry the duck in a cool, airy place for about 4 hours. The skin is sufficiently dry when it feels papery.
**3** Preheat the oven to 210°C (415°F/Gas 6–7). Cut an 8 cm (3¼ inch) section from the white end of each spring onion. Make fine parallel cuts from the top of the section towards the white end. Put the onion pieces in iced water — they will open into 'brushes'. Remove the seeds from the cucumber and slice into matchsticks.
**4** Roast the duck for 30 minutes, then turn it over carefully without tearing the skin and roast it for another 30 minutes. Remove the duck from the oven and leave for a minute or two, then place it on a warm dish.
**5** Meanwhile, to make the mandarin pancakes, put the flour and sugar in a bowl and pour in the boiling water. Stir the mixture a few times and leave until lukewarm. Knead the mixture, on a lightly floured surface, into a smooth dough. Cover and set aside for 30 minutes. Take two level tablespoons of dough and roll each one into a ball. Roll out to circles 8 cm (3¼ inches) in diameter. Lightly brush one of the circles with sesame oil and place another circle on top. Re-roll to make a thin pancake about 15 cm (6 inches) in diameter. Repeat with the remaining dough and oil to make about 10 'double' pancakes.
**6** Heat a small cast iron frying pan over medium heat and cook the double pancakes one at a time. When small bubbles appear on the surface, turn the pancake over and cook the second side, pressing the surface with a clean tea towel (dish towel). The pancake should puff up when done. Transfer the pancake to a plate. When cool enough to handle, peel the two halves of the double pancake apart. Stack them on a plate and cover them at once to prevent them drying out.
**7** To serve, thinly slice the duck. Place the pancakes and duck on separate serving plates. Arrange the cucumber batons and spring onion brushes on another serving plate. Put the hoisin sauce in a small dish. Each diner helps themselves to a pancake, spreads a little sauce on it and adds a couple of pieces of cucumber, a spring onion brush and, finally, a piece of duck. The pancake is then folded over into a neat envelope for eating.

china

# yum cha

Meaning literally 'to drink tea', this morning ritual is accompanied in tea houses throughout China with tiny steamed or fried parcels of dim sum, stuffed with fresh seafood, meats and vegetables.

### crabmeat dim sims

In a bowl, combine 200 g (7 oz) drained and flaked crabmeat, 250 g (9 oz) raw prawns (shrimp), peeled, deveined and chopped, 4 finely chopped spring onions (scallions), 3 chopped and soaked dried Chinese mushrooms, 3 tablespoons finely chopped bean sprouts, 1 tablespoon teriyaki sauce, 2 crushed garlic cloves and 2 teaspoons grated fresh ginger. Working with 1 won ton wrapper at a time (you will need about 20), place 1 tablespoon filling in the centre, gather up the corners and pinch together to seal. Keep the other won ton wrappers covered with a damp tea towel (dish towel) until needed. Line the base of a bamboo or metal steamer with a circle of baking paper. Arrange the dim sims on the paper, making sure they are not touching (you may need to cook them in batches). Cover and steam for 8 minutes. Serve immediately. Makes about 20.

### chicken moneybags

In a bowl, combine 375 g (13 oz) minced (ground) chicken, 90 g (3¼ oz) finely chopped ham, 4 finely chopped spring onions (scallions), 1 finely chopped celery stalk, 3 tablespoons chopped bamboo shoots, 1 tablespoon soy sauce, 1 crushed garlic clove and 1 teaspoon finely grated fresh ginger. Working with 1 won ton wrapper at a time (you will need about 40), place 2 teaspoons filling in the centre, gather up the corners and pinch together to form a pouch, leaving a frill at the top. Cut 20 chives in half and place in a heatproof bowl. Cover with boiling water for 1 minute; rinse and drain. Deep-fry the moneybags in hot oil for 4–5 minutes until crisp and golden; drain on paper towels. Tie a chive around each moneybag. Serve immediately. Makes about 40.

### prawn gow gees

In a bowl, mix 500 g (1 lb 2 oz) raw prawns (shrimp), peeled, deveined and chopped, 4 finely chopped spring onions (scallions), 1 tablespoon finely grated fresh ginger and 2 tablespoons chopped water chestnuts. Mix 3 teaspoons cornflour (cornstarch), 2 teaspoons sesame oil, 1 teaspoon soy sauce, ½ teaspoon caster (superfine) sugar and a little salt and pepper until smooth, and stir into the prawn mixture. Working with 1 gow gee (egg) dumpling wrapper at a time (you will need about 40), put 1 rounded teaspoon of mixture in the centre and press the edges together to form a semicircle. Twist the corners down to form a crescent shape. Line the base of a bamboo or metal steamer with a circle of baking paper. Arrange the gow gees on the paper, making sure they are not touching (you may need to cook them in batches). Steam, covered, for 8 minutes. Makes about 40.

### stuffed capsicums (peppers)

Mix together 500 g (1 lb 2 oz) peeled, deveined and finely chopped raw prawns (shrimp), 300 g (10½ oz) minced (ground) lean pork, 1 teaspoon salt, 3 finely chopped spring onions (scallions), 3 tablespoons finely chopped water chestnuts, 3 teaspoons soy sauce and 2 teaspoons dry sherry. Cut 3 capsicums (peppers) lengthways into 3–4 segments and remove the seeds and membrane. Fill the capsicum wedges with filling and cut in half. Heat 1 tablespoon oil in a wok. Cook the capsicum pieces in two batches over medium–high heat for 3–4 minutes, or until well browned. Turn over and cook for a further 3 minutes. Repeat with the remaining pieces. Serve immediately. Makes about 24.

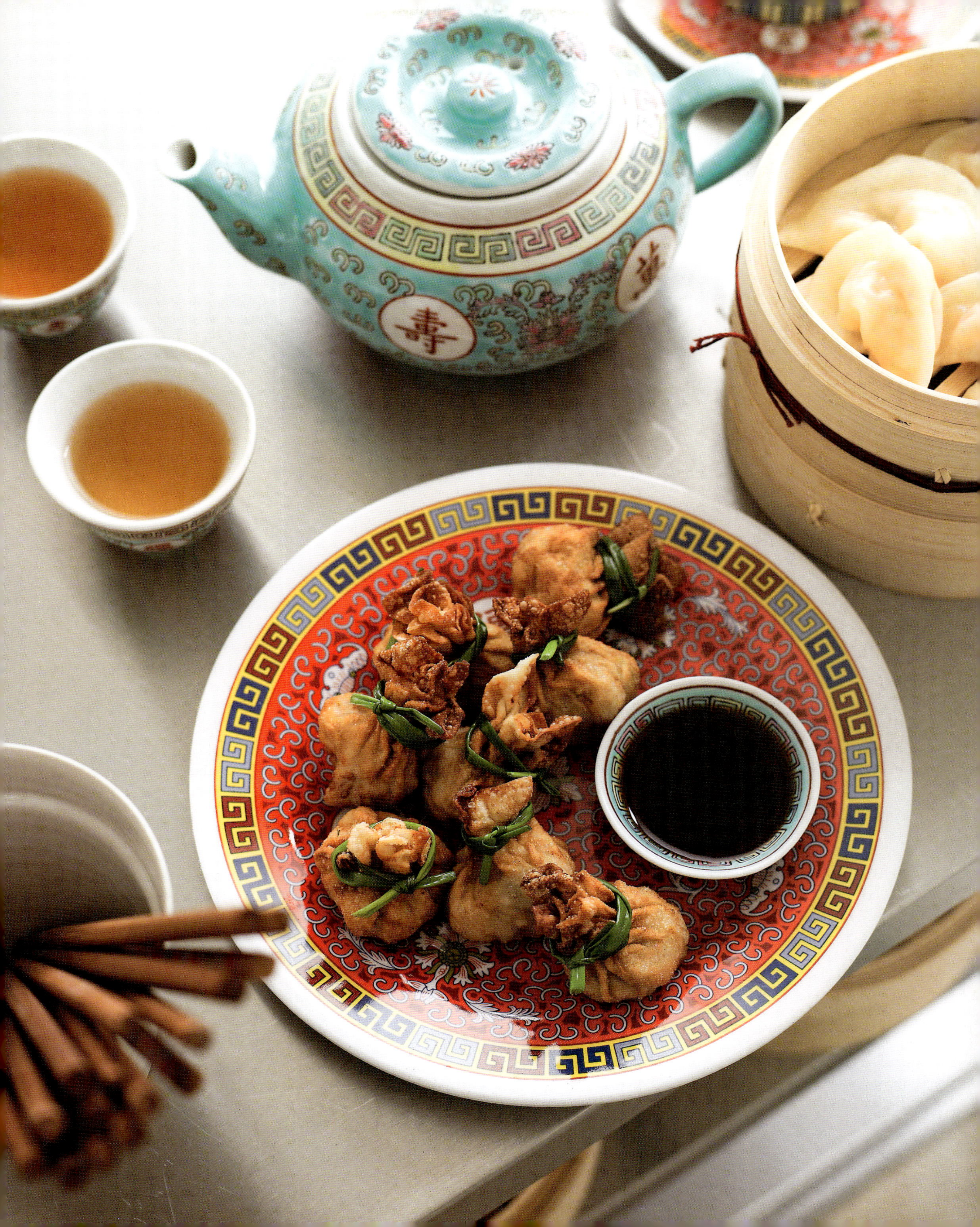
壽

## sichuan soup

✻

Preparation time: 20 minutes
Cooking time: 15 minutes
Serves 6–8

4 dried Chinese mushrooms
50 g (1¾ oz) thick dried rice stick noodles
1 litre (35 fl oz/4 cups) chicken stock
175 g (6 oz/1 cup) cooked chicken, chopped
225 g (8 oz) tin bamboo shoots, drained and chopped
1 teaspoon finely grated fresh ginger
1 tablespoon cornflour (cornstarch)
1 egg, lightly beaten
1 teaspoon tomato sauce (ketchup)
1 tablespoon soy sauce
1 tablespoon shaoxing rice wine (Chinese rice wine)
2 teaspoons sesame oil
2 spring onions (scallions), finely chopped
spring onion (scallion) (optional), extra, thinly sliced, to garnish

**1** Soak the mushrooms in hot water for 20 minutes. Drain, then squeeze to remove any excess liquid. Discard the stems and chop the caps finely. Soak the noodles in hot water for 20 minutes. Drain and cut into short lengths. Set aside.
**2** Heat the stock in a large saucepan and bring to the boil. Add the mushroom, noodles, chicken, bamboo shoots and ginger. Reduce the heat to a gentle simmer.
**3** Mix the cornflour with 80 ml (2½ fl oz/⅓ cup) water, add it to the soup and stir until clear. Add the egg to the soup in a fine stream, stirring the mixture constantly. Remove the pan from the heat. Add the tomato sauce, soy sauce, rice wine, sesame oil and spring onion. Season to taste. Serve topped with extra spring onion, if desired.

## black satin chicken

✻ ✻

Preparation time: 45 minutes
Cooking time: 1 hour
Serves 10

3 dried Chinese mushrooms
125 ml (4 fl oz/½ cup) dark soy sauce
3 tablespoons soft brown sugar
2 tablespoons shaoxing rice wine (Chinese rice wine)
1 tablespoon soy sauce
1 teaspoon sesame oil
¼ teaspoon ground star anise or 1 whole star anise
1.4 kg (3 lb 2 oz) whole chicken
4 cm (1½ inch) piece fresh ginger, finely grated
2 spring onions (scallions), thinly sliced, to garnish

**1** Soak the mushrooms in hot water for 20 minutes. Drain and reserve the liquid. Put the dark soy sauce, sugar, rice wine, soy sauce, sesame oil, star anise and reserved liquid in a small saucepan and bring to the boil, stirring continuously.
**2** Rub the inside of the chicken with ginger and 1 teaspoon salt. Place the chicken in a large saucepan. Cover with soy marinade and mushrooms, turning the chicken over so it is evenly coated. Cover and cook over low heat, turning regularly, for 55 minutes or until the juices run clear when pierced with a skewer. Remove the chicken and allow it to cool briefly.
**3** Boil the sauce over high heat until thick and syrupy. Discard the mushrooms.

# china

4  Chop the chicken Chinese-style (see page 11). Arrange the chicken pieces on a serving platter, brush lightly with the syrupy sauce and sprinkle over the spring onion. Alternatively you could serve the sauce separately, for dipping.

## honey prawns

Preparation time: 20 minutes
Cooking time: 12 minutes
Serves 4

16 raw king prawns (shrimp)
30 g (1 oz/¼ cup) cornflour (cornstarch)
40 g (1½ oz/¼ cup) white sesame seeds
oil, for deep-frying
90 g (3¼ oz/¼ cup) honey

BATTER
125 g (4½ oz/1 cup) self-raising flour
30 g (1 oz/¼ cup) cornflour (cornstarch)
¼ teaspoon lemon juice
1 tablespoon oil

1  Peel the prawns, leaving the tails intact. Gently pull out the dark vein from each prawn back, starting at the head end. Pat the prawns dry with paper towels, then lightly dust them with the cornflour.
2  Toast the sesame seeds in a dry frying pan over medium heat for 3–4 minutes, shaking the pan gently, until the seeds are golden brown; remove from the pan at once to prevent burning.
3  To make the batter, sift the flour and cornflour into a medium bowl. Combine 250 ml (9 fl oz/1 cup) water, the lemon juice and oil. Make a well in the centre of the flour and gradually add the liquid, beating well to make a smooth batter.
4  Heat the oil in a large, deep frying pan or wok until moderately hot. Working with a few prawns at a time, dip the prawns in the batter; drain any excess. Use tongs or a slotted spoon to place the prawns in the hot oil. Cook for 2–3 minutes or until the prawns are crisp and golden. Drain on paper towels and keep warm.
5  Place the honey in a large frying pan and warm over very low heat. (Don't overheat the honey or it will caramelise and lose some of its flavour.)
6  Place the cooked prawns in the pan with the warmed honey; toss gently to coat. Transfer to a serving plate and sprinkle over the sesame seeds. Serve immediately.

## sichuan cooking

The immense geographical and climatic diversity of China has led to the development of many distinct and varied regional cuisines. There are four major styles: Peking, Cantonese, Shanghai and Sichuan. The distinctive hot and spicy sichuan cuisine is a medley of many influences, one of the most important being the traders and Buddhist missionaries from India, who more than 2000 years ago brought cooking techniques, tangy spices and herbs, and a tradition of vegetarian dishes. Sichuan cooking makes liberal use of fiery chillies and most dishes include vinegar, sugar, salt and the unique spice, sichuan pepper (which has a numbing effect on the tongue, rather than a bite).

essential asian

## beef with capsicum and oyster sauce

Preparation time: 15 minutes
Cooking time: 10 minutes
Serves 6

500 g (1 lb 2 oz) rump steak
1 tablespoon soy sauce
1 egg white, lightly beaten
1 tablespoon cornflour (cornstarch)
2 tablespoons peanut oil
1 tablespoon finely grated fresh ginger
¼ teaspoon five-spice
1 small green capsicum (pepper), cut in diamond shapes
1 small red capsicum (pepper), cut in diamond shapes
2 celery stalks, thinly sliced
410 g (14½ oz) tin whole baby corn, drained
2 tablespoons oyster sauce
2 spring onions (scallions), thinly sliced, to garnish

1   Trim the beef of any fat and sinew, and slice it evenly across the grain into long, thin strips. Combine the soy sauce, egg white, cornflour and ¼ teaspoon ground black pepper in a bowl; add the beef, stirring to coat.
2   Heat 1 tablespoon of the peanut oil in a wok or heavy-based saucepan, swirling gently to coat the base and side. Add the ginger, five-spice, capsicum, celery and corn and stir-fry over high heat for 2 minutes or until just beginning to soften. Remove from the wok and keep warm.
3   Heat the remaining oil in the wok, swirling gently to coat the base and side. Cook the beef quickly in small batches over high heat until browned but not cooked through.
4   Return all the beef to the wok with the vegetables and add the oyster sauce. Stir-fry over high heat until the beef is cooked and the sauce is hot. Remove from the heat and serve immediately, sprinkled with the spring onion.

## chinese barbecued pork

Preparation time: 15 minutes + 30 minutes marinating time
Cooking time: 35 minutes
Serves 6

60 ml (2 fl oz/¼ cup) tomato sauce (ketchup)
1 tablespoon hoisin sauce
2 tablespoons honey
1 tablespoon malt extract or molasses
1 tablespoon chopped garlic
2 tablespoons caster (superfine) sugar
1 teaspoon five-spice
2 teaspoons cornflour (cornstarch)
750 g (1 lb 10 oz) pork neck or fillet
steamed rice sprinkled with crisp fried onion, to serve

1   Combine the tomato sauce, hoisin sauce, honey, malt extract, garlic, sugar and five-spice in a small saucepan. Mix

chinese barbecued pork

the cornflour in 1 tablespoon water and add to the mixture. Bring to the boil, then reduce to a simmer and stir for 2 minutes. Allow to cool.

**2** If using pork neck, cut it in half lengthways. Pork fillets do not need to be cut. Place the pork in the sauce, turning to coat; cover and marinate in the refrigerator for at least 30 minutes.

**3** Preheat the oven to 210°C (415°F/ Gas 6–7). Lift the pork from the marinade with a slotted spoon and reserve the marinade. Place the pork on a wire rack over a baking tray half-filled with hot water and cook for 15 minutes.

**4** Reduce the oven temperature to 180°C (350°F/Gas 4) and cook the pork for a further 15 minutes, basting it occasionally with the reserved marinade. Remove the pork from the oven and let it stand for 5 minutes before slicing and serving with steamed rice and crisp fried onion.

## crispy skin chicken

✹ ✹ ✹

Preparation time: 40 minutes
Cooking time: 40 minutes
Serves 4

1.3 kg (3 lb) whole chicken
1 tablespoon honey
1 whole star anise
1 strip dried mandarin or tangerine peel
oil, for deep-frying
spring onions (scallions), thinly sliced, to garnish
2 lemons (optional), cut into wedges, to serve

FIVE-SPICE SALT
2 tablespoons salt
1 teaspoon white peppercorns
½ teaspoon five-spice
½ teaspoon ground white pepper

**1** Put the chicken in a large saucepan and cover with cold water. Add the honey, star anise, mandarin peel and 1 teaspoon salt and bring to the boil. Reduce the heat to low and simmer for 15 minutes. Turn off the heat and leave the chicken, covered, for a further 15 minutes. Transfer the chicken to a plate to cool.

**2** Cut the chicken in half lengthways. Place it on paper towels, uncovered, in the refrigerator for 20 minutes.

**3** Fill a wok or deep heavy-based saucepan one-third full of oil and heat to 160°C (315°F), or until a cube of bread dropped into the oil turns golden brown in 30–35 seconds. Very gently lower in half of the chicken, skin side down. Cook for 6 minutes, then carefully turn the chicken over and cook for another 6 minutes, making sure all the skin comes in contact with the oil. Drain on paper towels. Repeat with the second chicken half.

**4** To make the five-spice salt, put the salt and peppercorns in a small frying pan and dry-fry until the mixture smells aromatic and the salt is slightly browned. Crush the mixture using a mortar and pestle or wrap in foil and crush it with a rolling pin. Mix with the five-spice and white pepper and place in a small, shallow dish.

**5** Use a cleaver or a large kitchen knife to chop the chicken halves into smaller pieces. Sprinkle over the five-spice salt and garnish with the spring onion. Serve with the lemon wedges, if desired.

NOTE: Any leftover five-spice salt can be stored in an airtight container for several months.

crispy skin chicken

essential asian

whole steamed fish with crisp finish

the capsicum into fine matchsticks 4 cm (1½ inches) long.

**3** Place a pair of wooden chopsticks in a cross in the base of a large wok (to act as a rack) and fill the wok with about 7 cm (2¾ inches) water. Score the fattest part of the fish three times, place on a heatproof dinner plate and sit the plate on top of the chopsticks. Cover and bring the water to the boil over high heat. Cook for 15–20 minutes; turn off the heat, scatter over the vegetables and leave, covered, for 3 minutes.

**4** Slide the steamed fish onto a warmed serving platter. Heat the oil in a small saucepan until it is very hot and slightly smoking, then carefully pour it over the vegetables. The vegetables or fish skin may crackle. Serve with small bowls of soy and chilli sauce and steamed rice.

NOTE: The oil must be very hot so it just crisps and brightens the vegetables. If desired, the oil can be poured over the fish at the table so the guests can watch; the crackling is quite spectacular.

## sweet and sour pork

✹ ✹

Preparation time: 35 minutes
Cooking time: 25 minutes
Serves 4

## whole steamed fish with crisp finish

✹ ✹

Preparation time: 25 minutes
Cooking time: 25 minutes
Serves 4

1 kg (2 lb 4 oz) whole snapper or bream, cleaned and scaled
½ teaspoon ground white pepper
3 cm (1¼ inch) piece fresh ginger, very finely sliced
1 tablespoon sesame oil
1 tablespoon soy sauce
3 spring onions (scallions)
1 celery stalk
½ red capsicum (pepper)
125 ml (4 fl oz/½ cup) oil
steamed rice, to serve

**1** Thoroughly wash the fish inside the cavity and out and pat dry with paper towels. Sprinkle the fish with ½ teaspoon salt and the white pepper and place the ginger inside the cavity. Combine the sesame oil and soy sauce and lightly brush over the fish.

**2** Cut the spring onions and celery into 4 cm (1½ inch) lengths, then finely shred them into long fine strips. Cut

350 g (12 oz) pork loin, cut into bite-sized pieces
2 eggs, lightly beaten
4 tablespoons cornflour (cornstarch)
oil, for deep-frying
1 carrot, very thinly sliced
1 onion, cut into thin wedges
160 g (5¾ oz/1 cup) chopped fresh pineapple
½ red capsicum (pepper), cut into bite-sized pieces
½ green capsicum (pepper), cut into bite-sized pieces
1 celery stalk, sliced
75 g (2½ oz/⅓ cup) sweet pickled Chinese vegetables, roughly chopped
60 ml (2 fl oz/¼ cup) white vinegar

- 60 ml (2 fl oz/¼ cup) soy sauce
- 2 tablespoons tomato paste (concentrated purée)
- 2 tablespoons caster (superfine) sugar
- 2 tablespoons orange juice
- 2 teaspoons cornflour (cornstarch), extra, mixed with 1 tablespoon water

**1** Mix ½ teaspoon salt through the pork. Dip each piece of pork in the egg, then roll it in the cornflour. Place the pork on a plate in a single layer.
**2** Heat the oil in a wok over medium heat, drop in 4 pieces of pork and cook for about 3 minutes or until golden brown. Remove the pork with a slotted spoon and drain it on paper towels. Repeat with the remaining pork.
**3** Remove all but 1 tablespoon of the oil from the wok, reheat and stir-fry the carrot, onion and pineapple for 2 minutes or until the carrot is just tender. Add the capsicum, celery and pickled vegetables and stir-fry for a further 2 minutes.
**4** Combine the vinegar, soy sauce, tomato paste, sugar and orange juice in a small bowl; stir in the cornflour mixture and mix well. Pour the sauce into the vegetables and stir constantly until the mixture boils and thickens slightly. Return the pork to the wok, stirring well to lightly coat the pork with the sauce. Arrange on a serving plate and serve immediately.

**NOTE:** Be sure to fry the pork quickly after coating it with the cornflour so it does not become sticky on standing.

## smoked five-spice chicken

❋ ❋

Preparation time: 30 minutes + 4 hours marinating time
Cooking time: 40 minutes
Serves 6

- 1.7 kg (3 lb 12 oz) whole chicken
- 60 ml (2 fl oz/¼ cup) soy sauce
- 1 tablespoon finely grated fresh ginger
- 2 strips dried mandarin or tangerine peel
- 1 star anise
- ¼ teaspoon five-spice
- 3 tablespoons soft brown sugar
- 1 spring onion (scallion), thinly sliced, to garnish
- 1 small handful coriander (cilantro) sprigs, to garnish

**1** Put the chicken in a large non-metallic bowl along with the soy sauce and ginger. Cover and marinate for at least 4 hours, or leave overnight in the refrigerator, turning occasionally.
**2** Put a small rack in the base of a saucepan large enough to hold the chicken. Add water up to the level of the rack. Place the chicken on the rack. Bring the water to the boil, cover tightly, then reduce the heat and steam for 15 minutes. Turn off the heat and allow the chicken to rest in the pan, covered, for another 15 minutes. Transfer the chicken to a bowl.
**3** Wash the pan and line it with three or four large pieces of foil. Use a mortar and pestle to pound the dried mandarin peel and star anise until the pieces are the size of coarse breadcrumbs, or process in a food processor. Add the five-spice and brown sugar. Spread the spice mixture over the foil in the pan.
**4** Replace the rack in the pan and place the chicken on it. Put the pan over medium heat and, when the spice mixture starts smoking, cover tightly. Reduce the heat to low and smoke the chicken for 20 minutes. Test if the chicken is cooked by piercing the thigh with a skewer; the juices should run clear. (The heat produced in this final step is very intense. When the chicken is removed from the pan, leave the pan on the stove to cool a little before handling it.)
**5** Remove the chicken from the pan and chop into smaller pieces using a cleaver or large knife. Transfer to a platter. Garnish with the spring onion and coriander.

smoked five-spice chicken

## chinese vegetables

✹

Preparation time: 10 minutes
Cooking time: 5 minutes
Serves 4

500 g (1 lb 2 oz) Chinese green vegetables (see Note)
2 teaspoons peanut oil
½ teaspoon finely chopped garlic
1 tablespoon oyster sauce
½ teaspoon caster (superfine) sugar
1 teaspoon sesame oil

**1** Bring a large saucepan of water to the boil.
**2** Wash the Chinese greens. Remove any tough leaves and trim the stems. Chop the greens into three equal portions.
**3** Add the greens to the pan of boiling water. Cook for 1–2 minutes, or until just tender but still crisp. Use tongs to remove the greens from the pan, drain well and place on a heated serving platter.
**4** Heat the peanut oil in a small saucepan and cook the garlic briefly. Add the oyster sauce, sugar, 2 tablespoons water and the sesame oil and bring to the boil. Pour over the greens and toss to coat. Serve immediately.

NOTE: Use choy sum, bok choy (pak choy) or Chinese broccoli (gai larn), or a combination of any two.

## pork with plum sauce

✹

Preparation time: 15 minutes
Cooking time: 15 minutes
Serves 4

3 tablespoons oil
2 garlic cloves, finely chopped
1 large onion, cut into thin wedges
500 g (1 lb 2 oz) pork loin, sliced
2 tablespoons cornflour (cornstarch)
½ teaspoon sugar

### adding cornflour

Cornflour (cornstarch) will thicken a sauce without affecting the flavour. Mix the cornflour with a little cold water or stock to make a thin, smooth paste. Remove the wok or pan containing the sauce from the heat for a minute or so, then stir the cornflour mixture immediately before adding it to the sauce, as the cornflour does not stay in suspension for long. Return the wok to the heat and, while stirring, quickly bring the sauce to the boil.

60 ml (2 fl oz/¼ cup) plum sauce
1 tablespoon soy sauce
2 teaspoons hoisin sauce

1  Heat 1 tablespoon of the oil in a wok and cook the garlic and onion until softened. Transfer to a plate and remove the wok from the heat.
2  Coat the pork lightly in the cornflour and season well with salt and pepper. Add the remaining oil to the wok and return to the heat. When the wok is extremely hot, stir-fry the pork in two batches until dark golden brown, then return all the pork and its juices to the wok.
3  Add the plum sauce, soy sauce and hoisin sauce and return the onion to the wok. Toss well to coat the pork with the sauce and serve immediately.

## stir-fried vegetables

✻

Preparation time: 5 minutes
Cooking time: 5 minutes
Serves 4

1 carrot
1 red capsicum (pepper)
125 g (4½ oz) green beans, trimmed
1 tablespoon oil
1 teaspoon finely chopped garlic
200 g (7 oz) straw mushrooms
1½ teaspoons cornflour (cornstarch)
80 ml (2½ fl oz/⅓ cup) chicken stock
1 teaspoon sesame oil
1 teaspoon caster (superfine) sugar
2 teaspoons soy sauce
steamed rice, to serve

1  Slice the carrot thinly. Seed the capsicum and cut it into 4 cm (1½ inch) pieces. Cut the beans in half.
2  Heat the oil in a wok or heavy-based frying pan, swirling gently to coat the base and side. Add the carrot and stir-fry it over high heat for 30 seconds. Stir in the garlic; add the remaining vegetables and stir-fry over high heat for 2 minutes — they should be very crisp and firm.
3  Dissolve the cornflour in a little of the stock; mix with the remaining stock, sesame oil, sugar and soy sauce. Add the cornflour mixture to the wok and stir until the sauce boils and thickens. Serve immediately with the steamed rice.

## sweet garlic eggplant

✻

Preparation time: 5 minutes
Cooking time: 15 minutes
Serves 4

3 eggplants (aubergines)
140 ml (4½ fl oz/7 tablespoons) oil
1½ teaspoons finely chopped garlic
6 teaspoons caster (superfine) sugar
1½ tablespoons soy sauce
1½ tablespoons cider vinegar
1 tablespoon dry sherry
steamed rice, to serve

1  Cut the eggplants in half lengthways and then slice into wedges about 3 cm (1¼ inches) wide. Cut the wedges into pieces about 3 cm (1¼ inches) long.
2  Heat 3 tablespoons of the oil in a wok or heavy-based frying pan, swirling gently to coat the base and side. Add half the eggplant and stir-fry over high heat for 5 minutes, or until browned and all the oil is absorbed. Transfer to a plate. Repeat the cooking procedure with another 3 tablespoons of the oil and the remaining eggplant.
3  Heat the remaining oil in the wok, swirling gently to coat the base and side. Add the garlic and cook slowly until just golden. Add the sugar, soy sauce, vinegar and sherry. Bring to the boil, stirring. Add the eggplant and simmer for 3 minutes to allow it to absorb the sauce. Serve with the steamed rice.

NOTE: This dish can be cooked up to 2 days ahead and refrigerated until required. Serve it at room temperature.

### chinese green vegetables

There are a number of Chinese green vegetables available in most fruit and vegetable markets. Choy sum, bok choy (pak choy) and Chinese broccoli (gai larn) are all easily prepared by cutting off the base, separating the leaves and rinsing in cold water. Roughly chop the vegetables into large pieces. The whole plant is used, including the stem — this requires longer cooking than the leaves, but don't overcook it or it will lose its lovely vibrant green colour.

# indonesia

The cuisine of Indonesia is rich and varied, a reflection of the many diverse influences that have shaped the country's history. Indonesian cooking combines the spicy flavours of chillies, herbs and other aromatic seasonings with the sweetness of fresh coconut, palm sugar and peanuts, and the sourness of limes, lemongrass and tamarind. Meals are often served with small bowls of sambal: spicy relishes made from combinations of coconut, chilli and shrimp paste.

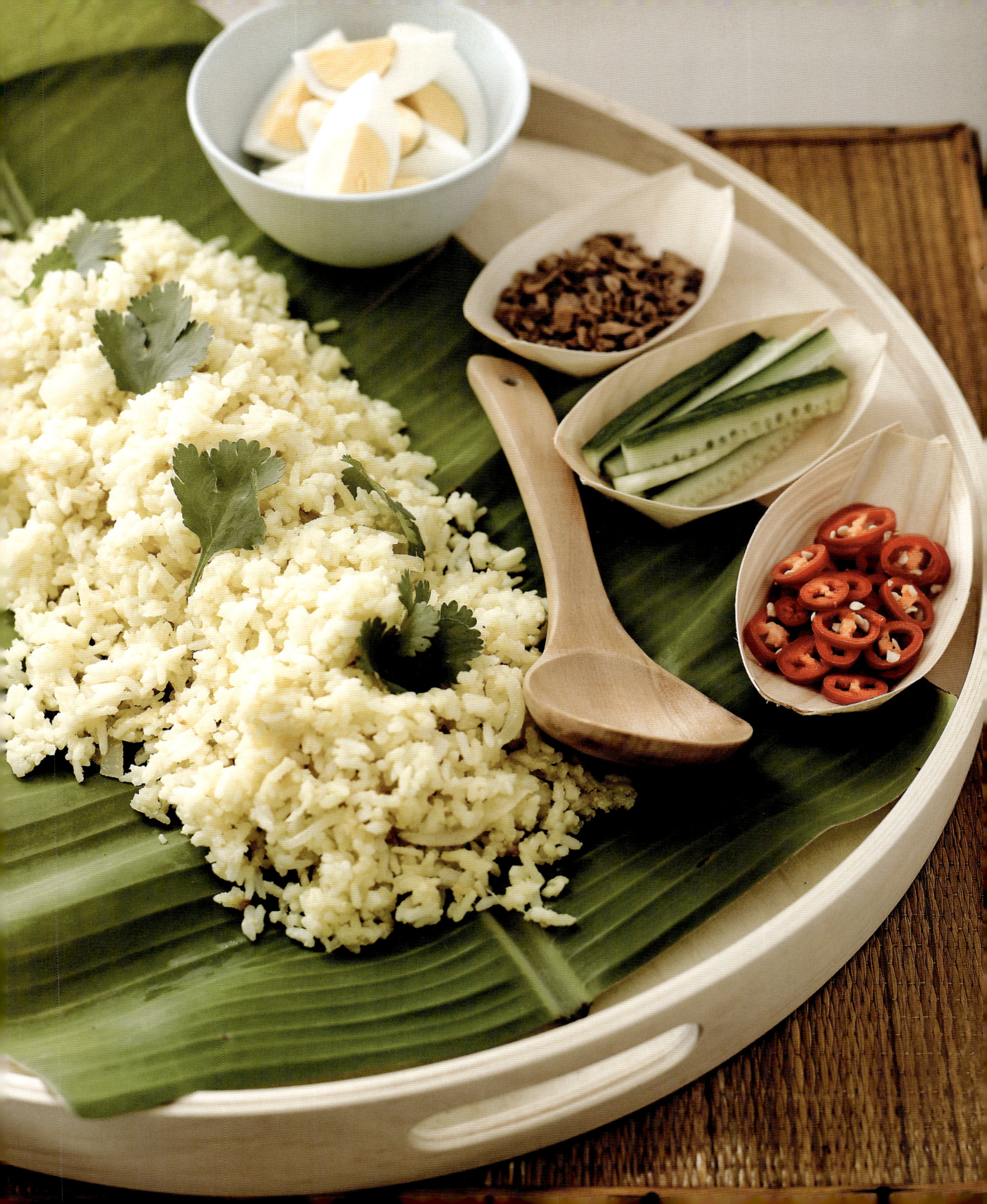

Remove the omelette from the pan with a spatula.

Process the garlic, onion, chilli, shrimp paste, coriander and sugar into a paste.

Stir-fry the steak and prawns until they change colour.

Stir-fry the rice, breaking up any lumps with a wooden spoon.

# nasi goreng (fried rice)

✹ ✹

Preparation time: 35 minutes
Cooking time: 30 minutes
Serves 4

2 eggs
80 ml (2½ fl oz/⅓ cup) oil
3 garlic cloves, finely chopped
1 onion, finely chopped
2 red chillies, seeded and very finely chopped
1 teaspoon shrimp paste
1 teaspoon coriander seeds
½ teaspoon sugar
400 g (14 oz) raw prawns (shrimp)
200 g (7 oz) rump steak, thinly sliced
200 g (7 oz/1 cup) long-grain rice, cooked and cooled
2 teaspoons kecap manis
1 tablespoon soy sauce
4 spring onions (scallions), finely chopped
½ lettuce, finely shredded
1 Lebanese (short) cucumber, thinly sliced, to garnish
3 tablespoons crisp fried onion, to garnish

**1** Beat the eggs and ¼ teaspoon salt until foamy. Heat a frying pan over medium heat and lightly brush with a little of the oil; pour about one-quarter of the egg mixture into the pan and cook for 1–2 minutes until the omelette sets. Turn the omelette over and cook the other side for 30 seconds. Remove the omelette from the pan and repeat three times with the remaining egg mixture. When the omelettes are cold, gently roll them up and cut them into fine strips; set aside.
**2** Peel the prawns and gently pull out the dark vein from each prawn back, starting at the head end. Combine the garlic, onion, chilli, shrimp paste, coriander seeds and sugar in a food processor or mortar and pestle, and process or pound until a paste is formed.
**3** Heat 1–2 tablespoons of the oil in a wok or large deep frying pan; add the paste and cook over high heat for 1 minute or until aromatic. Add the prawns and beef and stir-fry for 2–3 minutes, or until they change colour.
**4** Add the remaining oil and the cold rice to the wok. Stir-fry, breaking up any lumps, until the rice is heated through. Add the kecap manis, soy sauce and spring onion and stir-fry for another minute.
**5** Arrange the lettuce around the outside of a large platter. Place the rice in the centre, and garnish with the omelette strips, cucumber slices and crisp fried onion. Serve immediately.

# beef fillet in coconut

✹

Preparation time: 15 minutes + 1 hour marinating time
Cooking time: 10 minutes
Serves 4

2 garlic cloves, crushed
2 teaspoons finely grated lemon zest
1 teaspoon grated fresh ginger
2 teaspoons ground coriander
½ teaspoon ground turmeric
2 teaspoons grated palm sugar (jaggery) or soft brown sugar
3 tablespoons peanut oil
500 g (1 lb 2 oz) beef eye fillet, thinly sliced
45 g (1¾ oz/½ cup) desiccated coconut
3 spring onions (scallions), cut into thin strips
125 ml (4 fl oz/½ cup) coconut milk
steamed rice, to serve

**1** Mix together the garlic, lemon zest, ginger, coriander, turmeric, palm sugar and 2 tablespoons of the oil; add the beef and toss well to coat. Cover and refrigerate for 1 hour.
**2** Heat the remaining oil in a wok or frying pan; add the beef and stir-fry in batches until well browned. Add the coconut and spring onion and stir-fry for 1 minute. Return all the beef to the wok, add the coconut milk and stir until heated through. Serve with the steamed rice.

# indonesia

## deep-fried spiced tofu

✹ ✹

Preparation time: 10 minutes
Cooking time: 10 minutes
Serves 4

375 g (13 oz) firm tofu
90 g (3¼ oz/½ cup) rice flour
2 teaspoons ground coriander
1 teaspoon ground cardamom
1 garlic clove, crushed
vegetable oil, for deep-frying
lime wedges, to serve

**1** Drain the tofu and cut it into 1 cm (½ inch) thick slices, then halve the slices.
**2** Combine the flour, coriander, cardamom and garlic in a bowl; add 125 ml (4 fl oz/½ cup) water and stir until smooth.
**3** Heat the oil in a large saucepan. Dip the tofu slices into the spice mixture and coat thickly. Place the tofu slices into the oil, three at a time, and cook over medium heat for about 2 minutes, or until crisp and golden brown. Drain on paper towels. Serve with the lime wedges.

NOTE: Serve the tofu with stir-fried vegetables and any sauce of your choice; for example, peanut, chilli or soy sauce — the tofu soaks up the flavours.

deep-fried spiced tofu

## tofu

Tofu, or bean curd, is said to have been discovered more than 2000 years ago by a Chinese emperor who, while working with a group of scientists on new medicines, discovered the art of coagulating soy milk. In a region which has no tradition of dairy product consumption, tofu has long been valued for its high calcium and protein content. In addition, it is cheap to produce and extremely versatile.

essential asian

chicken soup with vermicelli and vegetables

# indonesia

## gado gado (vegetables with peanut sauce)

✼✼

Preparation time: 50 minutes
Cooking time: 25 minutes
Serves 4

250 g (9 oz) potatoes
2 carrots
200 g (7 oz) green beans, trimmed
¼ cabbage, shredded
3 hard-boiled eggs, peeled
200 g (7 oz) bean sprouts, trimmed
½ Lebanese (short) cucumber, sliced
150 g (5½ oz) firm tofu, cut into small cubes
80 g (2¾ oz/½ cup) unsalted roasted peanuts, roughly chopped, to garnish

PEANUT SAUCE
1 tablespoon oil
1 large onion, very finely chopped
2 garlic cloves, finely chopped
2 red chillies, very finely chopped
1 teaspoon shrimp paste, optional
250 g (9 oz) crunchy peanut butter
250 ml (9 fl oz/1 cup) coconut milk
2 teaspoons kecap manis
1 tablespoon tomato sauce (ketchup)

1  Cut the potatoes into thick slices; place in a medium saucepan, cover with cold water and bring to the boil. Reduce the heat and simmer for about 6 minutes or until just tender. Drain and allow to cool.
2  Cut the carrots into thick slices. Cut the beans into 4 cm (1½ inch) lengths. Bring a large saucepan of water to the boil, add the carrot and beans, and cook for 2–3 minutes. Remove the vegetables with a sieve and plunge briefly into a bowl of iced water. Drain well.
3  Plunge the shredded cabbage into the boiling water for about 20 seconds. Remove it from the pan and plunge it briefly into the iced water. Drain well.
4  Cut the eggs into quarters or halves. Arrange the eggs, potato, carrot, beans, cabbage, bean sprouts, cucumber and tofu in separate piles on a large serving platter. Cover the platter with plastic wrap and refrigerate.
5  To make the peanut sauce, heat the oil in a heavy-based saucepan, add the onion and garlic and cook over low heat for 8 minutes, stirring regularly. Add the chilli and shrimp paste to the pan and cook for another minute. Remove the pan from the heat and mix in the peanut butter. Return the pan to the heat and slowly stir in the combined coconut milk and 250 ml (9 fl oz/1 cup) water. Bring the sauce to the boil, stirring constantly over medium heat, and being careful the sauce does not stick and burn. Reduce the heat, add the kecap manis and tomato sauce, and simmer for another minute. Allow to cool.
6  Drizzle a little of the peanut sauce over the salad, garnish with the chopped peanuts and serve the remaining sauce in a bowl.

NOTE: Fresh peanut butter, available from health food stores, will give the sauce the best flavour. Be sure not to overcook the vegetables — they should be tender yet still crisp.

## chicken soup with vermicelli and vegetables

✼

Preparation time: 15 minutes
Cooking time: 35 minutes
Serves 4

1 kg (2 lb 4 oz) chicken pieces (such as drumsticks and thighs)
6 spring onions (scallions), chopped
2 cm (¾ inch) piece fresh ginger, very thinly sliced
2 bay leaves
2 tablespoons soy sauce
100 g (3½ oz) dried rice vermicelli
50 g (1¾ oz) spinach leaves, chopped
2 celery stalks, thinly sliced
200 g (7 oz) bean sprouts, trimmed
crisp fried onion, to garnish
chilli sauce, to serve

1  Combine the chicken and 1.5 litres (52 fl oz/6 cups) water in a saucepan and bring to the boil. Skim off any scum. Add the spring onion, ginger, bay leaves, soy sauce, ¼ teaspoon salt and ¼ teaspoon pepper, then reduce the heat and simmer for 30 minutes.
2  Meanwhile, cover the vermicelli with boiling water and leave to soak for 5 minutes or until soft; drain well.
3  Arrange the vermicelli, spinach, celery and bean sprouts on a platter. To serve, each diner places a serving of vermicelli and a selection of vegetables in large individual serving bowls. Pour the chicken soup, including a couple of chicken pieces, into each bowl. Sprinkle over the fried onion and season with the chilli sauce.

### grow your own bean sprouts

To grow your own sprouts, place ¼–½ cup mung beans in a large glass jar (the sprouts will take up 10 times as much space as the beans). Rinse well, then soak the beans in cold water for 12 hours. Drain off the water, cover the top of the jar with a piece of muslin (cheesecloth) held in place with a rubber band, and leave it in a dark place. Twice a day fill the jar with water, swirl, and then drain well, as any remaining water could cause the sprouts to rot. By the fourth or fifth day the beans should be well sprouted — about 2.5 cm (1 inch) long. Rinse again, transfer to a plastic bag and refrigerate.

## beef soup with rice noodles

✹ ✹

Preparation time: 30 minutes + 1 hour marinating time
Cooking time: 1 hour
Serves 4

350 g (12 oz) fillet steak
2 teaspoons soy sauce
60 ml (2 fl oz/¼ cup) coconut milk
1 tablespoon crunchy peanut butter
1 tablespoon grated palm sugar (jaggery) or soft brown sugar
2 teaspoons sambal oelek
1 teaspoon oil
125 g (4½ oz) dried rice vermicelli
1.5 litres (52 fl oz/6 cups) beef stock
2 tablespoons grated palm sugar (jaggery) or soft brown sugar, extra
2 tablespoons fish sauce
1 small Lebanese (short) cucumber
90 g (3¼ oz/1 cup) bean sprouts, trimmed
2 iceberg lettuce leaves, cut into small pieces
6 tablespoons finely chopped mint
80 g (2¾ oz/½ cup) unsalted roasted peanuts, finely chopped

**1** Trim the beef and slice it evenly across the grain into thin slices.
**2** Combine the beef, soy sauce, coconut milk, peanut butter, palm sugar and sambal oelek. Cover and marinate in the refrigerator for 1 hour.
**3** Heat the oil in a frying pan and cook the beef in small batches over high heat for 3 minutes, or until browned all over. Remove from the heat and cover.
**4** Cover the vermicelli with boiling water and leave to soak for 5 minutes; drain well.
**5** Place the stock in a large saucepan and bring to the boil. When the stock is boiling add the extra palm sugar and fish sauce.
**6** Cut the cucumber in quarters lengthways and then into thin slices. Place about 1 tablespoon of the cucumber slices in each individual serving bowl; divide the bean sprouts, pieces of lettuce and mint leaves evenly between the bowls. Place some vermicelli and then a ladleful of stock in each bowl. Top with slices of cooked beef, sprinkle with the peanuts and serve immediately.

## spicy roast chicken

✹

Preparation time: 20 minutes
Cooking time: 1 hour
Serves 4–6

1.6 kg (3 lb 8 oz) whole chicken
3 teaspoons chopped red chilli
3 garlic cloves
2 teaspoons peppercorns, crushed
2 teaspoons soft brown sugar
2 tablespoons soy sauce
2 teaspoons ground turmeric
1 tablespoon lime juice
30 g (1 oz) butter, chopped

**1** Preheat the oven to 180°C (350°F/Gas 4). Use a large cleaver to cut the chicken in half by cutting down the backbone and along the breastbone. To prevent the wings from burning, tuck them underneath. Put the chicken, skin side up, on a rack in a roasting tin and roast for 30 minutes.
**2** Meanwhile, combine the chilli, garlic, peppercorns and sugar in a food processor or use a mortar and pestle and process or pound until smooth. Add the soy sauce, turmeric and lime juice, and process in short bursts, or stir if using a mortar and pestle, until combined.
**3** Brush the spice mixture over the chicken, dot it with the butter pieces and roast for a further 25–30 minutes, or until cooked through and a rich red colour. Serve at room temperature.

beef soup with rice noodles

# indonesia

Cut the chicken in half by cutting down the backbone and along the breastbone.

Combine the chilli, garlic, peppercorns and sugar in a food processor.

Brush the spice mixture all over the chicken.

fiery prawn curry

## fiery prawn curry

✵ ✵

Preparation time: 45 minutes
Cooking time: 35 minutes
Serves 4

500 g (1 lb 2 oz) raw prawns (shrimp)
250 g (9 oz) fresh pineapple
250 g (9 oz) potatoes
1 tablespoon oil
250 ml (9 fl oz/1 cup) coconut milk
2 tablespoons tamarind concentrate
1 teaspoon sugar
steamed rice, to serve

SPICE PASTE
6 small dried red chillies
1 teaspoon shrimp paste
1 teaspoon coriander seeds
1 large red onion, roughly chopped
6 garlic cloves
4 small red chillies, roughly chopped
2 green chillies, roughly chopped
4 cm (1½ inch) piece fresh galangal, roughly chopped
1 lemongrass stem, white part only, sliced
6 candlenuts
½ teaspoon ground turmeric
1 tablespoon oil

**1** To make the spice paste, soak the dried chillies in hot water until soft, then drain. Wrap the shrimp paste in a small piece of foil and cook under a hot grill (broiler) for 3 minutes each side. Dry-fry the coriander seeds in a small frying pan until aromatic. Place the onion, garlic and drained dried red chillies in a food processor and process until just combined. Add the shrimp paste, coriander seeds, fresh red and green chilli, galangal and lemongrass and process until well combined, scraping down the sides of the bowl with a spatula. Add the candlenuts, turmeric and oil and process until a smooth paste is formed.

**2** Peel the prawns, leaving the tails intact. Gently pull out the dark vein from each prawn back, starting at the head end. Cut the pineapple into bite-sized pieces. Cut the potatoes into slightly larger pieces.

**3** Place the potato in a large saucepan with enough water to cover and cook for 5 minutes, or until just tender. Drain and set aside.

**4** Heat the oil in a large frying pan or wok; add the spice paste and cook over medium heat for 5 minutes, stirring. Add the pineapple, potato, coconut milk and 125 ml (4 fl oz/½ cup) water and bring to the boil. Reduce the heat, add the prawns and simmer for 5 minutes. Add the tamarind, sugar and 1 teaspoon salt. Serve with the steamed rice.

## baked spiced fish cutlets

✵

Preparation time: 15 minutes
Cooking time: 30 minutes
Serves 4

1 tablespoon oil
1 onion, very finely chopped
2 garlic cloves, finely chopped
5 cm (2 inch) piece fresh ginger, finely grated
1 teaspoon ground coriander
1 lemongrass stem, white part only, finely chopped
2 teaspoons tamarind concentrate
2 teaspoons very finely grated lemon zest
4 small fish cutlets, such as blue eye
lime wedges, to garnish
steamed rice, to serve

1 Preheat the oven to 160°C (315°F/Gas 2–3).
2 Heat the oil in a frying pan; add the onion, garlic, ginger, coriander and lemongrass, and stir over medium heat for 5 minutes or until aromatic.
3 Stir in the tamarind, lemon zest and season with black pepper, to taste. Remove from the heat and set aside until cool.
4 Line a baking dish with foil and grease it lightly to prevent the fish from sticking. Arrange the fish in the baking dish in a single layer and bake for 10 minutes. Turn the fish over gently, spread with the spice paste and bake for another 8 minutes, or until the flesh flakes when tested with a fork. Be sure not to overcook the fish or it will become dry. Garnish with the lime wedges and serve with the steamed rice.

NOTE: Adjust the cooking time if the cutlets are thick.

# mee goreng (fried noodles)

✹ ✹

Preparation time: 45 minutes
Cooking time: 20 minutes
Serves 4

1 kg (2 lb 4 oz) raw prawns (shrimp)
1 large onion, finely chopped
2 garlic cloves, finely chopped
2 red chillies, seeded and very finely chopped
2 cm (¾ inch) piece fresh ginger, finely grated
60 ml (2 fl oz/¼ cup) oil
350 g (12 oz) hokkien (egg) noodles, gently pulled apart
250 g (9 oz) rump steak, thinly sliced
4 spring onions (scallions), chopped
1 large carrot, cut into 4 cm (1½ inch) matchsticks
2 celery stalks, cut into 4 cm (1½ inch) matchsticks
1 tablespoon kecap manis
1 tablespoon soy sauce
1 tablespoon tomato sauce (ketchup)
spring onions (scallions), extra, thinly sliced, to garnish

1 Peel the prawns and gently pull out the dark vein from each prawn back, starting at the head end.
2 Combine the onion, garlic, chilli and ginger in a food processor or use a mortar and pestle, and process in short bursts, or pound, until a paste is formed, adding a little of the oil if necessary. Set aside until needed.
3 Heat about 1 tablespoon of the oil in a large wok; add the noodles and stir-fry over medium heat until they are plump and warmed through. Place the noodles on a serving plate and cover to keep warm.
4 Add another tablespoon of the oil to the wok; add the paste mixture and stir-fry until golden. Add the prawns, beef, spring onion, carrot and celery, and stir-fry for 2–3 minutes. Add the kecap manis, soy and tomato sauces, and season well with salt and pepper. Spoon the mixture over the noodles and garnish with the extra spring onion. Serve immediately.

indonesia

# satays & kebabs

To prevent the wooden skewers used for satays and kebabs burning before the meat is cooked, soak them in water for at least 30 minutes. The ends can also be wrapped in foil.

### chicken satays

Cut 500 g (1 lb 2 oz) chicken tenderloins in half lengthways. In a shallow non-metallic dish, combine 1 tablespoon honey, 60 ml (2 fl oz/¼ cup) soy sauce, 2 teaspoons sesame oil, 1 teaspoon ground coriander, 1 teaspoon ground turmeric and ½ teaspoon chilli powder. Thread the chicken lengthways onto soaked wooden skewers and place the skewers in the marinade. Cover and refrigerate for at least 2 hours. To make quick satay sauce, cook a small finely chopped onion in 1 tablespoon oil until softened and then stir in 125 g (4½ oz/½ cup) crunchy peanut butter, 2 tablespoons soy sauce, 125 ml (4 fl oz/½ cup) coconut cream and 2 tablespoons sweet chilli sauce. Cook gently until smooth and heated through. To cook the satays, cook the skewers under a preheated grill (broiler) for 5–7 minutes, turning and basting with the marinade frequently. Serve with the warm quick satay sauce. Makes 8 satays.

### teriyaki steak kebabs

Cut 750 g (1 lb 10 oz) lean rump steak into thin strips, 15 cm (6 inches) long and thread onto skewers. Combine 125 ml (4 fl oz/½ cup) soy sauce, 125 ml (4 fl oz/½ cup) sherry or sake, 1 crushed garlic clove and 1 teaspoon each ground ginger and sugar. Place the beef with the mixture in a non-metallic dish and marinate it for at least 1 hour in the refrigerator. Drain and place skewers on a preheated, oiled grill (broiler) tray or barbecue flatplate and cook for 3–4 minutes each side. Makes 24 kebabs.

### kofta on skewers

Combine 750 g (1 lb 10 oz) minced (ground) beef, 1 small grated onion, 30 g (1 oz/½ cup) chopped parsley, 2 tablespoons chopped coriander (cilantro) leaves, ½ teaspoon each ground cumin, nutmeg and cardamom, and ½ teaspoon each dried oregano and mint. Let stand for 1 hour. With wet hands, form the mixture into 24 sausage shapes; thread two koftas onto each skewer with a wedge of lime. Place the koftas on a preheated barbecue grill or flatplate, or under a hot grill (broiler) and cook for 10–12 minutes, turning frequently. Makes 12 skewers.

### malaysian lamb satays

Trim any fat or sinew from 500 g (1 lb 2 oz) lamb fillets. Slice the lamb across the grain into very thin strips (if you have time, put the lamb in the freezer for 30 minutes as this will make it easier to thinly slice). In a food processor, combine 1 roughly chopped onion, 2 crushed garlic cloves, 2 cm (¾ inch) lemongrass stem (white part only), 2 slices fresh galangal, 1 teaspoon chopped fresh ginger, 1 teaspoon ground cumin, ½ teaspoon ground fennel, 1 tablespoon ground coriander, 1 teaspoon turmeric, 1 tablespoon soft brown sugar and 1 tablespoon lemon juice and process until a smooth paste is formed. Transfer the paste to a shallow non-metallic dish and add the lamb, stirring to coat well. Cover and refrigerate overnight. Thread the lamb onto skewers and cook under a preheated grill (broiler) for 3–4 minutes on each side, or until cooked. Brush regularly with the remaining marinade while cooking. Makes 8 satays.

### chilli pork kebabs

Trim fat and sinew from 500 g (1 lb 2 oz) pork fillet and cut into small cubes. Combine 2 tablespoons sweet chilli sauce, 2 tablespoons tomato sauce (ketchup), 2 tablespoons hoisin sauce, 2 crushed garlic cloves, 60 ml (2 fl oz/¼ cup) lemon juice, 2 tablespoons honey and 2 teaspoons grated fresh ginger. Pour over pork and stir. Cover and refrigerate for several hours or overnight. Thread pork onto skewers; cook under a preheated, oiled grill (broiler) or barbecue flatplate for 3–4 minutes each side, until cooked. Brush with marinade while cooking. Serve with quick satay sauce (see Chicken satays). Makes 8 kebabs.

chicken satays and kofta on skewers

## cold vegetable salad with spice dressing

Preparation time: 15 minutes
Cooking time: 5 minutes
Serves 4

300 g (10½ oz) green or snake (yard-long) beans, trimmed
10 English spinach leaves
80 g (2¾ oz) snow pea (mangetout) sprouts
1 red capsicum (pepper)
1 red onion
100 g (3½ oz) bean sprouts, trimmed

SPICE DRESSING
2 tablespoons peanut oil
1 garlic clove, crushed
1 teaspoon finely grated fresh ginger
1 small red chilli, chopped
2 tablespoons desiccated coconut
1 tablespoon brown vinegar

1  Cut the beans into 10 cm (4 inch) lengths. Remove the stems from the spinach leaves and slice the leaves thinly. Remove about 1 cm (½ inch) of the long stems from the snow pea sprouts. Cut the capsicum into thin strips. Thinly slice the onion.
2  Put the beans in a large saucepan of boiling water and cook for 1 minute to blanch, then drain. Combine the beans, spinach, snow pea sprouts, bean sprouts, capsicum and onion in a bowl.
3  To make the spice dressing, heat the oil in a small frying pan. Add the garlic, ginger, chilli and coconut, and stir-fry over medium heat for 1 minute. Add the vinegar and 80 ml (2½ fl oz/⅓ cup) water, and simmer for 1 minute. Allow to cool.
4  To serve, add the dressing to the vegetables, and toss until combined.

NOTE: Snow pea (mangetout) sprouts are the growing tips and tendrils from the snow pea plant. Any blanched vegetables can be used in this salad. Try to use a variety of vegetables which result in a colourful appearance. The spice dressing can be added up to 30 minutes before serving.

## pork sambalan

Preparation time: 10 minutes
Cooking time: 10 minutes
Serves 4

400 g (14 oz) pork fillet
1–2 tablespoons Indonesian sambal paste (page 114)
1 tablespoon oil
375 ml (13 fl oz/1½ cups) coconut milk
spring onion (scallion), thinly sliced, to garnish
steamed rice, to serve

1  Slice the pork fillet into thin strips. Place the strips in a bowl with the sambal paste and oil, and toss until well combined.
2  Heat a wok to very hot; stir-fry the pork for about 2 minutes in two batches, until tender and lightly browned. Return all the pork to the wok.
3  Add the coconut milk and simmer, uncovered, for 2 minutes. Garnish with the spring onion and serve with the steamed rice.

NOTE: Two tablespoons of sambal paste will make this dish quite hot. Use less paste for a milder dish, if you prefer.

cold vegetable salad

# indonesia

## baked fish with spices

Preparation time: **15 minutes**
Cooking time: **30 minutes**
Serves **2**

2 whole white fish (such as bream or snapper), each about 300 g (10½ oz), cleaned and scaled
1 onion, chopped
1 garlic clove, crushed
1 teaspoon chopped fresh ginger
1 teaspoon chopped lemon zest
2 tablespoons tamarind concentrate
1 tablespoon light soy sauce
1 tablespoon peanut oil
spring onion (scallion), thinly sliced, and coriander (cilantro) sprigs, to garnish

**1** Preheat the oven to 180°C (350°F/Gas 4).
**2** Place the fish onto large pieces of foil. Make three deep incisions with a sharp knife on each side of the fish.
**3** Process the onion, garlic, ginger, lemon zest, tamarind, soy sauce and oil in a food processor until a smooth paste forms.
**4** Spread the onion mixture on the inside of the fish and on both sides.
**5** Wrap the foil around the fish and secure it firmly. Place the fish in a baking dish and bake for 30 minutes, or until the fish is just cooked. Garnish with spring onion and coriander.

baked fish with spices

## tamarind chicken

Preparation time: **15 minutes + 2 hours marinating time**
Cooking time: **35 minutes**
Serves **4**

4 boneless chicken thighs
4 chicken drumsticks
80 ml (2½ fl oz/⅓ cup) tamarind concentrate
2 teaspoons ground coriander
1 teaspoon ground turmeric
2 garlic cloves, crushed
2 tablespoons peanut oil
2 red chillies, finely chopped
6 spring onions (scallions), finely chopped
oil, for deep-frying

**1** Remove the skin from the chicken drumsticks. Put all the chicken in a large saucepan with enough water to cover it. Cover and simmer for 15 minutes, or until cooked through. Drain and cool.
**2** Combine the tamarind, coriander, turmeric and garlic. Add the tamarind mixture to the chicken and toss to coat. Cover and marinate in the refrigerator for at least 2 hours, or overnight.
**3** Heat the peanut oil in a frying pan; add the chilli and spring onion, and stir-fry over low heat for 3 minutes. Set aside.
**4** Heat the oil in a large, deep frying pan. Cook the chicken in three batches over medium heat for 5 minutes, or until the chicken is golden brown and heated through. Drain on paper towels, and keep warm while frying the remaining chicken. Serve the chicken pieces with a spoonful of the chilli mixture on the side.

essential asian

### grating coconut

To make grated fresh coconut, gently prise the flesh away from the shell using a flat-bladed knife. Use a vegetable peeler to remove the tough skin and then grate the flesh or use the vegetable peeler to flake it. Roast in a slow oven for 10–15 minutes to dry out before using.

## vegetable coconut curry

Preparation time: 40 minutes
Cooking time: 35 minutes
Serves 4 as part of a shared meal

300 g (10½ oz) pumpkin (winter squash)
200 g (7 oz) potatoes
250 g (9 oz) okra
1 onion
2 tablespoons oil
1 garlic clove, crushed
3 green chillies, seeded and very finely chopped
½ teaspoon ground turmeric
½ teaspoon fenugreek seeds
8 curry leaves
1 cinnamon stick
500 ml (17 fl oz/2 cups) coconut milk
steamed rice, to serve

1  Cut the pumpkin into 2 cm (¾ inch) cubes. Cut the potatoes into 2 cm (¾ inch) cubes. Trim the stems from the okra. Chop the onion.

2  Heat the oil in a large heavy-based saucepan. Add the garlic, chilli, turmeric, fenugreek seeds and onion, and cook over medium heat for 5 minutes, or until the onion is soft.

3  Add the pumpkin, potato, okra, curry leaves, cinnamon stick and coconut milk. Bring to the boil, then reduce the heat and simmer, uncovered, for 25–30 minutes, or until the vegetables are tender. Serve with the steamed rice.

# indonesia

## baked fish cakes

Preparation time: 20 minutes
Cooking time: 15 minutes
Serves 6 as an entrée

500 g (1 lb 2 oz) boneless white fish fillets
1 tablespoon Indonesian sambal paste (page 114)
2 tablespoons chopped lemongrass, white part only
2 cm (¾ inch) piece fresh ginger, finely grated
1 teaspoon ground cumin
3 spring onions (scallions), finely chopped
1 egg, lightly beaten
1 tablespoon chopped mint
lemon wedges, to serve

1  Preheat the oven to 180°C (350°F/Gas 4).
2  Place the fish, sambal paste, lemongrass, ginger, cumin and spring onion into a food processor and process until a smooth paste is formed.
3  Transfer the fish mixture to a bowl, and mix through the egg and mint.
4  Divide the mixture into 6 equal portions, and shape each portion into a sausage. Wrap each portion in a 15 x 25 cm (6 x 10 inch) piece of baking paper and bake for 15 minutes. Serve with a squeeze of lemon juice.

## indonesian rendang

Preparation time: 15 minutes
Cooking time: 2 hours 30 minutes
Serves 6

1.5 kg (3 lb 5 oz) chuck steak, trimmed
2 onions, roughly chopped
4 teaspoons crushed garlic
420 ml (14½ fl oz/1⅔ cups) coconut milk
2 teaspoons ground coriander
½ teaspoon ground fennel
2 teaspoons ground cumin
¼ teaspoon ground cloves
4 red chillies, chopped
1 lemongrass stem, white part only, or 4 strips lemon zest
1 tablespoon lemon juice
2 teaspoons grated palm sugar (jaggery) or soft brown sugar
steamed rice, to serve
red chilles, sliced, to serve
coriander (cilantro) sprigs, to garnish

1  Cut the beef evenly into small (about 3 cm/1¼ inch) cubes.
2  Place the onion and garlic in a food processor and process until smooth, adding water if necessary.
3  Place the coconut milk in a large saucepan and bring it to the boil, then reduce the heat to moderate and cook, stirring occasionally, until the milk is reduced by half and the oil is separated out. Do not allow the milk to brown.
4  Add the coriander, fennel, cumin and cloves, and stir for 1 minute. Add the beef and cook for 2 minutes until it changes colour. Add the onion mixture, chilli, lemongrass, lemon juice and palm sugar. Cook over moderate heat for 2 hours, or until the liquid is reduced and the mixture is quite thick. Stir frequently to prevent it catching on the bottom of the pan.
5  Cook until the oil from the coconut milk begins to emerge again, letting the curry develop colour and flavour. This dish needs constant attention to prevent it from burning. The curry is cooked when it is brown and dry. Serve with steamed rice, chillies and coriander.

NOTE: Like most curries, this one benefits from being made ahead of time. Prepare 2–3 days in advance and store, covered, in the refrigerator. Reheat over low heat. The curry can also be cooled in the refrigerator then frozen for up to 1 month.

indonesian rendang

## balinese fried rice

✹

Preparation time: 20 minutes
Cooking time: 20 minutes
Serves 6

500 g (1 lb 2 oz) raw prawns (shrimp)
2 teaspoons oil
2 eggs
2 onions, chopped
2 garlic cloves
3 tablespoons oil, extra
¼ teaspoon shrimp paste
125 g (4½ oz) rump steak, thinly sliced
1 cooked chicken breast, thinly sliced
300 g (10½ oz/1½ cups) long-grain rice, cooked and cooled
1 tablespoon soy sauce
1 tablespoon fish sauce
1 tablespoon sambal oelek
1 tablespoon tomato paste (concentrated purée)
6 spring onions (scallions), finely chopped
1 telegraph (long) cucumber sliced, to garnish

**1** Peel the prawns and gently pull out the dark vein from each prawn back, starting at the head end; chop the prawn meat.
**2** Heat the oil in a wok or heavy-based saucepan. Lightly beat the eggs and season with salt and pepper. Add the egg to the wok and cook over moderately high heat, pulling the cooked edges of the egg towards the centre. When set, transfer the omelette to a plate, cool, and cut into fine strips. Set aside.
**3** Place the onion and garlic in a food processor and process until finely chopped.
**4** Heat the extra oil in the wok; add the onion mixture and cook over medium heat, stirring frequently until it is reduced in volume and is translucent. Add the shrimp paste and cook a further minute. Add the prawns and beef and cook over high heat for 3 minutes. Add the chicken and rice and toss until heated.
**5** Combine the soy sauce, fish sauce, sambal oelek, tomato paste and spring onion and add to the rice mixture. Mix well. Remove the rice from the heat and transfer to a serving platter. Top with the omelette strips and garnish with the sliced cucumber.

## balinese fried fish

✹ ✹

Preparation time: 25 minutes
Cooking time: 30 minutes
Serves 4

750 g (1 lb 10 oz) firm white fish fillets (such as jewfish or ling)
oil, for shallow-frying
4 red Asian shallots, sliced lengthways
2.5 cm (1 inch) piece lemongrass, white part only, finely chopped
2 red chillies, finely chopped
2 cm (¾ inch) piece fresh ginger, grated
½ teaspoon shrimp paste
2 tablespoons kecap manis
1 tablespoon grated palm sugar (jaggery) or soft brown sugar
2 teaspoons lime juice
3 spring onions (scallions), finely chopped

balinese fried rice

# indonesia

### feasts in bali

Feasts are an important feature of Balinese family and community life. For temple festivals an entire community prepares foods and offerings. Pork (a largely forbidden food in the rest of Indonesia, where the population is mostly Muslim) is festive food in Bali, with babi guling — roast suckling pig — the usual feast centrepiece.

1   Preheat the oven to 160°C (315°F/Gas 2–3). Cut the fish into bite-sized pieces; sprinkle with ½ teaspoon salt and ½ teaspoon pepper.
2   Heat the oil, about 2 cm (¾ inch) deep, in a deep frying pan; add the fish 3–4 pieces at a time, and cook over moderately high heat for about 4 minutes, turning the pieces over, until they are light golden brown. Drain the fish on paper towels and place in the oven to keep warm.
3   In a small saucepan, heat 2 tablespoons of the fish frying oil; add the shallots, lemongrass, chilli, ginger and shrimp paste and cook for 3 minutes over low heat, stirring occasionally. Add 125 ml (4 fl oz/½ cup) water, the kecap manis and palm sugar, and stir until the sauce boils and thickens. Stir in the lime juice and spring onion. Drizzle the sauce over the fish and serve immediately.

NOTE: The fish must have a solid meaty texture or it will fall apart during the frying. Kecap manis is Indonesian soy sauce, and is slightly thicker and sweeter than Chinese soy sauce.

## sweet kecap pork

Preparation time: 20 minutes
Cooking time: 1 hour 30 minutes
Serves 4

500 g (1 lb 2 oz) diced pork
2 tablespoons oil
1 large onion, finely chopped
3 garlic cloves, finely chopped
5 cm (2 inch) piece fresh ginger, finely grated
3 red chillies, finely chopped
2 tablespoons kecap manis
250 ml (9 fl oz/1 cup) coconut milk
2 teaspoons lime juice
red chilli, thinly sliced, to serve
steamed rice, to serve
lime slices, to serve

**1** Mix together the pork, oil, ¼ teaspoon salt and ¼ teaspoon pepper and leave to stand for 10 minutes.
**2** Heat a wok or heavy-based frying pan and cook the pork in batches over medium heat, until well browned. Remove all the pork from the wok and set aside. Reduce the heat to low, add the onion, garlic, ginger and chilli and cook for 10 minutes, stirring occasionally until the onion is very soft and golden. Add the pork, kecap manis and coconut milk, and cook over low heat for 1 hour, stirring occasionally. Stir in the lime juice and serve with the chilli, steamed rice and lime slices.

## stir-fried hot beef

Preparation time: 25 minutes
Cooking time: 10 minutes
Serves 4

1 teaspoon coriander seeds
500 g (1 lb 2 oz) sirloin, fillet or topside steak, thinly sliced
1 tablespoon oil
2 tablespoons tamarind concentrate
2 teaspoons grated palm sugar (jaggery) or soft brown sugar
2 tablespoons coconut cream

SPICE PASTE
5 red chillies
2 cm (¾ inch) piece fresh galangal, sliced
1 teaspoon shrimp paste
10 red Asian shallots, roughly chopped
4 garlic cloves
2 tablespoons oil

**1** To make the spice paste, place all the paste ingredients in a food processor and process until a smooth paste forms, scraping down the sides of the bowl with a spatula regularly.
**2** Dry-fry the coriander seeds over low heat for 1 minute in a frying pan, shaking the pan constantly. Grind the seeds using a mortar and pestle or food processor.

# indonesia

**3** Combine the beef with the coriander and ½ teaspoon salt, mixing well. Set aside.

**4** Heat the oil in a wok or frying pan; add the spice paste and cook over high heat for 3 minutes, or until very aromatic and a little oily. Remove the spice paste from the wok.

**5** Reheat the wok to high: add the beef in two batches and stir-fry for 2–3 minutes or until just cooked. Add the spice paste, tamarind, palm sugar and coconut cream. Toss over very high heat for 1 minute and serve immediately.

## balinese chilli squid

✹ ✹

Preparation time: 25 minutes
Cooking time: 35 minutes
Serves 4

750 g (1 lb 10 oz) squid tubes
60 ml (2 fl oz/¼ cup) lime juice
2 tablespoons oil
1 large red chilli, seeded and sliced
3 spring onions (scallions), sliced
1 tablespoon oil, extra
1 tablespoon tamarind concentrate
1 lemongrass stem, white part only, thinly sliced
250 ml (9 fl oz/1 cup) chicken stock
5 Thai basil leaves, shredded
steamed rice, to serve

SPICE PASTE
2 large red chillies, seeded and chopped
2 garlic cloves, chopped
2 cm (¾ inch) piece fresh turmeric, chopped
2 cm (¾ inch) piece fresh ginger, chopped
3 spring onions (scallions), chopped
1 tomato, peeled, seeded and chopped
2 teaspoons coriander seeds
1 teaspoon shrimp paste

**1** Cut the squid into large pieces and score the tender inner flesh diagonally, in a criss-cross pattern, taking care not to cut all the way through. Place in a bowl with the lime juice and season to taste with salt and pepper. Cover and refrigerate.

**2** To make the spice paste, place all the ingredients in a food processor and process until a smooth paste forms, scraping down the sides of the bowl with a spatula regularly.

**3** Heat the oil in a wok and add the chilli and spring onion. Add the squid in batches and cook over moderate heat for 2 minutes. Remove from the wok.

**4** Heat the extra oil in the wok, add the spice paste, tamarind and lemongrass and cook over moderate heat, stirring, for 5 minutes.

**5** Return the squid to the wok and add the stock. Season with pepper and add the basil. Bring to the boil, then reduce the heat and simmer for 20 minutes. Serve with the steamed rice.

## shrimp paste

Shrimp paste is always cooked before it is eaten. This transforms its acrid flavour into an aromatic seasoning. If it is not to be fried with the spice paste, wrap it in foil and dry-fry in a frying pan or roast in the oven or under the grill (broiler) — this will prevent its overpowering odour filling the entire house.

## festive coconut rice

✹ ✹

Preparation time: 25 minutes
Cooking time: 40 minutes
Serves 6–8

3 tablespoons oil
1 onion, cut into thin wedges
4 cm (1½ inch) piece fresh ginger, finely grated
2 garlic cloves, finely chopped
500 g (1 lb 2 oz/2½ cups) long-grain rice
1 teaspoon ground turmeric
1 litre (35 fl oz/4 cups) coconut milk
6 curry leaves

GARNISHES
3 hard-boiled eggs, peeled, cut into quarters
35 g (1¼ oz/½ cup) crisp fried onion
1 Lebanese (short) cucumber, sliced into matchsticks
2 red chillies, thinly sliced
coriander (cilantro) sprigs

**1** Heat the oil in a large heavy-based saucepan; add the onion, ginger and garlic and fry over low heat for 5 minutes. Add the rice and turmeric, and cook for 2 minutes, stirring well.
**2** Place the coconut milk in a medium saucepan, and heat until nearly boiling.

# indonesia

Pour it over the rice, stirring constantly until the mixture comes to the boil. Add 1 teaspoon salt and the curry leaves. Cover with a tight-fitting lid, reduce the heat to very low and cook for 25 minutes or until all the coconut milk is absorbed.
**3** Remove the lid, stir well and cool for 10 minutes. Remove the curry leaves and pile the rice onto a platter (traditionally lined with banana leaves). Serve the egg, cucumber, chilli, fried onion and coriander separately, or over the top.

## fresh corn sambal

※ ※

Preparation time: 25 minutes
Cooking time: 10 minutes
Serves 8

3 corn cobs
1 tablespoon coriander seeds
1 teaspoon shrimp paste, crumbled into pieces
1 garlic clove
1 onion, roughly chopped
3 red chillies
3 tablespoons tamarind concentrate
3 teaspoons sugar
steamed rice, to serve

**1** Remove the husk and silks from the corn. Cut down the cobs with a sharp knife to remove the kernels. Dry-fry the corn kernels over medium heat for 5 minutes, in batches if necessary, shaking the pan regularly until the corn kernels turn golden but do not burn. Set aside.
**2** Dry-fry the coriander seeds and shrimp paste in a frying pan for 3 minutes or until aromatic. Roughly grind the coriander and shrimp paste using a mortar and pestle.
**3** Place the corn, ground coriander and shrimp paste, garlic, onion and chilli in a food processor and process until a rough paste forms. Add the tamarind, 2 tablespoons water, ½ teaspoon salt and the sugar and process again.
**4** Serve the sambal as an accompaniment to curries, fish and vegetable dishes with the steamed rice.

*mixed vegetables with tamarind*

## mixed vegetables with tamarind

※

Preparation time: 25 minutes
Cooking time: 30 minutes
Serves 4

250 g (9 oz) pumpkin (winter squash)
200 g (7 oz) potatoes
100 g (3½ oz) beans, trimmed
200 g (7 oz) cabbage
100 g (3½ oz) English spinach leaves
500 ml (17 fl oz/2 cups) vegetable stock
125 ml (4 fl oz/½ cup) tamarind concentrate
2 cinnamon sticks
2 bay leaves
4 garlic cloves, finely chopped
10 red Asian shallots, very thinly sliced
5 cm (2 inch) piece fresh ginger, finely grated
200 g (7 oz) baby corn
steamed rice, to serve
chilli, thinly sliced, to serve

**1** Roughly chop the pumpkin. Cut the potato into thick slices. Shred the cabbage and spinach leaves.
**2** Place the stock, tamarind, cinnamon, bay leaves, garlic, shallots and ginger in a large saucepan, and bring to the boil.
**3** Add the pumpkin and potato and simmer for 5 minutes. Add the corn and beans and cook for another 5 minutes.
**4** Add the cabbage and spinach and cook until just tender. Serve with the steamed rice as an accompaniment to a main meal, with thinly sliced chilli.

# singapore & malaysia

Separated by only a narrow strip of water, peninsular Malaysia and the island state of Singapore have many dishes in common. The Indian, Muslim and Chinese heritage of both countries can be seen in Indian-hot curries, Middle Eastern-inspired satays and Chinese noodles, stir-fries and roasted meats. These influences come together in dishes such as laksa, a creamy curry of seafood or chicken simmered in coconut milk. In Singapore, the mix of Malays and Chinese has created Nonya food — an exciting blend of Chinese balance and Malaysian heat.

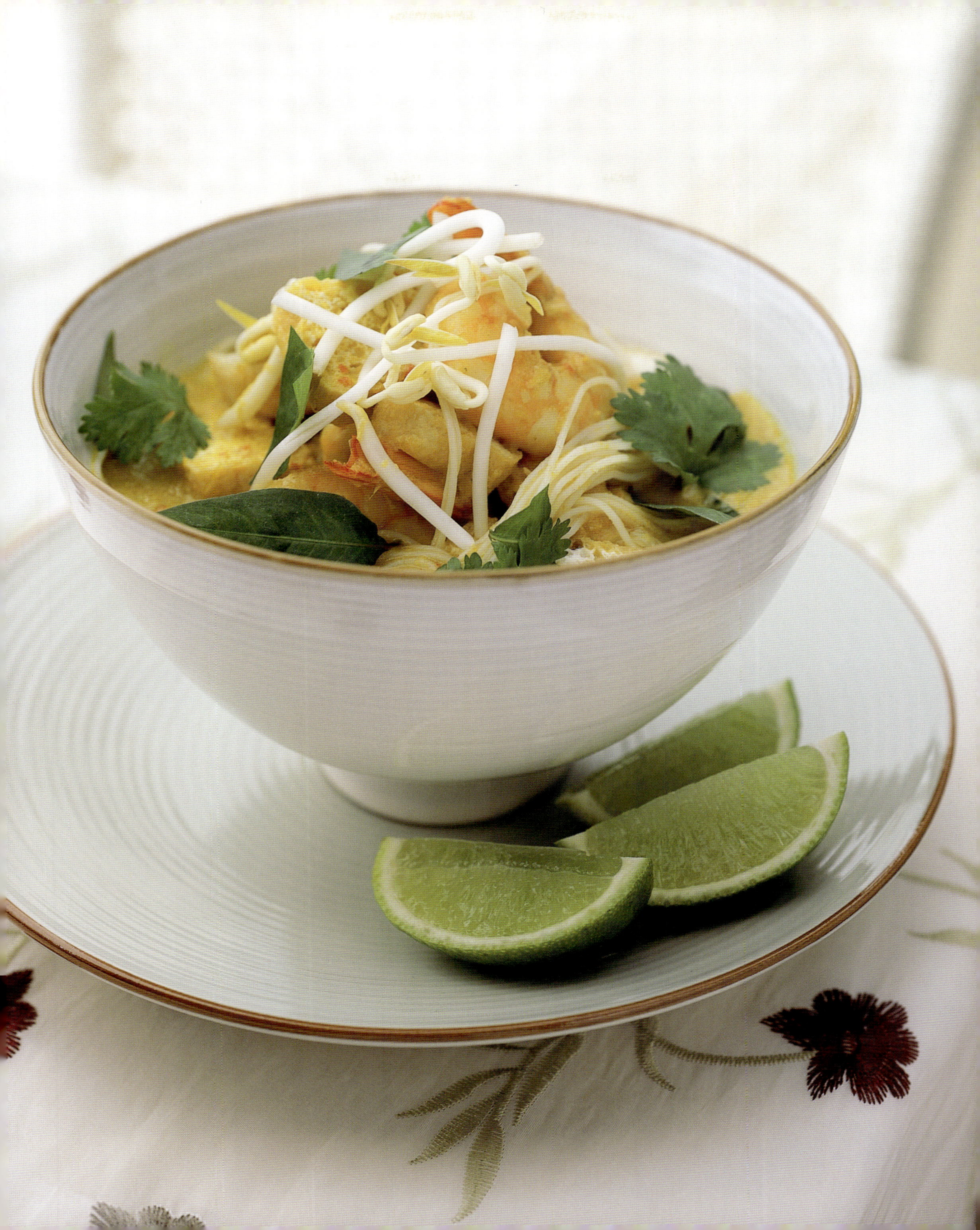

essential asian

Hit the legs and larger front nippers to crack the shells.

Turn the crab and hold it in oil until the shell just turns red.

# chilli crab

✹ ✹ ✹

Preparation time: 30 minutes
Cooking time: 45 minutes
Serves 2–4

2 fresh blue swimmer crabs, approximately 500 g (1 lb 2 oz) each
60 g (2¼ oz/½ cup) plain (all-purpose) flour
60 ml (2 fl oz/¼ cup) oil
1 onion, finely chopped
5 cm (2 inch) piece fresh ginger, finely grated
4 garlic cloves, finely chopped
3–5 red chillies, finely chopped
500 ml (17 fl oz/2 cups) tomato passata (puréed tomatoes)
2 tablespoons soy sauce
2 tablespoons sweet chilli sauce
1 tablespoon rice vinegar
2 tablespoons soft brown sugar
spring onion, thinly sliced, to garnish

1  Place the crabs in the freezer for 2 hours or until they are absolutely immobile and dead (this is the most humane way to kill crab or lobster).
2  Wash the crabs well and scrub the shells using a scourer. Use a large cleaver to cut the crabs in half and rinse well under cold water, carefully removing the yellow gills or spongy parts. Hit the legs and larger front nippers with the flat side of the cleaver to crack the shells (to make it easier to eat the meat inside).
3  Lightly and carefully coat the shells with a little flour. Heat about 2 tablespoons of the oil in a large wok, cook one crab half at a time, carefully turning and holding the crab in the hot oil until the shell just turns red. Repeat with the remaining crab halves.
4  Add the remaining oil to the wok; cook the onion, ginger, garlic and chilli for 5 minutes over medium heat, stirring regularly. Add the tomato passata, 250 ml (9 fl oz/1 cup) water, soy sauce, sweet chilli sauce, vinegar and sugar. Bring to the boil and cook for 15 minutes. Return the crab to the wok and simmer, turning carefully in the sauce for 8–10 minutes or until the crab meat turns white. Do not overcook. Garnish with the spring onion. Serve with steamed rice, if desired, and provide finger bowls.

NOTE: It is essential that only fresh crabs are used so order them from your fishmonger the day before required, and insist on having crabs that have been freshly caught. Live crabs can be killed by your fishmonger if you prefer. Don't buy cooked crabs for this recipe.

# singapore noodles

✹

Preparation time: 45 minutes
Cooking time: 15 minutes
Serves 2–4

300 g (10½ oz) dried rice vermicelli
600 g (1 lb 5 oz) raw prawns (shrimp)
2 tablespoons oil
2 garlic cloves, finely chopped
350 g (12 oz) pork loin, cut into strips
1 large onion, cut into thin wedges
1 tablespoon mild curry powder
150 g (5½ oz) green beans, trimmed, cut into 3–4 cm lengths
1 large carrot, cut into fine matchsticks
1 teaspoon caster (superfine) sugar
1 tablespoon soy sauce
200 g (7 oz) bean sprouts, trimmed
spring onion (scallion), thinly sliced, to garnish

1  Soak the vermicelli in boiling water for 5 minutes or until soft; drain well.
2  Peel the prawns and gently pull out the dark vein from each prawn back, starting at the head end. Chop the prawn meat.
3  Heat 1 tablespoon of the oil in a wok over high heat. When hot, add the prawn meat, garlic and pork. Stir-fry for 2 minutes or until just cooked; remove from the wok.
4  Reduce the heat to medium and heat another tablespoon of the oil; add the onion and curry powder and stir-fry for 2–3 minutes. Add the beans, carrot, sugar and 1 teaspoon salt, sprinkle with a little water and stir-fry for 2 minutes.
5  Add the vermicelli and soy sauce to the wok; toss with 2 wooden spoons. Add the bean sprouts and pork mixture, season with salt, pepper and sugar to taste, and then toss well. Serve garnished with the spring onion.

singapore noodles

## mixed vegetable salad

❄ ❄

Preparation time: 40 minutes
Cooking time: 5 minutes
Serves 4–6

300 g (10½ oz) fresh pineapple, chopped
1 telegraph (long) cucumber, sliced
250 g (9 oz) cherry tomatoes, halved
155 g (5½ oz) green beans, trimmed, thinly sliced
150 g (5½ oz) bean sprouts, trimmed
80 ml (2½ fl oz/⅓ cup) rice vinegar
2 tablespoons lime juice
2 red chillies, seeded and very finely chopped
2 teaspoons sugar
30 g (1 oz) dried shrimp, to garnish
small mint leaves, to garnish

1  Toss together the pineapple, cucumber, tomatoes, beans and sprouts in a bowl. Cover and refrigerate until chilled. Combine the vinegar, lime juice, chilli and sugar in a small bowl and stir until the sugar has dissolved.
2  Dry-fry the shrimp in a frying pan, shaking the pan constantly until the shrimp are light orange and fragrant. Process the shrimp in a food processor until finely chopped.
3  Arrange the chilled salad on a serving platter, drizzle the dressing over the top and garnish with the shrimp and mint leaves. Serve immediately.

## garlic prawns in chilli sauce

❄

Preparation time: 40 minutes
Cooking time: 10 minutes
Serves 4

1 kg (2 lb 4 oz) raw king prawns (shrimp)
2 garlic cloves, crushed
2 tablespoons peanut oil
3 teaspoons finely grated fresh ginger
1 celery stalk, diced
1 red capsicum (pepper), seeded and diced
1 tablespoon sweet chilli sauce
1 tablespoon hoisin sauce
2 tablespoons lime juice
1 teaspoon sugar
steamed rice, to serve

1  Peel the prawns, leaving the tails intact. Gently pull out the dark vein from each prawn back, starting at the head end. Place the prawns in a non-metallic bowl and mix in the garlic. Set aside.
2  Heat a wok over medium heat and add 1 tablespoon of the oil. Add the ginger, celery and capsicum and cook until softened. Remove from the wok. Heat the remaining oil and add the prawns. Cook over high heat until bright pink and cooked through. Spoon the celery and capsicum mixture back into the wok with the prawns and add the chilli sauce, hoisin sauce, lime juice and sugar. Season to taste with pepper. Heat through for a minute or so then serve with the steamed rice.

## siamese noodles with spicy coconut sauce

❄ ❄ ❄

Preparation time: 1 hour 10 minutes
Cooking time: 30 minutes
Serves 6

1 tablespoon dried tamarind pulp
1.25 litres (44 fl oz/5 cups) coconut milk

*mixed vegetable salad*

## singapore & malaysia

300 g (10½ oz) dried rice vermicelli
400 g (14 oz) fried tofu
oil, for shallow frying
400 g (14 oz) bean sprouts, trimmed
500 g (1 lb 2 oz) cooked prawns (shrimp), peeled and deveined, tails intact
125 g (4½ oz/ 1 cup) garlic chives, snipped
3 hard-boiled eggs, peeled, cut into quarters
2 red chillies (optional), seeded and finely sliced
3 limes, quartered, to serve

SPICE PASTE
10 dried red chillies, soaked in hot water until softened
10 red Asian shallots, chopped
1 lemongrass stem, white part only, chopped
1 teaspoon shrimp paste
3 tablespoons peanut oil
1 tablespoon sugar

**1** To make the spice paste, drain and seed the soaked chillies, reserving the water, and chop. Place the chillies in a food processor or blender along with the shallots, lemongrass and shrimp paste. Process until finely chopped, adding a little of the chilli water if necessary. Heat the peanut oil in a small frying pan and fry the paste over low heat for about 3 minutes. Add 1 teaspoon salt and the sugar. Set aside.
**2** Soak the tamarind in 125 ml (4 fl oz/½ cup) warm water for about 10 minutes.
**3** Take half the spice paste and place it in a saucepan along with the coconut milk. Strain the soaked tamarind and water through a nylon sieve into the coconut milk and discard any seeds and fibre. Bring the mixture to the boil and simmer for 3 minutes. Set aside.
**4** Soak the vermicelli in boiling water for 5 minutes or until soft; drain well. Cut the tofu into thick slices. Heat the oil in a small frying pan and fry the slices of tofu until golden on both sides. Remove and drain on paper towels.
**5** When ready to serve the dish, heat the remaining spice paste in a large wok and add the bean sprouts. Turn the heat up high and cook for about a minute. Add half the prawns and half the garlic chives. Add the drained vermicelli to the wok; toss until heated through. Reheat the coconut sauce and keep it hot.
**6** To serve, transfer the vermicelli mixture to a large warm serving platter and arrange the remaining prawns, the egg quarters and slices of tofu on top. Scatter over the sliced chilli, if desired, and remaining garlic chives. Pour the coconut sauce into a large warm soup tureen. Provide deep bowls for diners to fill with the vermicelli mixture, then ladle over some coconut sauce and a squeeze of lime juice.

### spring rolls

Spring rolls were originally eaten in China at festivities to celebrate the Lunar New Year, which heralds the coming of spring. Because no work should be done at this time, the rolls — which traditionally contained fresh bamboo shoots — were made ahead. Many varieties of spring roll are eaten throughout Southeast Asia.

# finger food

Asia has a delicious range of finger food, served with fragrant tea in the middle of the day, a cooling beer in the evening or bought piping hot from a street stall.

## thai spring rolls

Soak 30 g (1 oz) dried rice vermicelli in boiling water for 5 minutes or until soft. Drain well and cut into shorter lengths. Heat 1 tablespoon oil in a wok or pan and add 3 chopped garlic cloves, 2 teaspoons finely grated fresh galangal or ginger, 3 finely chopped coriander (cilantro) roots and 3 chopped spring onions (scallions). Stir-fry for 2 minutes. Add 200 g (7 oz) minced (ground) pork and 2 finely sliced celery stalks and stir-fry for 3 minutes to brown the pork, breaking up any lumps. Add 155 g (5½ oz/1 cup) grated carrot, 25 g (1 oz) chopped coriander (cilantro) leaves, 45 g (1¾ oz/¼ cup) finely chopped Lebanese (short) cucumber, 1 tablespoon sweet chilli sauce, 2 teaspoons fish sauce, 1 teaspoon brown sugar and the noodles and mix well. Cool completely. Place 1 spring roll wrapper at a time (you will need about 14), with a corner towards you, on a damp tea towel (dish towel). Wet the edges with a little water. Spread about 1½ tablespoons of the filling in the centre of the wrapper. Fold the edges towards the centre, roll up the spring roll tightly and seal the edge with water. Repeat with the remaining wrappers and filling. Half fill a deep saucepan with oil and heat until moderately hot. Fry the rolls, in batches, for 2–3 minutes or until golden brown. Drain and serve with sweet chilli sauce and soy sauce. Makes 14.

## prawn toasts

Peel and devein 350 g (12 oz) raw prawns (shrimp). Separate 2 eggs into small bowls and lightly beat the egg yolks. Place the prawn meat, egg whites, 1 garlic clove, 75 g (2¾ oz) drained, finely chopped tinned water chestnuts, 1 tablespoon chopped coriander (cilantro) leaves, 2 teaspoons grated fresh ginger, and ¼ teaspoon each ground white pepper and salt in a food processor. Process for 20–30 seconds, or until the mixture is smooth. Trim the crusts from 6 slices of white bread, cut in half diagonally then cut the halves in half again to form small triangles. Brush the top of each bread triangle with egg yolk, spread the prawn mixture evenly over the triangles and sprinkle each with white sesame seeds — you will need about 1 tablespoon. Half fill a deep saucepan with oil and heat until moderately hot. Fry the triangles in small batches, with the prawn mixture face down, for a few seconds, or until golden and crisp. Drain on paper towels. Serve hot. Makes 24.

## vegetarian won tons

Heat 1 tablespoon oil in a wok or frying pan and cook 2 chopped garlic cloves, 4 chopped spring onions (scallions) and 3 teaspoons grated fresh ginger for 2 minutes. Add 2 finely sliced celery stalks, 150 g (5½ oz/2 cups) finely shredded cabbage, 310 g (11 oz/2 cups) grated carrot, 125 g (4½ oz) finely sliced fried tofu, 125 g (4½ oz/1 cup) chopped, trimmed bean sprouts and 2 tablespoons drained, chopped tinned water chestnuts. Cover the wok and steam for 2 minutes. Mix 3 teaspoons cornflour (cornstarch), 1 tablespoon water, 2 teaspoons sesame oil, 2 teaspoons soy sauce and ½ teaspoon each of salt and ground white pepper and mix until smooth. Add to the vegetable mixture and stir for 2 minutes, or until the sauce thickens. Cool completely. Place 1 tablespoon of filling in the centre of each won ton wrapper (you will need about 40). Brush the edges with a little water and gather around the filling to form a pouch; twist and pinch the sides together. Deep-fry in hot oil for 4–5 minutes or steam in a bamboo or metal steamer for 25–30 minutes. Makes 40.

## seafood won tons

Make as for vegetarian won tons (above) but replace the celery, cabbage, carrot and tofu with 750 g (1 lb 10 oz) raw prawns (shrimp), peeled, deveined and chopped. After steaming, stir in 170 g (6 oz) drained tinned crabmeat and 2 tablespoons chopped coriander (cilantro) leaves. Makes 50.

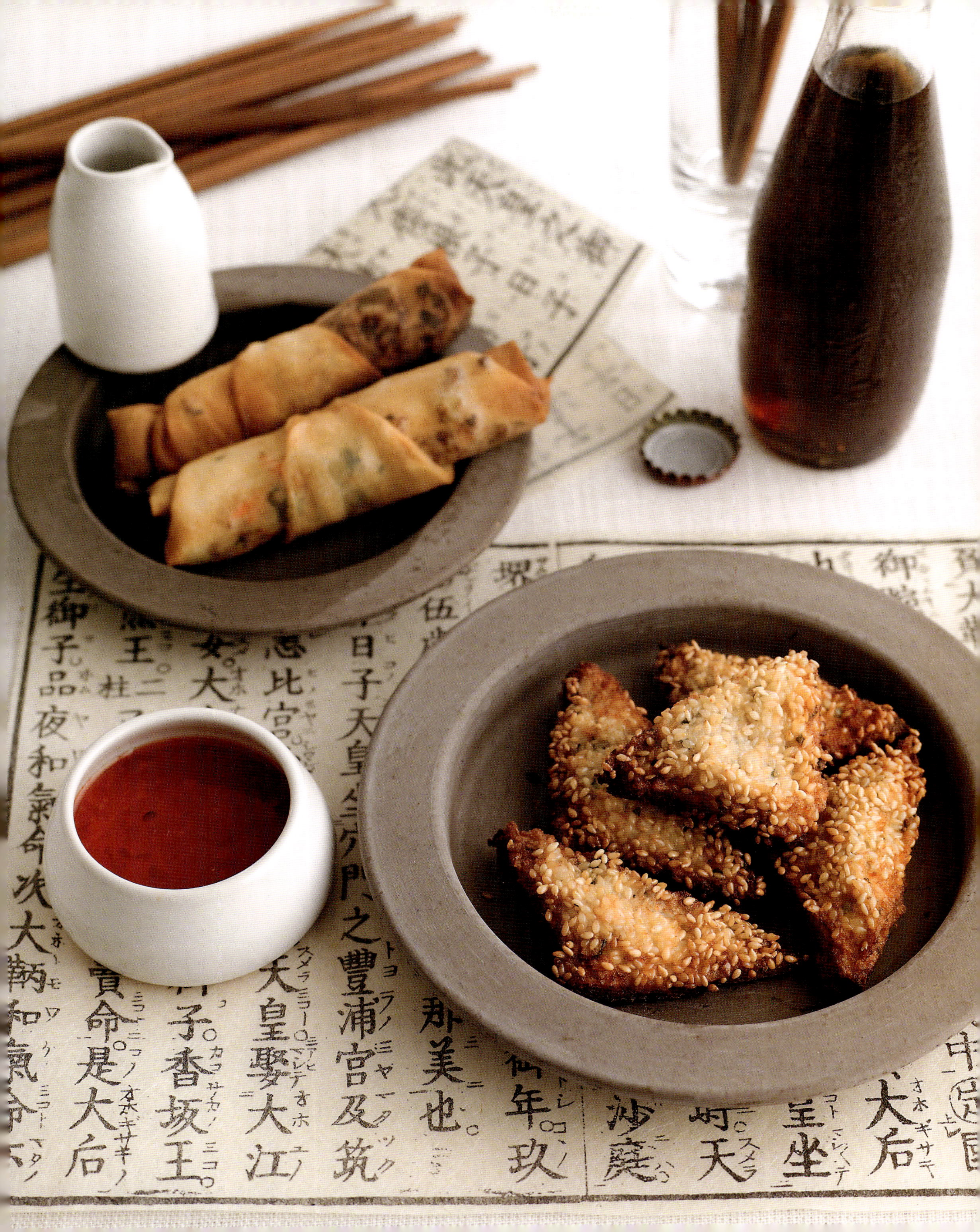

## malaysian coconut chicken

Preparation time: 25 minutes
Cooking time: 45–60 minutes
Serves 4–6

1.6 kg (3 lb 8 oz) chicken
1 tablespoon oil
2 onions, sliced
3 garlic cloves, crushed
2 red chillies, seeded and chopped
45 g (1¾ oz/½ cup) desiccated coconut
2 teaspoons ground turmeric
2 teaspoons ground coriander
2 teaspoons ground cumin
2 lemongrass stems, white part only, chopped
8 curry leaves
500 ml (17 fl oz/2 cups) coconut milk
cooked vermicelli noodles, to serve

**1** Cut the chicken into 8–10 pieces.
**2** Heat the oil in a large suacepan and cook the onion until soft. Add the garlic, chilli, coconut and turmeric. Stir the mixture for 1 minute. Add the coriander, cumin, lemongrass, curry leaves and coconut milk. Stir until well combined.
**3** Add the chicken pieces and stir until well coated with the sauce. Simmer, uncovered, for 45–60 minutes, or until the chicken is tender and the sauce is thickened. Serve with the noodles.

## rotis with spicy meat filling

Preparation time: 40 minutes + 2 hours resting time
Cooking time: 1 hour 30 minutes
Makes 12

375 g (13 oz/3 cups) roti flour or plain (all-purpose) flour
2 tablespoons ghee or oil
1 egg, lightly beaten
oil, to brush
1 egg, extra, beaten
½ red onion, finely chopped
extra ghee or oil, for frying

SPICY MEAT FILLING
1 tablespoon ghee
1 onion, finely chopped
3 garlic cloves, crushed
2 teaspoons ground cumin
1 teaspoon ground coriander
1 teaspoon ground turmeric
250 g (9 oz) lean minced (ground) beef or lamb
1 teaspoon finely chopped, seeded red chilli
1 tablespoon chopped coriander (cilantro) leaves

**1** Sift the flour into a large bowl and stir in 1 teaspoon salt. Rub in the ghee or pour in the oil. Add the egg and 250 ml (9 fl oz/1 cup) water and mix with a flat-bladed knife to form a moist mixture. Turn the mixture out on to a well-floured surface and knead for about 10 minutes until you have a soft dough, sprinkling with more flour as necessary. Form the dough into a ball and brush it with oil. Place it in an oiled bowl, cover with plastic wrap and leave to rest for 2 hours.
**2** To make the spicy meat filling, heat the ghee in a large frying pan and add the onion. Cook over low heat for about 5 minutes until soft and golden. Add the garlic, cumin, coriander and turmeric and cook for 1 minute. Turn up the heat, add the minced meat and brown well, using a fork to break up any lumps. Carry on cooking until the meat is cooked through, adding the chilli in the last few minutes of cooking. Remove from the heat, stir in the coriander and season with salt to taste.

3 Working on a floured work surface (use a clean bench top), divide the dough into 12 pieces and roll it into balls. Take one ball and, working with a little oil on your fingertips, hold the ball in the air and work around the edge pulling out the dough until a 15 cm (6 inch) round is formed. Lay the roti on a lightly floured surface and cover with plastic wrap so it doesn't dry out. Repeat with the other balls.

4 Heat a wide heavy frying pan or griddle and brush it with ghee or oil. Drape a roti over a rolling pin and carefully place the roti in the pan. Quickly brush the roti with some beaten egg and spoon over two heaped tablespoons of the meat filling. Cook until the underside of the roti is golden. This won't take long. Sprinkle the meat filling with some chopped onion, fold in two sides of the roti and then the other two sides, pressing to totally enclose the filling. Use a spatula to slide the roti onto a plate and brush the pan with some more ghee or oil. Return the roti to the heat to cook the other side. Cook until that side is golden. Cook the remaining rotis with the filling in the same way. Serve warm.

NOTE: Roti flour is a creamy-coloured flour available from Indian food stores. It is used in Indian unleavened breads. Plain flour can be used as a substitute.

## prawn and noodle soup

Preparation time: 40 minutes
Cooking time: 25 minutes
Serves 4

200 g (7 oz) baby spinach leaves
500 g (1 lb 2 oz) shanghai noodles
1 tablespoon oil
1 large onion, finely chopped
5 cm (2 inch) piece fresh ginger, finely grated
2 red chillies, finely chopped
1.5 litres (52 fl oz/6 cups) chicken stock
2 tablespoons soy sauce
2 teaspoons soft brown sugar
6 spring onions (scallions), chopped
300 g (10½ oz) small cooked prawns (shrimp), peeled and deveined, tails intact

GARNISHES
2 tablespoons crisp fried garlic
2 tablespoons crisp fried onion
90 g (3¼ oz/1 cup) bean sprouts, trimmed
2 teaspoons chilli flakes
1 tablespoon garlic chives, snipped

1 Wash and drain the spinach and snap off any long stems; set aside. Add the noodles to a saucepan of boiling water and cook for 3 minutes, or until plump and tender. Drain and set aside.

2 Heat the oil in a large saucepan and cook the onion and ginger over medium heat, stirring regularly, for 8 minutes. Add the chilli, stock, soy sauce and sugar and bring to the boil. Reduce the heat and leave to simmer for 10 minutes. Add the spring onion.

3 Transfer the noodles to large soup bowls and top with the prawns and spinach leaves. Pour the boiling stock over the top and serve immediately. Place the garnishes in small bowls, along with salt, pepper and sugar, for the diners to add according to their taste.

prawn and noodle soup

## fried rice noodles

❊

Preparation time: 20 minutes
Cooking time: 15 minutes
Serves 4

400 g (14 oz) raw prawns (shrimp)
2 Chinese dried pork sausages (see Note)
500 g (1 lb 2 oz) thick fresh rice noodles
2 tablespoons oil
2 garlic cloves, finely chopped
1 onion, finely chopped
3 red chillies, seeded and chopped
250 g (9 oz) Chinese barbecued pork (char siu), chopped
150 g (5½ oz) garlic chives, cut into short lengths, plus extra, to garnish
2 tablespoons kecap manis
3 eggs, lightly beaten
1 tablespoon rice vinegar
100 g (3½ oz) bean sprouts, trimmed, plus extra, to garnish

1 Peel the prawns and gently pull out the dark vein from each prawn back, starting at the head end. Slice the sausages on the diagonal into paper-thin slices. Use your fingertips to gently separate the noodles.
2 Heat the oil in a large wok or frying pan over high heat. Fry the sausage slices, tossing regularly, until they are golden and very crisp. Use a slotted spoon to remove from the wok and drain on paper towels.
3 Reheat the oil in the wok, add the garlic, onion, chilli and barbecued pork and stir-fry for 2 minutes. Add the prawns and toss constantly until they change colour. Add the noodles, chives and kecap manis and toss. Cook for 1 minute or until the noodles begin to soften. Pour the combined egg and vinegar over the top of the mixture and toss for 1 minute. Be careful not to let the egg-coated noodles burn on the base of the pan. Add the bean sprouts and toss.
4 Arrange the noodles on a large serving platter, scatter the drained pork sausages over the top and toss a little to mix a few slices among the noodles. Garnish with chives and bean sprouts and serve immediately.

NOTE: These spicy, dried pork sausages (lup chiang) are available from Asian food stores. They will keep for up to 3 months in the refrigerator.

## prawn laksa

❊ ❊

Preparation time: 30 minutes
Cooking time: 35 minutes
Serves 4–6

750 g (1 lb 10 oz) raw prawns (shrimp)
1½ tablespoons coriander seeds
1 tablespoon cumin seeds
1 teaspoon ground turmeric
1 onion, roughly chopped
2 teaspoons roughly chopped fresh ginger
3 garlic cloves
3 lemongrass stems, white part only, sliced
6 candlenuts or macadamia nuts, roughly chopped

# singapore & malaysia

## fish balls

These are small round balls made of finely minced fish, crab, prawns (shrimp) or scallops, and seasonings, bound with cornflour (cornstarch) or egg white, then kneaded, formed into balls and cooked. They are added to soups and braised dishes. Available ready-made from Asian food stores, they should be stored in the refrigerator and used within three days of purchase, or frozen.

- 4–6 small red chillies, roughly chopped
- 2–3 teaspoons shrimp paste
- 1 litre (35 fl oz/4 cups) chicken stock
- 60 ml (2 fl oz/¼ cup) vegetable oil
- 750 ml (26 fl oz/3 cups) coconut milk
- 4 kaffir lime (makrut) leaves
- 2½ tablespoons lime juice
- 2 tablespoons fish sauce
- 2 tablespoons grated palm sugar (jaggery) or soft brown sugar
- 250 g (9 oz) dried rice vermicelli
- 90 g (3¼ oz/1 cup) bean sprouts, trimmed
- 4 fried tofu puffs, cut into thin strips
- 3 tablespoons chopped Vietnamese mint
- 1 small handful coriander (cilantro) leaves
- lime wedges, to serve

1  Peel the prawns, leaving the tails intact. Gently pull out the dark vein from each prawn back, starting at the head end. Dry-fry the coriander seeds in a small frying pan over medium heat for 1–2 minutes, or until aromatic, tossing constantly. Grind finely using a mortar and pestle or spice grinder. Repeat the process with the cumin seeds.

2  Put the ground coriander and cumin, turmeric, onion, ginger, garlic, lemongrass, candlenuts, chilli and shrimp paste in a food processor or blender. Add 125 ml (4 fl oz/½ cup) of the stock and blend to a fine paste. Heat a wok over low heat, add the oil and swirl to coat the base and side. Cook the paste for 3–5 minutes, stirring constantly. Pour in the remaining stock and bring to the boil, then reduce the heat and simmer for 15 minutes, or until reduced slightly. Add the coconut milk, lime leaves, lime juice, fish sauce and palm sugar and simmer for 5 minutes. Add the prawns and simmer for 2 minutes, or until pink and cooked. Do not boil or cover.

3  Meanwhile, soak the vermicelli in boiling water for 5 minutes, or until soft. Drain well and divide among serving bowls along with most of the sprouts. Ladle on the hot soup then top with the tofu, mint, coriander and the remaining sprouts. Serve with lime wedges.

essential asian

# barbecued seafood

Preparation time: 35 minutes
Cooking time: 10 minutes
Serves 4

4 squid tubes
2 boneless firm white fish fillets, each about 300 g (10½ oz)
8 raw king prawns (shrimp)
banana leaves, to serve
lime cheeks, to serve

SPICE PASTE
1 onion, grated
4 garlic cloves, chopped
5 cm (2 inch) piece fresh ginger, grated
3 lemongrass stems, white part only, chopped
2 teaspoons ground turmeric
1 teaspoon dried shrimp paste
80 ml (2½ fl oz/⅓ cup) oil

**1** To make the spice paste, combine all the ingredients and ¼ teaspoon salt in a food processor or blender. Process in short bursts until a smooth paste forms.
**2** Cut the squid in half lengthways. Hold a sharp knife at a slight angle and make shallow, close cuts in one direction across the underside of each piece, then cut in the opposite direction, taking care not to cut all the way through. Then cut the squid into pieces about 3 x 4 cm (1¼ x 1½ inches).
**3** Wash all the seafood under cold running water and pat dry with paper towels. Brush the seafood lightly with the spice paste. Place the seafood on a tray and allow to stand for 15 minutes.
**4** Lightly brush a barbecue hotplate with oil and heat gently. When the plate is hot, arrange the fish fillets and prawns side by side on the plate. Cook for about 3 minutes on each side, turning them once only, or until the fish flesh is just firm and the prawns turn bright pink to orange. Add squid pieces and cook for about 2 minutes or until the flesh turns

Process all the ingredients for the spice paste until smooth.

Score a fine honeycomb pattern into the soft underside of the squid.

# singapore & malaysia

white and becomes firm. Take care not to overcook the seafood.

**5** Arrange seafood on a platter lined with banana leaves, add lime slices and serve.

## spicy prawns in sarongs

Preparation time: 30 minutes + 2 hours marinating time
Cooking time: 5 minutes
Serves 4 as an entrée

500 g (1 lb 2 oz) raw king prawns (shrimp)
1 tablespoon lime juice
2 teaspoons grated palm sugar (jaggery) or soft brown sugar
80 ml (2½ fl oz/⅓ cup) coconut milk
2 cm (¾ inch) wide strips of banana leaf (see Note), to wrap around each prawn
sweet chilli sauce (optional), to serve

SPICE PASTE
6 red Asian shallots, finely chopped
6 garlic cloves, crushed
3 candlenuts
2 teaspoons finely chopped fresh galangal
4 red chillies, seeded and finely chopped
1 teaspoon ground turmeric
1 teaspoon shrimp paste

**1** To make the spice paste, place all the ingredients in a food processor or blender. Process until a rough-textured paste forms.
**2** Peel the prawns and gently pull out the dark vein from each prawn back, starting at the head end. Place the prawns in a non-metallic bowl and sprinkle with the lime juice and ¼ teaspoon salt. Add the palm sugar and coconut milk and then stir through the spice paste. Combine well, cover and place in the refrigerator to marinate for 2 hours.
**3** Preheat the grill (broiler) to as hot as it will go. Tie a strip of banana leaf around each prawn and cook under the hot grill for about 2 minutes on each side or until the prawns are cooked. Serve with sweet chilli sauce, if desired.

NOTE: Banana leaves are available from speciality fruit and vegetable shops or from a friend who has a banana tree!

### coconut milk

Coconut milk is fundamental to Asian cooking and is made not from the liquid inside the coconut, but from the juice of the grated and pressed coconut flesh. The first extraction, which is the coconut cream, is very thick; the milk comes from a second pressing. Coconut milk is available in cans, tetra packs, or in powdered form.

## malaysian fish curry

Preparation time: 25 minutes
Cooking time: 25 minutes
Serves 4

1 tablespoon oil
1 tablespoon fish curry powder
250 ml (9 fl oz/1 cup) coconut milk
1 tablespoon tamarind concentrate
1 tablespoon kecap manis
350 g (12 oz) firm white fish fillets, cut into bite-sized pieces
2 ripe tomatoes, chopped
1 tablespoon lemon juice
steamed rice, to serve

SPICE PASTE
3–6 medium red chillies
1 onion, chopped
4 garlic cloves
3 lemongrass stems, white part only, sliced
4 cm (1½ inch) piece fresh ginger, sliced
2 teaspoons shrimp paste
1–2 tablespoons oil

**1** To make the spice paste, put the chillies, onion, garlic, lemongrass, ginger and shrimp paste in a food processor and roughly chop. Add enough oil to assist the blending and process until a smooth paste forms, regularly scraping down the sides of the bowl with a spatula.
**2** Heat the oil in a wok or heavy frying pan; add the spice paste and stir for 3–4 minutes over low heat, until very fragrant. Add the curry powder and stir for another 2 minutes.
**3** Add the coconut milk, 250 ml (9 fl oz/1 cup) water, tamarind and kecap manis. Bring to the boil, stirring occasionally, then reduce the heat and simmer for 10 minutes. Add the fish, tomato and lemon juice and season to taste with salt and pepper. Simmer for about 5 minutes or until the fish is just cooked. Serve with the steamed rice.

## malaysian rendang

Preparation time: 20 minutes
Cooking time: 1 hour 40 minutes
Serves 4–6

2 onions, chopped
4 garlic cloves, crushed
5 red chillies, seeded
1 tablespoon finely grated fresh ginger
500 ml (17 fl oz/2 cups) coconut milk
1 tablespoon oil
1 tablespoon ground coriander
1 tablespoon ground cumin
1 teaspoon ground turmeric
1 teaspoon ground cinnamon
¼ teaspoon ground cloves
¼ teaspoon chilli powder
1 large strip lemon zest
1 kg (2 lb 4 oz) chuck or skirt steak, cubed
1 tablespoon lemon juice

*malaysian fish curry*

### fish curry powder

Fish curry powder is a blend of coriander, cumin, fennel seeds, turmeric, peppercorns and chillies, particularly suitable for using in fish curries. Specific curry powders such as this one are usually only found in Asian food stores. If fish curry powder is not available, simply use a freshly ground mixture of the spices above. Avoid curry powders that are sold in cardboard packaging as the packaging tends to absorb the flavour and the aroma of the spice blend.

# singapore & malaysia

1 tablespoon soft brown sugar
1 teaspoon tamarind concentrate
steamed rice, to serve

1  Place the onion, garlic, chillies, ginger and 2 tablespoons of the coconut milk in a food processor, and process until a smooth paste has formed.
2  Heat the oil in a large saucepan, add the paste, coriander, cumin, turmeric, cinnamon, cloves, chilli powder, lemon zest and beef and stir until the beef is well coated with the spice mixture. Add the remaining coconut milk and bring to the boil, then simmer over low heat, stirring occasionally, for 1½ hours, or until the beef is tender and the mixture is almost dry.
3  When the oil starts to separate from the gravy, add the lemon juice, sugar and tamarind; stir until heated through. Serve with the steamed rice.

NOTE: This recipe produces a 'dry' curry which does not have much liquid. The spicy flavours are absorbed by the beef as it cooks. It tastes even better if it is made a day in advance.

## chicken kapitan

Preparation time: 35 minutes
Cooking time: 30 minutes
Serves 4–6

30 g (1 oz) dried shrimp
80 ml (2½ fl oz/⅓ cup) oil
4–8 red chillies, seeded and finely chopped
4 garlic cloves, finely chopped
3 lemongrass stems, white part only, finely chopped
2 teaspoons ground turmeric
10 candlenuts
2 large onions, chopped
500 g (1 lb 2 oz) boneless, skinless chicken thighs, chopped
250 ml (9 fl oz/1 cup) coconut milk
125 ml (4 fl oz/½ cup) coconut cream
2 tablespoons lime juice
steamed rice, to serve

*chicken kapitan*

1  Put the shrimp in a clean frying pan and dry-fry over low heat, shaking the pan regularly, for 3 minutes, or until the shrimp are dark orange and are giving off a strong aroma. Transfer the shrimp to a mortar and pound with a pestle until finely ground. Set aside.
2  Put half the oil with the chilli, garlic, lemongrass, turmeric and candlenuts in a food processor and process in short bursts until very finely chopped, regularly scraping down the sides of the bowl with a rubber spatula.
3  Heat the remaining oil in a wok or frying pan, add the onion and ¼ teaspoon salt and cook over low heat for 8 minutes, or until golden, stirring regularly. Take care not to let the onion burn. Add the spice mixture and nearly all of the ground shrimp meat, setting a little aside to use as a garnish. Stir for 5 minutes. If the mixture begins to stick to the bottom of the pan, add 2 tablespoons of the coconut milk to the mixture. It is important to cook the mixture thoroughly to fully develop the flavours.
4  Add the chicken to the wok and stir well. Cook for 5 minutes, or until the chicken begins to brown. Stir in the remaining coconut milk and 250 ml (9 fl oz/1 cup) water, and bring to the boil. Reduce the heat and simmer for 7 minutes, or until the chicken is cooked and the sauce is thick. Add the coconut cream and bring the mixture back to the boil, stirring constantly. Add the lime juice and serve immediately, sprinkled lightly with the reserved ground shrimp meat. Serve with the steamed rice.

essential asian

spicy eggs and snake beans

or until the mixture is heated through. Serve with the steamed rice.

NOTE: Use any combination of mushrooms up to the weight given. Some suitable mushrooms are button, oyster, shiitake or enoki.

## crunchy stuffed tofu puffs

Preparation time: 30 minutes
Cooking time: 5 minutes
Serves 6–8

12 deep-fried tofu puffs (see Note)
90 g (3¼ oz/1 cup) bean sprouts, trimmed
40 g (1½ oz/¼ cup) roasted peanuts, chopped
1 carrot, grated
1 tablespoon chopped coriander (cilantro) leaves

CHILLI SAUCE
2 small red chillies, finely chopped
2 garlic cloves, crushed
2 teaspoons soft brown sugar
1 tablespoon soy sauce
1 tablespoon white vinegar
125 ml (4 fl oz/½ cup) boiling water

## spicy eggs and snake beans

Preparation time: 20 minutes
Cooking time: 10 minutes
Serves 4

4 spring onions (scallions)
300 g (10½ oz) snake (yard-long) beans, trimmed
1 teaspoon sesame oil
1 tablespoon oil
2 garlic cloves, crushed
200 g (7 oz) mixed mushrooms (see Note)
8 eggs, lightly beaten
1 tablespoon kecap manis
2 teaspoons sambal oelek
3 tablespoons chopped mint
3 tablespoons chopped coriander (cilantro) leaves
steamed rice, to serve

**1** Chop the spring onions. Cut the snake beans into 5 cm (2 inch) lengths. Heat the combined oils in a wok or large frying pan, add the garlic and spring onion and cook over moderately high heat for 2 minutes.
**2** Add the beans and mushrooms and stir-fry for 1 minute. Remove from the wok. Add the combined eggs, kecap manis, sambal oelek, mint and coriander to the centre of the wok. Allow to set for 2 minutes.
**3** Return the vegetables to the wok and stir-fry, breaking up the egg, for 2 minutes

**1** To make the chilli sauce, combine all the ingredients in a small saucepan, bring to the boil, reduce the heat and simmer for 5 minutes, or until the sauce thickens slightly.
**2** Cut the tofu puffs in half. Cut a small slit in each half and open it up carefully to form a pocket.
**3** Place the bean sprouts, peanuts, carrot and coriander in a bowl, and toss until well mixed. Fill each pocket with a portion of the mixture. Serve drizzled with a little chilli sauce, and offer the rest of the sauce for dipping.

NOTE: Tofu puffs are cubes of tofu that have been deep-fried and are puffed and golden. They are available from Asian food stores.

# singapore & malaysia

## nonya lime chicken

✺ ✺

Preparation time: 20 minutes
Cooking time: 25 minutes
Serves 4–6

60 ml (2 fl oz/¼ cup) vegetable oil
1 kg (2 lb 4 oz) boneless, skinless chicken thighs, cut into 3 cm (1¼ inch) cubes
400 ml (14 fl oz) coconut milk
1 teaspoon finely grated lime zest
125 ml (4 fl oz/½ cup) lime juice
6 kaffir lime (makrut) leaves, finely shredded, plus extra, to garnish
2 tablespoons tamarind purée
steamed rice, to serve

CURRY PASTE
70 g (2½ oz/⅔ cup) red Asian shallots
4 garlic cloves
2 lemongrass stems, white part only, chopped
2 teaspoons finely chopped fresh galangal
1 teaspoon ground turmeric
2 tablespoons sambal oelek
1 tablespoon shrimp paste

**1** Combine all the curry paste ingredients in a food processor or blender and blend until a smooth paste forms.
**2** Heat a non-stick wok until very hot, add the oil and swirl to coat the base and side. Add the curry paste and stir-fry for 1–2 minutes, or until aromatic. Add the chicken and stir-fry for 5 minutes, or until browned. Add the coconut milk, lime zest and juice, lime leaves and tamarind purée.
**3** Reduce the heat and simmer for 15 minutes, or until the chicken is cooked and the sauce has reduced and thickened slightly. Season well with salt. Serve with the steamed rice and garnish with the extra lime leaves.

## nonya food

Nonya food is a mixture of Chinese ingredients with Malay spices and flavourings. The blending of the two cuisines evolved because Chinese merchants who settled in trading centres on the Straits of Malacca (Penang, Malacca and Singapore) were unable to bring Chinese women with them, so they married Malay wives. Nonya recipes are hot and spicy and often based on a rempah, a paste of hot chillies, shallots, lemongrass, candlenuts, galangal and turmeric. Coconut, unused in China, is an ingredient in many dishes, such as laksa, and the creamy coconut gravies of the Malacca region. To the north, around Penang, Nonya cooking shows Thai influences in the use of lime and tamarind.

## fish and herb salad

✻ ✻

Preparation time: 40 minutes
Cooking time: 15 minutes
Serves 4–6

500 g (1 lb 2 oz) smoked cod
60 ml (2 fl oz/¼ cup) lime juice
30 g (1 oz/½ cup) flaked coconut
200 g (7 oz/1 cup) jasmine rice, cooked and cooled
25 g (1 oz) Vietnamese mint, chopped
3 tablespoons chopped mint
25 g (1 oz/½ cup) chopped coriander (cilantro) leaves
8 kaffir lime (makrut) leaves, very finely shredded

DRESSING
1 tablespoon chopped coriander (cilantro) root
2 cm (¾ inch) piece fresh ginger, finely grated
1 red chilli, finely chopped
1 tablespoon chopped lemongrass, white part only
3 tablespoons chopped Thai basil
1 avocado, chopped
80 ml (2½ fl oz/⅓ cup) lime juice
2 tablespoons fish sauce
1 teaspoon soft brown sugar
125 ml (4 fl oz/½ cup) peanut oil

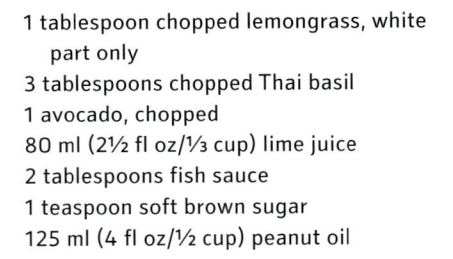

**1** Preheat the oven to 150°C (300°F/Gas 2). Put the cod in a large frying pan and cover with water. Add the lime juice and simmer for 15 minutes, or until the fish flakes when tested with a fork. Drain and set aside to cool slightly before breaking it into bite-sized pieces.
**2** Meanwhile, spread the coconut onto a baking tray and toast in the oven for 10 minutes, or until golden brown, shaking the tray occasionally. Remove the coconut from the tray immediately to prevent it burning.
**3** Put the fish, coconut, rice, Vietnamese mint, mint, coriander and lime leaves in a large bowl and mix to combine.
**4** To make the dressing, put the coriander root, ginger, chilli, lemongrass and basil in a food processor and process until combined. Add the avocado, lime juice, fish sauce, sugar and peanut oil and process until creamy. Pour the dressing over the salad and toss to coat the rice and fish. Serve immediately.

## singapore spare ribs

✻

Preparation time: 20 minutes + 4 hours marinating time
Cooking time: 50 minutes
Serves 6

2 teaspoons sesame oil
1 teaspoon finely chopped fresh ginger
3 garlic cloves, crushed
2 tablespoons soy sauce
2 tablespoons shaoxing rice wine (Chinese rice wine)
½ teaspoon five-spice

fish and herb salad

## singapore & malaysia

### chinese food in singapore

The food of Singapore, while sharing a similar heritage to Malaysia, also reflects the strong influence of the island's now predominantly Chinese population. Singapore–Chinese food is mostly Cantonese-style, with chicken, seafood and vegetables in clear sauces — a hint of chilli, tamarind and shrimp paste give it a Singaporean touch. Pork is popular, in contrast to largely Muslim Malaysia (converted to Islam in the early fifteenth century), where it is not eaten.

2 tablespoons honey
1 teaspoon sambal oelek
1.5 kg (3 lb 5 oz) pork spare ribs, cut into individual ribs (ask your butcher to do this), trimmed of excess fat
1 tablespoon snipped garlic chives
2 lemons, cut into wedges, to serve
steamed rice, to serve

1  Combine the sesame oil, ginger, garlic, soy sauce, rice wine, five-spice, honey, sambal oelek and ½ teaspoon salt in a large non-metallic bowl. Mix well.
2  Add the pork spare ribs and stir until the ribs are totally coated in the marinade. Cover and refrigerate for at least 4 hours or overnight so they absorb the flavour of the marinade.
3  Preheat the oven to 180°C (350°F/Gas 4). Place the ribs and marinade into an oiled baking dish and cook for 50 minutes, turning and basting with pan juices every 15 minutes. If the marinade begins to burn, add a few tablespoons of warm water to the dish during cooking.
4  Scatter the garlic chives over the spare ribs and serve with the wedges of lemon and steamed rice.

NOTE: Line the baking dish with thick foil to make the washing-up easier.

# the philippines

The 7000 islands of the Philippines owe much of their exciting cuisine to the sea that surrounds them. An abundance of fresh fish is hauled to shore daily in wooden outriggers and cooked in clay pots; Chinese merchants arriving by sea brought spring rolls and sticky noodles; while the Spanish, who colonised and later named the islands after their king, introduced foods such as spicy chorizo and empanadas. Filipino cooking often has a tart sharpness, with its meats and fish being marinated in vinegar or citrus fruit.

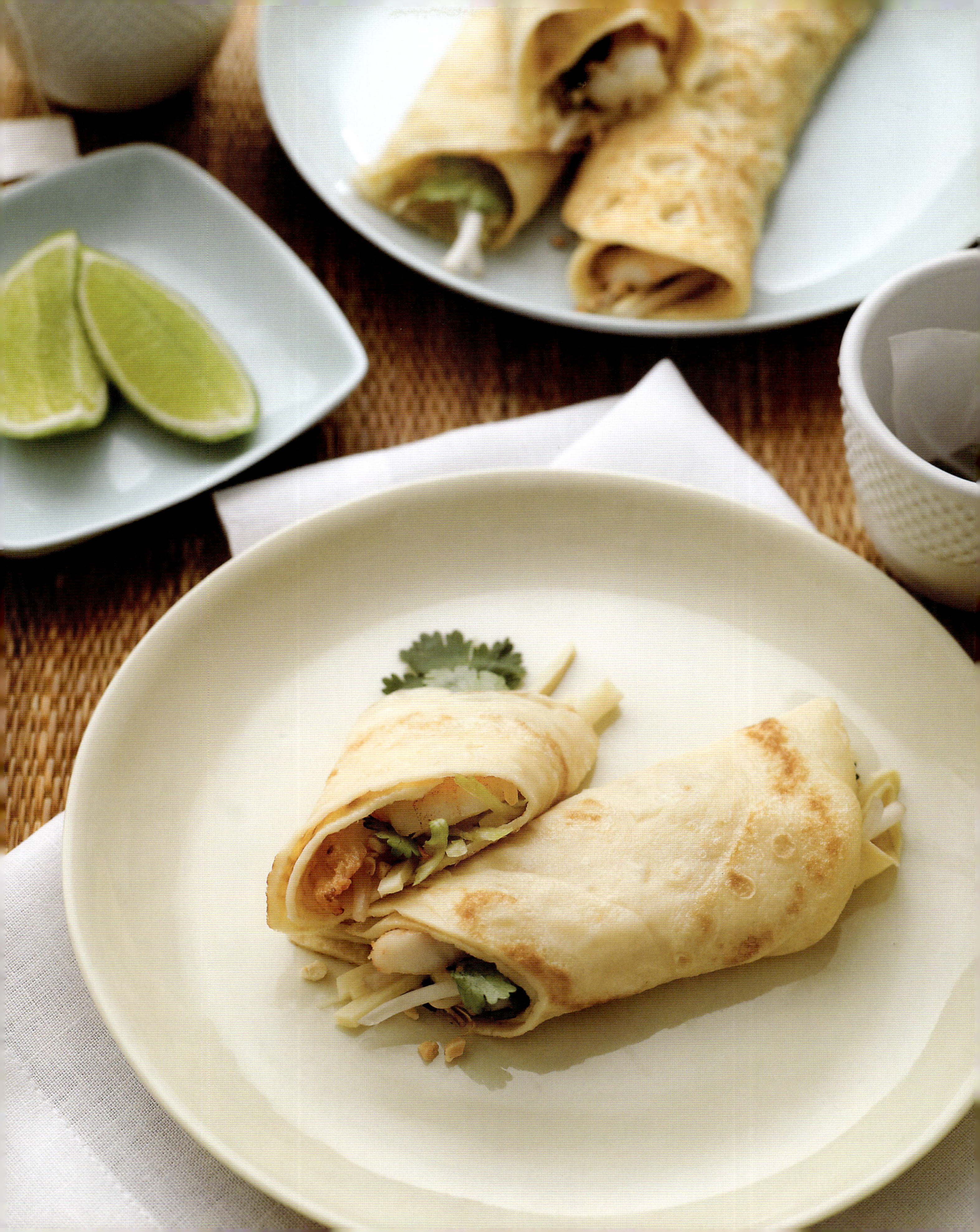

essential asian

## bagoong

Bagoong is a form of shrimp paste used mainly in the Philippines. The shrimps are salted and fermented in earthenware pots rather than being dried, as in other parts of Asia, and the paste has a runnier consistency.

## prawn fritters

☼

Preparation time: 30 minutes
Cooking time: 15 minutes
Serves 4–6

300 g (10½ oz) raw prawns (shrimp)
50 g (1¾ oz) dried rice vermicelli
1 egg
1 tablespoon fish sauce
125 g (4½ oz/1 cup) plain (all-purpose) flour
¼ teaspoon bagoong
3 spring onions (scallions), sliced
1 small red chilli, finely chopped
oil, for deep-frying
sweet chilli sauce, to serve

**1** Peel the prawns and gently pull out the dark vein from each prawn back, starting at the head end. Place half the prawns in a food processor and process until smooth. Chop the remaining prawns, place them in a bowl with the processed prawns and mix to combine.

**2** Soak the vermicelli in boiling water for 5 minutes, or until soft. Drain well and cut into short lengths.

**3** In a small jug, beat the egg, 185 ml (6 fl oz/¾ cup) water and the fish sauce. Sift the flour into a bowl; make a well in the centre, gradually add the egg mixture and stir until smooth.

**4** Add the prawn mixture, bagoong, spring onion, chilli and vermicelli to the bowl and mix to combine.

**5** Heat the oil in a large saucepan or wok; add tablespoons of the mixture to the pan and deep-fry for 3 minutes, or until the fritters are crisp and golden. Drain on paper towels. Repeat with the remaining mixture. Serve with the sweet chilli sauce.

# the philippines

## rice with chicken and seafood

✻ ✻

Preparation time: 30 minutes
Cooking time: 1 hour 5 minutes
Serves 4–6

500 g (1 lb 2 oz) black mussels
200 g (7 oz) squid tubes
500 g (1 lb 2 oz) raw prawns (shrimp)
¼ teaspoon saffron threads
2 tablespoons boiling water
4 large tomatoes
3 tablespoons oil
2 chorizo sausages, thickly sliced
500 g (1 lb 2 oz) chicken pieces
300 g (10½ oz) pork fillet, thickly sliced
4 garlic cloves, crushed
2 red onions, chopped
¼ teaspoon ground turmeric
440 g (15½ oz/2 cups) medium-grain rice
1.25 litres (44 fl oz/5 cups) chicken stock
125 g (4½ oz) green beans, trimmed, cut into 4 cm (1½ inch) lengths
1 red capsicum (pepper), cut into thin strips
155 g (5½ oz/1 cup) peas

**1** Scrub the mussels thoroughly and remove the hairy beards. Cut the squid tubes into ½ cm (¼ inch) thick slices. Peel the prawns, leaving the tails intact. Gently pull out the dark vein from each prawn back, starting at the head end. Soak the saffron threads in the boiling water for 15 minutes.
**2** Score a cross in the base of each tomato, place in a heatproof bowl, cover with boiling water and leave for 2 minutes. Plunge into cold water and then peel the skin away from the cross. Cut the tomatoes in half horizontally, scoop out the seeds with a teaspoon and chop the flesh.
**3** Heat 1 tablespoon of the oil in a large, heavy-based saucepan; add the chorizo slices and cook over medium heat for 5 minutes, or until browned. Drain on paper towels. Add the chicken pieces to the pan and cook for 5 minutes, or until golden, turning once. Drain on paper towels. Add the pork to the pan and cook for 3 minutes, or until browned, turning once. Drain on paper towels.
**4** Heat the remaining oil in the pan; add the garlic, onion, saffron and soaking liquid and turmeric, and cook over medium heat for 3 minutes or until the onion is golden. Add the tomato and cook for 3 minutes or until soft. Add the rice and stir for 5 minutes, or until the rice is translucent. Stir in the stock and bring to the boil; cover and simmer for 10 minutes.
**5** Return the chicken pieces to the pan, cover and continue cooking for 20 minutes. Add the pork, prawns, mussels, squid, chorizo and vegetables; cover and cook for 10 minutes or until the liquid has been absorbed.

Drain the browned chorizo slices on paper towels.

Cook the pork slices until they are browned, turning once.

## combination noodles with chorizo

✣ ✣

Preparation time: 25 minutes + 30 minutes drying time
Cooking time: 35 minutes
Serves 6

- 500 g (1 lb 2 oz) thin fresh egg noodles
- 500 g (1 lb 2 oz) raw prawns (shrimp)
- 3 tablespoons oil
- 4 garlic cloves, crushed
- 6 spring onions (scallions), thinly sliced
- 175 g (6 oz/1 cup) shredded cooked chicken
- 250 g (9 oz) chorizo sausage, sliced
- 75 g (2¾ oz/1 cup) shredded cabbage
- 3 tablespoons soy sauce
- 3 tablespoons coriander (cilantro) leaves
- lemon wedges, to serve

**1** Fill a large saucepan with salted water and bring it to the boil. Cook the noodles for 5 minutes or until tender. Rinse under cold water, drain and spread in a single layer on paper towels. Allow to dry for 30 minutes.

**2** Peel the prawns, reserving the heads, tails and shells. Gently pull out the dark vein from each prawn back, starting at the head end. Dry-fry the prawn heads, tails and shells in a frying pan for about 5 minutes, until they turn bright orange. Add 250 ml (9 fl oz/1 cup) water to the pan, bring to the boil, reduce the heat slightly and cook until the liquid has reduced to about a quarter. Add another 125 ml (4 fl oz/½ cup) water, bring to the boil, then reduce the heat and simmer for 3 minutes. Strain the liquid and set it aside, discarding all the prawn heads, tails and shells.

**3** Heat 1 tablespoon of the oil in a large wok. When the oil is very hot add a quarter of the noodles and fry until golden all over, turning when necessary. Remove the noodles from the wok and repeat three times with the remaining noodles, adding more oil when necessary.

**4** Add another tablespoon of the oil and fry the garlic and spring onion over low heat until soft; remove from the wok. Add the prawns and chicken and fry until golden; remove from the wok. Add the chorizo and cook until brown. Add the cabbage, soy sauce and prawn cooking liquid, and cook over high heat, stirring all the time until the liquid has reduced by a third.

**5** Return the noodles to the wok with the garlic, spring onion, chicken and prawns. Toss well until heated through. Season with salt and pepper, scatter over the coriander and serve immediately with the lemon wedges.

# the philippines

### spanish influence on the philippines

The chorizo used in the recipe on the opposite page gives an indication of the long-lasting impact the Spanish made on the people of the Philippines. Many of the traditional Spanish dishes they introduced — such as paella and empanadas — are popular to this day.

## beef pot roast

Preparation time: 15 minutes
Cooking time: 3 hours
Serves 6

75 g (2½ oz) pork fat
1.5 kg (3 lb 5 oz) topside beef
3 onions, quartered
4 tomatoes, quartered
125 ml (4 fl oz/½ cup) white vinegar
2 tablespoons soy sauce
2 bay leaves
3 potatoes, peeled, halved lengthwise and thickly sliced
3 sweet potatoes, peeled, halved lengthwise and thickly sliced

**1** Cut the pork fat into thin slivers. Use a sharp knife to make deep cuts evenly over the beef and then insert a sliver of the pork fat into each cut.
**2** Place the beef in a large saucepan with a tight-fitting lid. Add the onion, tomato, vinegar, soy sauce and bay leaves. Bring the liquid to the boil, then reduce the heat to a gentle simmer, cover and cook for 2 hours, until the beef is tender. Season with salt and pepper. Remove the lid and simmer for a further 30 minutes.
**3** Add the potato and sweet potato and simmer, uncovered, until tender. Remove the pan from the heat and remove the beef from the pan. Cut the beef into thin slices, drizzle with the gravy and serve with the potato and sweet potato. Garnish with the coriander and serve.

NOTE: Pork fat is available from butchers. If unavailable, lard can be used instead.

## oxtail and vegetable stew

Preparation time: 20 minutes
Cooking time: 2 hours 15 minutes
Serves 6

1.5 kg (3 lb 5 oz) oxtail, cut into 2 cm (¾ inch) lengths (ask your butcher to do this)
60 g (2¼ oz/¼ cup) lard
2 tablespoons annatto seeds (see Note)
4 garlic cloves, crushed
2 onions, finely sliced
1 bay leaf
1 tablespoon soy sauce
2 tablespoons fish sauce
2 turnips, chopped
250 g (9 oz/2 cups) trimmed, sliced green beans
2 slender eggplants (aubergines), sliced
2 large sweet potatoes, peeled and chopped
110 g (3¾ oz/½ cup) medium- or long-grain rice
80 g (2¾ oz/½ cup) unsalted raw peanuts

**1** Place the oxtail pieces into a large heatproof bowl, cover with salted boiling water and leave to stand for 5 minutes; remove and pat dry with paper towels.
**2** Heat the lard in a large frying pan, add the annatto seeds and cook over medium heat until the lard turns red. Add the garlic and onion to the pan and cook for 5 minutes. Remove the garlic and onion mixture from the pan with a slotted spoon and drain on paper towels.
**3** Heat a large deep saucepan, add the meat in batches and cook over medium heat for 5 minutes, or until brown on both sides. Return all the meat to the pan and add the onion and garlic mixture, 1.5 litres (52 fl oz/6 cups) water, the bay leaf, soy sauce and fish sauce. Bring to the boil, reduce the heat, cover and simmer for 1½ hours. Add the vegetables and simmer, covered, for 20 minutes, or until tender.
**4** Meanwhile, preheat the oven to 180°C (350°F/Gas 4). Spread the rice on a baking tray and roast for 15 minutes or until golden. Spread the peanuts on a baking tray and roast for 5 minutes or until lightly browned. Remove from the oven, cool slightly and process both in a food processor until the mixture resembles fine breadcrumbs. Sift the mixture to remove any large pieces, then add it to the stew and stir until the sauce thickens.

NOTE: If annatto seeds are unavailable, substitute 1 tablespoon of paprika combined with ½ teaspoon turmeric. The annatto seeds can be left in the dish but they are too hard to eat.

## fish with ginger and black pepper

Preparation time: 10 minutes
Cooking time: 35 minutes
Serves 4

2 whole firm white fish (such as snapper or bream), each about 500 g (1 lb 2 oz), cleaned and scaled
4 cm (1½ inch) piece fresh ginger, sliced
3 tablespoons oil
4 tablespoons finely chopped fresh ginger, extra
½ red onion, thinly sliced

# the philippines

1 tablespoon coriander (cilantro) leaves, to garnish
1 tablespoon thinly sliced spring onion (scallions), to garnish
steamed rice, to serve

**1** Preheat the oven to 180°C (350°F/Gas 4). Wash fish inside and out and pat dry. Place the ginger slices inside the fish.
**2** Heat the oil in a wok; add the chopped ginger and cook over low heat for 1–2 minutes, or until soft and aromatic. Stir in 1 teaspoon pepper.
**3** Place the fish in a baking dish, scatter over ½ teaspoon salt and pour in 250 ml (9 fl oz/1 cup) water. Place onion slices over the fish, cover the dish and bake for approximately 30 minutes or until the fish flakes when tested with a fork.
**4** Carefully lift out the fish and place it on a serving platter. Scatter over the coriander and spring onion. Pour the ginger mixture around the fish and serve with the steamed rice.

## chicken adobo

✷ ✷

Preparation time: 20 minutes + 2 hours marinating time
Cooking time: 1 hour
Serves 6

6 garlic cloves, crushed
250 ml (9 fl oz/1 cup) cider vinegar
375 ml (13 fl oz/1½ cups) chicken stock
1 bay leaf
1 teaspoon coriander seeds
1 teaspoon black peppercorns
1 teaspoon annatto seeds
3 tablespoons soy sauce
1.5 kg (3 lb 5 oz) chicken pieces
2 tablespoons oil
steamed rice, to serve
kaffir lime (makrut) leaves, to serve

**1** Combine the garlic, vinegar, stock, bay leaf, coriander seeds, black peppercorns, annatto seeds and soy sauce in a large bowl. Add the chicken, cover and leave to marinate in the refrigerator for 2 hours.
**2** Transfer the chicken mixture to a large heavy-based saucepan and bring to the boil. Reduce the heat, cover and simmer for 30 minutes. Remove the lid from the pan and continue cooking for 10 minutes, or until the chicken is tender. Remove the chicken from the pan and set aside. Bring the liquid to the boil again and cook over high heat for 10 minutes, or until the liquid is reduced by half.
**3** Heat the oil in a wok or large frying pan, add the chicken in batches and cook over medium heat for 5 minutes, or until crisp and brown. Pour the reduced stock mixture over the chicken, garnish with lime leaves and serve with steamed rice.

chicken adobo

### annatto seeds

Also known as achuete, these small red-brown seeds are used in Filipino cooking for their strong colour. They come from a small flowering tree native to Central and South America, which was introduced into the Philippines by Spanish traders. Annatto seeds are also used by the Chinese to colour barbecued pork.

# rice

As the staple of all Asian cuisines, this grain is of huge importance — in Thailand an invitation to a meal is 'kin khao', literally 'come and eat rice'.

## cooking methods

### rapid boiling
Bring a large saucepan of water to a fast boil. The quantity of water should be six times the quantity of rice. Add the rice and cook, uncovered, for 12–15 minutes, or until the swollen grains are tender and opaque. Drain.

### absorption
The most common method of cooking rice throughout Asia, it is easy to obtain good results if the water to rice ratio is correct. A quick and easy method is to place the quantity of rice required in a large saucepan and add enough water to reach the first joint of your index finger when the tip is on the top of the rice. For a more accurate measure, add 500 ml (17 fl oz/2 cups) water for the first 200 g (7 oz/1 cup) long-grain rice and 375 ml (13 fl oz/1½ cups) water for each additional 200 g of rice. For short-/medium-grain rice, add 375 ml water for the first 200 g rice and 250 ml (9 fl oz/1 cup) for each additional 200g of rice.

**saucepan:** Wash rice in a sieve until the water runs clear; place in a large saucepan with the water, bring to the boil and boil for 1 minute. Cover with a tight-fitting lid, then reduce the heat to as low as possible and cook for 10–15 minutes, or until all the water has been absorbed and the rice is tender. Steam tunnels will form holes on the surface. Turn off the heat and leave the pan, covered, for at least 10 minutes. Fluff the rice with a fork.

**electric rice cooker:** This appliance steams rice in the same way as the absorption method and is ideal for making large quantities. Wash rice in a sieve until the water runs clear, drain and add to the rice cooker with water. Follow the manufacturer's instructions for cooking times.

## rice varieties

### long-grain
Cultivated throughout Southeast Asia, this long slender grain is the favoured rice of the Chinese. When cooked, the grains separate easily and are non-starchy: perfect for fried rice.

### jasmine
Originating in Thailand, this variety of long-grain rice is now popular throughout Southeast Asia. It is a lightly aromatic rice that goes well with all kinds of Asian dishes.

### basmati
This aromatic, narrow, long-grain rice is grown in the foothills of the Himalayas. It is traditionally used for biryani and pilau dishes that utilise the firm texture of the cooked basmati rice.

### short-/medium-grain
These small oval grains, which are high in starch, are preferred by the Japanese and Koreans. Best cooked by the absorption method, this rice is slightly sticky.

### glutinous
**white glutinous:** This is the staple rice of the Laotians and northern Thais who use it as an accompaniment to savoury dishes. However, its main use is for leaf-wrapped snacks or Asian desserts. The grains are short and turn translucent when cooked. Ill-named because it contains no gluten, it has a high starch content and is commonly called 'sticky rice' or 'sweet rice'.
**black glutinous:** The layer of bran is left on this rice, giving it a dark colour, and it has a nutty flavour. It combines well with palm sugar (jaggery), coconut milk and sesame seeds, and is a popular dessert rice in Burma, Thailand, Indonesia and the Philippines. For best results, the rice should be soaked overnight.

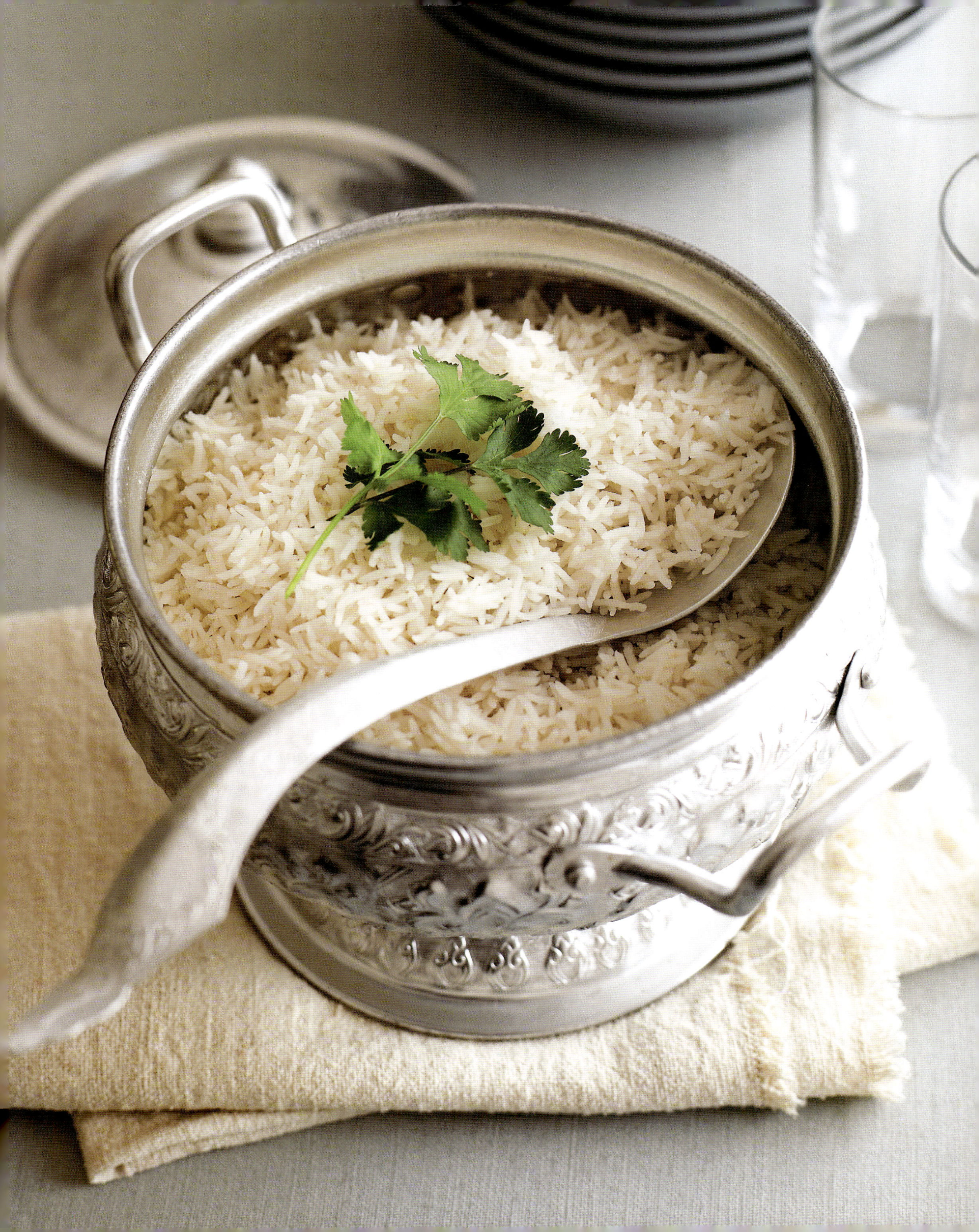

essential asian

## prawn crepes

✹ ✹

Preparation time: 1 hour
Cooking time: 20 minutes
Serves 4–6

5 eggs
2 tablespoons oil
60 g (2¼ oz/½ cup) cornflour (cornstarch)
60 g (2¼ oz/½ cup) plain (all-purpose) flour
oil, extra, for brushing
lime wedges, to serve

PRAWN FILLING
500 g (1 lb 2 oz) raw prawns (shrimp)
1 tablespoon oil
300 g (10½ oz) tinned bamboo shoots, cut into matchsticks
90 g (3¼ oz/1 cup) bean sprouts, trimmed
80 g (2¾ oz/½ cup) unsalted roasted peanuts, roughly chopped
½ iceberg lettuce, shredded
30 g (1 oz/1 cup) coriander (cilantro) leaves

1  Beat the eggs, 375 ml (13 fl oz/ 1½ cups) water and oil in a bowl until combined. Whisk in the cornflour and plain flour and beat the batter until smooth. Cover and set aside for 20 minutes.
2  Brush a small non-stick frying pan or crepe pan with oil, heat over low heat, add 2 tablespoons of the batter and swirl the pan to ensure the base has a very thin covering of batter; pour any excess batter back into the bowl. Cook the crepe for 2 minutes or until lightly golden. Turn and cook the other side for 2 minutes. Repeat with the remaining batter.
3  To make the prawn filling, peel the prawns and gently pull out the dark vein from each prawn back, starting at the head end. Cut the prawns in half lengthways if large. Heat the oil in a non-stick frying pan; add the prawns and cook over medium heat for 3 minutes or until they are bright pink. Arrange the prawns, bamboo shoots, bean sprouts, peanuts, lettuce and coriander on a platter.
4  On each crepe place a little shredded lettuce, a few coriander leaves, prawns, bamboo shoots, bean sprouts and peanuts; fold in the sides and roll up the crepe to enclose the mixture. Serve with the lime wedges.

## sour beef soup

✹ ✹

Preparation time: 30 minutes
Cooking time: 2 hours 30 minutes
Serves 6

500 g (1 lb 2 oz) chicken bones
500 g (1 lb 2 oz) lean stewing beef
250 g (9 oz) pork chops, fat removed
1 onion, finely diced
2 tomatoes, diced
1 tablespoon dried tamarind pulp
250 g (9 oz) sweet potato, peeled and cut into chunks
1 large daikon, thinly sliced
90 g (3¼ oz/2 cups) shredded Chinese cabbage (wong bok)
1 tablespoon fish sauce
1 lime, cut into wedges, to serve

Drain the bamboo shoots and cut them into matchsticks.

Fold in the sides and roll up the crepe to enclose the mixture.

# the philippines

1  Place chicken bones, beef, pork chops and 2.5 litres (87 fl oz/10 cups) water in a large saucepan. Stir in the onion, tomato and 1 teaspoon salt. Bring to the boil, then cover and simmer for 2 hours. Remove the chicken bones, beef and pork. Allow the beef and pork to cool and discard the chicken bones.
2  Pour 2 tablespoons boiling water over the tamarind pulp and soak it for 10 minutes. Stir and press the tamarind pulp with a spoon until it is fully dissolved, then strain it into the soup. Discard any seeds and fibre.
3  Dice the beef. Cut the meat from the pork chops, slice it thinly and discard the bones. Return the meat to the soup. Add the sweet potato and daikon and simmer for 20 minutes. Add the cabbage and fish sauce and serve immediately with the lime wedges.

## empanadas

✻ ✻

Preparation time: 30 minutes + 30 minutes standing time
Cooking time: 1 hour 15 minutes
Makes 24

FILLING
1 tablespoon oil
4 bacon slices, chopped
1 large onion, finely chopped
3 garlic cloves, chopped
150 g (5½ oz) minced (ground) pork and veal
150 g (5½ oz) minced (ground) chicken
2 tablespoons tomato paste (concentrated purée)
1 teaspoon soft brown sugar
2 hard-boiled eggs, chopped
4 gherkins (pickles) (optional), finely chopped
15 g (½ oz/½ cup) coriander (cilantro) leaves, chopped
1 egg white, beaten
oil, for shallow frying

PASTRY
560 g (1 lb 4 oz/4½ cups) plain (all-purpose) flour
2 eggs, beaten
2 teaspoons caster (superfine) sugar
100 g (3½ oz) butter, melted, plus extra, for brushing

1  To make the filling, heat the oil in a frying pan; add the bacon, onion and garlic and cook over medium heat for 5 minutes, stirring regularly. Add the pork and veal mince and the chicken mince and cook for another 5 minutes or until browned, breaking up any lumps with a fork or wooden spoon.
2  Add the tomato paste, sugar and 1 tablespoon water to the pan and bring the mixture to the boil, stirring constantly. Reduce the heat and simmer, uncovered, for 20 minutes. Add the egg, gherkin, if desired, and coriander. Set the mixture aside for at least 30 minutes to cool.
3  To make the pastry, combine the flour, 250 ml (9 fl oz/1 cup) water, the egg, sugar and butter in a food processor and process for 20–30 seconds or until the mixture comes together. Transfer the pastry to a floured surface and gather together into a ball. Cover with plastic wrap and set aside for 10 minutes.
4  Roll the pastry into a 20 x 30 cm (8 x 12 inch) rectangle. Brush with some extra melted butter and tightly roll up into a long sausage. Cut into 3 cm (1¼ inch) slices and cover with a clean tea towel (dish towel) to stop the pastry drying out.
5  Place 1 slice of pastry flat on a lightly floured surface; roll it out to a 12 cm (4½ inch) circle. Place 1 heaped tablespoon of filling in the centre and lightly brush the edges with egg white. Bring 1 side over to meet the other and press the edges to seal. Decorate the edge with a fork, if desired. Repeat with the remaining filling and pastry.
6  Heat 2 cm (¾ inch) of the oil in a large saucepan; add the empanadas in batches and cook over medium heat for 2–3 minutes each side. Drain on paper towels and serve.

# thailand

Every Thai meal is a delicate balancing act of bold flavours. The soups and curries are both tart and creamy sweet, flavoured with sour tamarind, scarlet-hot chillies, tangy lime leaves and handfuls of aromatic basil, coriander and mint. While the cooking of Thailand has borrowed from other countries — stir-fries and steamed dishes from China, spices from India — these influences have been shaped into a cuisine whose tastes and aromas are uniquely Thai.

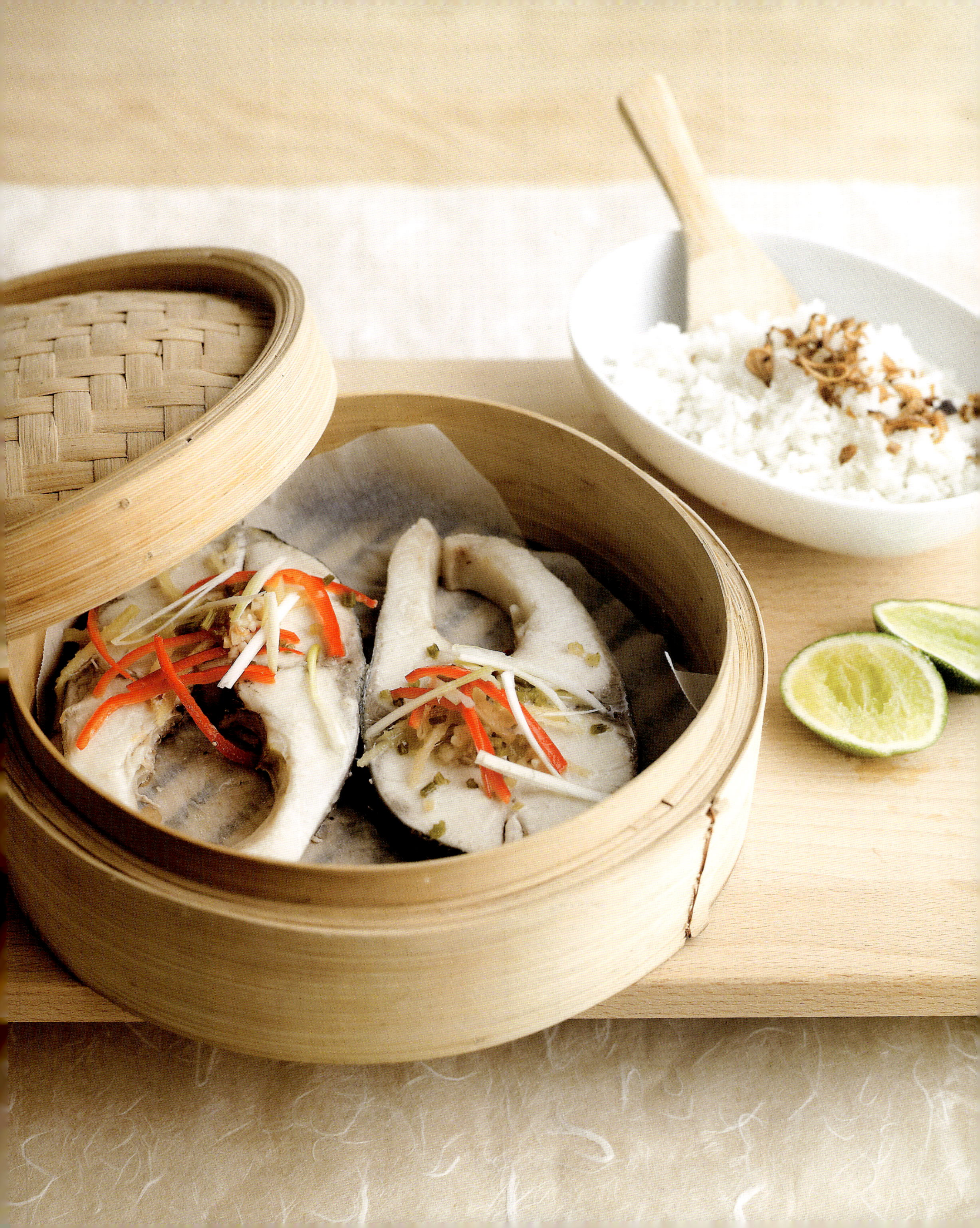

essential asian

## using dried galangal

If fresh galangal is not available, use a similar amount of dried galangal. Cover the galangal with boiling water for 10 minutes; drain. The soaking water can be substituted for the stock in the recipe.

## tom kha gai

☀

Preparation time: 20 minutes
Cooking time: 20 minutes
Serves 4

5 cm (2 inch) piece fresh galangal, thinly sliced
500 ml (17 fl oz/2 cups) coconut milk
250 ml (9 fl oz/1 cup) chicken stock
600 g (1 lb 5 oz) boneless, skinless chicken breasts, cut into thin strips
1–2 teaspoons finely sliced red chilli, plus extra slices, to garnish
2 tablespoons fish sauce
1 teaspoon soft brown sugar
10 g (¼ oz/⅓ cup) coriander (cilantro) leaves
coriander (cilantro) sprigs, to garnish

Combine the galangal, coconut milk and stock in a saucepan. Bring to the boil, then reduce the heat and simmer over low heat for 10 minutes, stirring occasionally. Add the chicken and chilli to the pan and simmer for 8 minutes. Add the fish sauce and sugar and stir to combine. Add the coriander leaves and serve immediately, garnished with coriander sprigs and chilli slices.

tom kha gai

## golden prawn puffs

☀

Preparation time: 15 minutes + 30 minutes resting time
Cooking time: 10 minutes
Serves 4–6

750 g (1 lb 10 oz) raw prawns (shrimp)
4 red chillies, finely chopped
15 g (½ oz/½ cup) coriander (cilantro) leaves
2 egg whites
1 tablespoon finely grated fresh ginger
2 garlic cloves, chopped
1 tablespoon fish sauce
60 g (2¼ oz/⅓ cup) rice flour or cornflour (cornstarch)
125 ml (4 fl oz/½ cup) oil
chilli sauce, to serve

**1** Peel the prawns and gently pull out the dark vein from each prawn back, starting at the head end.
**2** Place the prawns, chilli, coriander leaves, egg whites, ginger, garlic and fish sauce in a food processor and process for 10 seconds or until the mixture is well combined.
**3** Transfer the mixture to a bowl and stir in the flour. Refrigerate the prawn mixture for at least 30 minutes, or until you are ready to fry the puffs.
**4** Heat the oil in a heavy-based frying pan. Very gently drop rounded teaspoons

# thailand

### tamarind pulp

If tamarind concentrate is not available, soak a piece of tamarind pulp in hot water — 3 tablespoons pulp to 125 ml (4 fl oz/½ cup) hot water — and work with your fingertips until soft. Strain, using the back of a spoon to force the liquid from the seeds and fibre. The liquid should have the consistency of a light sauce. Any leftover liquid can be frozen in convenient measures and stored in the freezer.

of the mixture into the hot oil and cook for 2 minutes, carefully turning them with tongs until golden brown on all sides. Drain the puffs on paper towels and serve immediately with the chilli sauce.

NOTE: Do not overprocess or overcook the mixture or it will become tough.

## tom yum goong

Preparation time: 25 minutes
Cooking time: 45 minutes
Serves 4–6

500 g (1 lb 2 oz) raw prawns (shrimp)
1 tablespoon oil
2 tablespoons red curry paste (pages 102–3)
2 tablespoons tamarind concentrate
2 teaspoons ground turmeric
1 teaspoon chopped red chilli (optional)
4–8 kaffir lime (makrut) leaves, shredded
2 tablespoons fish sauce
2 tablespoons lime juice
2 teaspoons soft brown sugar
10 g (¼ oz ⅓ cup) coriander (cilantro) leaves, to garnish
red chilli, thinly sliced, to serve

**1** Peel the prawns and gently pull out the dark vein from each prawn back, starting at the head end, leaving the tails intact. Reserve the shells and heads.
**2** Heat the oil in a large saucepan, add the prawn shells and heads to the pan and cook for 10 minutes over high heat, tossing frequently, until the shells and heads are deep orange in colour.
**3** Have 2 litres (70 fl oz/8 cups) water ready. Add 250 ml (9 fl oz/1 cup) of the water and the curry paste to the pan. Boil for 5 minutes, until the liquid is reduced slightly. Add the remaining water and simmer for 20 minutes. Drain the stock, discarding the prawn heads and shells.
**4** Return the drained stock to the pan. Add the tamarind concentrate, turmeric, chilli and lime leaves, bring to the boil and cook for 2 minutes. Add the prawns to the pan and cook for 5 minutes or until the prawns turn pink. Add the fish sauce, lime juice and sugar and stir to combine. Serve immediately, sprinkled with the coriander leaves and chilli slices.

## red vegetable curry

Preparation time: 25 minutes
Cooking time: 30 minutes
Serves 4

1 tablespoon oil
1 onion, chopped
1–2 tablespoons red curry paste (see below) or ready-made paste
375 ml (13 fl oz/1½ cups) coconut milk
350 g (12 oz) potatoes, chopped
200 g (7 oz) cauliflower florets
6 kaffir lime (makrut) leaves
150 g (5½ oz) snake (yard-long) beans, trimmed, cut into 3 cm (1¼ inch) pieces
½ red capsicum (pepper), cut into strips
10 baby corn, cut in half lengthways
1 tablespoon green peppercorns, roughly chopped
15 g (½ oz/½ cup) Thai basil, finely chopped
2 tablespoons fish sauce
1 tablespoon lime juice
2 teaspoons soft brown sugar
green peppercorn stems or extra Thai basil leaves (optional), to garnish
steamed rice, to serve

**1** Heat the oil in a large wok or frying pan. Cook the onion and curry paste for 4 minutes over medium heat, stirring.

**2** Add the coconut milk and 250 ml (9 fl oz/1 cup) water, bring to the boil and simmer, uncovered, for 5 minutes. Add the potato, cauliflower and lime leaves, and simmer for 7 minutes. Add the snake beans, capsicum, corn and peppercorns and cook for 5 minutes or until the vegetables are tender.

**3** Stir in the basil, fish sauce, lime juice and sugar. Garnish as desired and serve with the steamed rice.

## red curry paste

Preparation time: 20 minutes
Cooking time: 10 minutes
Makes approximately 250 ml (9 fl oz/1 cup)

1 tablespoon coriander seeds
2 teaspoons cumin seeds
1 teaspoon black peppercorns
2 teaspoons shrimp paste
1 teaspoon freshly ground nutmeg
12 dried or fresh red chillies, roughly chopped
20 red Asian shallots, chopped
2 tablespoons oil
4 lemongrass stems, white part only, finely chopped
12 small garlic cloves, chopped
2 tablespoons coriander (cilantro) roots, chopped
2 tablespoons coriander (cilantro) stems, chopped
6 kaffir lime (makrut) leaves, chopped
2 teaspoons finely grated lime zest
2 teaspoons salt
2 teaspoons ground turmeric
1 teaspoon paprika

red vegetable curry

# thailand

1  Place the coriander and cumin seeds in a dry frying pan and roast over medium heat for 2–3 minutes, shaking the pan constantly.
2  Place the roasted spices and peppercorns in a mortar and use a pestle to pound until finely ground.
3  Wrap the shrimp paste in a small piece of foil and cook under a hot grill (broiler) for 3 minutes, turning the package twice.
4  Place the ground spices, shrimp paste, nutmeg and chilli in a food processor and process for 5 seconds. Add the remaining ingredients and process for 20 seconds at a time, scraping down the sides of the bowl each time with a spatula, until a smooth paste forms.

## green chicken curry

Preparation time: 20 minutes
Cooking time: 30 minutes
Serves 4

1 tablespoon oil
1 onion, chopped
1–2 tablespoons green curry paste (pages 110–11) or ready-made paste
375 ml (13 fl oz/1½ cups) coconut milk
500 g (1 lb 2 oz) boneless, skinless chicken thighs, cut into bite-sized pieces
100 g (3½ oz) green beans, trimmed, cut into short pieces
6 kaffir lime (makrut) leaves
1 tablespoon fish sauce
1 tablespoon lime juice
1 teaspoon finely grated lime zest
2 teaspoons soft brown sugar
10 g (¼ oz/⅓ cup) coriander (cilantro) sprigs

1  Heat the oil in a wok or heavy-based saucepan. Add the onion and curry paste to the wok and cook for 1 minute, stirring constantly. Add the coconut milk and 125 ml (4 fl oz/½ cup) water to the wok and bring to the boil.
2  Add the chicken pieces, beans and lime leaves to the wok, stirring to combine. Reduce the heat and simmer for 15–20 minutes or until the chicken is tender.
3  Add the fish sauce, lime juice, lime zest and sugar to the wok; stir to combine. Sprinkle with coriander sprigs just before serving. Serve with steamed rice, if desired.

NOTE: Boneless, skinless chicken thighs are sweet in flavour and have a good texture for curries, but you can use boneless, skinless chicken breasts if you prefer. Do not overcook breasts or they will become tough.

## larb (spicy pork salad)

Preparation time: 20 minutes
Cooking time: 10 minutes
Serves 4–6

1 tablespoon oil
2 lemongrass stems, white part only, thinly sliced
2 green chillies, finely chopped
500 g (1 lb 2 oz) lean minced (ground) pork or beef
60 ml (2 fl oz/¼ cup) lime juice
2 teaspoons finely grated lime zest
2–6 teaspoons chilli sauce
lettuce leaves, to serve
10 g (¼ oz) chopped coriander (cilantro) leaves
5 g (⅛ oz) chopped mint
1 small red onion, thinly sliced
50 g (1¾ oz/⅓ cup) unsalted roasted peanuts, chopped
25 g (1 oz/¼ cup) crisp fried garlic

1  Heat the oil in a wok and stir-fry the lemon grass, chilli and mince over high heat for 6 minutes, until the mince is cooked, breaking up any lumps. Transfer to a bowl; allow to cool.
2  Add the lime juice, zest and chilli sauce to the mince mixture. Arrange the lettuce leaves on a serving plate. Stir most of the coriander, mint, onion, peanuts and fried garlic through the mince, spoon over the lettuce and sprinkle the rest of the coriander, mint, onion, peanuts and garlic over the top.

larb (spicy pork salad)

## fish fillets in coconut milk

Preparation time: 15 minutes
Cooking time: 15 minutes
Serves 4

2 long green chillies
2 small red chillies
400 g (14 oz) firm white fish fillets
2 lemongrass stems, white part only
2 coriander (cilantro) roots, finely chopped
4 kaffir lime (makrut) leaves
2 cm (¾ inch) piece fresh ginger, grated
2 garlic cloves, crushed
3 spring onions (scallions), white part only, thinly sliced
1 teaspoon soft brown sugar
250 ml (9 fl oz/1 cup) coconut milk
125 ml (4 fl oz/½ cup) coconut cream
1 tablespoon fish sauce
2–3 tablespoons lime juice
kaffir lime (makrut) leaves, extra, to garnish

1  Heat a wok until hot. Add the whole chillies and roast until just beginning to brown all over. Remove the green chillies, cool and slice.
2  Cut the fish into cubes. Bruise the lemongrass by crushing with the flat side of a knife.
3  Add the lemongrass, coriander roots, lime leaves, ginger, garlic, spring onion, sugar and coconut milk to the wok. Bring to the boil, then simmer for 2 minutes. Add the fish pieces and simmer gently for 2–3 minutes, or until the fish is tender. Stir in the coconut cream.
4  Stir through the sliced green chilli, fish sauce, lime juice and salt to taste. Remove the lemongrass and whole chillies to serve. Sprinkle with the extra lime leaves.

# thailand

## watercress and duck salad with lychees

Preparation time: 25 minutes
Cooking time: 30 minutes
Serves 4

2 large duck breasts, skin on
1 tablespoon soy sauce
½ each red, green and yellow capsicum (pepper)
250 g (9 oz) watercress
12 fresh or tinned lychees
2 tablespoons pickled shredded ginger
1–2 tablespoons green peppercorns in brine (optional), rinsed and drained
1 tablespoon white vinegar
2 teaspoons soft brown sugar
1–2 teaspoons chopped red chilli
1 large handful coriander (cilantro) leaves

**1** Preheat the oven to 210°C (415°F/Gas 6–7). Brush the duck breasts with the soy sauce and put on a rack in a roasting tin. Bake for 30 minutes. Remove from the oven and allow to cool.
**2** Slice the capsicums into thin strips. Discard any tough woody stems from the watercress. Peel the fresh lychees and remove the seeds. If you are using tinned lychees, drain them thoroughly.
**3** Arrange the capsicum strips, watercress, lychees and ginger on a large serving platter. Slice the duck into thin pieces and toss gently through the salad.
**4** In a small bowl, combine the peppercorns, if using, vinegar, sugar, chilli and coriander. Serve this on the side for spooning over the salad.

## hot pork curry with pumpkin

Preparation time: 20 minutes
Cooking time: 25 minutes
Serves 4

1 tablespoon oil
1–2 tablespoons red curry paste (pages 102–3) or ready-made paste
500 g (1 lb 2 oz) lean pork, cut into thick strips or chunks
250 ml (9 fl oz/1 cup) coconut milk
350 g (12 oz) butternut pumpkin (squash), cut into small chunks
6 kaffir lime (makrut) leaves
60 ml (2 fl oz/¼ cup) coconut cream
1 tablespoon fish sauce
1 teaspoon soft brown sugar
2 red chillies, thinly sliced
basil leaves (optional), to serve
steamed rice, to serve

1  Heat the oil in a wok or heavy-based saucepan; add the curry paste and stir for 1 minute. Add the pork and stir-fry over moderately high heat until golden brown.
2  Add the coconut milk, 125 ml (4 fl oz/½ cup) water, pumpkin and lime leaves, reduce the heat and simmer for 20 minutes, or until the pork is tender.
3  Add the coconut cream, fish sauce and sugar to the wok and stir to combine. Scatter the chilli over the top. Garnish with sprigs of basil, if desired, and serve with the steamed rice.

## prawns in lime coconut sauce

Preparation time: 20 minutes
Cooking time: 35 minutes
Serves 4

15 g (½ oz/¼ cup) shredded coconut
500 g (1 lb 2 oz) raw prawns (shrimp)
1 teaspoon shrimp paste
250 ml (9 fl oz/1 cup) coconut milk
2 lemongrass stems, white part only, finely chopped
2–4 kaffir lime (makrut) leaves
2 teaspoons chopped red chilli
2 tablespoons tamarind concentrate
2 teaspoons fish sauce
1 teaspoon soft brown sugar
2 limes, zest finely shredded
steamed rice, to serve

1  Preheat the oven to 150°C (300°F/Gas 2). Spread the coconut on a baking tray and toast it in the oven for 10 minutes, or until it is dark golden, shaking the tray occasionally. Peel the prawns, leaving the tails intact. Gently pull out the dark vein from each prawn back, starting at the head end.
2  Meanwhile, wrap the shrimp paste in a piece of foil and cook under a hot grill (broiler) for 3 minutes, turning twice.

# thailand

**3** Combine the coconut milk and 250 ml (9 fl oz/1 cup) water in a wok or frying pan and cook over medium heat until just boiling. Add the lemongrass, lime leaves and chilli; reduce the heat and simmer for 7 minutes. Add the shrimp paste, tamarind, fish sauce and sugar and simmer for 8 minutes.
**4** Add the prawns to the sauce and cook for 5 minutes or until they turn pink. Sprinkle with the coconut and long, thin shreds of lime zest just before serving with the steamed rice.

NOTE: The prawns can be cooked and served in their shells. If so, provide a finger bowl and napkin for each diner.

## chicken and peanut penang curry

Preparation time: 25 minutes
Cooking time: 30–40 minutes
Serves 4

1 tablespoon oil
1 large red onion, chopped
1–2 tablespoons ready-made penang curry paste
250 ml (9 fl oz/1 cup) coconut milk
500 g (1 lb 2 oz) boneless, skinless chicken thighs, cut into bite-sized pieces
4 kaffir lime (makrut) leaves
60 ml (2 fl oz/¼ cup) coconut cream
1 tablespoon fish sauce
1 tablespoon lime juice
2 teaspoons soft brown sugar
80 g (2¾ oz/½ cup) unsalted roasted peanuts, chopped
15 g (½ oz/¼ cup) Thai basil leaves
80 g (2¾ oz/½ cup) chopped fresh pineapple
basil leaves, to garnish
1 Lebanese (short) cucumber, sliced, to serve

**1** Heat the oil in a wok or large frying pan; add the onion and curry paste and stir over medium heat for 2 minutes. Add the coconut milk and bring to the boil.
**2** Add the chicken and lime leaves to the wok; reduce the heat and cook for 15 minutes. Remove the chicken with a wire mesh strainer or slotted spoon. Simmer the sauce for 5 minutes or until it is reduced and quite thick.
**3** Return the chicken to the wok. Add the coconut cream, fish sauce, lime juice and sugar and cook for 5 minutes. Stir in the peanuts, basil and pineapple. Garnish with the basil leaves. Serve with the sliced cucumber on the side, as well as chilli sauce and steamed rice, if desired.

NOTE: Penang curry paste is based on ground nuts (usually peanuts). Penang curry originated in Malaysia but is now also found in both Thai and Indonesian cuisines.

essential asian

## stuffed prawn omelettes

Preparation time: 25 minutes
Cooking time: 15 minutes
Makes 8

500 g (1 lb 2 oz) raw prawns (shrimp)
1½ tablespoons oil
4 eggs, lightly beaten
2 tablespoons fish sauce
8 spring onions (scallions), chopped
6 coriander (cilantro) roots, chopped
2 garlic cloves, chopped
1 small red chilli, seeded and chopped
2 teaspoons lime juice
2 teaspoons grated palm sugar (jaggery) or soft brown sugar
3 tablespoons chopped coriander (cilantro) leaves
1 small red chilli, extra, finely sliced, to garnish
coriander (cilantro) sprigs, to garnish
sweet chilli sauce, to serve

1  Peel the prawns and gently pull out the dark vein from each prawn back, starting at the head end; chop the prawn meat.
2  Heat a wok over high heat, add 2 teaspoons of the oil and swirl to coat. Combine the egg with half of the fish sauce. Add 2 tablespoons of the mixture to the wok and swirl to a 16 cm (6¼ inch) round. Cook for 1 minute, then gently lift out. Repeat with the remaining egg mixture to make eight omelettes.
3  Heat the remaining oil in the wok. Add the prawns, spring onion, coriander root, garlic and chilli. Stir-fry for 3–4 minutes, or until the prawns are cooked. Stir in the lime juice, palm sugar, coriander leaves and the remaining fish sauce.
4  Divide the prawn mixture among the omelettes and fold each into a small firm parcel. Cut a slit in the top and garnish with the chilli and coriander sprigs. Serve with the sweet chilli sauce.

## crisp fried whole fish with sour pepper and coriander sauce

Preparation time: 20 minutes
Cooking time: 15 minutes
Serves 4

1 kg (2 lb 4 oz) whole firm sweet fish (such as snapper or red emperor), cleaned and scaled
oil, for deep-frying
4 spring onions (scallions), chopped
5 cm (2 inch) piece fresh ginger, grated
2–4 teaspoons fresh green peppercorns, crushed
2 teaspoons chopped red chilli
125 ml (4 fl oz/½ cup) coconut milk
1 tablespoon tamarind concentrate
1 tablespoon fish sauce
iceberg lettuce leaves, to serve
30 g (1 oz) coriander (cilantro) leaves
sweet chilli sauce, to serve

1  Cut a shallow, criss-cross pattern on both sides of the fish. Use kitchen scissors or a sharp knife to trim the fins if they are very long.
2  Heat the oil in a large wok or heavy-based, deep frying pan. Place the whole fish in the oil and cook for 4–5 minutes on each side, moving it around in the oil to ensure the whole fish is crisp and cooked (including the tail and head). Drain the fish well on paper towels and keep warm.

stuffed prawn omelettes

# thailand

**3** Drain almost all the oil from the wok. Heat the wok over medium heat, add the spring onion, ginger, peppercorns and chilli and stir-fry for 3 minutes. Add the coconut milk, tamarind and fish sauce and cook for 2 minutes.

**4** Place the fish on a bed of lettuce on a serving plate and pour over the sauce. Sprinkle with the coriander leaves and serve with the sweet chilli sauce.

NOTE: To serve, use tongs or a small spatula to lift pieces of fish away from the bones. Then remove the bones, or turn the fish over, and lift pieces of fish from the underside.

## stir-fried cauliflower and snake beans

✹

Preparation time: 15 minutes
Cooking time: 10 minutes
Serves 4

4 coriander (cilantro) roots, chopped, or 1 tablespoon chopped leaves and stems
1 teaspoon soft brown sugar
½ teaspoon ground turmeric
2 garlic cloves, crushed
2 tablespoons fish sauce
400 g (14 oz) cauliflower
6 spring onions (scallions)
200 g (7 oz) snake (yard-long) beans, trimmed
2 tablespoons oil
4 garlic cloves, extra, sliced lengthways
20 spinach leaves, coarsely shredded
1 tablespoon lime juice

**1** Use a mortar and pestle or a blender to blend the coriander, sugar, turmeric, crushed garlic and 1 tablespoon of the fish sauce to make a smooth paste.

**2** Cut the cauliflower into florets. Cut the spring onions in half lengthways, then cut the white parts into short lengths, reserving some of the green tops for a garnish. Cut the snake beans into short lengths.

**3** Heat half the oil in a large saucepan or wok, add the extra sliced garlic and stir-fry for 30 seconds or until just beginning to brown. Reserve some of the garlic for a garnish.

**4** Add the spinach to the pan and stir-fry for another 30 seconds or until just wilted. Add ½ teaspoon pepper and the remaining fish sauce and mix well. Arrange on a serving plate; keep warm.

**5** Heat the remaining oil in the same pan; add the paste and cook over high heat for 1 minute or until aromatic. Add the cauliflower and stir-fry until well combined. Add 125 ml (4 fl oz/½ cup) water, bring to the boil, reduce the heat and simmer, covered, for 3 minutes. Add the beans, cover and cook for another 3 minutes. Add the spring onion and stir until just wilted. Spoon the vegetables over the spinach, drizzle with the lime juice and sprinkle over the reserved fried garlic and spring onion.

crisp fried whole fish

essential asian

1 Line a bamboo steaming basket with banana leaves or baking paper (this is so the fish will not stick or taste of bamboo).
2 Arrange the fish cutlets in the basket and top with the ginger, garlic, chilli and coriander. Cover and steam over a wok or large saucepan of boiling water for 5–6 minutes.
3 Remove the lid and sprinkle the spring onion and lime juice over the fish. Cover and steam for 30 seconds, or until the fish is cooked. Serve immediately with the steamed rice and wedges of lime, if desired.

## green curry paste

☼

Preparation time: 20 minutes
Cooking time: 10 minutes
Makes approximately 250 ml (9 fl oz/1 cup)

1 tablespoon coriander seeds
2 teaspoons cumin seeds
1 teaspoon black peppercorns
2 teaspoons shrimp paste
8 large green chillies, roughly chopped
20 red Asian shallots
5 cm (2 inch) piece fresh galangal, chopped
12 small garlic cloves, chopped
100 g (3½ oz) chopped coriander (cilantro) leaves, stems and roots
6 kaffir lime (makrut) leaves, chopped
3 lemongrass stems, white part only, finely chopped
2 teaspoons finely grated lime zest
2 teaspoons salt
2 tablespoons oil

1 Place the coriander and cumin seeds in a dry frying pan and roast over medium heat for 2–3 minutes, shaking the pan constantly.
2 Pound the roasted spices and peppercorns using a mortar and pestle until finely ground.
3 Wrap the shrimp paste in a small piece of foil and cook under a hot grill (broiler) for 3 minutes, turning the package twice.

*steamed fish cutlets with ginger and chilli*

## steamed fish cutlets with ginger and chilli

☼

Preparation time: 15 minutes
Cooking time: 10 minutes
Serves 4

banana leaves (optional), for steaming
4 firm white fish cutlets (such as snapper), each approximately 200 g (7 oz)
5 cm (2 inch) piece fresh ginger, cut into fine shreds
2 garlic cloves, chopped
1 long red chilli, seeded and cut into thin strips
2 tablespoons finely chopped coriander (cilantro) stems
3 spring onions (scallions), cut into fine shreds each 4 cm (1½ inches) long
2 tablespoons lime juice
steamed rice, to serve

# thailand

4  Place the ground spices and shrimp paste in a food processor and process for 5 seconds. Add the remaining ingredients and process for 20 seconds at a time, scraping down the sides of the bowl with a spatula each time, until a smooth paste forms.

## thai curry pastes

Thai curry pastes are traditionally made of fresh herbs that grow in the house gardens or nearby fields, rather than the dry spices (those of the spice trade — cumin, coriander seeds, cardamom, cinnamon and cloves) used in Indian cooking. Throughout Thailand, market stalls provide a variety of pastes, each freshly made, for the home cook. The deceptively cool-coloured green curry paste is the most searingly hot; the colour comes from fresh green chillies and coriander (cilantro) leaves. Red curry paste is only marginally milder; here, the colour is derived mainly from dried or fresh red chillies.

## coriander pork with fresh pineapple

☀

Preparation time: 25 minutes
Cooking time: 15 minutes
Serves 4

400 g (14 oz) pork loin or fillet
¼ medium pineapple
1 tablespoon oil
4 garlic cloves, chopped
4 spring onions (scallions), chopped
1 tablespoon fish sauce
1 tablespoon lime juice
15 g (½ oz/½ cup) coriander (cilantro) leaves
15 g (½ oz/¼ cup) chopped mint
steamed rice, to serve
red chilli, sliced, to serve

1  Partially freeze the pork until it is just firm, then slice it thinly. Trim the skin from the pineapple and cut the flesh into bite-sized pieces.
2  Heat the oil in a wok or heavy-based frying pan over medium-high heat. Add the garlic and spring onion and cook for 1 minute. Remove from the wok.
3  Heat the wok to very hot; add the pork in two or three batches and stir-fry each batch for 3 minutes or until the pork is just cooked. Return the pork, garlic and spring onion to the wok and then add the pineapple pieces, fish sauce and lime juice. Toss well. Just before serving, sprinkle over the coriander leaves and mint and toss lightly. Serve with the steamed rice and red chilli on the side.

coriander pork with fresh pineapple

essential asian

## steamed mussels with lemongrass, basil and wine

✹

Preparation time: 30 minutes
Cooking time: 15 minutes
Serves 4–6

1 kg (2 lb 4 oz) black mussels
1 tablespoon oil
1 onion, chopped
4 garlic cloves, chopped
2 lemongrass stems, white part only, chopped
1–2 teaspoons chopped red chilli
250 ml (9 fl oz/1 cup) white wine or water
1 tablespoon fish sauce
30 g (1 oz/⅔ cup) Thai basil, chopped

1  Discard any open mussels. Scrub the outside of the mussels with a brush. Remove and discard the hairy beards. Soak the mussels in a bowl of cold water for 10 minutes; drain.
2  Heat the oil in a wok or large saucepan. Add the onion, garlic, lemongrass and chilli, and cook for 4 minutes over low heat, stirring occasionally. Add the wine and fish sauce and cook for 3 minutes.
3  Add the mussels to the wok and toss well. Cover the wok, increase the heat and cook for 3–4 minutes or until the mussels open. (Do not overcook or the mussels will become tough.) Discard any which have not opened after 4 minutes. Add the basil, toss well and serve with steamed rice, if desired.

## mee grob

✹

Preparation time: 30 minutes
Cooking time: 15 minutes
Serves 4–6

4 dried Chinese mushrooms
8 raw prawns (shrimp)
oil, for deep-frying
100 g (3½ oz) dried rice vermicelli
100 g (3½ oz) fried tofu puffs, cut into thin strips
4 garlic cloves, crushed
1 onion, chopped
200 g (7 oz) boneless, skinless chicken breast, thinly sliced
8 green beans, trimmed, sliced on the diagonal
6 spring onions (scallions), thinly sliced
30 g (1 oz/⅓ cup) bean sprouts, trimmed
coriander (cilantro) leaves, to garnish

SAUCE
1 tablespoon light soy sauce
60 ml (2 fl oz/¼ cup) white vinegar
60 ml (2 fl oz/¼ cup) fish sauce
1 tablespoon sweet chilli sauce
110 g (3¾ oz/½ cup) sugar

1  Soak the mushrooms in hot water for 20 minutes. Drain, then squeeze to remove any excess liquid. Discard the stems and chop the caps finely.
2  Peel the prawns and gently pull out the dark vein from each prawn back, starting at the head end.
3  Fill a wok or heavy-based saucepan one-third full of oil and heat to 180°C (350°F), or until a cube of bread dropped into the oil browns in 15 seconds. Cook the vermicelli in batches for 5 seconds, or until puffed and crispy. Drain on paper towels.
4  Add the tofu to the wok in batches and deep-fry for 1 minute, or until crisp.

Drain on paper towels. Cool the oil slightly and carefully remove all but 2 tablespoons of the oil.

**5** Reheat the wok over high heat until very hot. Add the garlic and onion and stir-fry for 1 minute. Add the mushrooms, chicken, green beans and half the spring onion and stir-fry for 2 minutes, or until the chicken is almost cooked through. Add the prawns and stir-fry for a further 2 minutes, or until the prawns just turn pink.

**6** To make the sauce, combine all the ingredients, stirring to dissolve the sugar. Add to the wok and stir-fry for 2 minutes, or until the sauce is syrupy and the chicken and prawns are tender. Remove the wok from the heat and stir in the vermicelli, tofu and bean sprouts. Garnish with the coriander and the remaining spring onion.

## pad thai

Preparation time: **30 minutes**
Cooking time: **10 minutes**
Serves 4–6

250 g (9 oz) dried rice stick noodles
1 tablespoon tamarind purée
1 small red chilli, chopped
2 garlic cloves, chopped
2 spring onions (scallions), sliced
1½ tablespoons sugar
2 tablespoons fish sauce
2 tablespoons lime juice
2 tablespoons oil
2 eggs, beaten
8 raw large prawns (shrimp)
150 g (5½ oz) pork fillet, thinly sliced
100 g (3½ oz) fried tofu puffs, cut into thin strips
90 g (3¼ oz/1 cup) bean sprouts
40 g (1½ oz/¼ cup) chopped unsalted roasted peanuts, to garnish
3 tablespoons coriander (cilantro) leaves, to garnish
1 lime, cut into wedges, to garnish
dried chilli flakes, to serve

**1** Put the noodles in a heatproof bowl, cover with warm water and soak for 15–20 minutes, or until soft and pliable. Drain well.

**2** Combine the tamarind with 1 tablespoon water. Put the chilli, garlic and spring onion in a spice grinder or use a mortar and pestle and grind to a smooth paste. Transfer the mixture to a bowl. Stir in the tamarind mixture along with the sugar, fish sauce and lime juice, stirring until combined.

**3** Heat a wok until very hot, add 1 tablespoon of the oil and swirl to coat the base and side. Add the egg, swirl to coat and cook for 1–2 minutes, or until set. Remove, roll up and cut into thin slices.

**4** Peel the prawns and gently pull out the dark vein from each prawn back, starting at the head end.

**5** Heat remaining oil in the wok, stir in chilli mixture and stir-fry for 30 seconds. Add the pork and stir-fry for 2 minutes, or until tender. Add prawns and stir-fry for a further minute, or until pink and curled.

**6** Stir in the noodles, egg, tofu and bean sprouts and gently toss together until heated through. Serve immediately topped with the peanuts, coriander, lime wedges and chilli flakes.

pad thai

# curry pastes & powders

The secret to making authentic Asian curries is to grind your own fresh spices into dry powder or wet pastes. Just a few minutes over high heat unlocks the aromas into the air.

## ceylon curry powder

In a small frying pan, dry-fry 6 tablespoons coriander seeds, 3 tablespoons cumin seeds, 1 teaspoon fennel seeds and ½ teaspoon fenugreek seeds for 8–10 minutes, or until the spices are dark brown, stirring occasionally to prevent the spices from burning. Place the roasted spices with 3 small dried chillies, 3 cloves, ¼ teaspoon cardamom seeds, 1 crushed cinnamon stick and 2 dried curry leaves in a food processor and grind to a fine powder. Cool and transfer to an airtight jar. Store in a cool, dark place for up to 3 months.

## indonesian sambal paste

Soak 12 large dried red chillies in hot water for 30 minutes; drain. Place the chillies, 2 roughly chopped large red onions, 6 garlic cloves, 1 teaspoon shrimp paste and 125 ml (4 fl oz/½ cup) oil in a food processor and mix into a smooth paste, scraping down the sides regularly. Heat a heavy-based saucepan over low heat and cook the paste for 10 minutes, stirring regularly, until very oily. Stir in 185 ml (6 fl oz/¾ cup) tamarind concentrate, 1 tablespoon grated palm sugar (jaggery) or soft brown sugar, 2 teaspoons salt and 1 teaspoon pepper. Bring to the boil and simmer for 2 minutes. Pour into warm sterilised jars, seal and cool. Store in the refrigerator for up to 2 weeks or freeze for up to 3 months.

## garam masala

Put 4 tablespoons coriander seeds, 3 tablespoons cardamom pods, 2 tablespoons cumin seeds, 1 tablespoon whole black peppercorns, 1 teaspoon whole cloves and 3 cinnamon sticks in a frying pan and dry-fry over moderate heat until aromatic. Open the cardamom pods, retaining the seeds only. Put the fried spices in a food processor or blender with a grated whole fresh nutmeg and process to a powder. Store in an airtight jar in a cool, dark place for up to 3 months.

## balti masala paste

Put 4 tablespoons coriander seeds, 2 tablespoons cumin seeds, 2 crumbled cinnamon sticks, 2 teaspoons each of fennel seeds, black mustard seeds and cardamom seeds, 1 teaspoon fenugreek seeds, 6 whole cloves, 4 bay leaves and 20 dried curry leaves in a small frying pan or balti. Dry-fry over moderate heat until the spices just start to become aromatic. Transfer to a mortar, then allow to cool before grinding to a powder using a pestle. Add 4 teaspoons each ground turmeric and garlic powder, 2 teaspoons ground ginger, 1½ teaspoons chilli powder and 250 ml (9 fl oz/1 cup) vinegar. Heat 250 ml (9 fl oz/1 cup) oil in the pan, add the paste and stir-fry for 5 minutes. Pour into warm sterilised jars, seal and cool. Store in the refrigerator for up to 2 weeks.

## chilli paste

Remove the stalks from 200 g (7 oz) small red chillies. Place in a small saucepan with 250 ml (9 fl oz/1 cup) water and bring to the boil. Reduce the heat and simmer, partially covered, for 15 minutes, then cool slightly. Transfer the chillies and liquid to a food processor; add 1 teaspoon each of salt and sugar, and 1 tablespoon each of vinegar and oil. Process until finely chopped. Store in a sealed container in the refrigerator for up to 2 weeks.

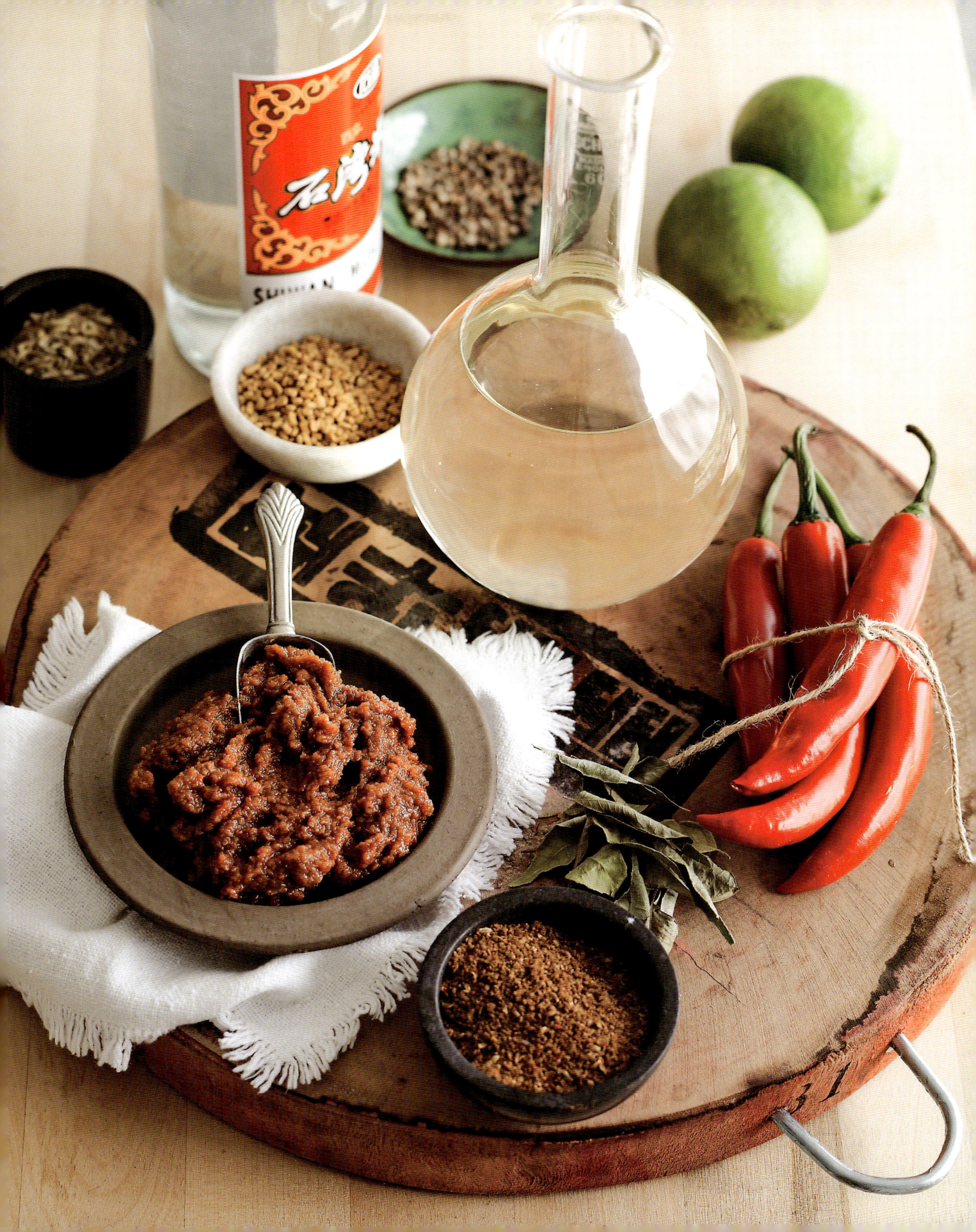

essential asian

chicken and vegetable salad

frying pan. Bring the mixture to the boil, reduce the heat slightly and simmer for 5 minutes.

**2** Add the chicken to the pan and cook in the hot liquid for 5 minutes, stirring occasionally. Drain and allow to cool. Discard the liquid.

**3** Bring a large saucepan of water to the boil and cook the broccolini, corn, snow peas, capsicum and spring onion for 2 minutes. Drain and plunge into iced water, then drain again.

**4** Combine the sweet chilli sauce, honey, lime juice and zest in a small bowl and mix well. Arrange the vegetables and chicken in a serving bowl. Pour the sauce over the top and gently toss. Sprinkle with the coriander leaves.

NOTE: To trim snow peas, cut or break both ends off and then pull away any strings from along the sides.

## curried rice noodles with chicken

Preparation time: 25 minutes
Cooking time: 10–15 minutes
Serves 4–6

200 g (7 oz) dried rice vermicelli
1½ tablespoons oil
1 tablespoon red curry paste (pages 102–3) or ready-made paste
450 g (1 lb) boneless, skinless chicken thighs, cut into fine strips
1–2 teaspoons chopped red chilli
2 tablespoons fish sauce
2 tablespoons lime juice
100 g (3½ oz) bean sprouts
80 g (2¾ oz) chopped unsalted roasted peanuts
20 g (¾ oz/¼ cup) crisp fried onion
25 g (1 oz/¼ cup) crisp fried garlic
25 g (1 oz/¾ cup) coriander (cilantro) leaves

**1** Cook the vermicelli in a saucepan of rapidly boiling water for 2 minutes. Drain and then toss with 2 teaspoons of the

## chicken and vegetable salad

Preparation time: 30 minutes
Cooking time: 20 minutes
Serves 4

3 slices fresh ginger
2 lemongrass stems, white part only, roughly chopped
2 tablespoons fish sauce
400 g (14 oz) boneless, skinless chicken breasts, cut into short, thin strips
250 g (9 oz) broccolini, cut into florets
150 g (5½ oz) baby corn
100 g (3½ oz) snow peas (mangetout), trimmed
1 red capsicum (pepper), cut into strips
3 spring onions (scallions), cut into strips
125 ml (4 fl oz/½ cup) sweet chilli sauce
2 tablespoons honey
2 tablespoons lime juice
2 teaspoons finely grated lime zest
1 handful coriander (cilantro) leaves, to garnish

**1** Put the ginger, lemongrass, fish sauce and 250 ml (9 fl oz/1 cup) water in a

oil to prevent the strands from sticking together; set aside.

**2** Heat the remaining oil in a wok. Add the curry paste and stir for 1 minute or until aromatic. Add the chicken in batches and stir-fry for 2 minutes or until golden brown. Return all the chicken to the pan.

**3** Add the chilli, fish sauce and lime juice; bring to the boil and simmer for 1 minute. Add the bean sprouts and vermicelli and toss well. Arrange the mixture on a serving plate and sprinkle with peanuts, onion, garlic and coriander leaves. Serve immediately.

## spicy roasted eggplant with tofu

Preparation time: **15 minutes**
Cooking time: **15 minutes**
Serves **4**

4 slender eggplants (aubergines) (about 400 g/14 oz)
250 g (9 oz) firm tofu
2–4 small red or green chillies
4 garlic cloves, crushed
4 coriander (cilantro) roots, chopped
1 small onion, chopped
3 teaspoons soft brown sugar
2 tablespoons lime juice
2 tablespoons fish sauce
1 tablespoon oil
15 g (½ oz/¼ cup) Thai basil
2 teaspoons dried shrimp (optional), finely chopped, to garnish

**1** Heat a medium frying pan or wok until hot. Add the eggplant and cook until the skin begins to char, turning to cook all sides. Remove from the heat and cool. Slice the eggplant diagonally into 2 cm (¾ inch) thick slices. Drain the tofu and cut into 3 cm (1¼ inch) cubes.

**2** Blend the chillies, garlic, coriander, onion, sugar, lime juice and fish sauce in a food processor or blender until smooth.

**3** Heat the oil in the same frying pan or wok, add the paste and stir over high heat for 1 minute or until fragrant. Add the eggplant, stir to combine and cook, covered, for 3 minutes or until just tender.

**4** Add the tofu and half the basil and gently stir through. Serve garnished with the remaining basil and dried shrimp, if desired.

NOTE: This dish can be eaten hot or as a cold accompaniment. If you prefer a milder, less spicy dish, use only 2 chillies.

### storing fresh coriander

To store a bunch of fresh coriander (cilantro), stand it, unwashed, in a container of suitable size with the roots in 1 cm (½ inch) water. Enclose the leaves and stems with a large plastic supermarket carrier bag and tie the handles together around the container, then stand the whole thing in the refrigerator. It should keep for up to 2 weeks — break off leaves as you need them. The roots will also freeze well.

## green pawpaw and peanut salad

Preparation time: 25 minutes
Cooking time: 5 minutes
Serves 4

50 g (1¾ oz) dried shrimp (see Note)
100 g (3½ oz) green beans, trimmed
1 small iceberg lettuce
½ green pawpaw, peeled and grated (see Note)
60 ml (2 fl oz/¼ cup) lime juice
2 tablespoons fish sauce
2 teaspoons soft brown sugar
1–2 teaspoons chopped red chilli
80 g (2¾ oz/½ cup) unsalted roasted peanuts, chopped
1 red chilli, extra, finely chopped

1  Use a mortar and pestle to pound the shrimp, or chop finely. Cut the beans into short pieces and cook them in a saucepan of boiling water for 2 minutes. Drain, then plunge them into iced water and drain again. Shred the lettuce and arrange it on a serving plate. Top with the shrimp, beans and pawpaw.
2  Combine the lime juice, fish sauce, sugar and chilli in a small bowl and mix well. Pour over the salad and sprinkle the peanuts and extra chilli over the top.

NOTE: Dried shrimp and green pawpaw are available at Asian food stores.

## fresh spring rolls

Preparation time: 30 minutes
Cooking time: nil
Makes 8

16 cooked prawns (shrimp)
50 g (1¾ oz) dried mung bean vermicelli
8 dried rice paper wrappers
16 Thai basil leaves
30 g (1 oz/1 cup) coriander (cilantro) leaves
1 carrot, cut into short thin strips
1 tablespoon finely grated lime zest
2 tablespoons sweet chilli sauce

DIPPING SAUCE
1 teaspoon sugar
2 tablespoons fish sauce
1 tablespoon white vinegar
1 small red chilli (optional), finely chopped
1 tablespoon chopped coriander (cilantro) leaves and stems

1  To make the dipping sauce, place 80 ml (2½ fl oz/⅓ cup) cold water in a small bowl; add the sugar and stir until it has dissolved. Stir in the fish sauce, vinegar, chilli, if desired, and coriander leaves and stems.
2  Peel the prawns and gently pull out the dark vein from each prawn back, starting at the head end. Soak the vermicelli in 500 ml (17 fl oz/2 cups) hot water for 10 minutes and then drain. Dip a rice paper wrapper into lukewarm water until it softens and place it on a work surface. Place 2 prawns side by side in the centre of the wrapper and top with 2 basil leaves, 1 tablespoon coriander, a few carrot strips, a little lime zest and a small amount of vermicelli. Spoon a little sweet chilli sauce over the top.
3  Press the filling down to flatten it a little; fold in two sides, then roll up the parcel. Lay seam-side down on a serving plate and sprinkle with a little water; cover with plastic wrap. Repeat with the remaining ingredients. Serve with the dipping sauce and a little extra sweet chilli sauce.

NOTE: Rice paper wrappers must be kept moist or they become brittle. Continue to sprinkle cold water on them while rolling them up or if they are left for any length of time before serving.

# thailand

Place 2 prawns side by side in the centre of the wrapper and top with the other ingredients.

Fold in the sides of the wrapper then roll it up to form a parcel.

# steamed fish in banana leaves

Preparation time: **45 minutes**
Cooking time: **10 minutes**
Makes **10**

2 large banana leaves
350 g (12 oz) firm white fish fillets, cut into thin strips
1–2 tablespoons red curry paste (pages 102–3) or ready-made paste
250 ml (9 fl oz/1 cup) coconut cream
banana leaves, extra, or cabbage leaves, for steaming
150 g (5½ oz/2 cups) finely shredded cabbage
2 tablespoons fish sauce
2 tablespoons lime juice
1–2 tablespoons sweet chilli sauce
1 red chilli (optional), chopped

**1** Cut the banana leaves into squares 10 x 10 cm (4 x 4 inches) and make a 3 cm (1¼ inch) cut towards the centre on each corner. Fold in the corners, then staple and/or tie around with a piece of string to form a cup. Trim the corners to neaten, if necessary.
**2** Put the fish in a bowl with the curry paste and coconut cream and stir gently to combine. Place spoonfuls of the fish mixture in each banana leaf cup.
**3** Line a large steaming basket with the extra banana leaves or cabbage leaves and place the prepared cups in the basket. Top each piece of fish with shredded cabbage and a little fish sauce. Place the basket over a wok of simmering water and steam, covered, for about 7 minutes. Drizzle lime juice and sweet chilli sauce over the top and serve immediately, sprinkled with the chilli, if desired.

NOTE: The fish can be cooked in foil cups instead of banana leaves.

# thailand

## spicy beef curry

✻

Preparation time: 20 minutes
Cooking time: 30–35 minutes
Serves 4

1 tablespoon oil
1 large onion, chopped
1–2 tablespoons green curry paste (pages 110–11) or ready-made paste
500 g (1 lb 2 oz) round or blade steak, cut into thick strips
185 ml (6 fl oz/¾ cup) coconut milk
6 kaffir lime (makrut) leaves
100 g (3½ oz) pea eggplants (aubergines)
2 tablespoons fish sauce
1 teaspoon soft brown sugar
2 teaspoons finely grated lime zest
15 g (½ oz/½ cup) coriander (cilantro) leaves
30 g (1 oz/½ cup) shredded basil
steamed rice, to serve

**1** Heat the oil in a wok or large frying pan. Add the onion and curry paste and stir for 2 minutes over medium heat until aromatic.
**2** Heat the wok until it is very hot. Add the beef in two batches and stir-fry until brown. Return all the beef to the wok. Add the coconut milk, 60 ml (2 fl oz/¼ cup) water and the lime leaves. Bring to the boil, reduce the heat, cover and simmer for 10 minutes. Add the eggplants and simmer, uncovered, for another 10 minutes or until both the beef and eggplants are tender.
**3** Add the fish sauce, sugar and lime zest to the wok and mix well. Stir in the coriander and basil. Serve immediately with the steamed rice.

NOTE: Use thinly sliced slender eggplants if pea eggplants are not available.

## son-in-law eggs

✻

Preparation time: 15 minutes
Cooking time: 20 minutes
Serves 4

**son-in-law eggs**

8 eggs
2 tablespoons oil
2 tablespoons grated palm sugar (jaggery) or soft brown sugar
1 tablespoon fish sauce
2 tablespoons tamarind concentrate
1 teaspoon chopped red chilli (optional)

**1** Place the eggs in a saucepan of cold water. Bring the water to the boil and cook the eggs for 7 minutes (begin timing when the water boils). Drain and run under cold water until cool. Remove the shells.
**2** Heat the oil in a wok or frying pan. Add the eggs to the wok in batches and turn frequently over medium heat. When they are golden brown and blistered, remove the eggs from the wok and keep warm.
**3** Remove the excess oil from the wok and add the palm sugar, fish sauce, tamarind concentrate and chilli, if using. Bring to the boil and boil rapidly for 2 minutes, or until the mixture resembles a syrup. Serve the eggs with the syrup poured over them.

Add the cornflour, fish sauce, egg, coriander, curry paste and chilli. Process for 10 seconds or until well combined.
**2** Transfer the fish mixture to a large bowl. Add the beans and spring onion and mix well. Using wet hands, form 2 rounded tablespoons of the mixture at a time into fairly flat patties.
**3** Heat the oil in a heavy-based frying pan over medium heat. Cook four fish cakes at a time until they are dark golden brown on both sides. Drain on paper towels and serve immediately with the dipping sauce.

NOTE: The fish cakes can be prepared ahead up to the end of Step 2 and stored, covered, in the refrigerator for up to 4 hours.

# ginger chicken with black fungus

Preparation time: 40 minutes
Cooking time: 15 minutes
Serves 4

10 g (¼ oz/¼ cup) dried black fungus
1 tablespoon oil
3 garlic cloves, chopped
6 cm (2½ inch) piece fresh ginger, cut into fine shreds
500 g (1 lb 2 oz) boneless, skinless chicken breasts, sliced
4 spring onions (scallions), chopped
1 tablespoon golden mountain sauce
1 tablespoon fish sauce
2 teaspoons soft brown sugar
½ red capsicum (pepper), finely sliced
15 g (½ oz/½ cup) coriander (cilantro) leaves
25 g (1 oz) chopped Thai basil

**1** Place the fungus in a heatproof bowl, cover with hot water, and leave for 15 minutes until it is soft and swollen; drain and chop roughly.

*thai fish cakes*

# thai fish cakes

Preparation time: 25 minutes
Cooking time: 5–10 minutes
Serves 4–6

450 g (1 lb) firm white fish fillets
3 tablespoons cornflour (cornstarch) or rice flour
1 tablespoon fish sauce
1 egg, beaten
15 g (½ oz/½ cup) coriander (cilantro) leaves
3 teaspoons red curry paste (pages 102–3) or ready-made paste
1–2 teaspoons chopped red chilli (optional)
100 g (3½ oz) green beans, trimmed, very thinly sliced
2 spring onions (scallions), finely chopped
125 ml (4 fl oz/½ cup) oil
dipping sauce (page 118), to serve

**1** Place the fish in a food processor and process for 20 seconds or until smooth.

# thailand

2  Heat the oil in a large wok, add the garlic and ginger and stir-fry for 1 minute. Add the chicken in batches, stir-frying over high heat until it changes colour. Return all the chicken to the wok. Add the spring onion and golden mountain sauce and stir-fry for 1 minute.

3  Add the fish sauce, sugar and fungus to the wok. Stir thoroughly; cover and steam for 2 minutes. Serve immediately with the capsicum, coriander and basil scattered on top.

## a thai meal

A traditional Thai meal consists of a variety of dishes — usually a soup, a curry or stewed dish, a stir-fry and a salad. These dishes are selected for a balance of flavours (sweet, sour, hot, bitter and salty), as well as textures and colours. All dishes are served at the same time and eaten warm or at room temperature; diners help themselves and eat using a knife and fork. Rice is always served, and a number of tasty sauces and dips add even more flavour to the dishes. The main meal is sometimes followed by a platter of fresh tropical fruits and desserts made of mung bean flour, rice, palm sugar, coconut and eggs. Tea and water accompany the meal.

## cucumber salad with peanuts and chilli

Preparation time: 25 minutes + 45 minutes marinating time
Cooking time: nil
Serves 4–6

3 Lebanese (short) cucumbers
2 tablespoons white vinegar
2 teaspoons sugar
1–2 tablespoons chilli sauce
½ red onion, chopped
1 large handful coriander (cilantro) leaves
160 g (5¾ oz/1 cup) unsalted roasted peanuts, chopped
2 tablespoons crisp fried garlic
½ teaspoon chopped chilli
1 tablespoon fish sauce

1  Peel the cucumbers and slice in half lengthways. Remove the seeds with a teaspoon and slice thinly.

2  Combine the vinegar and sugar in a small bowl, and stir until the sugar has dissolved. Transfer to a large bowl and toss with the cucumber, chilli sauce, onion and coriander. Allow to marinate for 45 minutes.

3  Just before serving, add the peanuts, garlic, chilli and fish sauce. Toss lightly to combine.

## green curry with sweet potato and eggplant

✳

Preparation time: 15 minutes
Cooking time: 20 minutes
Serves 4–6

1 onion
1 eggplant (aubergine)
1 orange sweet potato
1 tablespoon vegetable oil
1–2 tablespoons green curry paste (see pages 110–11)
375 ml (13 fl oz/1½ cups) coconut milk
250 ml (9 fl oz/1 cup) vegetable stock
6 kaffir lime (makrut) leaves
2 teaspoons grated palm sugar (jaggery) or soft brown sugar
2 tablespoons lime juice
2 teaspoons finely grated lime zest
coriander (cilantro) leaves, to garnish
kaffir lime (makrut) leaves (optional), extra, to garnish
steamed rice, to serve

1  Chop the onion. Quarter and slice the eggplant and cut the sweet potato into cubes. Heat the oil in a large wok. Add the onion and green curry paste and cook, stirring, over medium heat for 3 minutes. Add the eggplant and cook for a further 4–5 minutes, or until softened. Pour in the coconut milk and stock, bring to the boil, then reduce the heat and simmer for 5 minutes. Add the lime leaves and sweet potato and cook, stirring occasionally, for 10 minutes, or until the eggplant and sweet potato are very tender.
2  Mix in the palm sugar, lime juice and lime zest until well combined with the vegetables. Season to taste with salt. Garnish with the coriander leaves and extra lime leaves, if desired, and serve with the steamed rice.

green curry with sweet potato and eggplant

## fried rice with coriander and basil

✳

Preparation time: 20 minutes + overnight standing time
Cooking time: 20 minutes
Serves 4

100 g (3½ oz) pork loin
300 g (10½ oz) boneless, skinless chicken thighs
2 tablespoons oil
3 cm (1¼ inch) piece pork fat, chopped
4 garlic cloves, chopped
4 cm (1½ inch) piece fresh ginger, finely grated
2 teaspoons chopped red chilli
500 g (1 lb 2 oz/2½ cups) jasmine rice, cooked and cooled (see Note)
1 tablespoon fish sauce
2 teaspoons golden mountain sauce
2 spring onions (scallions), chopped
30 g (1 oz/⅔ cup) Thai basil, chopped
15 g (½ oz/½ cup) coriander (cilantro) leaves, chopped

1  Dice the pork and the chicken.
2  Heat the oil in a wok or large heavy-based frying pan. When the oil is very

hot, add the pork fat, garlic, ginger and chilli; stir for 2 minutes.

**3** Add the diced chicken and pork to the wok and stir-fry for 3 minutes or until the meat changes colour. Break up any lumps in the rice and add it to the wok; toss well using two wooden spoons. When the rice is warmed, add the fish sauce and golden mountain sauce and toss through with the spring onion, basil and most of the coriander, reserving some for garnish. Serve immediately, garnished with the remaining coriander leaves.

NOTE: If possible, cook the rice a day ahead and refrigerate it overnight before making the fried rice so the finished dish is not gluggy.

## thai beef salad

Preparation time: 20 minutes
Cooking time: 5 minutes
Serves 6

500 g (1 lb 2 oz) lean beef fillet
2 tablespoons peanut oil
2 garlic cloves, crushed
1 tablespoon grated palm sugar (jaggery) or soft brown sugar
3 tablespoons finely chopped coriander (cilantro) roots and stems
80 ml (2½ fl oz/⅓ cup) lime juice
2 tablespoons fish sauce
¼ teaspoon ground white pepper
2 small red chillies, seeded and thinly sliced
2 red Asian shallots, thinly sliced
2 telegraph (long) cucumbers, sliced into thin ribbons
2 large handfuls mint
90 g (3¼ oz/1 cup) bean sprouts, trimmed
40 g (1½ oz/¼ cup) chopped unsalted roasted peanuts

**1** Thinly slice the beef across the grain. Heat a wok over high heat, then add 1 tablespoon of the oil and swirl to coat the side of the wok. Add half the beef and cook for 1–2 minutes, or until medium–rare. Remove from the wok and put on a plate. Repeat with remaining oil and beef.

**2** Put the garlic, palm sugar, coriander, lime juice, fish sauce, white pepper and ¼ teaspoon salt in a bowl, and stir until the sugar has dissolved. Add the chilli and shallots and mix well.

**3** Pour the sauce over the hot beef, mix together well, then allow the beef to cool to room temperature.

**4** In a separate bowl, toss together the cucumber and mint, and refrigerate until required.

**5** Pile up a bed of the cucumber and mint on a serving platter, then top with the beef and the marinade, then the bean sprouts and peanuts.

### thai salads

Most Thai salads are a subtle combination of apparently opposing tastes and textures — crisp raw vegetables and chilli-hot meat or seafood — and are made with a range of ingredients, from rose petals to squid. Raw or rare beef salads are a traditional feature of northeastern Thailand.

# laos & cambodia

The cuisine of these two neighbours owes much to the influence of the country that they both border, Thailand, and the abundance of fresh fish caught in the Mekong River in landlocked Laos or the Gulf of Thailand in Cambodia. The fish are cooked simply with aromatic herbs or citrus marinades, while other soups, meat and vegetable dishes may be flavoured with garlic, ginger, chilli, galangal and lime leaves and scattered with fresh basil, coriander and mint.

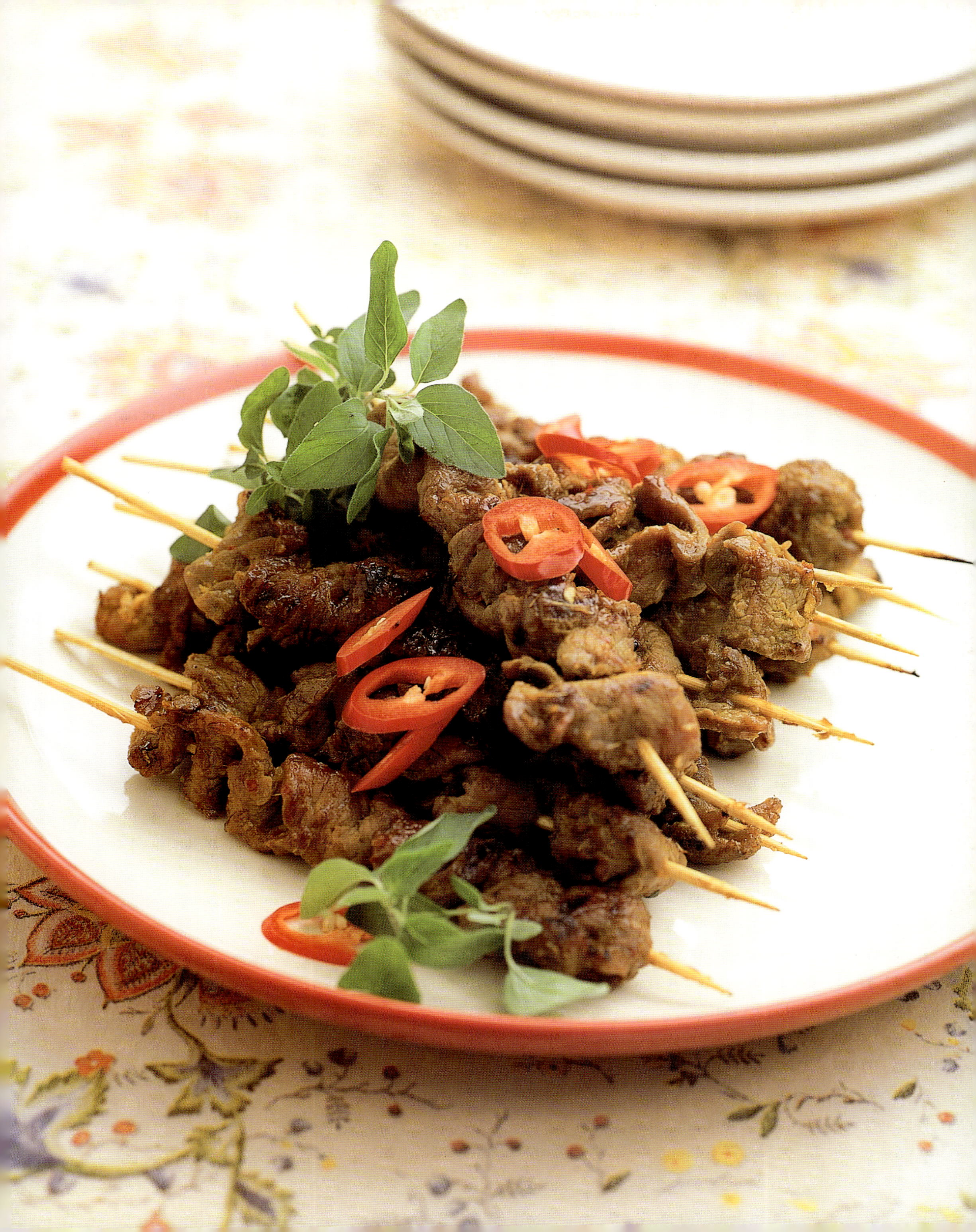

essential asian

1  Score a cross in the base of the tomatoes. Put in a heatproof bowl and cover with boiling water. Leave for 30 seconds, then transfer to cold water and peel the skin away from the cross. Cut the tomatoes in half, scoop out the seeds and chop the flesh.
2  Peel the prawns and gently pull out the dark vein from each prawn back, starting at the head end.
3  Heat the oil in a large saucepan. Add the ginger, lemongrass, chilli and onion and stir over medium heat for 5 minutes or until the onion is golden.
4  Add the tomato to the pan and cook for 3 minutes. Stir in the stock, 750 ml (26 fl oz/3 cups) water, the lime leaves, pineapple, tamarind, palm sugar, lime juice and fish sauce. Cover, bring to the boil, then reduce the heat and simmer for 15 minutes.
5  Add the fish, prawns and coriander to the pan, and simmer for 10 minutes or until the seafood is tender. Serve immediately.

## laotian fish balls

❊

Preparation time: 30 minutes
Cooking time: 10 minutes
Makes 24 balls

500 g (1 lb 2 oz) firm white fish fillets
2 tablespoons fish sauce
3 red chillies, seeded and finely chopped
1½ teaspoons finely chopped lemongrass, white part only
4 garlic cloves, crushed
3 spring onions (scallions), finely chopped
4 tablespoons chopped coriander (cilantro) leaves
1 egg, beaten
2 tablespoons rice flour
oil, for deep-frying
1 lemon, cut into wedges, to serve

1  Finely chop the fish. Alternatively, chop the fish in a food processor but be careful not to overwork it or the fish will be tough. Combine the fish and fish sauce in

## seafood soup

❊

Preparation time: 30 minutes
Cooking time: 40 minutes
Serves 6

4 tomatoes
500 g (1 lb 2 oz) raw prawns (shrimp)
1 tablespoon oil
5 cm (2 inch) piece fresh ginger, grated
3 tablespoons finely chopped lemongrass, white part only
3 small red chillies, finely chopped
2 onions, chopped
750 ml (26 fl oz/3 cups) fish stock
4 kaffir lime (makrut) leaves, finely shredded
165 g (5¾ oz/1 cup) chopped pineapple
1 tablespoon tamarind concentrate
1 tablespoon grated palm sugar (jaggery) or soft brown sugar
2 tablespoons lime juice
1 tablespoon fish sauce
500 g (1 lb 2 oz) firm white fish fillets, cut into 2 cm (¾ inch) cubes
2 tablespoons chopped coriander (cilantro) leaves

# laos & cambodia

a bowl. Add the chilli, lemongrass, garlic, spring onion and half the coriander and mix well. Add the egg and rice flour and mix until thoroughly combined.

2  With slightly damp hands, make small balls from the mixture, each with a diameter of approximately 3 cm (1¼ inches).

3  Fill a deep heavy-based saucepan or deep-fryer one-third full of oil and heat to 180°C (350°F), or until a cube of bread dropped into the oil browns in 15 seconds. Add the fish balls in two batches and cook until golden. Drain on paper towels. Sprinkle the remaining coriander over the fish balls and serve immediately with the lemon wedges.

## chicken and pumpkin stew

✹ ✹

Preparation time: 20 minutes
Cooking time: 50 minutes
Serves 6

110 g (3¾ oz/½ cup) medium-grain rice
2 tablespoons oil
1 kg (2 lb 4 oz) chicken pieces
3 garlic cloves, crushed
3 tablespoons finely chopped lemongrass, white part only
2 teaspoons grated fresh turmeric or 1 teaspoon ground turmeric
2 tablespoons grated fresh galangal
6 kaffir lime (makrut) leaves, finely shredded
6 spring onions (scallions), chopped
1 litre (35 fl oz/4 cups) chicken stock
500 g (1 lb 2 oz) pumpkin (winter squash), cubed
1 small green pawpaw, peeled and chopped
125 g (4½ oz) snake (yard-long) beans, trimmed, cut into short lengths

1  Preheat the oven to 180°C (350°F/Gas 4). Spread the rice on a baking tray and roast it for 15 minutes or until golden. Remove the rice from the oven, allow it to cool slightly and then process it in a food processor until finely ground.

2  Heat the oil in a large saucepan; add the chicken pieces in batches and cook for 5 minutes, or until brown. Drain on paper towels.

3  Add the garlic, lemongrass, turmeric, galangal, lime leaves and spring onion to the pan; cook over medium heat for 3 minutes or until spring onion is golden. Return the chicken to the pan; add the stock, cover and simmer for 20 minutes.

4  Add the pumpkin and pawpaw, and simmer, covered, for 10 minutes. Add the beans and simmer, covered, for another 10 minutes, or until the chicken is tender. Stir in the ground rice, bring to the boil, then reduce the heat and simmer, uncovered, for 5 minutes or until the mixture thickens slightly.

NOTE: Green pawpaw is available at Asian food stores. If it is not available, green mango can be substituted.

chicken and pumpkin stew

essential asian

## fish and noodle soup

✹

Preparation time: 15 minutes
Cooking time: 25 minutes
Serves 4

200 g (7 oz) dried rice vermicelli
1 tablespoon oil
2.5 cm (1 inch) piece fresh ginger, grated
3 small red chillies, finely chopped
4 spring onions (scallions), chopped
875 ml (30 fl oz/3½ cups) coconut milk
2 tablespoons fish sauce
2 tablespoons tomato paste (concentrated purée)
500 g (1 lb 2 oz) firm white fish fillets, cubed
2 ham steaks, diced
150 g (5½ oz) snake (yard-long) beans, trimmed, chopped
185 g (6½ oz) bean sprouts, trimmed
1 small handful mint
80 g (2¾ oz/½ cup) unsalted roasted peanuts

**1** Soak the vermicelli in boiling water for 6–7 minutes, or until soft, then drain well. Set aside.
**2** Heat the oil in a large, heavy-based saucepan and cook ginger, chilli and spring onion for 3 minutes, or until golden. Stir in the coconut milk, fish sauce and tomato paste, cover and simmer for 10 minutes. Add the fish, ham and beans and simmer for 10 minutes, or until fish is tender.
**3** Divide the vermicelli among four bowls and top with the bean sprouts and mint. Spoon the soup into the bowls and sprinkle with peanuts.

## steamed spicy chicken

✹ ✹

Preparation time: 40 minutes
Cooking time: 30 minutes
Serves 4

125 ml (4 fl oz/½ cup) coconut cream
2 teaspoons grated palm sugar (jaggery) or soft brown sugar
1 tablespoon fish sauce
2 kaffir lime (makrut) leaves, shredded
500 g (1 lb 2 oz) boneless, skinless chicken breasts, cut into 5 cm (2 inch) strips
180 g (6 oz/4 cups) shredded silverbeet (Swiss chard) or spinach

SPICE PASTE
7 dried chillies, seeded
4 lemongrass stems, white part only, finely chopped
1 slice fresh galangal, finely chopped
1 slice fresh turmeric, finely chopped
6 cm (2½ inch) strip makrut (kaffir lime) zest, chopped
1 teaspoon shrimp paste
4 garlic cloves, chopped
4 red Asian shallots, chopped

**1** To make the spice paste, soak the chillies in hot water for 30 minutes or until soft; drain. Place the softened chillies and ½ teaspoon salt in a food processor and process until a smooth paste has formed. Add all the other paste ingredients one at a time while continuing to run the processor.

steamed spicy chicken

# laos & cambodia

2 Combine the coconut cream, palm sugar, fish sauce and lime leaves in a large bowl. Add the spice paste and stir together until well combined. Stir in the chicken strips.

3 Select a round heatproof serving dish which will fit into a large, deep saucepan. Put the silverbeet onto the serving dish. Spoon the spicy chicken mixture over the silverbeet.

4 Place a saucer or rack on the base of the pan and pour in enough boiling water to cover it. Place the dish on top of the saucer or rack, cover the pan with a tight-fitting lid and steam over medium heat for about 30 minutes or until the chicken is cooked. Check from time to time that there is enough water in the pan. Serve with steamed rice, if desired.

## prawns steamed in banana leaves

✹ ✹

Preparation time: 25 minutes + 2 hours marinating time
Cooking time: 15 minutes
Serves 4

1 kg (2 lb 4 oz) raw prawns (shrimp)
8 small banana leaves
1 tablespoon sesame seeds
2.5 cm (1 inch) piece fresh ginger, grated
2 small red chillies, finely chopped
4 spring onions (scallions), finely chopped
2 lemongrass stems, white part only, finely chopped
2 teaspoons soft brown sugar
1 tablespoon fish sauce
2 tablespoons lime juice
2 tablespoons chopped coriander (cilantro) leaves

1 Peel the prawns and gently pull out the dark vein from each prawn back, starting at the head end. Put the banana leaves in a large heatproof bowl, cover with boiling water and leave them to soak for 3 minutes, or until softened. Drain and pat dry. Cut the banana leaves into squares, about 18 cm (7 inches). Toast the sesame seeds in a dry frying pan over medium heat for 3–4 minutes, shaking the pan gently, until the seeds are golden brown. Remove from the pan at once to prevent the seeds burning.

2 Place the ginger, chilli, spring onion and lemongrass in a food processor, and process in short bursts until a paste forms. Transfer the paste to a bowl; stir in the sugar, fish sauce, lime juice, sesame seeds and coriander and mix well. Add the prawns and toss to coat. Cover the bowl and marinate for 2 hours in the refrigerator.

3 Divide the mixture into eight, and place a portion on each banana leaf. Fold the leaf to enclose the mixture, and then secure the parcels with a wooden skewer.

4 Cook the parcels in a bamboo steamer over simmering water for 8–10 minutes or until the prawn filling is cooked.

NOTE: Banana leaves are available from Asian food stores and speciality fruit and vegetable stores or a banana tree!

*Cut the banana leaves into 18 cm (7 inch) squares.*

*Fold the leaf to enclose the filling, then secure the parcel with a wooden skewer.*

## containers for marinating

As a marinade usually contains an acid, such as vinegar, rice wine, lime juice or lemon juice, always use a non-metallic container to marinate food as acid will react with metal. A dish of glass or glazed china is best. Use a wooden spoon to stir or turn the food.

chicken mince with herbs and spices

## chicken mince with herbs and spices

Preparation time: 30 minutes
Cooking time: 30 minutes
Serves 4–6

55 g (2 oz/¼ cup) medium-grain white rice
1 kg (2 lb 4 oz) boneless, skinless chicken thighs
2 tablespoons peanut oil
4 garlic cloves, crushed
2 tablespoons grated fresh galangal
2 small red chillies
4 spring onions (scallions), finely chopped
60 ml (2 fl oz/¼ cup) fish sauce
1 tablespoon shrimp paste
3 tablespoons chopped Vietnamese mint
2 tablespoons chopped basil
4 tablespoons lime juice
lettuce leaves, to serve

1 Preheat the oven to 180°C (350°F/Gas 4). Spread the rice on a baking tray and roast for 15 minutes or until golden. Cool slightly, then transfer the rice to a food processor and process until finely ground. Set aside.
2 Place the chicken in a food processor and process until finely minced.
3 Heat the oil in a wok or frying pan; add the garlic, galangal, chilli and spring onion and cook over medium heat for 3 minutes. Add the minced (ground) chicken to the wok and stir for 5 minutes, or until the mince is browned, breaking up any large lumps with a wooden spoon. Stir in the fish sauce and shrimp paste and bring to the boil, then reduce the heat and simmer for 5 minutes.
4 Remove the wok from the heat, stir in the rice, mint, basil and lime juice, and mix to combine. Serve with lettuce leaves.

## laotian beef salad

Preparation time: 15 minutes + 2 hours marinating time
Cooking time: 10 minutes
Serves 4

500 g (1 lb 2 oz) rump steak
3 tablespoons lemon juice
2 tablespoons finely chopped lemongrass, white part only
1 tablespoon fish sauce
1 onion, thinly sliced
2 tablespoons chopped coriander (cilantro) leaves
1 tablespoon chopped mint, plus mint leaves, extra, to garnish
2 Lebanese (short) cucumbers, chopped
½ small Chinese cabbage (wong bok), shredded

# laos & cambodia

1 Chargrill the beef for 3 minutes on each side or until cooked to medium-rare. Remove, cover and set aside for 5 minutes. Use a sharp knife to cut the beef into 5 mm (¼ inch) thick slices.
2 Heat 4 tablespoons water in a wok, add the sliced beef and cook over medium heat for 2 minutes. Do not overcook. Transfer the beef and liquid to a non-metallic bowl.
3 Add the lemon juice, lemongrass, fish sauce, onion, coriander and mint and mix until well combined. Cover and leave in the refrigerator for 2 hours to marinate.
4 Stir in the chopped cucumber. Serve the salad on a bed of shredded cabbage, garnished with the extra mint leaves.

NOTE: If you prefer your beef more well done, increase the chargrilling time.

## laotian dried beef with green pawpaw salad

✸

Preparation time: 30 minutes + 4 hours marinating time
Cooking time: 5 hours 5 minutes
Serves 6

1 kg (2 lb 4 oz) piece topside steak, partially frozen
2 teaspoons salt
¼ teaspoon chilli powder
1 teaspoon ground black pepper
1 tablespoon soft brown sugar
4 garlic cloves, crushed
2 teaspoons sesame oil
1 tablespoon peanut oil

GREEN PAWPAW SALAD
1 small green pawpaw, peeled and seeded
1 carrot
2 garlic cloves, crushed
6 cm (2½ inch) piece fresh ginger, finely grated
2 small red chillies
2 tablespoons fish sauce
4 kaffir lime (makrut) leaves, finely shredded
1 tablespoon lime juice
2 teaspoons soft brown sugar
1 teaspoon sesame oil
30 g (1 oz/1 cup) coriander (cilantro) leaves
160 g (5¾ oz/1 cup) unsalted roasted peanuts

1 Preheat the oven to 120°C (235°F/Gas ½).
2 Trim any excess fat from the beef. Cut the beef into 3 mm (⅛ inch) thick slices, then into strips. Mix the salt, chilli powder, pepper, sugar, garlic, sesame oil and peanut oil in a bowl. Add the beef and, using your fingertips, toss it in the oil mixture until coated. Cover and marinate for 4 hours in the refrigerator.
3 Place the beef on a rack in a large baking dish and bake for 5 hours, or until it is dried out.
4 To make the green pawpaw salad, cut the papaya and carrot into shreds, using a citrus zester if you have one. Combine the pawpaw and carrot in a bowl with the remaining ingredients and toss lightly.
5 Cook the beef under a hot grill (broiler) for 3 minutes, then serve with the green pawpaw salad.

NOTE: The dried beef will keep for 3 weeks in an airtight container in the refrigerator or can be frozen for up to 6 months.

laotian dried beef with green pawpaw salad

## grilled pork

Preparation time: 10 minutes + 4 hours marinating time
Cooking time: 15 minutes
Serves 4

1 kg (2 lb 4 oz) pork chops
8 garlic cloves, crushed
2 tablespoons fish sauce
1 tablespoon soy sauce
2 tablespoons oyster sauce
2 tablespoons finely chopped spring onion (scallion)

**1** Place the pork in a large glass bowl and add the garlic, fish sauce, soy sauce, oyster sauce and ½ teaspoon ground black pepper. Stir well so that all the meat is covered with the marinade; cover and marinate for 4 hours in the refrigerator.
**2** Preheat a grill (broiler) to hot; cook the pork on both sides until browned and cooked through. If the meat starts to burn, move it further away from the grill element. Alternatively, you can cook the pork on a hot barbecue grill.
**3** Arrange the pork on a serving platter and scatter over the spring onion.

## spicy eggplant and fish purée in salad leaves

Preparation time: 45 minutes
Cooking time: 1 hour
Serves 6

1 large eggplant (aubergine), approximately 800 g (1 lb 12 oz)
12 garlic cloves, unpeeled
4 red Asian shallots, unpeeled
600 g (1 lb 5 oz) white fish fillets
peanut oil, to brush
100 g (3½ oz) dried mung bean vermicelli
2 tablespoons fish sauce
3 red chillies, seeded and finely chopped
2 tablespoons mint, roughly chopped
2 tablespoons coriander (cilantro) leaves, roughly chopped
1 mignonette lettuce
1 butter lettuce
50 g (1¾ oz) coriander (cilantro) sprigs

SAUCE
3 tablespoons fish sauce
3 tablespoons lime juice
1 teaspoon caster (superfine) sugar
1 red chilli, seeded and thinly sliced

**1** Preheat the oven to 180°C (350°F/Gas 4). Place the eggplant on a baking tray and bake for 50 minutes, or until soft and tender. Add the garlic and shallots to the baking tray after 15 minutes of cooking. Allow to cool.
**2** Brush the fish with the oil and cook under a hot grill (broiler) until cooked through. Allow the fish to cool, then break into pieces.

## laos & cambodia

3  Place the vermicelli in boiling water and cook for 1–2 minutes or until tender. Drain, cool and chop roughly.

4  Cut the eggplant in half, scoop out the soft flesh and place it in a food processor. Squeeze six of the soft garlic cloves and all the shallots from their skins into the food processor. Add the fish, fish sauce, chilli, mint and coriander, and process until a fine-textured purée forms. Transfer the purée to a bowl, season to taste with salt, and stir in the vermicelli.

5  To make the sauce, place all the ingredients in a food processor. Squeeze the remaining cloves of garlic into the food processor and process until a smooth sauce forms. Heat the sauce in a small saucepan, stirring to dissolve the sugar, and then allow it to cool to room temperature.

6  To serve, place the bowl containing the purée onto a platter and surround it with the lettuce leaves and coriander sprigs. Place the sauce in a separate bowl. The diners help themselves — each takes a lettuce leaf and places a sprig of coriander on top of it. They then place a spoonful of purée and a teaspoon of the sauce on the leaves and roll them up to eat.

# lemongrass beef skewers

❋

Preparation time: 15 minutes + 4 hours marinating time
Cooking time: 5 minutes
Serves 4

500 g (1 lb 2 oz) sirloin steak
2 teaspoons chilli flakes
4 lemongrass stems, white part only, chopped
2 slices fresh galangal, chopped
2 slices fresh turmeric, chopped
4 garlic cloves, peeled
1 tablespoon grated palm sugar (jaggery) or soft brown sugar
125 ml (4 fl oz/½ cup) oyster sauce
2 tablespoons oil
lemon basil, to garnish
sliced red chilli, to garnish

1  Soak 10–12 wooden skewers in water for 30 minutes to prevent them burning during cooking.

2  Cut the beef into long, thin strips and put in a non-metallic bowl. Use a mortar and pestle to pound the chilli, lemongrass, galangal, turmeric and garlic to form a paste. Add the palm sugar, oyster sauce, 1 teaspoon salt and the oil and combine well. Spoon the marinade over the beef and mix well. Cover with plastic wrap and refrigerate for 4 hours.

3  Thread the beef onto the skewers. Heat a barbecue grill or hotplate and cook the skewers for 5 minutes, or until browned and cooked through. Serve garnished with the lemon basil and red chilli.

### laotian purées

Unique to Laotian cooking are its puréed dishes — raw meat or cooked fish pounded to a smooth, soft consistency, seasoned with chilli and herbs and then served with lettuce and leafy herbs. Another feature of the cuisine is the method of using slow-cooked eggplant as a thickening agent for stewed dishes.

# vietnam

The lush greenness of Vietnam produces a wide range of vegetables and herbs that impart a fresh taste and fragrance to its cooking. Bunches of coriander and mint are scattered over steaming bowls of pho, a soupy noodle and meat dish which can be bought on every street corner. The basic flavour of many Vietnamese dishes comes from nuoc mam, a fish sauce that is added to soups and stir-fries, or used in marinades with lemongrass, lemon juice and chillies to give a tangy, pungent flavour to meat and fish.

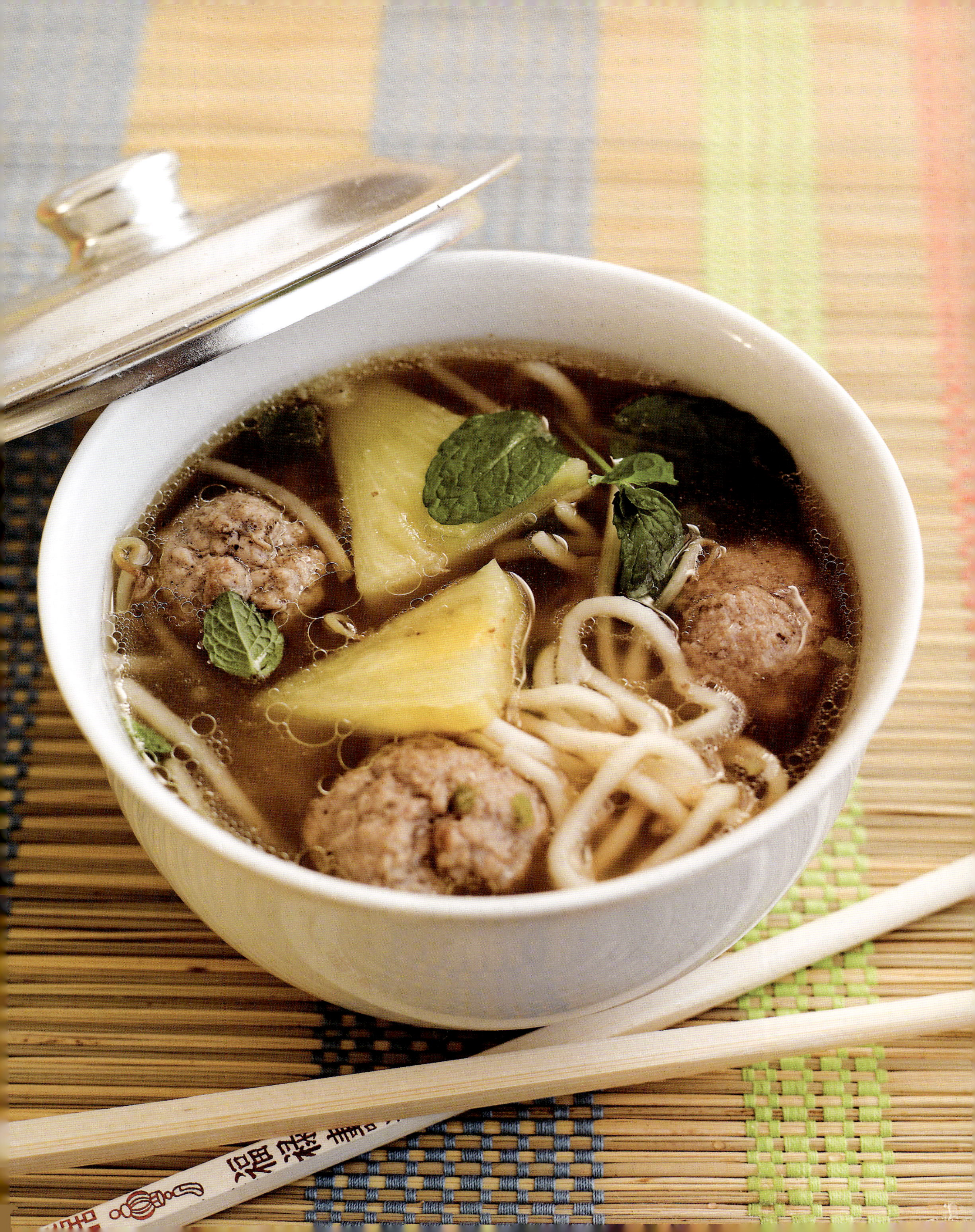
福祿

essential asian

### lemongrass

This long, grass-like herb has a citrus aroma and taste. Trim the base, remove the tough outer layers and thinly slice, finely chop or pound the white interior. For pastes and salads, use the tender, white portion just above the root. The whole stem, trimmed, washed and bruised with the back of a knife, can be added to simmering curries and soups (remove before serving). Dried lemongrass is rather flavourless, so you may prefer to use lemon zest, although either is a poor substitute for the real thing.

2 teaspoons sugar
1 tablespoon fish sauce
coriander (cilantro) and Vietnamese mint leaves, finely chopped, to garnish

**1** Heat the oil in a heavy-based frying pan or wok over medium heat. Add the onion, garlic, ginger, lemongrass and chilli and stir-fry for 3–5 minutes, or until the mixture is lightly golden. Take care not to burn the mixture or it will become bitter.
**2** Increase the heat to high and when the pan is very hot, add the chicken and toss. Sprinkle the sugar over the chicken and cook for about 5 minutes, tossing regularly until the chicken is just cooked. Add the fish sauce, cook for a further 2 minutes, then serve immediately, garnished with the coriander and Vietnamese mint.

## crab, prawn and potato fritters

❋

Preparation time: **25 minutes**
Cooking time: **20 minutes**
Makes **18 fritters**

200 g (7 oz) raw prawns (shrimp)
200 g (7 oz) tin crabmeat
200 g (7 oz) potatoes
60 g (2¼ oz/½ cup) self-raising flour
250 ml (9 fl oz/1 cup) coconut milk
2 teaspoons fish sauce
1 teaspoon sugar
oil, for shallow frying
iceberg lettuce leaves, to serve
mint leaves, chopped, to garnish
Vietnamese dipping sauce (see page 148), to serve

stir-fried chicken with lemongrass, ginger and chilli

## stir-fried chicken with lemongrass, ginger and chilli

❋

Preparation time: **30 minutes**
Cooking time: **15 minutes**
Serves **4**

2 tablespoons oil
2 brown onions, roughly chopped
4 garlic cloves, finely chopped
5 cm (2 inch) piece fresh ginger, finely grated
3 lemongrass stems, white part only, thinly sliced
2 teaspoons chopped green chilli
500 g (1 lb 2 oz) boneless, skinless chicken thighs, thinly sliced

**1** Peel the prawns and gently pull out the dark vein from each prawn back, starting at the head end. Finely chop the prawn meat. Drain the crabmeat. Finely grate the potatoes, squeezing out as much water as possible.
**2** Place the prawn meat, crabmeat, potato, flour, coconut milk, fish sauce,

# vietnam

½ teaspoon salt, ½ teaspoon pepper and sugar in a large bowl and combine well.

**3** Heat the oil in a frying pan or wok until hot; cook tablespoons of the mixture, about 3 at a time, tossing gently until golden brown. Drain the fritters on paper towels.

**4** Arrange the fritters on a bed of lettuce leaves and garnish with the mint leaves. Serve with the Vietnamese dipping sauce.

NOTE: Grate the potatoes just before cooking to keep them from going brown.

## caramelised prawns

✹ ✹

Preparation time: 25 minutes
Cooking time: 15 minutes
Serves 4

500 g (1 lb 2 oz) raw prawns (shrimp)
6 spring onions (scallions)
1 tablespoon oil
3 garlic cloves, finely chopped
2 tablespoons caramel sauce (see Note)
1 tablespoon fish sauce
1 tablespoon lime juice
1 tablespoon soft brown sugar
¼ red capsicum (pepper), cut into fine strips, to garnish

**1** Remove the prawn heads and, using a fine needle, devein the prawns, leaving the tails, shells and legs intact. Rinse the prawns under running water and pat dry with paper towels.

**2** Finely chop half the spring onions. Cut the rest into 4 cm (1½ inch) long pieces and then finely shred the pieces into thin strips.

**3** Heat the oil in a heavy-based frying pan; add the garlic, chopped spring onion and prawns, and cook over medium heat for about 3 minutes, tossing the prawns until they turn pink. Drizzle the caramel sauce and fish sauce over the top and cook for 1 minute. Add the lime juice, sugar, ½ teaspoon salt and remaining spring onion. Toss well and serve immediately, garnished with the capsicum. If the prawn shells are tender, they can be eaten, but supply finger bowls and napkins at the table so your diners can peel the prawns if they prefer.

NOTE: To make the caramel sauce, combine 4 tablespoons sugar and 60 ml (2 fl oz/¼ cup) water in a small saucepan. Stir over low heat, without boiling, until the sugar has dissolved. Bring the syrup to the boil, reduce the heat and simmer gently for about 5 minutes, until the syrup turns dark golden. Take care not to burn it. Remove the pan from the heat and add 80 ml (2½ fl oz/⅓ cup) water — it will spit and sizzle, and the caramel will form hard lumps. Return the pan to the heat and cook, stirring, until the lumps become liquid again. The sauce can be stored in the refrigerator for up to 1 week.

When water is added to the caramel sauce, hard lumps will form.

Toss the unpeeled prawns in the pan until they turn pink.

Add the lime juice, sugar, salt and remaining spring onion to the pan.

essential asian

# vietnam

## whole barbecued fish

☀

Preparation time: 40 minutes
Cooking time: 20 minutes
Serves 4–6

750 g (1 lb 10 oz) snapper or bream, cleaned and scaled
2 teaspoons green peppercorns
2 teaspoons chopped red chilli
3 teaspoons fish sauce
1 tablespoon oil
2 onions, thinly sliced
4 cm (1½ inch) piece fresh ginger, thinly sliced
3 garlic cloves, thinly sliced
2 teaspoons sugar
4 spring onions (scallions), cut into 4 cm (1½ inch) pieces, then finely shredded
lemon and garlic dipping sauce (page 148), to serve
lime cheeks, to serve

**1** Wash the fish inside and out and pat dry with paper towels. Cut two diagonal slashes into the thickest part of the fish on both sides.
**2** Put the peppercorns, chilli and fish sauce in a food processor and process until a paste forms. Alternatively, use a mortar and pestle. Brush the paste lightly over the fish, cover and refrigerate for 20 minutes.
**3** Heat a barbecue hotplate until very hot and lightly brush it with oil. Cook the fish for 8 minutes on each side, or until the flesh flakes easily when tested with a fork.
**4** While the fish is cooking, heat the oil in a frying pan over medium heat. Add the onion and cook, stirring, for about 5 minutes, or until golden. Add the ginger, garlic and sugar and cook for a further 3 minutes.
**5** Place the fish on a serving plate, top with the onion mixture, sprinkle over the spring onion and serve immediately with the lemon and garlic dipping sauce and lime wedges.

## beef pho (beef soup)

☀ ☀

Preparation time: 15 minutes
Cooking time: 35 minutes
Serves 4

2 litres (70 fl oz/8 cups) beef stock
1 whole star anise
4 cm (1½ inch) piece fresh ginger, sliced
2 pigs' trotters (cut in half)
½ onion, studded with 2 whole cloves
2 lemongrass stems, bruised
2 garlic cloves, crushed
¼ teaspoon ground white pepper
1 tablespoon fish sauce, plus extra, to serve
200 g (7 oz) fresh thin rice noodles
300 g (10½ oz) beef fillet, partially frozen, thinly sliced
90 g (3¼ oz/1 cup) bean sprouts, trimmed
2 spring onions (scallions), thinly sliced
25 g (1 oz/½ cup) chopped coriander (cilantro) leaves, plus extra, to serve
4 tablespoons chopped Vietnamese mint, plus extra, to serve
1 red chilli, thinly sliced, plus extra, to serve
2 limes, quartered

**1** Put the stock, star anise, ginger, pigs' trotters, onion, lemongrass, garlic and white pepper in a wok and bring to the boil. Reduce the heat to very low and simmer, covered, for 30 minutes. Strain, return to the wok and stir in the fish sauce.
**2** Meanwhile, put the noodles in a heatproof bowl, cover with boiling water and gently separate. Drain well then refresh under cold running water. Divide the noodles among four deep soup bowls then top with beef strips, bean sprouts, spring onion, coriander, mint and chilli. Ladle over the broth.
**3** Place the extra fish sauce, chilli, mint and coriander and the lime quarters in small bowls on a platter, serve with the soup and allow your guests to help themselves.

essential asian

## vietnamese chicken salad

Preparation time: 40 minutes
Cooking time: 5 minutes
Serves 4

600 g (1 lb 5 oz) boneless, skinless chicken thighs, cooked
125 g (4½ oz/1 cup) thinly sliced celery
2 carrots, cut into 5 cm (2 inch) lengths
75 g (2¾ oz/1 cup) finely shredded cabbage
1 small onion, sliced
3 tablespoons coriander (cilantro) leaves
3 tablespoons finely shredded mint

DRESSING
3 tablespoons caster (superfine) sugar
2 tablespoons water
1 tablespoon fish sauce
1 teaspoon crushed garlic
2 tablespoons white vinegar
1 red chilli, seeded and finely chopped

TOPPING
2 tablespoons peanut oil
1½ teaspoons chopped garlic
50 g (1¾ oz/⅓ cup) unsalted roasted peanuts, finely chopped
1 tablespoon soft brown sugar or 2 teaspoons caster (superfine) sugar

**1** Slice the chicken into long, thin strips. Combine the chicken, celery, carrot, cabbage, onion, coriander and mint in a large bowl.
**2** To make the dressing, place all the ingredients in a small bowl. Whisk until the sugar has dissolved and the ingredients are well combined.
**3** To make the topping, heat the oil in a wok; add the garlic and cook over moderate heat, stirring, until pale golden. Stir in the peanuts and sugar.
**4** Pour the dressing over the chicken mixture and toss to combine. Place the chicken salad on a serving plate, and sprinkle over the topping just before serving.

## eggplant slices in black bean sauce

Preparation time: 20 minutes
Cooking time: 35 minutes
Serves 4

500 g (1 lb 2 oz) eggplants (aubergines)
80 ml (2½ fl oz/⅓ cup) oil
4 garlic cloves, finely chopped
4 cm (1½ inch) piece fresh ginger, grated
2 onions, finely chopped
80 ml (2½ fl oz /⅓ cup) chicken stock
2 teaspoons tinned black beans, rinsed well, roughly chopped
2 tablespoons oyster sauce
1 tablespoon soy sauce
2 teaspoons fish sauce
4 spring onions (scallions), thinly sliced

**1** Slice the eggplants into long slices and lightly brush each side with oil.
**2** Heat a frying pan over moderately low heat; add the eggplant, four to five slices at a time, and cook until golden on both sides; remove from the pan. Do

eggplant slices in black bean sauce

# vietnam

not hurry this process as cooking the eggplant slowly allows the natural sugars to caramelise and produces a wonderful flavour. If the eggplant begins to burn, reduce the heat and sprinkle it with a little water.

**3** Increase the heat to moderately high and add any remaining oil, the garlic, ginger, onion and about 1 tablespoon of the stock; cover and cook for 3 minutes. Add the remaining stock, black beans, oyster sauce, soy sauce and fish sauce. Bring to the boil and cook for 2 minutes. Return the eggplant to the pan and simmer for 2 minutes or until it is heated through. Scatter over the spring onion and serve.

NOTE: Always rinse black beans very well before using, as they are extremely salty. They will keep indefinitely if refrigerated after opening.

## vermicelli and crabmeat stir-fry

❋

Preparation time: 40 minutes
Cooking time: 15 minutes
Serves 4

200 g (7 oz) dried mung bean vermicelli
2 tablespoons oil
10 red Asian shallots, very thinly sliced
3 garlic cloves, finely chopped
2 lemongrass stems, white part only, very thinly sliced
1 red capsicum (pepper), cut into 4 cm (1½ inch) matchsticks
170 g (6 oz) tin crabmeat, well drained
2 tablespoons fish sauce
2 tablespoons lime juice
2 teaspoons sugar
3 spring onions (scallions), thinly sliced

**1** Soak the noodles in hot water for 20 minutes or until softened; drain. Use scissors to cut the noodles into short lengths for easy eating.

**2** Heat the oil in a wok or heavy-based saucepan; add the shallots, garlic and lemongrass and stir-fry over high heat for 2 minutes. Add the capsicum and cook for 30 seconds, tossing well. Add the vermicelli and toss. Cover and steam for 1 minute, or until the vermicelli is heated through.

**3** Add the crabmeat, fish sauce, lime juice and sugar and toss well, using two wooden spoons. Season with salt and pepper to taste, sprinkle with the spring onion and serve.

### crabmeat

Fresh crabmeat is always best, but it is expensive and not always easily available. Tinned crabmeat has a slightly different flavour and texture to fresh — salt will have been added. After draining, use a knife or your finger to check for pieces of membrane or shell, and remove. Note that when drained, the crabmeat is only about half the weight shown on the tin.

essential asian

pork and lettuce parcels

# vietnam

## pork and lettuce parcels

Preparation time: 1 hour
Cooking time: 1 hour
Serves 4–6

500 g (1 lb 2 oz) pork loin
5 cm (2 inch) piece fresh ginger, thinly sliced
1 tablespoon fish sauce
20 thin spring onions (scallions)
2 soft-leaf lettuces, such as butter lettuce
1 Lebanese (short) cucumber, thinly sliced
3 tablespoons mint leaves
3 tablespoons coriander (cilantro) leaves
2 green chillies (optional), seeded and very thinly sliced
2 teaspoons caster (superfine) sugar
Lemon and garlic dipping sauce (page 148), to serve

**1** Put the pork, ginger and fish sauce in a large saucepan and cover with cold water. Bring to the boil, then reduce the heat and simmer, covered, for about 45 minutes, or until the pork is tender. Remove the pork and allow to cool. Discard the liquid.
**2** Trim both ends from the spring onions so you have long stems of equal length. Bring a large saucepan of water to the boil and blanch the spring onions, two or three at a time, for about 2 minutes, until softened. Remove the spring onions from the hot water with tongs and place in a bowl of iced water. Drain and lay them flat and straight on a tray.
**3** Separate the lettuce into leaves. If the leaves have a firm section at the base, trim this away (or making a neat parcel will be difficult).
**4** When the pork is cool enough to handle, cut it into thin slices and finely shred each slice. Spread out a lettuce leaf and place about 1 tablespoon of the shredded pork in the centre of the leaf. Top with a few slices of cucumber, a few mint and coriander leaves, a little green chilli, if desired, and a light sprinkling of sugar. Fold a section of the lettuce over the filling, bring in the sides to meet each other, and carefully roll up the parcel. Tie one of the spring onions around the parcel, trim off the excess or tie it into a bow. Repeat with the remaining ingredients.
**5** Arrange the pork and lettuce parcels on a serving platter and serve with the Lemon and garlic dipping sauce.

## seared pork skewers

Preparation time: 35 minutes
Cooking time: 15 minutes
Serves 4

500 g (1 lb 2 oz) pork fillet, cut into 2 cm (¾ inch) cubes
5 cm (2 inch) piece fresh ginger, finely grated
2 garlic cloves, finely chopped
2 tablespoons fish sauce
1 tablespoon dry sherry
2 teaspoons oil
mint, to garnish
Vietnamese dipping sauce (page 148), to serve
steamed rice or cooked rice noodles, to serve

**1** Soak eight wooden skewers in water for 30 minutes to prevent burning.
**2** Place the pork in a bowl with the ginger, garlic, fish sauce, sherry, ½ teaspoon salt and ½ teaspoon pepper and marinate for 20 minutes. Drain the pork and reserve the marinade. Dry the skewers with paper towels and thread the meat onto them.
**3** Brush a heavy-based frying pan with oil and heat until extremely hot. Cook the skewers of pork, three at a time, for 3–4 minutes; turn the skewers regularly until the pork becomes a dark golden brown and sprinkle over a little of the marinade. Do not overcook the pork or it will become very dry.
**4** Garnish with the mint and serve with the Vietnamese dipping sauce and steamed rice or cooked rice noodles.

## warm beef and watercress salad

Preparation time: 25 minutes + 30 minutes marinating time
Cooking time: 10 minutes
Serves 4

350 g (12 oz) fillet steak, partially frozen (optional) (see Note)
1 tablespoon green peppercorns, roughly chopped
4 garlic cloves, crushed
3 lemongrass stems, white part only, very thinly sliced
3 tablespoons oil
250 g (9 oz) watercress
125 g (4½ oz) cherry tomatoes, halved
4 spring onions (scallions), chopped
2 tablespoons lime juice

**1** Cut the beef into thin slices. Place the beef, peppercorns, garlic, lemongrass, 2 tablespoons of the oil, ¼ teaspoon salt and ¼ teaspoon pepper in a bowl. Mix well, cover and marinate in the refrigerator for 30 minutes.
**2** Remove the watercress sprigs from the tough stems, break them into small pieces, and wash and drain them well. Arrange the watercress on a serving platter and place the tomatoes on top, around the outside edge.
**3** Heat the remaining oil in a wok or heavy-based frying pan until very hot and lightly smoking. Add the beef mixture and stir-fry it quickly until the beef is just cooked. Add the spring onion and toss through. Remove the beef mixture from the pan, pile it up in the centre of the watercress and sprinkle the lime juice over the top. Serve immediately.

NOTE: Partially freezing the meat for 30 minutes makes it easier to slice thinly.

## braised duck with mushrooms

✸ ✸

Preparation time: 20 minutes
Cooking time: 1 hour 10 minutes
Serves 6

15 g (½ oz) dried Chinese mushrooms
1.5 kg (3 lb 5 oz) whole duck
2 teaspoons oil
2 tablespoons soy sauce
2 tablespoons shaoxing rice wine (Chinese rice wine)
2 teaspoons sugar
2 wide strips orange zest
125 g (4½ oz) watercress

**1** Soak the mushrooms in hot water for 20 minutes. Drain well, discard the stems and thinly slice the caps.
**2** Remove the neck and any large pieces of fat from inside the duck carcass. Using a large heavy knife or cleaver, chop the duck into small pieces, cutting through the bone. Arrange the pieces on a rack and pour boiling water over them — the water will plump up the skin and help keep the duck succulent. Drain and pat dry with paper towel.
**3** Heat the oil in a wok over medium heat and add the duck. Cook, in batches, for about 8 minutes, turning regularly, until browned. (The darker the browning at this stage, the better the colour when finished.) Between each batch, wipe out the pan with crumpled paper towels to remove excess oil.
**4** Wipe the pan with paper towels again and return all the duck to the pan. Add the mushrooms, soy sauce, rice wine, sugar and orange zest.
**5** Bring the mixture to the boil, reduce the heat, cover and simmer gently for 35 minutes or until the duck is tender. Season, to taste, and stand for 10 minutes, covered, before serving.
**6** Remove the duck from the sauce and discard the orange zest. Pick off small sprigs of the watercress and arrange them on one side of a large serving platter. Carefully place the duck segments on the other side of the platter — try not to place the duck on the watercress as it will become soggy. Carefully spoon a little of the sauce over the duck and serve.

**NOTE:** Braising the duck over low heat produces tender, melt-in-the-mouth meat and a delicious sauce. If the heat is too high, the duck will dry out and lose its flavour.

## vietnamese coleslaw

✸

Preparation time: 55 minutes
Cooking time: 10 minutes
Serves 4

500 g (1 lb 2 oz) boneless, skinless chicken breasts
350 g (12 oz) Chinese cabbage (wong bok), finely shredded
3 celery stalks, thinly sliced
1 carrot, cut into fine matchsticks
1½ tablespoons oil
2 tablespoons shredded Vietnamese mint
1 tablespoon chopped garlic chives
1 tablespoon crisp fried onion

DRESSING
4 tablespoons rice vinegar
2 tablespoons caster (superfine) sugar
1 tablespoon fish sauce
1 tablespoon lime juice
1 onion, finely sliced

# vietnam

1  Place the chicken in a frying pan with enough water to just cover it. Poach the chicken over low heat for 8–10 minutes or until it is cooked — do not let the water boil; it should just simmer gently. Drain and cool. When the chicken is cool enough to touch, shred it into fine pieces using your fingertips.

2  To make the dressing, place the vinegar, sugar, fish sauce, lime juice, ½ teaspoon salt, ½ teaspoon pepper and the onion in a small bowl and toss well to combine. Let it stand for at least 20 minutes so that the onion absorbs all the flavours.

3  Place the chicken, cabbage, celery, carrot, oil and dressing in a bowl and toss well. Arrange the salad on a serving plate, scatter over the mint, chives and crisp fried onion, and serve immediately.

## vietnamese spring rolls

✷ ✷

Preparation time: 50 minutes
Cooking time: 20 minutes
Makes 20

50 g (1¾ oz) dried mung bean vermicelli
2 tablespoons black fungus
500 g (1 lb 2 oz) raw prawns (shrimp)
20 rice paper wrappers
150 g (5½ oz) minced (ground) pork
4 spring onions (scallions), chopped
45 g (1¾ oz/½ cup) bean sprouts, trimmed, roughly chopped
1 teaspoon sugar
1 egg, beaten
oil, for deep-frying
20 lettuce leaves, to serve
90 g (3¼ oz/1 cup) bean sprouts, extra, trimmed
1 large handful mint
Vietnamese dipping sauce (page 148), to serve

1  Put the vermicelli and fungus in separate heatproof bowls. Cover with hot water and soak for 10 minutes, or until soft. Drain both, and chop the fungus roughly. Peel the prawns and gently pull out the dark vein from each prawn back, starting at the head end. Finely chop the prawn meat.

2  Use a pastry brush to brush both sides of each rice paper wrapper liberally with water. Allow to stand for 2 minutes, or until they become soft and pliable. Stack the wrappers on a plate. Sprinkle over a little extra water and cover the plate with plastic wrap to keep the wrappers moist until needed.

3  Combine vermicelli, fungus, prawn meat, pork, spring onion, bean sprouts, sugar and salt and pepper in a bowl.

4  Put 1 tablespoon of the filling along the base of a wrapper. Fold in the sides, roll the wrapper up tightly, and brush the seam with the egg. Repeat with the remaining wrappers and filling.

5  Press the rolls with paper towels to remove any excess water. Heat 4–5 cm (1½–2 inches) oil in a wok or deep frying pan to 180°C (350°F), or until a cube of bread dropped in the oil browns in 15 seconds. Add the spring rolls in batches and cook for 2–3 minutes, or until dark golden brown. Drain on paper towels.

6  To serve, put a spring roll in each lettuce leaf, top with 1 tablespoon bean sprouts and two mint leaves, and roll up to form a neat parcel. Serve with the Vietnamese dipping sauce.

# dipping sauces

A small bowl of one of these delicious sauces will enhance the flavour of dishes ranging from spring rolls, satays and fritters, to noodles and fish dishes.

### sweet chilli sauce

Remove the seeds from 6 large red chillies and soak for 15 minutes in hot water. Process with 1 tablespoon chopped red chilli, 60 ml (2 fl oz/¼ cup) white vinegar, 250 g (9 oz/1 cup) caster (superfine) sugar, 1 teaspoon salt and 4 chopped garlic cloves until smooth. Transfer to a saucepan and cook over medium heat for 15 minutes, stirring frequently until thickened. Cool. Stir in 2 teaspoons fish sauce.

### sesame seed sauce

Toast 100 g (3½ oz) Japanese white sesame seeds in a dry frying pan over medium heat for 3–4 minutes, shaking the pan gently, until theseeds are golden brown; remove from the pan at once to prevent burning. Grind the seeds using a mortar and pestle until a paste is formed. Add 2 teaspoons oil, if necessary, to assist in forming a paste. Mix the paste with 125 ml (4 fl oz/½ cup) Japanese soy sauce, 2 tablespoons mirin, 3 teaspoons caster (superfine) sugar, ½ teaspoon instant dashi granules and 125 ml (4 fl oz/½ cup) warm water. Store, covered, in the refrigerator and use within 2 days of preparation.

### soy and ginger sauce

In a bowl combine 1 tablespoon grated fresh ginger, 2 teaspoons sugar and 250 ml (9 fl oz/1 cup) soy sauce. Mix well and serve immediately.

### peanut satay sauce

Place 160 g (5¾ oz/1 cup) unsalted roasted peanuts in a food processor and process until finely chopped. Heat 2 tablespoons oil in a medium saucepan. Add 1 chopped onion and cook over medium heat for 5 minutes or until softened. Add 2 crushed garlic cloves, 2 teaspoons grated fresh ginger, ½ teaspoon chilli powder, 2 teaspoons curry powder and 1 teaspoon ground cumin, and cook, stirring, for 2 minutes. Add 420 ml (14½ fl oz/1⅔ cups) coconut milk, 3 tablespoons soft brown sugar and chopped peanuts. Reduce the heat and cook for 5 minutes or until the sauce thickens. Add 1 tablespoon lemon juice, season and serve. (For a smoother sauce, process in a food processor for 30 seconds.)

### lemon and garlic dipping sauce

In a small bowl, stir 60 ml (2 fl oz/¼ cup) lemon juice, 2 tablespoons fish sauce and 1 tablespoon caster (superfine) sugar until the sugar has dissolved. Stir in 2 chopped small red chillies and 3 finely chopped garlic cloves.

### vietnamese dipping sauce

In a bowl, mix together 2 tablespoons fish sauce, 2 tablespoons cold water, 2 tablespoons chopped coriander (cilantro) leaves, 1 teaspoon chopped red chilli and 1 teaspoon soft brown sugar.

### thai dipping sauce

In a small saucepan, combine 125 g (4½ oz/½ cup) sugar, 125 ml (4 fl oz/½ cup) water, 60 ml (2 fl oz/¼ cup) white vinegar, 1 tablespoon fish sauce and 1 small chopped red chilli. Bring to the boil and simmer, uncovered, for 5 minutes or until slightly thickened. Remove from the heat and cool slightly. Stir in ¼ small, peeled, seeded and finely chopped Lebanese (short) cucumber, ¼ small finely chopped carrot, and 1 tablespoon chopped roasted peanuts.

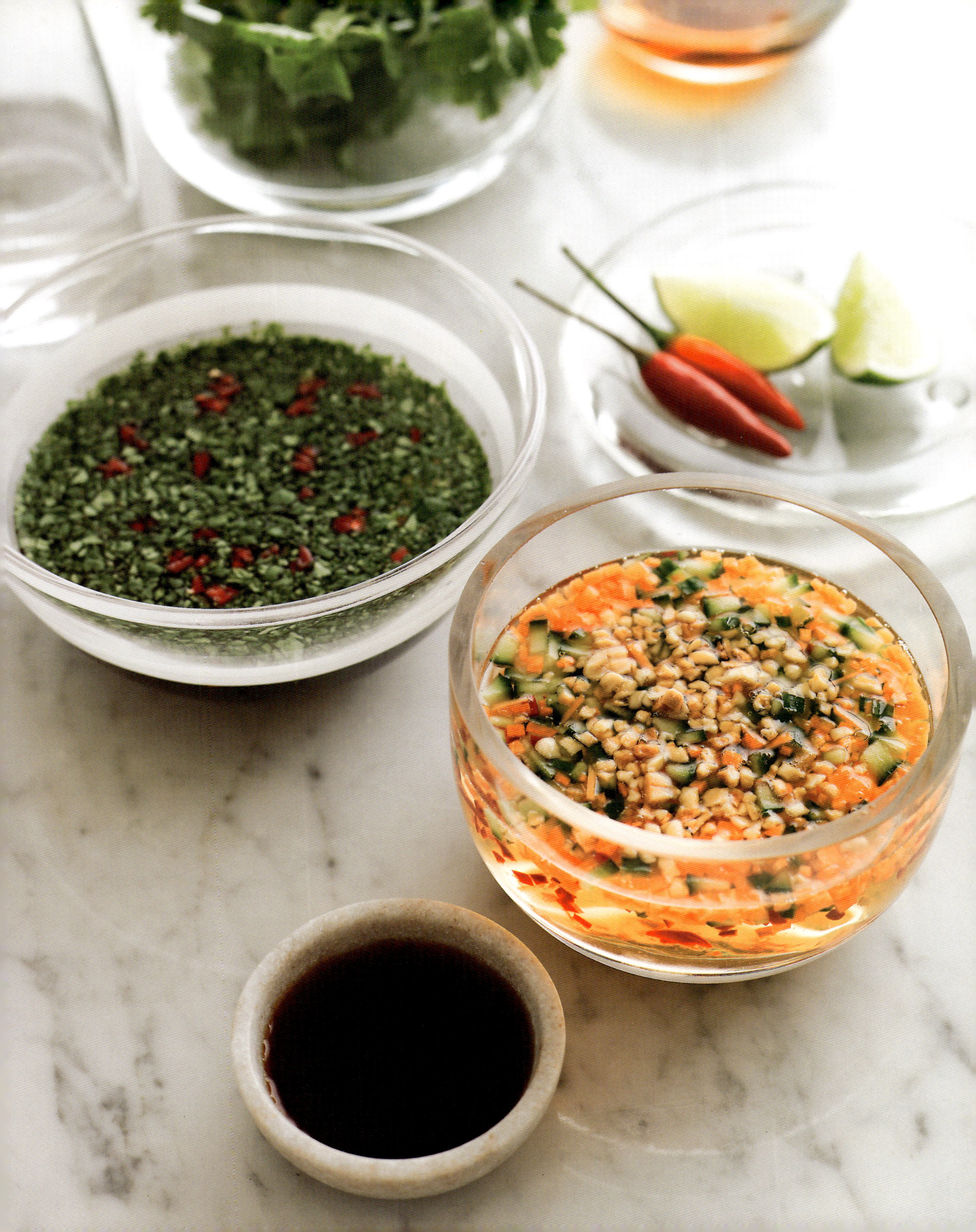

essential asian

fried rice noodle pancake with garlic beef

## mung bean vermicelli

Mung bean vermicelli, made by extruding a paste of mung bean flour and water, readily absorb the flavours of other foods and are popular throughout China, Southeast Asia and Japan. For vegetarians, the boiled noodles can be mixed with herbs, spices and flavourings to take the place of meat or prawns in stuffings or salads. In Indonesia, Malaysia and Singapore they are used as an ingredient in some sweet drinks and desserts.

## fried rice noodle pancake with garlic beef

✺ ✺

Preparation time: 20 minutes + 30 minutes marinating time
Cooking time: 25 minutes
Serves 4–6

350 g (12 oz) fillet steak, thinly sliced
1 red capsicum (pepper), cut into short, thin strips
6 garlic cloves, finely chopped
4 tablespoons oil
400 g (14 oz) thick fresh rice noodles
1 tablespoon sugar
2 tablespoons fish sauce
125 ml (4 fl oz/½ cup) beef stock
2 teaspoons cornflour (cornstarch)
4 spring onions (scallions), thinly sliced

1  Place the beef, capsicum, garlic, ¼ teaspoon pepper and half the oil in a large bowl; mix well to combine and marinate for 30 minutes.
2  Gently separate the noodles. Heat the remaining oil in a heavy-based frying pan over medium heat, swirling the oil to coat the pan well. Add the noodles and press them down firmly with a spatula to form a large flat pancake the size of the pan. Cook the noodles for 10–15 minutes, pressing down occasionally, until the base is very crisp and golden. Do not disturb or lift the noodles as they need to form a solid pancake. Run a spatula underneath to loosen the base then turn it over with 2 spatulas and cook the other side. Be patient because if the pancake is moved before it sets it will break up. Transfer to a plate, cover and keep warm.
3  Heat a heavy-based saucepan or wok. Sprinkle the sugar and fish sauce over the beef mixture. Add the beef mixture to the pan in two batches, and toss it over high heat for 2–3 minutes. Place the stock and cornflour in a bowl and stir until a smooth paste forms. Add the cornflour mixture to the meat and toss for 1 minute. Do not overcook the meat or it will become tough.
4  Place the pancake on a large serving plate, cut it into serving wedges and place the beef mixture on top, piling it up in the centre. Garnish with the spring onion and serve immediately.

## green pawpaw, chicken and fresh herb salad

✺

Preparation time: 40 minutes
Cooking time: 10 minutes
Serves 4

# vietnam

- 350 g (12 oz) boneless, skinless chicken breasts
- 1 large green pawpaw
- 20 g (¾ oz/1 cup) Vietnamese mint
- 15 g (½ oz/½ cup) coriander (cilantro) leaves
- 2 red chillies, seeded and thinly sliced
- 2 tablespoons fish sauce
- 1 tablespoon rice vinegar
- 1 tablespoon lime juice
- 2 teaspoons sugar
- 2 tablespoons finely chopped unsalted roasted peanuts

**1** Place the chicken in a frying pan with enough water to just cover it. Simmer gently for 8–10 minutes or until cooked. Remove from the liquid, cool completely, then slice thinly.
**2** Peel the pawpaw, then grate the flesh into long shreds. Mix gently with the mint, coriander, chilli, fish sauce, vinegar, lime juice and sugar.
**3** Arrange the pawpaw mixture on a serving plate and top with the chicken. Scatter with the peanuts and serve immediately.

**NOTE:** Green pawpaw is underripe pawpaw, used for tartness and texture.

## chicken with pineapple and cashews

Preparation time: 35 minutes
Cooking time: 30 minutes
Serves 4

- 2 tablespoons shredded coconut
- 80 g (2¾ oz/½ cup) raw cashews
- 2 tablespoons oil
- 1 large onion, cut into large chunks
- 4 garlic cloves, finely chopped
- 2 teaspoons chopped red chilli
- 350 g (12 oz) boneless, skinless chicken thighs, chopped
- ½ red capsicum (pepper), chopped
- ½ green capsicum (pepper), chopped
- 2 tablespoons oyster sauce
- 1 tablespoon fish sauce
- 1 teaspoon sugar
- 320 g (11¼ oz/2 cups) chopped fresh pineapple
- 3 spring onions (scallions), chopped

**1** Preheat the oven to 150°C (300°F/Gas 2). Spread the coconut on a baking tray and toast in the oven for 10 minutes or until dark golden, shaking the tray occasionally. Remove the coconut from the tray immediately, to prevent burning, and set aside.
**2** Increase the heat to 180°C (350°F/Gas 4). Roast the cashews on a baking tray in the oven for about 15 minutes, until deep golden. Remove the cashews from the tray and set aside to cool.
**3** Heat the oil in a wok or large, deep frying pan; add the onion, garlic and chilli and stir-fry over medium heat for 2 minutes, then remove from the wok. Increase the heat to high; add the chicken and red and green capsicum, in two batches, and stir-fry until the chicken is light brown. Return the onion mixture to the wok; add the oyster sauce, fish sauce, sugar and pineapple and toss for 2 minutes. Toss the cashews through.
**4** Arrange the chicken mixture on a serving plate, scatter the toasted coconut and the spring onion over the top, and serve immediately.

chicken with pineapple and cashews

## chilli prawn and snake bean stir-fry

Preparation time: 35 minutes
Cooking time: 10 minutes
Serves 4

300 g (10½ oz) raw prawns (shrimp)
250 g (9 oz) snake (yard-long) beans
2 tablespoons oil
2 onions, very thinly sliced
5 garlic cloves, finely chopped
2 lemongrass stems, white part only, very thinly sliced
3 red chillies, seeded and very thinly sliced
2 teaspoons sugar
1 tablespoon fish sauce
1 tablespoon rice vinegar
garlic chives, snipped, to garnish

1  Peel the prawns and gently pull out the dark vein from each prawn back, starting at the head end. Top and tail the beans and cut them into 2 cm (¾ inch) pieces.
2  Heat the oil in a large heavy-based wok, add the onion, garlic, lemongrass and chilli and stir-fry over moderately high heat for 4 minutes, or until the onion is soft and golden.
3  Add the beans to the wok and stir-fry for 2–3 minutes or until they become bright green. Add the prawns and sugar and toss gently for 2 minutes. Add the fish sauce and vinegar, toss well and serve immediately, sprinkled with the garlic chives.

NOTE: The equivalent weight of green beans may be used if snake beans are unavailable.

## sweet braised pumpkin

Preparation time: 20 minutes
Cooking time: 15 minutes
Serves 4

750 g (1 lb 10 oz) pumpkin (winter squash)
1½ tablespoons oil
3 garlic cloves, finely chopped
4 cm (1½ inch) piece fresh ginger, finely grated
6 red Asian shallots, chopped
1 tablespoon soft brown sugar
125 ml (4 fl oz/½ cup) chicken stock
2 tablespoons fish sauce
1 tablespoon lime juice

1  Peel the pumpkin and cut it into large chunks.
2  Heat the oil in a heavy-based frying pan; add the garlic, ginger and shallots and cook over medium heat for 3 minutes, stirring regularly.
3  Add the pumpkin and sprinkle with the sugar. Cook for 7–8 minutes, turning the pieces regularly, until the pumpkin is golden and just tender.
4  Add the stock and fish sauce, bring to the boil, then reduce the heat and simmer until all the liquid has evaporated, turning the pumpkin over regularly. Sprinkle with the lime juice, season to taste with salt and pepper, and serve. Delicious as an accompaniment to meat dishes such as curries, or on its own with plenty of steamed rice.

NOTE: The sweeter pumpkins, such as butternut (squash) and jap, will produce a dish with a delicious flavour and a soft texture.

sweet braised pumpkin

# vietnam

## vietnamese pancakes in lettuce leaves

✳ ✳ ✳

Preparation time: 20 minutes + 45 minutes standing time
Cooking time: 30 minutes
Makes 10

175 g (6 oz/1 cup) rice flour
2 teaspoons cornflour (cornstarch)
½ teaspoon curry powder (see Note)
½ teaspoon ground turmeric
250 ml (9 fl oz/1 cup) coconut milk
60 ml (2 fl oz/¼ cup) coconut cream
300 g (10½ oz) raw prawns (shrimp)
2 teaspoons oil
150 g (5½ oz) pork ribs, boned and thinly sliced
4 spring onions (scallions), chopped
150 g (5½ oz) bean sprouts, trimmed
10 large lettuce leaves
20 g (¾ oz/1 cup) mint

DIPPING SAUCE
2 tablespoons fish sauce
2 tablespoons lime juice
1–2 teaspoons chopped fresh red chilli
½ teaspoon sugar

**1** Place the rice flour, cornflour, curry powder, turmeric, coconut milk, 125 ml (4 fl oz/½ cup) water and coconut cream in a food processor, and process for 30 seconds or until smooth. Cover and set aside for 45 minutes so the batter thickens. Peel the prawns and gently pull out the dark vein from each prawn back, starting at the head end. Finely chop the prawn meat.
**2** Heat 1 teaspoon of the oil in a heavy-based frying pan; cook the pork in batches over moderately high heat for 1–2 minutes or until browned.
**3** Stir the batter well. Heat the remaining oil and add 2 tablespoons of the batter to the pan, swirling it to form a small round pancake. Cook the pancake for 30 seconds or until it begins to crisp on the underside. Place 2 pieces of pork, 1 tablespoon of the prawn meat, 1 tablespoon of the spring onion and 1 tablespoon of the bean sprouts in the centre of the pancake. Cover the pan and cook for 1–2 minutes, or until the prawns are pink and the vegetables soften. (The base of the pancake will be very crisp, the top side will be set but soft.) Place the pancake on a platter and repeat with the remaining ingredients.
**4** Place each cooked pancake inside a lettuce leaf and top with 2 mint leaves. Fold the lettuce to form a parcel. Serve with the dipping sauce.
**5** To make the dipping sauce, combine all the ingredients in a bowl and whisk until well blended.

NOTE: Use a mild Asian curry powder labelled 'for meat', available from Asian food stores. A standard supermarket curry powder is not suitable for this recipe.

### chopping pork mince

For some dishes, such as meatballs, you need a really finely chopped minced (ground) meat, which will hold together well and keep its shape during cooking. If you have bought minced (ground) meat from your butcher, chopping it at home will give it this finer texture.

spicy grilled fish pieces

paste forms, adding the oil to help with the grinding.
**2** Cut the fish into large bite-sized pieces. Place the fish in a bowl with the spice paste, toss well and cover and refrigerate for 15 minutes.
**3** Place the fish on a foil-lined grill tray and cook under a hot grill (broiler) for 3–4 minutes, turning the pieces over so the fish browns on all sides.
**4** Arrange the fish on a serving plate. Sprinkle over the fish sauce and garnish with the watercress or coriander leaves. Serve immediately with steamed rice, if desired.

# vermicelli with stir-fried squid and tomatoes

Preparation time: 35 minutes
Cooking time: 20 minutes
Serves 4

100 g (3½ oz) dried mung bean vermicelli
350 g (12 oz) squid tubes, cut into rings
2 tablespoons fish sauce
2 tablespoons oil
3 garlic cloves, finely chopped
3 lemongrass stems, white part only, thinly sliced
2 teaspoons sugar
1 red onion, thinly sliced
2 ripe tomatoes, diced
2 tablespoons lime juice
2 tablespoons snipped garlic chives

**1** Soak the vermicelli in hot water for 5 to 10 minutes or until softened; drain.
**2** Place the squid in a bowl with 1 tablespoon of the fish sauce, 1 tablespoon of the oil, half the garlic, half the lemongrass, and the sugar, ¼ teaspoon salt and ¼ teaspoon pepper. Mix well to combine and marinate for 15 minutes.
**3** Heat a wok until it is extremely hot; add the squid in two batches, stir-fry until

# spicy grilled fish pieces

Preparation time: 30 minutes
Cooking time: 10 minutes
Serves 4

3 garlic cloves
4 red Asian shallots
3 lemongrass stems, white part only, thinly sliced
1 teaspoon ground turmeric
1 teaspoon galangal powder
2 red chillies
2 tablespoons oil
500 g (1 lb 2 oz) boneless white fish fillets
1 tablespoon fish sauce
watercress or coriander (cilantro) leaves, to garnish

**1** Place the garlic, shallots, lemon grass, turmeric, galangal powder, chillies, ¼ teaspoon salt and ¼ teaspoon pepper in a food processor and process until a

# vietnam

it just changes colour, and remove it from the wok. Reheat the wok until hot; add the remaining oil, garlic, lemongrass and onion, and stir-fry for 1 minute. Add the tomato and toss well. Add the vermicelli and return the squid (with any juices) to the wok, and toss well. Add the lime juice, chives and remaining fish sauce, and serve immediately.

## vietnamese pork and prawn salad

Preparation time: 30 minutes + 1 hour marinating time
Cooking time: 10 minutes
Serves 6–8

250 g (9 oz) pork fillet
300 g (10½ oz) raw prawns (shrimp)
60 ml (2 fl oz/¼ cup) white vinegar
1 tablespoon sugar
1 carrot, cut into matchsticks
1 Lebanese (short) cucumber, cut into matchsticks
1 red capsicum (pepper), cut into matchsticks
1 Chinese cabbage (wong bok), finely shredded
1 tablespoon oil
100 g (3½ oz) unsalted roasted peanuts, roughly chopped

DRESSING
2 red Asian shallots, finely chopped
1 garlic clove, crushed
1 tablespoon fish sauce
1 tablespoon lime juice
1 teaspoon brown sugar
1 teaspoon sesame oil
1 tablespoon chopped Vietnamese mint

**1** Cut the pork into thin strips. Peel the prawns, leaving the tails intact. Gently pull out the dark vein from each prawn back, starting at the head end.
**2** Place the vinegar, 125 ml (4 fl oz/½ cup) water and sugar into a bowl and mix to combine. Add the carrot, cucumber, capsicum and Chinese cabbage and toss to coat in the marinade. Cover and refrigerate for 1 hour.
**3** Heat the oil in a wok; stir-fry the pork in two batches over high heat for 3 minutes or until browned. Remove the pork from the wok. Add the prawns and stir-fry over high heat for 3 minutes or until bright pink.
**4** Remove the vegetables from the marinade and drain thoroughly. Combine the vegetables with the pork, prawns and peanuts and toss well. Pour the dressing over the salad and toss to coat.
**5** To make the dressing, combine the shallots, garlic, fish sauce, lime juice, brown sugar and sesame oil. Add the Vietnamese mint and mix together well.

## pork ball soup with noodles

✻

Preparation time: 25 minutes
Cooking time: 35 minutes
Serves 4

250 g (9 oz) pork bones
5 cm (2 inch) piece fresh ginger, thinly sliced
6 spring onions (scallions), chopped
300 g (10½ oz) shanghai noodles
250 g (9 oz) minced (ground) pork
2 tablespoons fish sauce
150 g (5½ oz) fresh pineapple, cut into small chunks
100 g (3½ oz) bean sprouts, trimmed
2 tablespoons shredded mint

1  Place the pork bones, ginger, 1 teaspoon salt, 1 teaspoon pepper and 1 litre (35 fl oz/4 cups) water in a saucepan, and bring it to the boil. Skim off any scum, add the spring onion and simmer for 20 minutes. Remove and discard the bones then set the stock aside.
2  Cook the noodles in a saucepan of boiling water for 5 minutes. Drain and rinse in cold water.
3  Chop the pork very finely with a cleaver or large knife for 3 minutes or until the meat feels very soft and spongy. Wet your hands and roll 2 teaspoons of pork at a time into small balls.
4  Return the stock to the heat and bring it to the boil. Add the pork balls and cook for 4 minutes. Add the fish sauce and pineapple.
5  Place the noodles in individual soup bowls and ladle the hot stock over them, making sure each bowl has pork balls and pineapple. Scatter the bean sprouts and mint over the soup, and serve immediately.

pork ball soup with noodles

## peppery pork with vegetables

✻✻

Preparation time: 1 hour
Cooking time: 20 minutes
Serves 4

2 teaspoons black peppercorns
350 g (12 oz) pork loin
1 tablespoon fish sauce
4 garlic cloves, very thinly sliced
4 spring onions (scallions), finely chopped
3 tablespoons oil
8 red Asian shallots, thinly sliced
200 g (7 oz) baby corn, cut in half lengthways
100 g (3½ oz) green beans, trimmed, cut into short lengths
1 teaspoon sugar
150 g (5½ oz) broccoli, cut into small florets
200 g (7 oz) bean sprouts, trimmed
steamed rice, to serve

1  Dry-fry the peppercorns in a hot frying pan for 2 minutes, shaking the pan constantly. Place the peppercorns in a mortar and using a pestle pound until roughly ground.
2  Cut the pork into thin pieces. Place the pork, pepper, fish sauce, garlic,

¼ teaspoon salt, spring onion and half the oil in a bowl. Mix well to combine and refrigerate, covered, for 20 minutes.
**3** Heat a wok to extremely hot and stir-fry the pork in three batches for about 1½ minutes, or until just golden brown, reheating the wok between batches.
**4** Heat the remaining oil in the wok; add the shallots, corn and beans and stir-fry over medium heat for 1 minute. Sprinkle over 1 tablespoon water and the sugar; cover and steam for 1 minute. Add the broccoli and steam for 1 minute more. Return the pork and any juices to the wok, add the bean sprouts and stir-fry for 30 seconds. Serve with the steamed rice.

## beef fondue with rice paper wrappers and salad

✲✲

Preparation time: 20 minutes
Cooking time: 30 minutes
Serves 4

1 red onion, thinly sliced
185 ml (6 fl oz/¾ cup) rice vinegar
3 red chillies, finely chopped
2 tablespoons fish sauce
2 tablespoons lime juice
6 garlic cloves, finely chopped
2 tablespoons sugar
500 g (1 lb 2 oz) beef fillet
410 g (14½ oz) tinned chopped tomatoes
12 rice paper wrappers (plus a few extras to allow for breakages)
75 g (2¾ oz) iceberg lettuce leaves, shredded
10 g (¼ oz/½ cup) mint leaves
1 small Lebanese (short) cucumber, sliced

**1** Place the onion and 3 tablespoons of the vinegar in a small bowl; mix to combine and set aside. To make a dipping sauce, place the chilli, fish sauce, lime juice, half the garlic and half the sugar in a small bowl; mix to combine and set aside for the flavours to mingle. Cut the beef into thin slices, season with ½ teaspoon pepper and set aside.
**2** Place 1 litre (35 fl oz/4 cups) water in a large saucepan and bring it to the boil. Add the tomatoes and the remaining garlic, sugar and vinegar, and simmer for 20 minutes.
**3** Use a pastry brush to brush both sides of each rice paper wrapper liberally with water. Allow to stand for 2 minutes or until they become soft and pliable. Stack the wrappers on a plate. Sprinkle over a little extra water and cover with plastic wrap to keep the wrappers moist until needed.
**4** Place the tomato mixture in a food processor and process until smooth.

Return the tomato stock to the pan and reheat to simmering point. Add the beef in batches to the simmering stock, and cook it quickly, just until it changes colour, then place it in a serving bowl.
**5** To serve, place the rice paper wrappers, shredded lettuce, mint leaves and sliced cucumber on a serving platter in separate piles. Each diner takes a wrapper, places a few slices of beef on it along with a little of the lettuce, mint, cucumber and the marinated onion, then rolls it up and dips it in the dipping sauce to eat.

# korea

Caught between Japan and China, Korean food is a wonderful combination of the two, mixed with its own distinctive elements. The food has a warming robustness that defies the winter ice and snow, most notably in its national dish, kimchi, a spicy pickle served at every meal. Korean meals are made up of many small, tempting dishes, flavoured with soy sauce, ginger, bean paste and toasted sesame seeds, while the centrepiece may be a steaming hotpot or thinly sliced meat, grilled at the table.

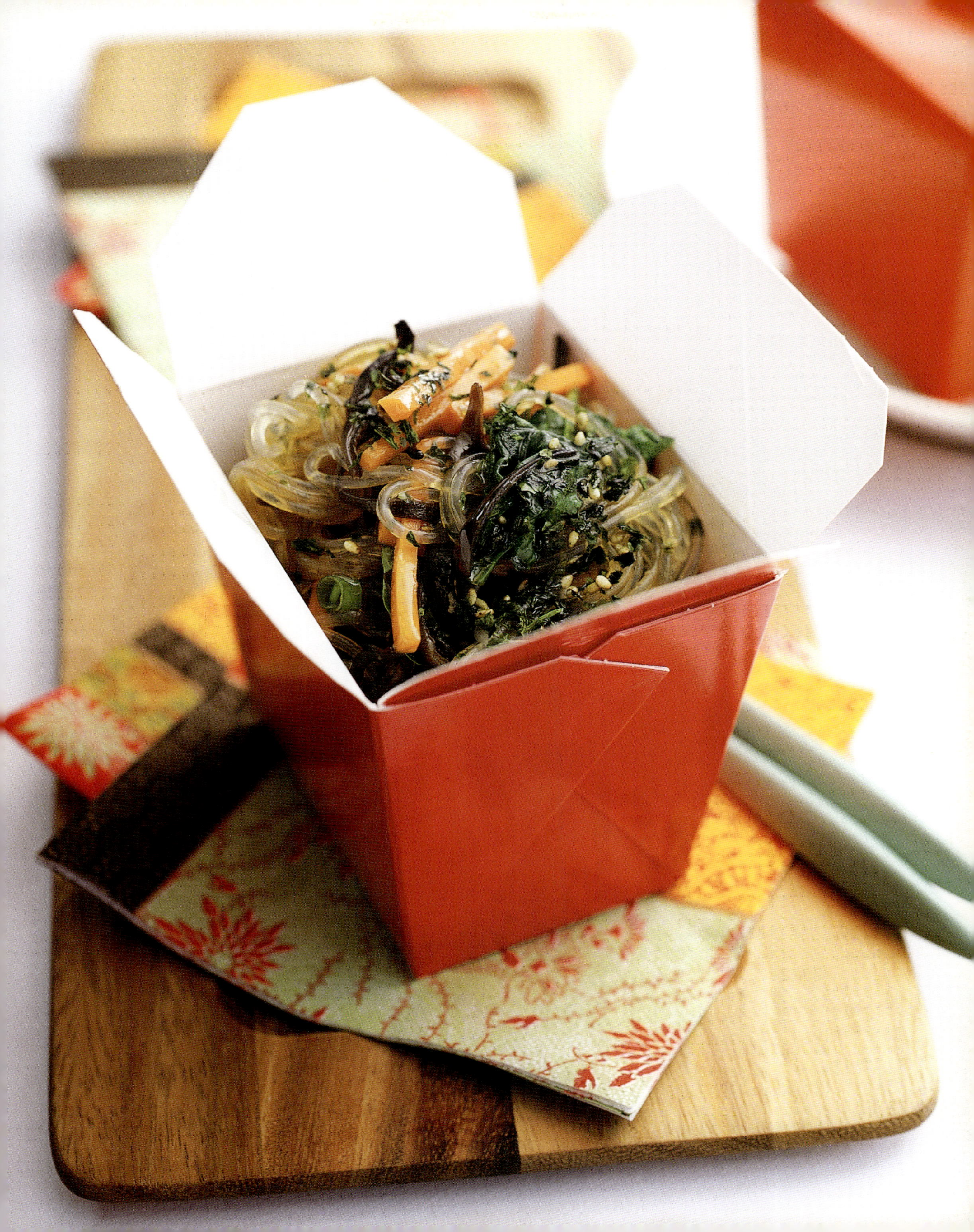

## egg strip bundles

✽ ✽

Preparation time: 25 minutes
Cooking time: 15 minutes
Serves 4

1 tablespoon white sesame seeds
10 spring onions (scallions)
5 eggs
¼ teaspoon white pepper
3 teaspoons oil
2 tablespoons rice vinegar
2 tablespoons Japanese soy sauce (shoshoyu)

**1** Toast the sesame seeds in a dry frying pan over medium heat for 3–4 minutes, shaking the pan gently, until the seeds are golden brown; remove from the pan at once to prevent burning.
**2** Trim the white ends from the spring onions and discard; take off the outside layer and discard. Make a bunch of the green stems, then trim them all to the same size, cutting off the skinny tip. Plunge 2 spring onions at a time into a large saucepan of boiling water and cook for about 30 seconds or until softened; remove with tongs and place in iced water. Repeat for all the spring onions. Drain well and dry lightly on paper towels. Cut each spring onion in half lengthways using a small sharp knife.
**3** Beat the eggs with ¼ teaspoon salt and pepper, to taste, until they are foamy.
**4** Brush a medium-sized frying pan with the oil, and place it over medium heat. Pour in half the eggs, cover and cook for 2 minutes. Run a spatula around the edge of the omelette to loosen it, then turn the omelette over and cook it for a further 2 minutes. Remove the omelette from the pan, and cook the remaining egg mixture. Trim the curved edges from the omelettes to make a square shape. Cut thin strips of omelette about 7 cm (2¾ inches) long and 5 mm (¼ inch) wide.
**5** Gather together eight strips of egg, carefully wrap one piece of spring onion four or so times around the middle of the bundle, tucking in the ends. Repeat with the remaining egg strips and arrange the bundles on a serving platter. Combine the vinegar, soy sauce and sesame seeds, drizzle over the bundles and serve.

## barbecued beef

✽

Preparation time: 15 minutes + 30 minutes freezing + 2 hours marinating time
Cooking time: 15 minutes
Serves 4–6

500 g (1 lb 2 oz) scotch fillet or sirloin steak
40 g (1½ oz/¼ cup) sesame seeds
125 ml (4 fl oz/½ cup) soy sauce
2 garlic cloves, finely chopped
3 spring onions (scallions), finely chopped
1 tablespoon sesame oil
1 tablespoon vegetable oil
kimchi, to serve (see Note)

**1** Freeze the beef for 30 minutes. Remove from the freezer and slice into long, thin strips, cutting across the natural grain of the beef.
**2** Toast the sesame seeds in a dry frying pan over medium heat for 3–4 minutes, shaking the pan gently, until the seeds are golden brown. Remove from the pan at

barbecued beef

once to prevent burning. Crush the seeds in a food mill or use a mortar and pestle.

**3** Combine the beef, soy sauce, garlic, spring onion and half the sesame seeds in a bowl, mixing well. Cover and refrigerate for 2 hours.

**4** Combine the sesame and vegetable oils and brush a little oil onto a chargrill pan, heavy-based frying pan or barbecue hotplate. Heat to very hot and cook the beef in three batches, searing each side for about 1 minute (don't overcook the beef or it will become chewy). Brush the pan with more oil and allow it to reheat to very hot between batches. Sprinkle the remaining crushed sesame seeds over the beef before serving. Serve with ready-made or homemade kimchi, if desired.

NOTE: Pickled vegetables are a popular accompaniment to meals in Korea. Most common is kimchi, made with pickled cabbage leaves and spiced with chilli. Ready-made kimchi is found in the refrigerator in Korean grocery stores and large Asian grocery stores.

# kimchi

Preparation time: **9 days**
Cooking time: **nil**
Makes **about 3 cups**

1 large Chinese cabbage (wong bok)
160 g (5¾ oz/½ cup) sea salt
½ teaspoon cayenne pepper
5 spring onions (scallions), finely chopped
2 garlic cloves, finely chopped
5 cm (2 inch) piece fresh ginger, finely grated
3 teaspoons–3 tablespoons chopped fresh chilli (see Note)
1 tablespoon caster (superfine) sugar

**1** Cut the cabbage in half, then into large bite-sized pieces. Place a layer of cabbage in a large bowl and sprinkle with a little salt. Continue with layers of cabbage and salt, finishing with a salt layer. Cover with a dinner plate that will fit as snugly as possible over the top of the cabbage. Weigh down the plate with tins or a small brick and leave the bowl in a cool place for 5 days.

**2** Remove the weights and plate, pour off any liquid, then rinse the cabbage well under cold running water. Squeeze out any excess water and combine the cabbage with the cayenne pepper, spring onion, garlic, ginger, chilli and sugar. Mix well to combine before spooning the cabbage into a large sterilised jar. Pour 625 ml (21½ fl oz/2½ cups) cold water over the top and seal with a tight-fitting lid. Refrigerate for 3–4 days before eating.

NOTE: Kimchi is an accompaniment eaten with Korean main meals and with steamed rice. For an authentic flavour, use 3 tablespoons chilli. Bottled chopped chilli can be used instead of fresh chilli.

# pickles & chutneys

Just a spoonful of these spicy relishes will lift an Indian dish, while the pickled vegetables and ginger are traditional in Japanese and Korean meals.

### lime oil pickle

Cut 12 limes into eight thin wedges each, sprinkle with salt and set aside. In a medium frying pan, dry roast 3 teaspoons mustard seeds and 2 teaspoons each ground turmeric, cumin seeds, fennel seeds and fenugreek seeds for 1–2 minutes. Remove and grind to a fine powder using a mortar and pestle. Over low heat, fry 5 chopped green chillies, 4 sliced garlic cloves and 2 teaspoons grated fresh ginger in 1 tablespoon oil until golden brown. Add 500 ml (17 fl oz/2 cups) oil, 1 tablespoon sugar, the lime wedges and spices; simmer over low heat for 10 minutes, stirring occasionally. Spoon into warm sterilised jars, seal and cool. Store in the refrigerator for up to 3 months.

### sweet mango chutney

Peel 3 large green mangoes, remove stones, slice, and sprinkle with salt. Seed 2 red chillies; chop finely. Blend ½ teaspoon garam masala with 330 g (11½ oz/1½ cups) raw (demerara) sugar and place in a large saucepan with 250 ml (9 fl oz/1 cup) white vinegar; bring to the boil. Reduce the heat and simmer for 5 minutes. Add the mango, chilli, 1 tablespoon finely grated fresh ginger and 95 g (3¼ oz/½ cup) finely chopped dates. Simmer for 1 hour or until the mango is tender. Pour into warm sterilised jars, seal and cool. Store in the refrigerator for up to 3 months.

### pickled vegetables

Put 80 ml (2½ fl oz/⅓ cup) rice (or white) vinegar, 2 teaspoons salt and 1 teaspoon sugar into a large non-metallic bowl. Pour over 500 ml (17 fl oz/2 cups) boiling water, mix well and allow to cool until lukewarm. Cut 250 g (9 oz) cabbage into 4 cm (1½ inch) strips, 1 small Lebanese (short) cucumber and 2 carrots into matchsticks and 1 white onion into thick rings, and add to the warm pickling mixture. Put a flat plate on top of the vegetables. Place a small bowl filled with water on top of the plate to weigh it down and submerge the vegetables. Leave for 3 days in the refrigerator. Place into sterilised jars, seal and store in the refrigerator for up to 1 month.

### eggplant pickle

Cut 1 kg (2 lb 4 oz) slender eggplants (aubergines) lengthways and sprinkle lightly with salt. In a food processor, place 6 garlic cloves, 2.5 cm (1 inch) piece roughly chopped fresh ginger, 4 teaspoons garam masala, 1 teaspoon ground turmeric, 1 teaspoon chilli powder and 1 tablespoon oil; process until a paste forms. Rinse the salt off the eggplant and pat dry. Heat 80 ml (2½ fl oz/⅓ cup) oil in a large frying pan and fry the eggplant for 5 minutes or until golden brown. Add the paste and fry for 2 minutes. Stir in 420 ml (14½ fl oz/1⅔ cups) oil and cook, uncovered, for 10–15 minutes, stirring occasionally. Spoon into warm sterilised jars, seal and cool. Store in a cool, dark place for up to 2 months. Refrigerate after opening.

### pickled ginger

Cut 125 g (4½ oz) fresh ginger into 2.5 cm (1 inch) pieces. Sprinkle with 2 teaspoons salt, cover and refrigerate for 1 week. With a very sharp knife, cut into paper-thin slices across the grain. Over low heat dissolve 2 tablespoons sugar in 125 ml (4 fl oz/½ cup) rice vinegar and 2 tablespoons water. Bring to the boil and simmer for 1 minute. Place the ginger in sterilised jars, cover with the marinade, seal and refrigerate for 1 week before using. The ginger will turn pale pink or it can be coloured using 1 teaspoon grenadine. Store in the refrigerator for up to 3 months.

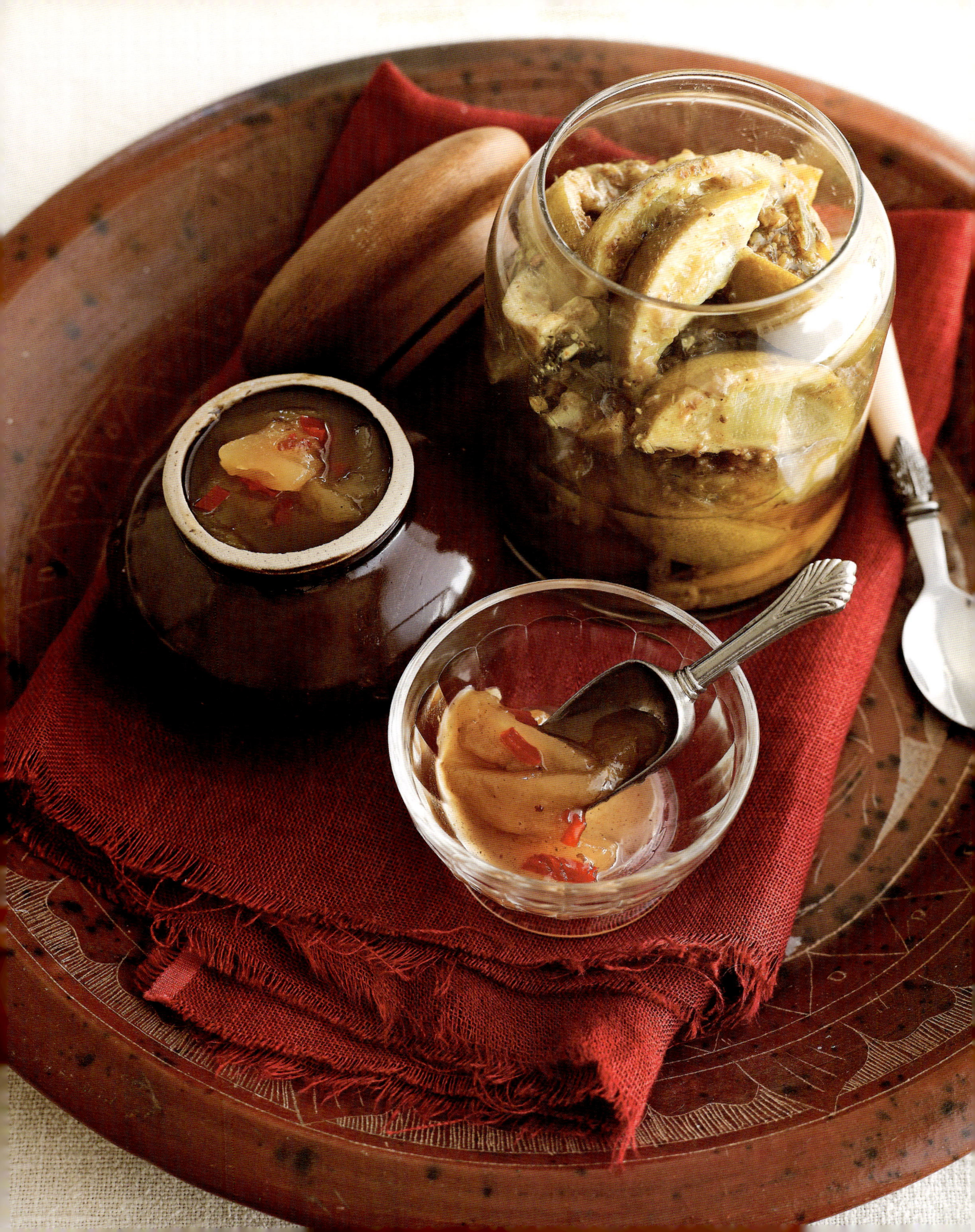

shredded potato pancakes

with the garlic, spring onion, soy sauce, white wine, sesame oil, sugar and chilli. Mix well and then place in a serving bowl.

**2** Peel the potatoes and grate them on the coarse side of a grater. Place the potato in a large bowl with the onion, egg and cornflour, and season with salt and pepper to taste. Stir very well, making certain that the cornflour is mixed in thoroughly.

**3** Heat the oil in a large heavy-based frying pan (an electric frying pan is good for this). Drop about 1 rounded tablespoon of mixture onto the hot surface and spread it out gently with the back of a spoon so the pancake is about 6 cm (2½ inches) in size. Cook for 2–3 minutes or until golden brown. Turn it over with a spatula and cook another 2 minutes on the other side. Cook four to five pancakes, or as many as you can fit in the pan at one time. Do not have the pan too hot or the pancakes will burn and not cook through. Keep the cooked pancakes warm in a 120°C (235°F/Gas 1–2) oven while cooking the remaining pancakes.

**4** Serve with the dipping sauce as a snack or with rice and kimchi (page 161) as part of a meal.

NOTE: Have all the ingredients ready before the potatoes are grated as they discolour quickly.

## shredded potato pancakes

❋ ❋

Preparation time: 25 minutes
Cooking time: 30 minutes
Makes about 18

500 g (1 lb 2 oz) potatoes
1 large onion, very finely chopped
2 eggs, beaten
2 tablespoons cornflour (cornstarch)
60 ml (2 fl oz/¼ cup) oil

DIPPING SAUCE
2 teaspoons white sesame seeds
2 garlic cloves, finely chopped
2 spring onions (scallions), very thinly sliced
60 ml (2 fl oz/¼ cup) soy sauce
1 tablespoon white wine
1 tablespoon sesame oil
2 teaspoons caster (superfine) sugar
1 teaspoon chopped red chilli

**1** To make the dipping sauce, toast the sesame seeds in a dry frying pan over medium heat for 3–4 minutes, shaking the pan gently, until they are golden brown; remove from the pan at once to prevent burning and cool for 5 minutes. Combine

## pork with spinach

❋ ❋

Preparation time: 20 minutes
Cooking time: 15 minutes
Serves 4

1 tablespoon white sesame seeds
400 g (14 oz) English spinach
2 garlic cloves, very thinly sliced
3 spring onions (scallions), chopped
½ teaspoon cayenne pepper
300 g (10½ oz) pork loin, cut into thick strips
2 tablespoons oil
2 teaspoons sesame oil
2 tablespoons Japanese soy sauce (shoshoyu)
2 teaspoons sugar

# korea

1 Toast the sesame seeds in a dry frying pan over medium heat for 3–4 minutes, shaking the pan gently, until the seeds are golden brown; remove from the pan at once to prevent burning.
2 Trim the ends from the spinach, roughly chop the leaves and wash to remove grit.
3 Combine the garlic, spring onion, cayenne pepper and pork, mixing well. Heat the oils in a heavy-based frying pan and stir-fry the pork quickly in three batches over very high heat until golden. Remove the pork and set aside.
4 Add the soy sauce, sugar and spinach, and toss lightly. Cover and cook for 2 minutes or until the spinach is just soft. Return the pork to the pan, add sesame seeds, toss well and serve immediately.

## meat dumpling soup

✻ ✻

Preparation time: 45 minutes
Cooking time: 35 minutes
Serves 4–6

1 tablespoon white sesame seeds
2 tablespoons oil
2 garlic cloves, finely chopped
150 g (5½ oz) lean minced (ground) pork
200 g (7 oz) lean minced (ground) beef
200 g (7 oz) Chinese cabbage (wong bok), finely shredded
100 g (3½ oz) bean sprouts, trimmed and chopped
100 g (3½ oz) mushrooms, finely chopped
3 spring onions (scallions), finely chopped
150 g (5½ oz) gow gee dumpling wrappers

SOUP
2.5 litres (87 fl oz/10 cups) beef stock
2 tablespoons soy sauce
3 cm (1¼ inch) piece fresh ginger, very thinly shredded
4 spring onions (scallions), chopped

1 To make the filling, toast the sesame seeds in a dry frying pan over medium heat for 3–4 minutes, shaking the pan gently, until the seeds are golden brown. Remove from the pan at once to prevent burning. Crush the seeds in a food mill or use a mortar and pestle.
2 Heat the oil in a saucepan. Cook the garlic and the pork and beef over medium heat until the meat changes colour, breaking up any lumps with a fork. Add the cabbage, bean sprouts, mushrooms and 80 ml (2½ fl oz/⅓ cup) water. Cook, stirring occasionally, for 5–6 minutes, or until the water evaporates and the vegetables soften. Add the spring onion, crushed sesame seeds and season, to taste. Set aside.
3 Work with one gow gee wrapper at a time and keep the extra wrappers covered with a damp tea towel (dish towel). Place 1 teaspoon of filling on a wrapper, just off-centre, and gently smooth out the filling a little. Brush the edges of the wrapper with a little water and fold it over the filling to form a semi-circle. Press the edges together to seal. Repeat with the extra wrappers and filling.
4 To make the soup, combine the stock, soy sauce, ginger and half the spring onion in a large saucepan. Bring to the boil and simmer for 15 minutes.
5 Drop the dumplings into the soup and cook gently for 5 minutes, or until they change colour and look plump. Garnish with the remaining spring onion and serve immediately.

## potato noodles with vegetables

Preparation time: 25 minutes
Cooking time: 15 minutes
Serves 4

4 spring onions (scallions)
2 carrots
500 g (1 lb 2 oz) baby bok choy (pak choy) or 250 g (9 oz) spinach
300 g (10½ oz) dried potato starch noodles (see Note)
10 g (¼ oz/⅓ cup) black fungus (see Note)
60 ml (2 fl oz/¼ cup) sesame oil
2 tablespoons vegetable oil
3 garlic cloves, finely chopped
4 cm (1½ inch) piece fresh ginger, finely grated
60 ml (2 fl oz/¼ cup) Japanese soy sauce (shoshoyu) (see Note)
2 tablespoons mirin
1 teaspoon sugar
2 tablespoons sesame and seaweed sprinkle (see Note)

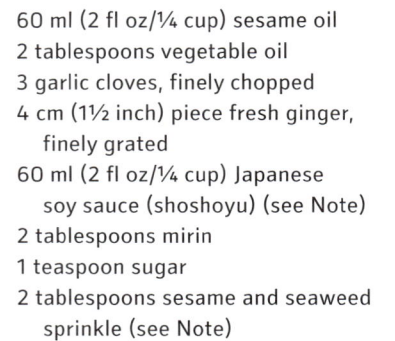

**1** Finely chop two of the spring onions. Slice the remaining spring onions into 4 cm (1½ inch) pieces. Cut the carrots into 4 cm (1½ inch) batons. Roughly chop the baby bok choy.
**2** Cook the noodles in a large saucepan of boiling water for about 5 minutes, or until they are translucent. Drain and rinse thoroughly under cold running water until the noodles are cold (this will also remove any excess starch). Use scissors to roughly chop the noodles into shorter lengths (this will make them easier to eat with chopsticks).
**3** Pour hot water over the black fungus and soak for about 10 minutes.
**4** Heat 1 tablespoon of the sesame oil with the vegetable oil in a large heavy-based frying pan or wok. Cook the garlic, ginger and finely chopped spring onion for 3 minutes over medium heat, stirring regularly. Add the carrot and stir-fry for 1 minute. Add the drained cooled noodles, sliced spring onion, baby bok choy, remaining sesame oil, soy sauce, mirin and sugar. Toss well to coat the noodles with the sauce. Cover and cook over low heat for 2 minutes. Add the drained fungus, then cover and cook for 2 minutes. Scatter over the sesame and seaweed sprinkle and serve immediately.

NOTE: Potato starch noodles are also known as Korean pasta and are available from Asian food stores. Dried black fungus, Japanese soy sauce and sesame and seaweed sprinkle are all available from Asian food stores.

# korea

### sesame and seaweed sprinkle

Also known as gomashio, this combination of finely chopped nori, black sesame seeds and salt is used in Japanese and Korean cooking sprinkled on noodles, salads and egg dishes. It is available in shaker containers from Japanese food stores.

## spare ribs with sesame seeds

Preparation time: 30 minutes
Cooking time: 1 hour
Serves 4–6

1 tablespoon white sesame seeds
1 kg (2 lb 4 oz) pork spare ribs, cut into 3 cm (1¼ inch) pieces
2 tablespoons oil
2 spring onions (scallions), finely chopped
4 cm (1½ inch) piece fresh ginger, grated
3 garlic cloves, finely chopped
2 tablespoons caster (superfine) sugar
2 tablespoons sake
1 tablespoon soy sauce
2 teaspoons sesame oil
2 teaspoons cornflour (cornstarch)
steamed rice, to serve
kimchi (optional), to serve

**1** Toast the sesame seeds in a dry frying pan over medium heat for 3–4 minutes, shaking the pan gently, until the seeds are golden brown. Remove the seeds from the pan immediately, to prevent them burning. Crush the seeds in a food mill or use a mortar and pestle.

**2** Trim the pork of excess fat. Heat the oil in a heavy-based frying pan. Brown the spare ribs over high heat, turning regularly, until dark golden brown. Drain any excess oil from the pan. Add half the sesame seeds, the spring onion, ginger, garlic, sugar, sake, soy sauce, sesame oil and 310 ml (10¾ fl oz/1¼ cup) hot water; stir well to evenly coat the ribs. Bring to the boil over medium heat, then cover and simmer 45–50 minutes, stirring occasionally.

**3** Mix the cornflour with a little water and add to the pan, stirring constantly, until it boils and thickens. Sprinkle with remaining sesame seeds. Serve with the steamed rice and kimchi (page 161), if desired.

NOTE: Make sure the rib pieces can be held easily with chopsticks — if necessary, cut them into smaller pieces.

essential asian

*When the peas and rice are cool, purée them in a food processor.*

*When the base is cooked, gently lift and turn the pancakes and cook them for another 2 minutes.*

*split pea and rice pancakes with vegetables*

## split pea and rice pancakes with vegetables

❋ ❋

Preparation time: 30 minutes
Cooking time: 1 hour
Makes about 15

200 g (7 oz) dried split green peas
100 g (3½ oz) medium-grain rice
60 g (2¼ oz/½ cup) plain (all-purpose) flour
2 eggs, beaten
1 carrot
½ green capsicum (pepper)
½ red capsicum (pepper)
6 spring onions (scallions)
3 cm (1¼ inch) piece fresh ginger
2 garlic cloves
2 teaspoons soy sauce
2 tablespoons oil
1 tablespoon sesame oil
spring onions (scallions), thinly sliced, to garnish
sweet chilli sauce, to serve

1  Wash the peas and rice in a colander under cold running water until the water runs clear. Place in a saucepan, cover with cold water and bring to the boil. Cook for 25 minutes, adding more water if necessary, or until the peas are very soft. Cool, then purée in a food processor. Add the flour, eggs and most of 250 ml (9 fl oz/1 cup) water and pulse until a smooth batter forms, adding more water until it is a thick pouring consistency. (You may need to add a little extra water.)
2  Cut the carrot, capsicums and spring onions into fine matchsticks about 3 cm (1¼ inches) long. Finely grate the ginger and chop the garlic. Pour the batter into a bowl and stir in the vegetables, ginger, garlic and soy sauce.
3  Heat a heavy-based frying pan over medium heat. When hot, brush with a little oil and sesame oil. Pour in 2 tablespoons of batter and cook for 3–5 minutes. When the base is cooked, gently run a spatula around the bottom of the pancake to release it from the pan. Turn the pancake over and cook the other side for 2 minutes. Cover the pan for about 30 seconds to ensure the pancake is cooked, then place it on a plate. Keep it warm in a very slow oven while the other pancakes cook.
4  Scatter the spring onion over the pancakes. Serve with sweet chilli sauce.

## vermicelli with stir-fried beef and vegetables

❋ ❋

Preparation time: 40 minutes
Cooking time: 25 minutes
Serves 4

8 dried Chinese mushrooms
150 g (5½ oz) dried mung bean vermicelli
1 tablespoon white sesame seeds
150 g (5½ oz) sirloin steak, partially frozen
4 garlic cloves, finely chopped
2 tablespoons soy sauce
2 teaspoons sesame oil
1–2 teaspoons chopped red chilli

# korea

1 large carrot
½ red capsicum (pepper)
75 g (2½ oz) asparagus spears
2 tablespoons oil
6 spring onions (scallions), thinly sliced
soy sauce and sesame oil, extra, to serve

**1** Soak the mushrooms in hot water for 20 minutes. Drain, then squeeze to remove any excess liquid. Discard the stems and chop the caps finely, reserving 2 tablespoons of the soaking liquid. Soak the vermicelli for 10 minutes; drain.
**2** Toast the sesame seeds in a dry frying pan over medium heat for 3–4 minutes, shaking the pan gently, until the seeds are golden brown; remove from the pan at once to prevent burning.
**3** Slice the beef into very thin strips. Combine the beef, garlic, soy sauce, 2 tablespoons water, sesame oil and chilli; marinate for 15 minutes. Cut the carrot, capsicum and asparagus into thin strips about 4 cm (1½ inches) long. Mix the mushrooms with the beef; drain off any liquid and set aside.
**4** Heat a wok or large heavy-based frying pan over medium heat until very hot. Add a little oil; stir-fry the beef and mushroom mixture in two batches. Sear the beef quickly, but do not overcook it; remove from the wok. Add a little oil; stir-fry the vegetables for 2 minutes, then cover with a lid and steam for 1 minute, or until just softened. Add vermicelli, reserved liquid and spring onion; toss well. Return beef to the wok, cover and steam for 1 minute.
**5** Divide the vermicelli among four bowls, sprinkle with the sesame seeds and serve with the extra soy sauce and sesame oil.

## chicken stew

✻

Preparation time: 30 minutes
Cooking time: 50 minutes
Serves 4

1.6 kg (3 lb 8 oz) whole chicken
6 garlic cloves, finely chopped
4 spring onions (scallions), chopped
1 teaspoon Korean chilli powder
2 tablespoons Japanese soy sauce (shoshoyu)
2 tablespoons sesame oil
1 tablespoon rice vinegar
2 zucchini (courgettes), thickly sliced
steamed rice, to serve

**1** Using a cleaver or large cook's knife, cut the chicken into quarters, then into small eating pieces, chopping straight through the bone.
**2** Combine the chicken, garlic, spring onion, chilli powder, soy sauce, sesame oil, vinegar and zucchini in a heavy-based saucepan or flameproof casserole dish. Toss the chicken well to coat it in the sauce. Cover and cook over a low heat for 45–50 minutes or until the chicken is very tender. The chicken should come off the bone easily, so it can be eaten with chopsticks. Serve with the steamed rice.

**NOTE:** Korean chilli powder may be replaced with 1 teaspoon of cayenne pepper and sweet paprika for each teaspoon of chilli powder.

# japan

Japanese food is a treat for the eye as well as the palate. Meals are beautifully presented and only the freshest of ingredients are used. Japanese food contains few spices; instead chefs concentrate on bringing out the natural taste of the individual ingredients in a dish. The characteristic flavour of Japanese food comes from dashi, a stock made from dried fish and dried kelp; the rice wines mirin and sake; and miso, tofu and Japanese soy sauce (shoshoyu), all products of soy beans.

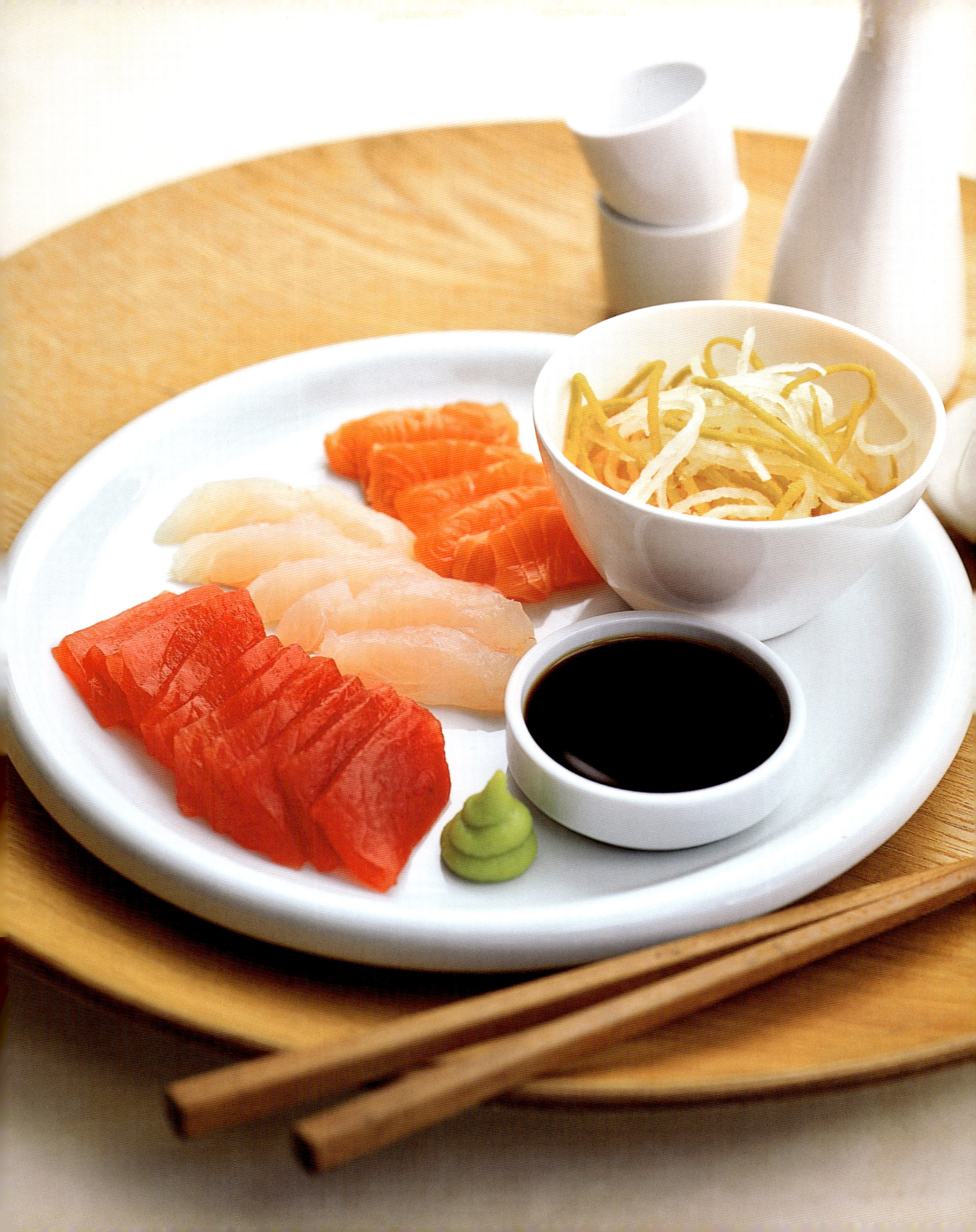

## salmon sushi roll

✹✹✹

Preparation time: 45 minutes + 1 hour draining time
Cooking time: 15 minutes
Makes about 30

220 g (7¾ oz/1 cup) Japanese medium-grain rice
1 tablespoon rice vinegar
2 teaspoons caster (superfine) sugar
125 g (4½ oz) sashimi-grade salmon
1 small Lebanese (short) cucumber, peeled
½ small avocado
4 sheets roasted nori (dried seaweed), 18 x 20 cm (7 x 8 inches)
wasabi paste
3 tablespoons pickled ginger
Japanese soy sauce (shoshoyu), to serve

1 Wash the rice under cold running water until the water runs clear, then drain thoroughly. Leave the rice in the strainer to drain for 1 hour. Put the rice in a saucepan and cover with 300 ml (10½ fl oz) water. Cover the pan and bring the water to the boil, then reduce the heat to very low and simmer for 10 minutes. Remove the pan from the heat, remove the lid and put a clean cloth across the top to absorb excess moisture. Set aside for 10 minutes.
2 To make the sushi dressing, combine the vinegar, sugar and ¼ teaspoon salt in a small bowl.
3 Spread the rice over the base of a non-metallic dish or bowl, pour the sushi dressing over the top and use a rice paddle or spatula to mix the dressing through the rice. Fan the rice until it cools to room temperature. Cover with a damp cloth and set it aside, but do not refrigerate.
4 Using a very sharp knife, cut the salmon into thin strips. Cut the cucumber and avocado into matchstick strips about 5 cm (2 inches) in length.
5 Put a nori sheet on a sushi mat, with the nori shiny side down and with the longest sides at the top and bottom. Top with a quarter of the rice, spreading it over the nori, leaving a 2 cm (¾ inch) gap at the edge furthest away from you. Spread a very small amount of wasabi along the centre of the rice. Arrange a quarter of the pieces of salmon, cucumber, avocado and ginger along the top of the wasabi. Starting with the end nearest to you, tightly roll up the mat and the nori, making sure you do not tuck the edge of the mat under the roll. When you have finished rolling, press the mat to make a round roll and press the nori edges together to seal. Repeat with the remaining ingredients.
6 Use a sharp knife to trim the ends and cut the rolls into 2.5 cm (1 inch) rounds. Serve the sushi with small bowls of soy sauce and extra wasabi — your guests can mix them together to their taste for a dipping sauce.

NOTE: Sushi can be made up to 4 hours in advance and kept on a plate, covered with plastic wrap. Keep the large rolls intact and slice just before serving. Don't refrigerate or the rice will become hard.

## steamed sake chicken

✹

Preparation time: 25 minutes + 30 minutes marinating time
Cooking time: 20 minutes
Serves 4

500 g (1 lb 2 oz) boneless chicken breasts, with skin on
80 ml (2½ fl oz/⅓ cup) sake
2 tablespoons lemon juice
4 cm (1½ inch) piece fresh ginger, cut into very thin matchsticks
steamed rice, optional, to serve

SAUCE
2 tablespoons Japanese soy sauce (shoshoyu)
1 tablespoon mirin
1 teaspoon sesame oil
1 spring onion (scallion), sliced

GARNISH
2 spring onions (scallions)
½ small red capsicum (pepper)

salmon sushi roll

# japan

mixed sashimi

## sashimi and sushi

The fortuitous discovery that fresh fish fillets stored on rice sprinkled with rice vinegar not only remained fresh but took on a pleasing flavour is said to have been made in the huts of humble Japanese fishermen. Today, specialist sushi bars are devoted to the dish; sashimi, accompanied by sake, is traditionally served as first course, and an array of sushi with various toppings follow. The chefs who slice the fish and prepare the delicacies are highly skilled masters of their art.

**1** Use a fork to prick the skin on the chicken in several places. Put the chicken, skin side up, in a shallow non-metallic dish and sprinkle with 1 teaspoon salt. Combine the sake, lemon juice and ginger in a bowl. Pour over the chicken, then cover and marinate in the refrigerator for 30–40 minutes.
**2** To make the sauce, combine the soy sauce, mirin, sesame oil and spring onion in a small bowl.
**3** To make the garnish, peel the outside layer from the spring onions, then cut thinly into diagonal pieces. Lay the capsicum flat on a board, skin side down. Holding a knife in a horizontal position, cut just under the membrane surface to remove the top layer, then discard it. Cut the capsicum into very thin 3 cm (1¼ inch) long strips.
**4** Line the base of a bamboo or metal steamer with baking paper. Remove the chicken from the marinade and arrange it, skin side up, in the steamer. Fill a wok or frying pan with 500 ml (17 fl oz/ 2 cups) water and bring to the boil. Sit the steamer in the wok, cover and cook over gently boiling water for 15–20 minutes, or until the chicken is cooked.
**5** Cut the chicken into bite-sized pieces (remove the skin if you prefer) and arrange in the centre of a serving plate. Drizzle over the sauce. Arrange the capsicum strips in a bundle on the side of the plate and scatter the spring onion over the chicken. Serve warm or cold, with rice if desired.

## mixed sashimi

✳ ✳

Preparation time: **30 minutes**
Cooking time: **nil**
Serves **4**

500 g (1 lb 2 oz) sashimi-grade fish (such as tuna, salmon, kingfish, ocean trout, snapper, whiting, bream and/or jewfish)
1 carrot
1 daikon, peeled
Japanese soy sauce (shoshoyu), to serve
wasabi paste, to serve

**1** Use a very sharp, flat-bladed knife to remove any skin from the fish. Place the fish in the freezer and chill it until it is just firm enough to be cut thinly and evenly into slices, about 5 mm (¼ inch) in width. Try to make each cut one motion in one direction, taking care not to saw the fish.
**2** Use a zester to scrape the carrot and daikon into long fine strips, or cut them into thin matchstick strips. Arrange the sashimi on a platter. Garnish with the carrot and daikon and serve with the soy sauce and wasabi.

essential asian

## smoked salmon rice balls

❋ ❋

**Preparation time:** 20 minutes + 1 hour draining time
**Cooking time:** 15 minutes
**Makes** about 20 balls

275 g (9¾ oz/1¼ cups) Japanese medium-grain rice
55 g (2 oz) smoked salmon, chopped
2 tablespoons finely chopped pickled ginger
2 spring onions (scallions), finely chopped
2 teaspoons black sesame seeds, toasted

**1** Wash the rice under cold running water until the water runs clear, then drain thoroughly. Leave the rice in the strainer to drain for 1 hour. Put the rice in a saucepan with 330 ml (11¼ fl oz/1⅓ cups) water. Cover the pan and bring to the boil, then reduce the heat to very low and simmer for 10 minutes. Remove the pan from the heat, remove the lid and put a clean cloth across the top to absorb excess moisture. Set aside for 10 minutes.
**2** Combine the salmon, ginger and spring onion in a small bowl. Using wet hands, form 1 heaped tablespoon of rice into a ball, push 2 teaspoons of the salmon mixture into the centre of the rice and remould the ball around it. Repeat with the remaining rice and salmon, keeping your hands wet to prevent the rice from sticking. Arrange all the balls on a serving platter and sprinkle with sesame seeds.

## tofu miso soup

❋

**Preparation time:** 10 minutes
**Cooking time:** 15 minutes
**Serves** 4

80 g (2¾ oz/½ cup) dashi granules
100 g (3½ oz) miso paste
1 tablespoon mirin
250 g (9 oz) firm tofu, cubed
1 spring onion (scallion), sliced, to garnish

**1** Use a wooden spoon to combine 1 litre (35 fl oz/4 cups) water and the dashi granules in a small saucepan and bring to the boil.
**2** Combine the miso paste and mirin in a small bowl, then add to the pan. Stir the miso over medium heat, taking care not to let the mixture boil once the miso has dissolved, or it will lose flavour. Add the tofu cubes to the hot stock and heat, without boiling, over medium heat for 5 minutes. Serve in individual bowls, garnished with the spring onion.

> ### making dashi stock from granules
> Dashi, Japanese soup stock, can be made from granules (dashi-no-moto) which are dissolved in hot water. The strength of the granules varies according to the brand. However, as a general rule use 80 g (2¾ oz/½ cup) of granules to 1 litre (35 fl oz/4 cups) water. This can be strengthened or diluted to taste.

# japan

## sukiyaki

✺ ✺ ✺

Preparation time: 1 hour
Cooking time: 15 minutes
Serves 6

- 500 g (1 lb 2 oz) scotch fillet, partially frozen
- 3 small white onions, each cut into 6 wedges
- 5 spring onions (scallions), white part only, cut into 4 cm (1½ inch) lengths
- 1 large carrot, cut into 4 cm (1½ inch) matchsticks
- 400 g (14 oz) small button mushrooms, stalks discarded, caps halved
- ½ small Chinese cabbage (wong bok), cut into bite-sized pieces
- 180 g (6¼ oz/2 cups) bean sprouts, trimmed
- 225 g (8 oz) tin bamboo shoots, drained, trimmed into even-sized pieces
- 100 g (3½ oz) firm tofu, cut into 2 cm (¾ inch) cubes
- 100 g (3½ oz) fresh shirataki noodles
- 60 ml (2 fl oz/¼ cup) oil
- 6 eggs

SAUCE
- 80 ml (2½ fl oz/⅓ cup) Japanese soy sauce (shoshoyu)
- 60 ml (2 fl oz/¼ cup) beef stock
- 60 ml (2 fl oz/¼ cup) sake
- 60 ml (2 fl oz/¼ cup) mirin
- 2 tablespoons caster (superfine) sugar

**1** Use a very sharp knife to slice the partially frozen beef as thinly as possible, then arrange the slices on a large tray or platter, leaving room for the vegetables, tofu and noodles. Cover the beef and refrigerate the platter while preparing the remaining ingredients.
**2** Arrange the prepared vegetables and tofu on the platter with the beef.
**3** Cook the noodles in a saucepan of boiling water for about 3 minutes, or until just soft; do not overcook them or they will fall apart. Drain thoroughly and, if you like, use scissors to cut the cooked noodles into shorter lengths that can be picked up easily with chopsticks. Arrange the noodles on the platter with the meat and vegetables.
**4** To make the sauce, combine the soy sauce, stock, sake, mirin and sugar in a small bowl and stir until the sugar has dissolved.
**5** Set the table with individual place settings, each with a serving bowl, a bowl of rice (see Note), a bowl to break an egg into, chopsticks and napkins. Place an electric frying pan on the table so it is within easy reach of each diner.
**6** When all the diners are seated, heat the frying pan and brush it lightly with a little of the oil. When the pan is very hot, take about a third of each of the vegetables and cook them quickly for about 2 minutes, tossing constantly. Push the vegetables to the side of the pan. Add about a third of the beef in one layer and sear the slices for 30 seconds on each side, taking care not to overcook them. Drizzle a little of the sauce over the meat. Add some of the noodles and tofu to the pan and gently toss with the other ingredients.
**7** Each diner breaks an egg into their bowl and whisks it with chopsticks. Mouthfuls of sukiyaki are then selected from the hot pan, dipped into the egg and eaten. When the diners are ready for more, the pan is reheated and the cooking process repeated.

NOTE: Some people prefer to have sukiyaki on rice but it is not traditionally served with rice.

## sukiyaki

Buddhist prohibitions against eating flesh meant that red meat was not part of the Japanese diet until the mid-nineteenth century when, weakened by foreign influence, the taboo was abandoned. The beef dish sukiyaki dates from this time. A feature of the dish is the thin, translucent, jelly-like noodles (called shirataki noodles) which are made from the starchy root of a plant known in Japan as devil's tongue. Shirataki noodles are also available dried.

## savoury egg custard

✳

Preparation time: 20 minutes
Cooking time: 30 minutes
Serves 6

200 g (7 oz) boneless, skinless chicken breasts, cut into bite-sized pieces
2 teaspoons sake
2 teaspoons Japanese soy sauce (shoshoyu)
2 leeks, sliced
1 small carrot, sliced
200 g (7 oz) English spinach, chopped

CUSTARD
1 litre (35 fl oz/4 cups) boiling water
80 g (2¾ oz/½ cup) dashi granules
2 tablespoons Japanese soy sauce (shoshoyu)
6 eggs

**1** Place the chicken pieces into six heatproof bowls. Combine the sake and soy sauce, and pour the mixture over the chicken.
**2** Divide the vegetables between the six bowls.
**3** To make the custard, combine the water and dashi granules in a heatproof bowl and stir to dissolve; cool completely. Combine the dashi, soy sauce and eggs, and strain equal amounts into the six bowls.
**4** Cover the bowls with foil, place them in a steamer, and cook over high heat for 20–30 minutes. Test the custard by inserting a fine skewer into the centre; it is cooked when the skewer comes out with no moisture clinging to it. Serve immediately.

## prawn and vegetable tempura

✳ ✳

Preparation time: 40 minutes
Cooking time: 15 minutes
Serves 4

20 raw large prawns (shrimp)
plain or tempura flour, for coating
215 g (7½ oz/1¾ cups) tempura flour
435 ml (15¼ fl oz/1¾ cups) iced water
2 egg yolks
oil, for deep frying
1 large zucchini (courgette), cut into strips
1 red capsicum (pepper), cut into strips
1 onion, cut into rings
Japanese soy sauce (shoshoyu), to serve

**1** Peel the prawns, leaving the tails intact. Gently pull out the dark vein from each prawn back, starting at the head end. Make a shallow incision in the underside of the prawns and then open up the cut to straighten the prawns out.
**2** Coat the prawns lightly with flour, leaving the tail uncoated, and shake off the excess. In a bowl, gently mix the tempura flour, water and egg yolks and use at once (the batter will be lumpy — don't overmix).
**3** Heat the oil in a deep saucepan or wok to moderately hot. Working with a few at a time, dip each prawn into the batter, still leaving the tail uncoated. Fry briefly in the hot oil until lightly golden; remove from the pan and drain well on paper towels. Repeat this process with the vegetable pieces, doing about 2–3 pieces at a time. Serve immediately with soy sauce. Add strips of fresh ginger to the soy sauce if you like.

NOTE: Tempura flour is available from Asian food stores, and makes the lightest tempura batter. Plain (all-purpose) flour can be used but the batter will be slightly heavier.

savoury egg custard

japan

essential asian

## steak in roasted sesame seed marinade

✹ ✹

Preparation time: 25 minutes + 30 minutes marinating time
Cooking time: 15 minutes
Serves 4

2 tablespoons white Japanese sesame seeds
1 garlic clove, crushed
3 cm (1¼ inch) piece fresh ginger, finely grated
2 tablespoons Japanese soy sauce (shoshoyu)
1 tablespoon sake
1 teaspoon caster (superfine) sugar
500 g (1 lb 2 oz) scotch fillet, cut into 4 steaks
3 spring onions (scallions), to garnish
1 tablespoon oil
steamed rice, to serve

DIPPING SAUCE
4 cm (1½ inch) piece fresh ginger
½ teaspoon shichimi togarashi (see far right)
125 ml (4 fl oz/½ cup) Japanese soy sauce (shoshoyu)
2 teaspoons dashi granules

**1** Toast the sesame seeds in a dry frying pan over moderately low heat for 2 minutes, shaking the pan constantly, until the seeds begin to pop. Crush the toasted seeds in a mortar and pestle.
**2** Place the crushed sesame seeds, garlic, ginger, soy sauce, sake and sugar in a bowl and whisk until the sugar has dissolved. Place the beef in a shallow dish; spoon the marinade over the top and marinate for 30 minutes.
**3** To make the dipping sauce, cut the ginger lengthways into very fine strips about 4 cm (1½ inches) long. Place the ginger, shichimi togarashi, soy sauce, dashi and 2 tablespoons water in a small bowl and whisk lightly until well combined.
**4** Cut the spring onions lengthways into very fine strips about 4 cm (1½ inches) long. Place the strips in a bowl of iced water and leave until they are crisp and curled; drain.
**5** Lightly brush the oil over the beef and then grill (broil) or fry them for 4–6 minutes on each side — don't overcook or the beef will become very tough. Set the beef aside for 5 minutes before cutting into diagonal slices. Arrange the slices on serving plates and then drizzle over a little of the dipping sauce. Garnish with the spring onion curls and serve with steamed rice and the remaining dipping sauce.

## tonkatsu

✹ ✹

Preparation time: 35 minutes + 2 hours chilling time
Cooking time: 15 minutes
Makes 40–50 slices

500 g (1 lb 2 oz) pork schnitzels, trimmed of sinew
60 g (2¼ oz/½ cup) plain (all-purpose) flour
5 egg yolks
120 g (4¼ oz/2 cups) Japanese breadcrumbs (panko)
1 sheet nori (dried seaweed)
oil, for shallow frying
250 ml (9 fl oz/1 cup) tonkatsu sauce (see far right)

**1** Sprinkle the pork with a good pinch each of salt and pepper, and lightly coat with the flour.
**2** Beat the egg yolks with 2 tablespoons water. Dip each schnitzel in the egg, then in the breadcrumbs, pressing them on to ensure an even coating. Refrigerate the pork in a single layer on a plate, uncovered, for at least 2 hours.
**3** Use a sharp knife to shred the nori very finely and then break into strips about 4 cm (1½ inches) long. Set aside until serving time.

# japan

**4** Heat 2 cm (¾ inch) oil in a deep, heavy-based saucepan to 180°C (350°F), or until a cube of bread browns in 15 seconds. Cook two or three schnitzels at a time until golden brown on both sides, then drain on crumpled paper towels. Repeat the process with the remaining schnitzels.

**5** Slice the schnitzels into 1 cm (½ inch) strips and reassemble into the original shape. Sprinkle with the nori strips and serve with the tonkatsu sauce.

## chilled soba noodles

Preparation time: 25 minutes
Cooking time: 15 minutes
Serves 4

250 g (9 oz) dried soba (buckwheat) noodles
4 cm (1½ inch) piece fresh ginger
1 carrot
4 spring onions (scallions), outside layer removed
1 sheet nori, to garnish
pickled ginger, to garnish
pickled daikon, thinly sliced, to garnish

DIPPING SAUCE
3 tablespoons dashi granules
125 ml (4 fl oz/½ cup) Japanese soy sauce (shoshoyu)
80 ml (2½ fl oz/⅓ cup) mirin

**1** Put the noodles in a large saucepan of boiling water. When the water returns to the boil, pour in 250 ml (9 fl oz/1 cup) cold water. Bring the water back to the boil and cook the noodles for 2–3 minutes, or until just tender — take care not to overcook them. Drain the noodles in a colander and then cool under cold running water. Drain thoroughly and set aside.

**2** Cut the ginger and carrot into fine matchsticks about 4 cm (1½ inches) long. Slice the spring onions very thinly. Bring a small saucepan of water to the boil, add the ginger, carrot and spring onion and blanch for about 30 seconds. Drain and place in a bowl of iced water to cool. Drain again when the vegetables are cool.

**3** To make the dipping sauce, combine 375 ml (13 fl oz/1½ cups) water, the dashi granules, soy sauce, mirin and a good pinch each of salt and pepper in a small saucepan. Bring the sauce to the boil, then cool completely. When ready to serve, pour the sauce into four small dipping bowls.

**4** Gently toss the cooled noodles and vegetables to combine. Arrange in four individual serving bowls.

**5** Toast the nori by holding it with tongs over low heat and moving it back and forth for about 15 seconds. Cut it into thin strips with scissors, and scatter the strips over the noodles. Place a little pickled ginger and daikon on the side of each plate. Serve the noodles with the dipping sauce. The noodles should be dipped into the sauce before being eaten.

### japanese condiments

*Shichimi togarashi* ('seven spice red pepper') contains a roughly ground mixture of red chilli flakes, Japanese pepper (sansho), white sesame seeds, black sesame seeds (in some mixtures replaced by mustard seeds), the dried seaweed nori, dried tangerine or mandarin peel and white poppy seeds. *Tonkatsu sauce* is a type of barbecue sauce that usually contains tomato sauce (ketchup), dark soy sauce, sake, worcestershire sauce and mustard. Both are available from Asian food stores.

# teas

It was China that first introduced tea to the rest of the world. Whether black or green, plain or highly spiced, tea is an important part of the meal in most Asian countries.

## black tea
Mainly produced in India, China and Sri Lanka, black tea leaves undergo fermentation which gives them their characteristic full, aromatic flavour and rich colour and strength.
**Assam:** Grown in north east India, this classic tea has a strong, full-flavoured malty taste and is ideal for drinking with milk.
**Darjeeling:** Grown in the foothills of the Himalayas, this prized tea has a subtle 'muscatel' flavour and a reddish-brown colour.
**Ceylon:** Produced in the high-altitude areas of Sri Lanka and known for its excellent quality, this tea has a strong rich flavour.
**Lapsang souchong:** A famous tea from China and Taiwan, this is rich and full-bodied, with a distinctive smoky, tarry taste due to the unique smoking process it undergoes.
**Yunnan:** Often used in blended teas, this Chinese tea produces a sweet light golden liquid, considered to have health-giving properties.

## oolong tea
Semi-fermented oolong teas are stronger than green teas but milder than black. They are often scented with jasmine, gardenia or rose petals and are then known as pouchong. Oolong tea originated in China, but the highest grade is now produced in Taiwan.
**Formosa:** These Taiwanese leaves produce a dark tea with a natural fruity flavour.

## green tea
A favourite in the East, green tea is served with meals in many Asian restaurants and is believed to aid digestion. It is always made weak: only 1 teaspoon of tea for the whole pot. Sugar and milk are never added.
**Gunpowder:** A high-quality, small Chinese leaf which yields a very pale green, fruity and slightly bitter tea.
**Jasmine:** This Chinese green tea is scented with jasmine petals and traditionally served with yum cha.
**Sencha:** A Japanese tea with a delicate, light flavour and colour.
**Genmai-cha:** This blend of rolled Japanese green tea leaves and toasted, puffed rice is a nutty-flavoured tea.

## blended tea
Blended teas are a combination of 15–20 different tea leaves. They were introduced to avoid by fluctuations in availability.
**English breakfast:** A mix of a number of strong Indian leaves and Ceylon tea which produces a full-flavoured, fragrant tea.
**Irish breakfast:** A strong, fragrant tea which is a combination of Assam and Ceylon leaves.
**Russian caravan:** Originally transported from India to Russia by camels, this is a blend of Keemun, Assam and Chinese green leaves.
**Earl Grey:** Scented with oil of bergamot, this blend of Keemun and Darjeeling leaves produces a pale tea with a citrus flavour.

## brewing the perfect cup of tea
1  Use a china or glazed earthenware teapot that will retain the heat, and warm it by swirling a little hot water around the sides and emptying it out.
2  Measure out the tea carefully: 1 heaped teaspoon leaves for each cup and 1 for the pot.
3  Follow the old adage 'bring your teapot to the kettle, not the kettle to the teapot' to ensure the water is still on the boil when it is poured onto the tea leaves. This will agitate the leaves and release the full flavour of the tea.
4  Put the lid on the pot and leave for 5 minutes to infuse.
5  If using, add milk to the cup before the tea. The scalding tea will slightly cook the milk and blend the flavours.
6  Stir the pot and pour tea through a strainer into each cup. Add sugar to taste and a slice of lemon if desired.

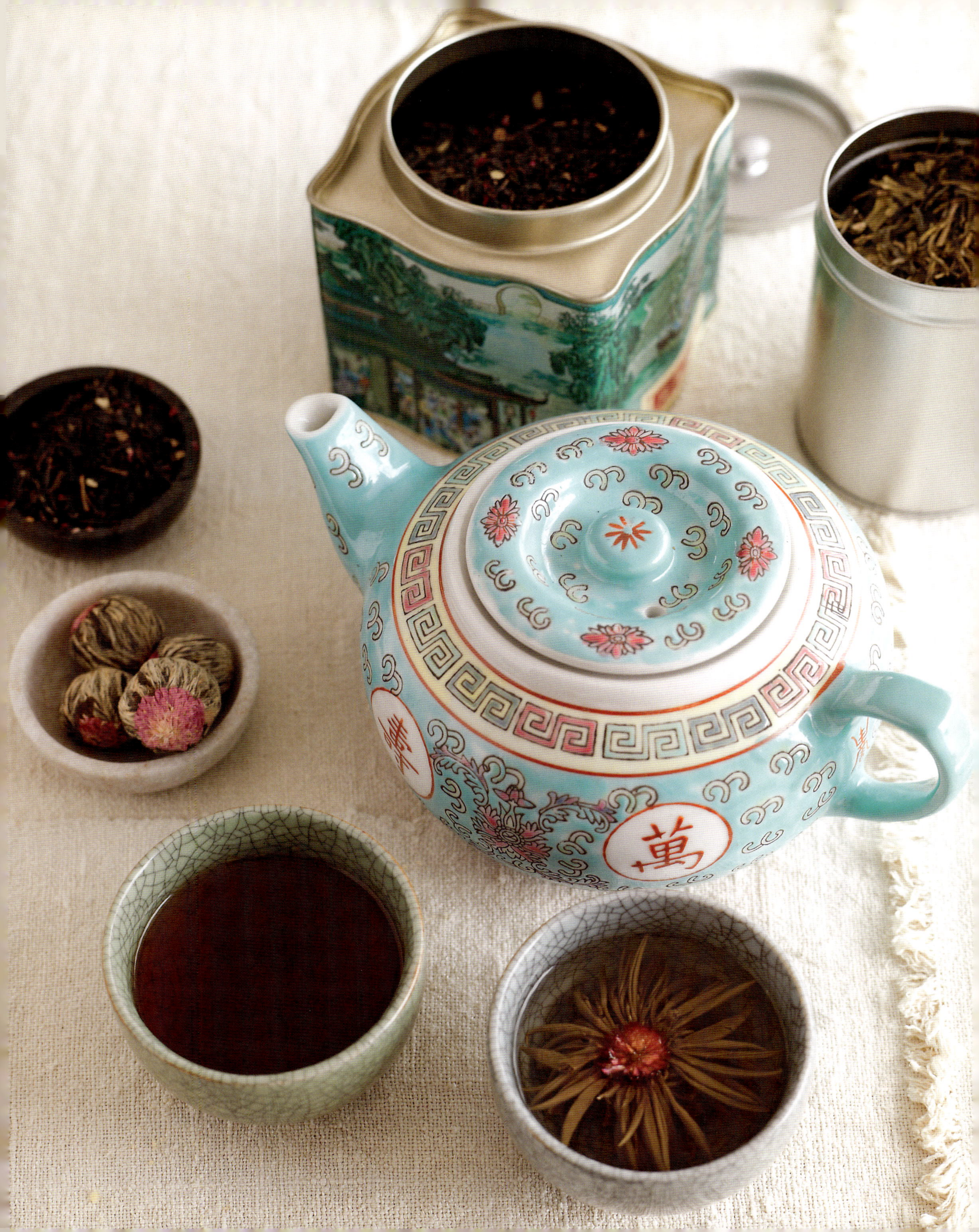
萬

essential asian

udon noodle soup

# japan

## udon noodle soup

Preparation time: 20 minutes
Cooking time: 15 minutes
Serves 4

400 g (14 oz) dried udon noodles
3 teaspoons dashi granules
2 leeks, white part only, thinly sliced
200 g (7 oz) pork loin, cut into thin strips
125 ml (4 fl oz/½ cup) Japanese soy sauce (shoshoyu)
2 tablespoons mirin
4 spring onions (scallions), finely chopped, plus extra, to garnish
shichimi togarashi (see Note), to serve

1  Cook the noodles in a large saucepan of rapidly boiling water for 5 minutes, or until tender. Drain and cover to keep warm.
2  Combine 1 litre (35 fl oz/4 cups) water and the dashi in a large saucepan and bring to the boil. Add the leek, reduce the heat and simmer for 5 minutes. Add the pork, soy sauce, mirin and spring onion and simmer for 2 minutes, or until the pork is cooked. Divide the noodles among four serving bowls and ladle the soup over the top. Garnish with spring onion and sprinkle with the shichimi togarashi.

NOTE: Shichimi togarashi is a Japanese spice mix containing seven flavours. Ingredients can vary, but it always contains togarashi, a hot Japanese chilli. It is available in Asian or Japanese food stores.

## eggs scrambled with prawns and peas

Preparation time: 25 minutes
Cooking time: 10 minutes
Serves 4

10 g (¼ oz/¼ cup) dried shiitake mushrooms
250 g (9 oz) raw prawns (shrimp)
4 eggs
1 teaspoon dashi granules
2 teaspoons Japanese soy sauce (shoshoyu)
2 teaspoons sake
2 teaspoons oil
100 g (3½ oz) frozen peas
3 spring onions (scallions), thinly sliced
steamed rice, to serve

1  Soak the mushrooms in hot water for 15 minutes; drain and slice. Peel the prawns and gently pull out the dark vein from each prawn back, starting at the head end.
2  Place the eggs, dashi, soy sauce and sake in a bowl and beat until well combined.
3  Heat the oil in a frying pan; add the prawns and stir-fry over medium heat for 2 minutes or until just cooked. Add the peas, cover and steam for 2 minutes.
4  Pour in the egg mixture; cook over low heat until lightly set, stirring gently occasionally so the egg sets in large curds. Sprinkle over the spring onions and serve immediately with steamed rice.

## chicken domburi

Preparation time: 35 minutes
Cooking time: 35 minutes
Serves 4

2 cups (440 g/15½ oz) medium-grain rice
2 tablespoons oil
200 g (7 oz) boneless, skinless chicken breast, cut into thin strips
2 onions, thinly sliced
80 ml (2½ fl oz/⅓ cup) Japanese soy sauce (shoshoyu)
2 tablespoons mirin
1 teaspoon dashi granules
5 eggs, lightly beaten
2 sheets nori
2 spring onions (scallions), sliced

1  Wash the rice in a colander under cold running water until the water runs clear. Place the rice in a medium-sized heavy-based pan, add 600 ml (21 fl oz) water and bring to the boil over high heat. Cover the pan with a tight-fitting lid, reduce the heat to as low as possible (otherwise the rice in the bottom of the pan will burn) and cook for 15 minutes. Turn the heat to very high for 15–20 seconds then remove the pan from the heat. Set the pan aside for 12 minutes, without lifting the lid (don't allow the steam to escape).
2  Heat the oil in a frying pan over high heat, and stir-fry the chicken until golden and tender; set aside. Reheat the pan, add the onion and cook, stirring occasionally, for 3 minutes or until beginning to soften. Add 80 ml (2½ fl oz/⅓ cup) water, soy sauce, mirin and dashi. Stir to dissolve the dashi and bring the stock to the boil. Cook for 3 minutes or until onion is tender.
3  Return the chicken to the pan and pour in the egg, stirring gently to just break up the egg. Cover and simmer over very low heat for 2–3 minutes or until the eggs are just set. Remove the pan from the heat.
4  Toast the nori by holding it over low heat and moving it back and forth for about 15 seconds; crumble it into small pieces.
5  Transfer the rice to an earthenware dish, carefully spoon over the chicken and egg mixture and sprinkle over the nori. Garnish with the spring onion.

NOTE: Domburi is an earthenware dish, but the food served in the dish has also taken on the name.

### a noisy affair

While etiquette dictates that Japanese mealtimes should be silent affairs, an exception is made for noodles, which may be eaten with gusto and much lip-smacking. Some say this allows an intake of air to cool the noodles, but chilled noodles, a favourite summer dish in Japan, are eaten with the same enthusiastic slurping.

## marinated salmon strips

❋

Preparation time: 15 minutes + 1 hour marinating time
Cooking time: nil
Serves 4

2 sashimi-grade salmon fillets, each about 400 g (14 oz), skinned
4 cm (1½ inch) piece fresh ginger, finely grated
1 garlic clove, finely chopped
3 spring onions (scallions), finely chopped
1 teaspoon sugar
2 tablespoons Japanese soy sauce (shoshoyu)
125 ml (4 fl oz/½ cup) sake
pickled ginger, to garnish
pickled cucumber, to garnish

**1** Cut the salmon into thin strips and arrange them in a single layer in a large deep dish.
**2** Put the ginger, garlic, spring onion, sugar, 1 teaspoon salt, soy sauce and sake in a small bowl and stir to combine. Pour the marinade over the salmon, cover and refrigerate for 1 hour.
**3** Arrange the salmon, strip by strip, on a serving plate. Garnish with the pickled ginger and cucumber and serve chilled.

## inari sushi

❋ ❋

Preparation time: 10 minutes
Cooking time: 40 minutes + 15 minutes
Makes 6

220 g (7¾ oz/1 cup) medium-grain rice
2 tablespoons Japanese white sesame seeds
2 tablespoons rice vinegar
1 tablespoon caster (superfine) sugar
1 teaspoon mirin
6 inari pouches (see Note)

**1** Wash the rice under cold running water until the water runs clear; drain thoroughly. Place the rice and 500 ml (17 fl oz/2 cups) water in a medium saucepan, and bring to the boil. Reduce the heat and simmer, uncovered, for 4–5 minutes or until the water is absorbed. Cover, reduce the heat to very low and cook for another 4–5 minutes. Remove the pan from the heat and let stand, covered, for 10 minutes.
**2** Toast the sesame seeds in a dry frying pan over medium heat for 3–4 minutes, shaking the pan gently, until the seeds are golden brown; remove the seeds from the pan at once to prevent burning.
**3** Add the combined vinegar, sugar, mirin and 1 teaspoon salt to the rice, tossing with a wooden spoon until the rice is cool.
**4** Gently separate the inari pouches and open them up. Place a ball of the rice mixture inside. Sprinkle the rice with the toasted sesame seeds and press the inari closed with your fingers. Serve on a plate, cut side down.

NOTE: Inari are small 'pouches' made from bean curd and are available from Japanese food shops.

## hand-shaped tuna sushi

❋ ❋

Preparation time: 20 minutes
Cooking time: 30 minutes + 10 minutes cooling
Makes about 30

220 g (7¾ oz/1 cup) medium-grain rice
2 tablespoons rice vinegar
1 tablespoon caster (superfine) sugar
300 g (10½ oz) very fresh tuna
wasabi, to taste
Japanese soy sauce (shoshoyu), and wasabi, extra, to serve

**1** Wash the rice under cold running water until the water runs clear; drain thoroughly. Place the rice and 500 ml (17 fl oz/2 cups) water in a medium saucepan and bring it to the boil. Reduce the heat; simmer, uncovered, for 4–5 minutes or until the water is absorbed. Reduce the heat to very low. Cover and cook for another 4–5 minutes. Remove the pan from the heat and let stand, covered, for 10 minutes.
**2** Add the combined vinegar, sugar and 1 teaspoon salt to the rice, tossing with a wooden spoon until the rice is cool.
**3** Cut the tuna into strips about 5 cm (2 inches) long. Place a little wasabi on each.
**4** Use your hands to roll a tablespoon of rice into a ball. Place the rice ball onto a strip of fish and then gently mould the tuna around the rice. Flatten the ball slightly to elongate. Repeat with the remaining ingredients. Serve with the soy sauce and wasabi.

inari sushi

# japan

Grate the piece of fresh ginger.

Use a sharp knife to cut the salmon into thin strips.

Place all the ingredients for the marinade in a small bowl and stir together well.

**marinated salmon strips**

essential asian

grilled fish steaks

1   Finely grate the ginger. Squeeze the ginger firmly with your fingertips to remove all the juice; reserve the juice and discard the dry pulp. Place the ginger juice, soy sauce, mirin, spring onion and sugar in a small bowl and stir until the sugar has dissolved.
2   Place the fish in a shallow dish. Pour the marinade over the fish and marinate for 15 minutes. Drain the fish, reserving the marinade, and place it on a foil-lined grill (broiler) tray.
3   Cook the fish under medium heat for about 3 minutes each side, carefully turning the fish over with spatulas.
4   Pour the reserved marinade into a small saucepan and boil it over high heat for 2 minutes until thickened. Drizzle the marinade over the fish, garnish with the cucumber and pickled ginger, and serve with steamed rice if desired.

## teriyaki chicken

✺

Preparation time: 15 minutes
Cooking time: 40 minutes
Serves 6

125 ml (4 fl oz/½ cup) Japanese
   soy sauce (shoshoyu)
2 tablespoons mirin
1 tablespoon sugar
2 tablespoons oil
12 chicken drumsticks
steamed rice, to serve

1   Place the soy sauce, mirin and sugar in a small saucepan and stir over low heat until the sugar has dissolved. Bring to the boil, reduce the heat and simmer, uncovered, for 2 minutes.
2   Heat the oil in a large heavy-based frying pan; add the chicken drumsticks in batches and cook over high heat until browned on both sides.
3   Return all the chicken to the pan, add the sauce, cover and cook for 20 minutes or until the chicken is tender. Serve with the steamed rice.

## grilled fish steaks

✺ ✺

Preparation time: 30 minutes
Cooking time: 10 minutes
Serves 4

5 cm (2 inch) piece fresh ginger
3 tablespoons Japanese soy sauce
   (shoshoyu)
1 tablespoon mirin
3 spring onions (scallions), very finely
   chopped
3 teaspoons sugar
4 small fish cutlets (such as tuna, blue eye,
   jewfish), each about 150 g (5½ oz)
cucumber slices, to garnish
pickled ginger (page 162),
   to garnish
steamed rice (optional), to serve

# japan

## eggplant kebabs with miso

Preparation time: 15 minutes
Cooking time: 15 minutes
Makes 10

2 eggplants (aubergines), cut into 2 cm (¾ inch) cubes
2 tablespoons Japanese white sesame seeds
140 g (5 oz/½ cup) red miso paste
2 tablespoons mirin
2 tablespoons sake
60 ml (2 fl oz/¼ cup) oil
steamed rice, to serve

**1** Soak 10 wooden skewers in water for 30 minutes to ensure they don't burn during cooking. Put the eggplant in a colander and sprinkle generously with salt. Set aside for 15 minutes, or until the moisture is drawn out of the eggplant (this removes the bitterness). Rinse thoroughly and pat dry with paper towels.
**2** Drain the skewers and dry with paper towels. Thread the eggplant cubes onto the skewers.
**3** Put the sesame seeds in a dry frying pan over medium heat and toast for 3–4 minutes, shaking the pan gently, until the seeds are golden brown. Remove the seeds from the pan at once to prevent burning.
**4** Combine the miso, mirin and sake in a small saucepan. Bring to the boil, then reduce the heat and simmer for 5 minutes.
**5** Heat the oil on a barbecue hotplate and cook the eggplant skewers for 5 minutes, turning frequently until golden brown. Spread the miso topping over the eggplant skewers and sprinkle with the sesame seeds. Serve with steamed rice.

## green beans in sesame seed sauce

✻✻

Preparation time: 10 minutes
Cooking time: 10 minutes
Serves 4

500 g (1 lb 2 oz) green beans, trimmed
2 tablespoons Japanese white sesame seeds (see Note)
6 cm (2½ inch) fresh ginger, finely sliced
1 tablespoon Japanese soy sauce (shoshoyu)
1 tablespoon mirin
3 teaspoons sugar
1 teaspoon Japanese white sesame seeds, extra

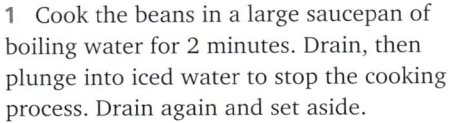

**1** Cook the beans in a large saucepan of boiling water for 2 minutes. Drain, then plunge into iced water to stop the cooking process. Drain again and set aside.
**2** Toast the sesame seeds in a dry frying pan, over medium heat, for 3–4 minutes, shaking the pan gently, until the seeds are golden brown; remove the seeds from the pan at once to prevent browning. Pound the seeds using a mortar and pestle until a paste forms (the mixture will become damp as oil is released from the seeds).
**3** Combine the sesame seed paste with the ginger, soy sauce, mirin and sugar. Pour the sauce over the beans, scatter over the extra sesame seeds and serve.

**NOTE:** Japanese sesame seeds are plump and large, with a fuller flavour than other sesame seeds. The beans can be marinated in the sauce overnight.

## yakitori (skewered chicken)

✻

Preparation time: 20 minutes
Cooking time: 10 minutes
Makes 25 skewers

1 kg (2 lb 4 oz) boneless, skinless chicken thighs
6 spring onions (scallions)
125 ml (4 fl oz/½ cup) sake
185 ml (6 fl oz/¾ cup) soy sauce (see Note)
125 ml (4 fl oz/½ cup) mirin
2 tablespoons sugar

**1** Soak 25 wooden skewers in water for 30 minutes to ensure they don't burn during cooking. Cut the chicken into bite-sized pieces. Trim the spring onions, then cut diagonally into 2 cm (¾ inch) lengths.
**2** Combine the sake, soy sauce, mirin and sugar in a small saucepan. Bring to the boil, then remove from the heat and set aside.
**3** Drain the skewers and dry with paper towels. Thread the chicken and spring onion pieces alternately onto the skewers. Place the skewers on a foil-lined tray and

*green beans in sesame seed sauce*

cook under a preheated moderate grill (broiler), turning and brushing frequently with the sauce, for 7–8 minutes, or until the chicken is cooked through. Yakitori is traditionally served as a snack with beer.

NOTE: For this dish, it is best to use a darker soy sauce rather than the lighter Japanese one.

## salmon nabe

✸ ✸

Preparation time: 20 minutes
Cooking time: 40 minutes
Serves 3–4

12 dried shiitake mushrooms
250 g (9 oz) firm tofu
½ Chinese cabbage (wong bok)
4 salmon cutlets
2 x 5 cm (2 inch) pieces tinned bamboo shoots
2 litres (70 fl oz/8 cups) dashi
80 ml (2½ fl oz/⅓ cup) Japanese soy sauce
60 ml (2 fl oz/¼ cup) mirin or sake

SESAME SEED SAUCE
100 g (3½ oz) white sesame seeds
2 teaspoons oil
125 ml (4 fl oz/½ cup) Japanese soy sauce (shoshoyu)
2 tablespoons mirin
3 teaspoons caster (superfine) sugar
½ teaspoon instant dashi granules

**1** Soak the mushrooms in warm water for 15 minutes, then drain. Remove stems. Cut the tofu into 12 squares. Roughly shred the cabbage into 5 cm (2 inch) wide pieces.
**2** Place the mushrooms, tofu, cabbage, salmon, bamboo shoots, dashi, soy sauce, mirin and a pinch of salt in a large saucepan and bring to the boil. Reduce the heat, cover and simmer over medium heat for 15 minutes. Turn the salmon cutlets over and simmer for a further 15 minutes, or until tender.
**3** To make the sesame seed sauce, toast the sesame seeds in a frying pan over medium heat for 3–4 minutes, shaking the pan gently, until the seeds are golden brown. Remove from the pan at once to prevent burning. Grind the seeds using a mortar and pestle until a paste is formed. Add the oil, if necessary, to assist in forming a paste. Mix the paste with the soy sauce, mirin, sugar, dashi granules and 125 ml (4 fl oz/½ cup) warm water.
**4** Pour the salmon nabe into warmed serving bowls and serve with the sesame seed sauce.

NOTE: This dish is traditionally cooked in a clay pot over a burner and served in the same pot. Diners dip the fish and vegetable pieces into the accompanying sauce and the broth is served in small bowls at the end of the meal.

salmon nabe

essential asian

**noodle-coated prawns**

1  Peel the prawns, leaving the tails intact. Gently pull out the dark vein from each prawn back, starting at the head end. Make a shallow incision in the underside of the prawns and then open up the cut to straighten the prawns out. Cut the nori into strips about 7 cm (2¾ inches) long and 1.5 cm (⅝ inch) wide. To make the batter, put the flour, egg yolk and water in a bowl and whisk until just combined. To make the sauce, combine all ingredients in a small bowl and mix well.

2  Break the noodles so that they are the same length as the prawns, not including the tails. Place the noodles on a board. Dip a prawn into the batter, then lay it, lengthways, on the noodles and gather up the noodles to cover the prawns all around. Press so they stick to the prawn. Wrap a strip of nori around the centre of the prawn, dampen the ends with a little water and press to seal. Repeat with the rest of the prawns.

3  Fill a deep-fryer or heavy-based saucepan one-third full of oil and heat to 170°C (325°F), or until a cube of bread dropped into the oil browns in 20 seconds. Cook the prawn bundles in two batches, until the noodles are golden brown. Serve immediately with the sauce.

## rice with chicken and mushrooms

❋

Preparation time: 30 minutes
Cooking time: 40 minutes
Serves 4–6

500 g (1 lb 2 oz) medium-grain white rice
8 dried shiitake mushrooms
2 tablespoons Japanese soy sauce (shoshoyu)
2 tablespoons sake
2 teaspoons sugar
600 g (1 lb 5 oz) boneless, skinless chicken breasts, cut into strips
200 g (7 oz) frozen peas
2 eggs, lightly beaten

## noodle-coated prawns

❋ ❋

Preparation time: 20 minutes
Cooking time: 15 minutes
Serves 2

6 raw large prawns (shrimp)
¼ sheet nori
100 g (3½ oz) somen noodles
oil, for deep-frying

BATTER
125 g (4½ oz/1 cup) plain (all-purpose) flour
1 egg yolk
250 ml (9 fl oz/1 cup) iced water

SOY AND GINGER SAUCE
1 tablespoon finely grated fresh ginger
2 teaspoons sugar
250 ml (9 fl oz/1 cup) soy sauce

1 Wash the rice thoroughly in a sieve under cold running water until the water runs clear. Place the rice in a heavy-based saucepan with 600 ml (21 fl oz) water and bring it to the boil. Reduce the heat to very low, cover and cook for 15 minutes. Remove the pan from the heat and leave, with the lid on, for 20 minutes.
2 Soak mushrooms in hot water for about 15 minutes, until soft. Drain well and slice into thin strips, discarding the hard stem.
3 Combine the soy sauce, sake and sugar in a frying pan. Cook over low heat stirring until the sugar has dissolved. Add the mushrooms, chicken and peas. Cover and cook for 5 minutes until the chicken is cooked. Set aside and cover to keep warm.
4 Heat a non-stick frying pan; pour in the egg and cook over medium heat, swirling the pan gently until the egg sets. Turn the omelette over and cook the other side. Remove the omelette from the pan and cut it into thin strips.
5 Arrange the rice in individual serving bowls, spoon over the chicken mixture with a little of the soy liquid and scatter over the egg strips. Serve immediately.

## skewers of beef, capsicum and spring onion

✳ ✳

Preparation time: 25 minutes + 20 minutes marinating time
Cooking time: 20 minutes
Makes 12

60 ml (2 fl oz/¼ cup) Japanese soy sauce (shoshoyu)
2 tablespoons mirin
2 teaspoons sesame oil
1 teaspoon sugar
2 tablespoons Japanese white sesame seeds
350 g (12 oz) scotch fillet, cut into bite-sized cubes
1 green capsicum (pepper), cut into small bite-sized pieces
6 spring onions (scallions), white part only, cut into short lengths
oil, for shallow frying
2 eggs, beaten
60 g (2¼ oz/½ cup) plain (all-purpose) flour

1 Soak 12 small wooden skewers in water for 30 minutes to ensure they don't burn during cooking.
2 Put the soy sauce, mirin, sesame oil, sugar and half the sesame seeds in a large bowl. Add the beef to the marinade, toss to combine, and marinate for 20 minutes.

Drain the beef and gently pat dry with paper towels. Thread a piece of beef, capsicum and spring onion onto each skewer, repeating this pattern once more.
3 Heat 1 cm (½ inch) of oil in a deep heavy-based frying pan until hot. Roll each skewer in the beaten egg, then lightly coat it in the flour. Add the skewers to the pan in two or three batches and fry until golden brown, turning each skewer regularly. Sprinkle over the remaining sesame seeds and serve immediately.

# india & pakistan

At the heart of Indian and Pakistani cooking are the spices, which are ground up to produce masalas, aromatic blends created freshly for each different dish. The variety of food reflects the religious, cultural and geographic diversity of the sub-continent itself. In Pakistan and the north of India, the cooking is meat-based: curries, tikkas and koftas mopped up with fresh breads. The dishes of the south are predominantly vegetarian, spicy-hot and bursting with colour. Special dishes are prepared for religious or cultural events, from a festive pan of biryani, flavoured with aromatic saffron, to coconut sweets, served up at weddings and other celebrations.

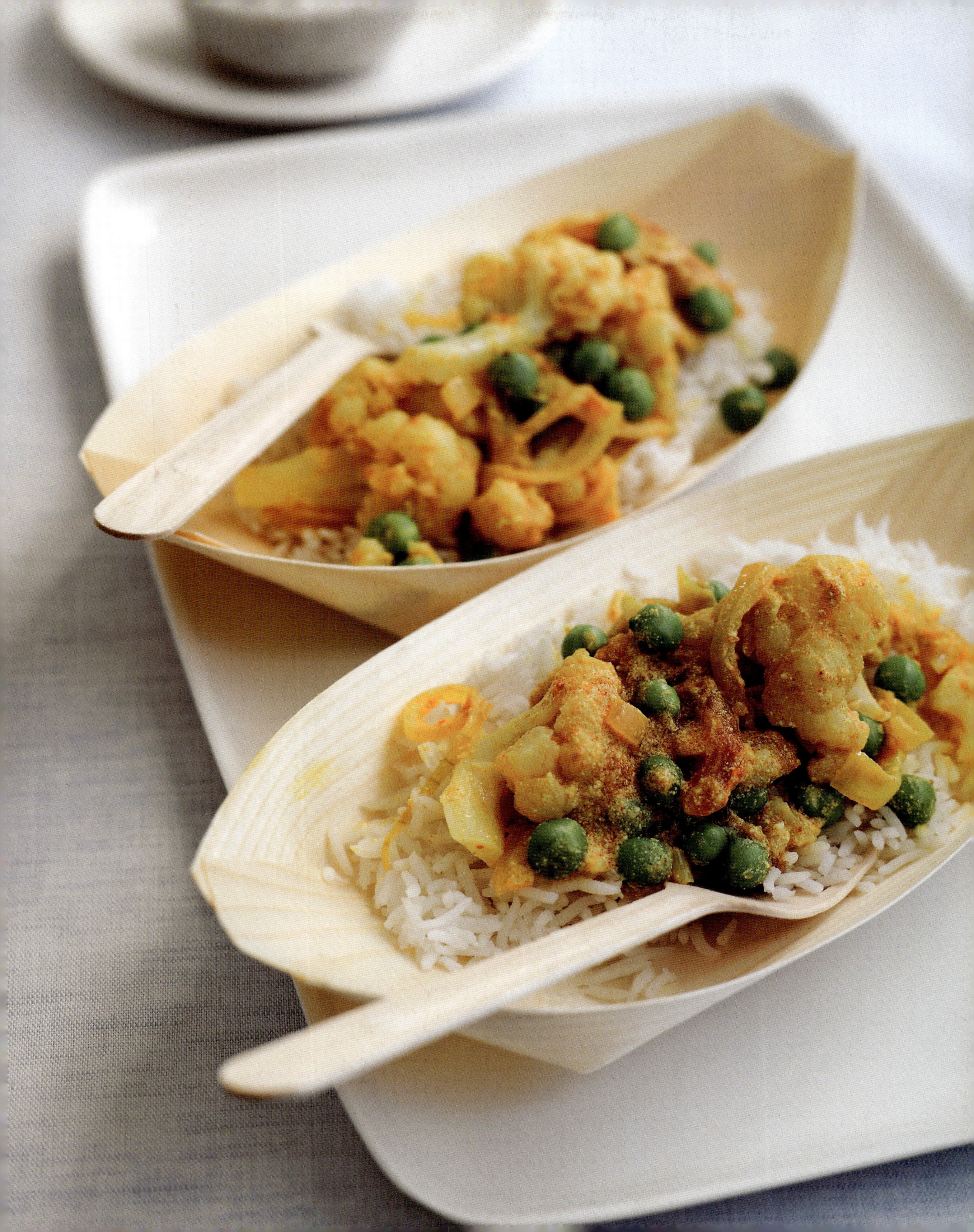

# madras curry

Preparation time: 20 minutes
Cooking time: 1 hour 30 minutes
Serves 4

1 kg (2 lb 4 oz) skirt or chuck steak
1 tablespoon ground coriander
1½ tablespoons ground cumin
1 teaspoon brown mustard seeds
½ teaspoon cracked black peppercorns
1 teaspoon chilli powder
1 teaspoon ground turmeric
2 teaspoons crushed garlic
2 teaspoons grated fresh ginger
2–3 tablespoons white vinegar
1 tablespoon oil or ghee
1 onion, chopped
60 g (2¼ oz/¼ cup) tomato paste (concentrated purée)
250 ml (9 fl oz/1 cup) beef stock
steamed rice, to serve

**1** Trim the excess fat and sinew from the beef, and cut it into 2.5 cm (1 inch) cubes.

**2** Put the coriander, cumin, mustard seeds, peppercorns, chilli powder, turmeric, garlic, ginger and 1 teaspoon salt in a small bowl and stir to combine. Add the vinegar and mix to a smooth paste.

**3** Heat the oil in a large frying pan. Add the onion and cook over medium heat until just soft. Add the spice paste and stir for 1 minute. Add the beef and cook, stirring, until it is coated with the spice paste. Add the tomato paste and stock. Simmer, covered, for about 1 hour 30 minutes, or until the meat is tender. Serve with steamed rice.

# india & pakistan

## hot lentil soup

✺

Preparation time: 15 minutes
Cooking time: 45 minutes
Serves 6

95 g (3¼ oz/½ cup) brown lentils (see Note)
2 tablespoons ghee or oil
1 onion, finely chopped
½ teaspoon finely grated fresh ginger
1 large potato, cut into small cubes
2 large tomatoes, chopped
2 teaspoons ground coriander
1 teaspoon ground cumin
½ teaspoon ground turmeric
½ teaspoon chilli flakes
2 tablespoons desiccated coconut
1–2 teaspoons tamarind concentrate
150 g (5½ oz) finely shredded cabbage
1 tablespoon chopped coriander (cilantro) or mint leaves (optional), to garnish
chapattis, to serve

**1** Place the lentils in a medium saucepan, cover with water, bring to the boil and simmer, uncovered, for about 20 minutes or until tender. Drain well.
**2** Heat the ghee in a large saucepan; add the onion and ginger and cook over medium heat until deep brown. Add the potato and tomato, and cook for 5 minutes, then add the ground coriander, cumin, turmeric, chilli and coconut and cook for another 2–3 minutes.
**3** Add the drained lentils and 1 litre (35 fl oz/4 cups) water and bring to the boil. Simmer until the lentils and potato begin to break up. Add the tamarind and cabbage. Cook until the cabbage is soft. Season with black pepper to taste. Serve with chopped coriander or mint as a garnish, if desired, and chapattis.

NOTE: Red or yellow lentils, which require less cooking time, can be used instead of brown.

## dry potato and pea curry

✺

Preparation time: 15 minutes
Cooking time: 30 minutes
Serves 4

2 onions
750 g (1 lb 10 oz) potatoes
2 teaspoons brown mustard seeds
2 tablespoons ghee or oil
2 garlic cloves, crushed
2 teaspoons finely grated fresh ginger
1 teaspoon ground turmeric
½ teaspoon chilli powder
1 teaspoon ground cumin
1 teaspoon garam masala
100 g (3½ oz/⅔ cup) peas
2 tablespoons chopped mint leaves
steamed rice, to serve

**1** Slice the onion and cut the potatoes into cubes. Put the mustard seeds in a large dry saucepan and cook over medium heat until the seeds start to pop. Add the ghee, onion, garlic and ginger, and cook, stirring, until the onion is soft.
**2** Add the turmeric, chilli powder, cumin, garam masala and potato. Stir until the potato is coated. Add 125 ml (4 fl oz/½ cup) water, cover and simmer for 15–20 minutes, or until the potato is just tender, stirring occasionally.
**3** Add the peas and stir until combined. Season to taste. Simmer, covered, for 3–5 minutes, or until the potato is cooked through and the liquid is absorbed. Stir in the mint and serve with steamed rice.

dry potato and pea curry

## the tandoor oven

Tandoori is the name given to food that is traditionally threaded onto spits and cooked in a tandoor or clay oven. Barrel-shaped and often as high as a man, the ovens are usually set into the ground with a small circular opening at the top. Long spits, laden with meats marinated in an aromatic spice paste, are lowered in to roast over the white-hot coals.

Brush the skinned chicken thighs with lemon juice.

Add several drops of red food colouring to the spice and yoghurt mixture.

## tandoori chicken

Preparation time: 25 minutes + 4 hours 30 minutes marinating time
Cooking time: 45 minutes
Serves 4–6

6 boneless, skinless chicken thighs
60 ml (2 fl oz/¼ cup) lemon juice
½ small onion, chopped
4 garlic cloves
1 tablespoon finely grated fresh ginger
3 teaspoons coriander seeds
1 tablespoon cumin seeds
1 tablespoon lemon juice, extra
¼ teaspoon paprika
pinch of chilli powder
250 g (9 oz/1 cup) plain yoghurt
red food colouring
steamed rice, to serve
cooked poppadoms, to serve

**1** Remove the skin from the chicken pieces and brush the flesh with the lemon juice; cover and marinate in the refrigerator for 30 minutes.
**2** Place the onion, garlic, ginger, coriander and cumin seeds, extra lemon juice and 1 teaspoon salt in a food processor and process until a smooth paste forms. Combine the spice paste with the paprika, chilli powder and yoghurt, and mix together until smooth. Add enough drops of food colouring to make the mixture a deep red colour.
**3** Place the chicken pieces in a large shallow dish, and spread liberally with the spicy yoghurt mixture. Cover with plastic wrap and refrigerate. Marinate the chicken for at least 4 hours or overnight.
**4** Preheat the oven to 180°C (350°F/Gas 4). Place the chicken pieces on a wire rack over a large baking dish. Bake for 45 minutes, or until the chicken pieces are tender and cooked through. Serve with steamed rice and poppadoms.

# india & pakistan

## onion bhaji

✹✹

Preparation time: 20 minutes
Cooking time: 15 minutes
Makes 25–30

80 g (2¾ oz/¾ cup) besan (chickpea flour)
60 g (2¼ oz/½ cup) plain (all-purpose) flour
1½ teaspoons bicarbonate of soda (baking soda)
1 teaspoon chilli powder
1 egg, lightly beaten
4 large onions, halved and thinly sliced
4 garlic cloves, chopped
oil, for shallow frying
chilli sauce or mango chutney, to serve

**1** Sift the flours, bicarbonate of soda and chilli powder into a bowl. Make a well in the centre, add the combined egg and 310 ml (10¾ fl oz/1¼ cups) water and stir to make a smooth creamy batter, adding a little more water if necessary. Add the onion and garlic and mix well.
**2** Heat the oil, about 1 cm (½ inch) deep, in a wide flat frying pan. Drop in tablespoons of the mixture and press into patties. Fry the bhaji on both sides until golden brown and cooked through; drain on paper towels. Serve hot with chilli sauce or mango chutney.

NOTE: Use sweet paprika instead of chilli powder for a milder taste.

pork vindaloo

## pork vindaloo

✹

Preparation time: 20 minutes
Cooking time: 1 hour 55 minutes
Serves 4

1 kg (2 lb 4 oz) pork fillets
60 ml (2 fl oz/¼ cup) vegetable oil
2 onions, finely chopped
4 garlic cloves, finely chopped
1 tablespoon finely chopped fresh ginger
1 tablespoon garam masala
2 teaspoons brown mustard seeds
4 tablespoons ready-made vindaloo curry paste
1 tablespoon white vinegar
steamed rice, to serve
cooked poppadoms, to serve

**1** Trim the pork of any excess fat and sinew and cut into bite-sized pieces.
**2** Heat a wok over medium heat, add the oil and swirl to coat the base and side. Add the pork in small batches and cook for 5–7 minutes, or until browned. Remove from the wok.
**3** Add the onion, garlic, ginger, garam masala and mustard seeds to the wok, and cook, stirring, for 5 minutes, or until the onion is soft. Add the vindaloo paste and cook for 2 minutes.
**4** Return all the pork to the wok, add 750 ml (26 fl oz/3 cups) water and bring to the boil. Reduce the heat and simmer, covered, for 1½ hours, or until the pork is tender. Stir in the vinegar 15 minutes before serving and season to taste with salt. Serve with steamed rice and poppadoms.

## yoghurt

In India, yoghurt is known as dahi and is served with almost every meal, either as raita or lassi (a smooth drink). It is also stirred into sauces to thicken and flavour, or mixed with spices and used as a marinade. The Aryans introduced cattle to India in the second millennium BC and with them came dairy products, namely cream and yoghurt. Today, yoghurt in India and Sri Lanka is produced from buffalo milk, which is far higher in butterfat than Western cow's milk. Coconut milk is still more popular in the south of India, with its largely vegetarian population.

rogan josh

## rogan josh

Preparation time: 25 minutes
Cooking time: 1 hour 30 minutes
Serves 4–6

1 kg (2 lb 4 oz) lamb
1 tablespoon ghee or oil
2 onions, chopped
125 g (4½ oz/½ cup) plain yoghurt
1 teaspoon chilli powder
1 tablespoon ground coriander
2 teaspoons ground cumin
1 teaspoon ground cardamom
½ teaspoon ground cloves
1 teaspoon ground turmeric
3 garlic cloves, crushed
1 tablespoon finely grated fresh ginger
400 g (14 oz) tin chopped tomatoes
3 teaspoons garam masala
30 g (1 oz/¼ cup) slivered almonds
coriander (cilantro) leaves, to garnish

1  Cut the lamb into 2.5 cm (1 inch) cubes.
2  Heat the ghee in a large saucepan; add the onion and cook, stirring, until soft. Add the yoghurt, chilli powder, coriander, cumin, cardamom, cloves, turmeric, garlic and ginger. Combine well. Add 1 teaspoon salt and the undrained tomatoes, and simmer, uncovered, for 5 minutes.
3  Add the lamb and stir until coated. Cover and cook over low heat for 1 to 1½ hours, or until the lamb is tender, stirring occasionally. Uncover and simmer until the liquid is thick.
4  Meanwhile toast the almonds in a dry frying pan over medium heat for 3–4 minutes, shaking the pan gently, until the nuts are golden brown; remove from the pan at once to prevent burning.
5  Sprinkle the lamb with the garam masala and mix through. Serve with the almonds sprinkled over and garnished with coriander, on a bed of steamed rice.

## chicken tikka

Preparation time: 30 minutes + 4 hours marinating time
Cooking time: 15 minutes
Makes 12

750 g (1 lb 10 oz) boneless, skinless chicken thighs
¼ onion, chopped
2 garlic cloves, crushed
1 tablespoon finely grated fresh ginger
2 tablespoons lemon juice
3 teaspoons ground coriander
3 teaspoons ground cumin
3 teaspoons garam masala
90 g (3¼ oz/⅓ cup) plain yoghurt

1  Cut the chicken into 3 cm (1¼ inch) cubes. Soak 12 wooden skewers in water for 30 minutes to ensure they don't burn during cooking.

# india & pakistan

2 Place the onion, garlic, ginger, lemon juice and spices in a food processor and process until finely chopped. Add the yoghurt and 1 teaspoon salt and process briefly to combine.

3 Thread the chicken pieces onto the skewers. Place the skewers in a large baking dish; coat the chicken with the spice mixture, and marinate for at least 4 hours or overnight, covered, in the refrigerator.

4 Cook the chicken on a hot barbecue grill or in a large, well-greased frying pan over high heat for about 5 minutes each side, or until golden brown and cooked through.

## lentil bhuja casserole

✹✹

Preparation time: 40 minutes + overnight soaking + 30 minutes chilling time
Cooking time: 1 hour 10 minutes
Serves 4–6

375 g (13 oz/2 cups) green lentils
2 carrots
1 large onion
1 large potato
1 teaspoon ground cumin
1 teaspoon ground coriander
1 teaspoon ground turmeric
90 g (3¼ oz/¾ cup) plain (all-purpose) flour
oil, for pan-frying
2 tablespoons oil, extra
2 garlic cloves, crushed
1 tablespoon finely grated fresh ginger
250 ml (9 fl oz/1 cup) tomato passata (puréed tomatoes)
500 ml (17 fl oz/2 cups) vegetable stock
250 ml (9 fl oz/1 cup) pouring (whipping) cream
200 g (7 oz) green beans, trimmed
pitta bread, to serve

1 Cover the lentils with cold water and soak overnight. Drain well.

2 Slice the carrots. Grate the onion and potato and drain the excess liquid. Combine the lentils, onion, potato, cumin, coriander, turmeric and flour in a bowl, and mix well. Roll the mixture into walnut-sized balls and place them on a foil-lined tray. Cover and refrigerate for 30 minutes.

3 Heat the oil, about 2 cm (¾ inch) deep, in a frying pan. Add the lentil balls in small batches and fry over high heat for 5 minutes, or until golden brown. Drain on paper towels.

4 Heat the extra oil in a large saucepan. Add the garlic and ginger and cook, stirring, over medium heat for 1 minute. Stir in the tomato passata, stock and cream. Bring to the boil, reduce the heat and simmer, uncovered, for 10 minutes. Add the lentil balls, beans and carrot, cover and simmer for 35 minutes, stirring occasionally. Serve with pitta bread.

NOTE: Make sure your hands are dry when shaping the lentil mixture into balls. The lentil balls can be made a day ahead and stored in an airtight container in the refrigerator.

lentil bhuja casserole

Roll the lentil mixture into walnut-sized balls.

Fry the lentil balls over high heat until they are golden brown.

Add the lentil balls, beans and carrot to the curry sauce.

## chickpea curry

Preparation time: 20 minutes
Cooking time: 30 minutes
Serves 4–6

2 x 400 g (14 oz) tins chickpeas (garbanzo beans)
3 tablespoons ghee, oil or butter
2 onions, finely chopped
1 teaspoon finely grated fresh ginger
½ teaspoon crushed garlic
1–2 green chillies, seeded and finely chopped
½ teaspoon ground turmeric
2 large, ripe tomatoes, seeded and chopped
1 tablespoon ground coriander
2 teaspoons garam masala
2 tablespoons lemon juice
2–3 tablespoons chopped coriander (cilantro) leaves

**1** Drain the chickpeas, reserving the liquid.

**2** Heat the ghee in a large saucepan; add the onion, ginger, garlic, chilli and turmeric and cook over medium heat until the onion is soft and golden.

**3** Add the tomato and cook until soft. Add the coriander and chickpeas, and cook for 10 minutes. Add 250 ml (9 fl oz/1 cup) of the reserved chickpea liquid and cook for a further 10 minutes.

**4** Add the garam masala, lemon juice and coriander, and cook gently for 2–3 minutes, adding more liquid, if needed, to make a sauce. Pour the chickpeas into a serving dish.

## vegetable korma

Preparation time: 20 minutes
Cooking time: 50 minutes
Serves 4–6

3 tomatoes
1 onion
300 g (10½ oz) cauliflower
300 g (10½ oz) pumpkin (winter squash)
3 slender eggplants (aubergines)
2 carrots
125 g (4½ oz) green beans, trimmed
2 tablespoons oil
2 tablespoons ready-made green masala paste
1 teaspoon chilli powder
1 tablespoon finely grated fresh ginger
375 ml (13 fl oz/1½ cups) vegetable stock
steamed rice, to serve

**1** Score a cross in the base of each tomato. Put in a heatproof bowl and cover with boiling water. Leave for 30 seconds, then transfer to cold water, drain and peel the skin away from the cross. Cut the tomatoes in half, scoop out the seeds and chop the flesh. Chop the onion. Cut the cauliflower into florets. Cut the pumpkin, eggplants and carrots into large pieces. Chop the beans.

**2** Heat the oil in a large heavy-based saucepan. Add the masala paste and cook over medium heat for 2 minutes, or until the oil separates from the paste. Add the

### garam masala

Although one of the best known Indian spice mixtures, garam masala does not contain turmeric, the ingredient that gives many curries their characteristic yellow colour. Garam masala was popularised in northern India during the Moghul reign of the seventeenth and eighteenth centuries; curries there are usually brown or pale in colour. (See recipe on page 114.)

# india & pakistan

chilli powder, ginger and onion, and cook for 3 minutes, or until the onion softens.

**3** Add the cauliflower, pumpkin, eggplant and carrot and stir to coat in the paste mixture. Stir in the tomato and stock and bring to the boil, then reduce the heat and simmer, uncovered, for 30 minutes. Add the beans and cook for 10 minutes or until the vegetables are tender. Serve with steamed rice.

## lamb kofta

Preparation time: **25 minutes**
Cooking time: **50 minutes**
Serves 4–6

1 kg (2 lb 4 oz) minced (ground) lamb
1 onion, finely chopped
2 green chillies, finely chopped
3 teaspoons finely grated fresh ginger
3 garlic cloves, crushed
1 teaspoon ground cardamom
1 egg
25 g (1 oz/⅓ cup) fresh breadcrumbs
2 tablespoons ghee or oil
steamed rice, to serve

SAUCE
1 tablespoon ghee or oil
1 onion, sliced
1 green chilli, finely chopped
3 teaspoons finely grated fresh ginger
2 garlic cloves, crushed
1 teaspoon ground turmeric
3 teaspoons ground coriander
2 teaspoons ground cumin
1 teaspoon chilli powder
2 tablespoons white vinegar
185 g (6½ oz/¾ cup) plain yoghurt
310 ml (10¾ fl oz/1¼ cups) coconut milk

**1** Line a baking tray with baking paper. Place the lamb in a large bowl. Add the onion, chilli, ginger, garlic, cardamom, egg and breadcrumbs, and season well. Mix until combined. Roll level tablespoons of the mixture into balls, and place them on the prepared tray.

**2** Heat the ghee in a frying pan, add the meatballs in two batches and cook over medium heat for 5 minutes at a time, or until browned all over. Transfer the meatballs to a large bowl.

**3** To make the sauce, heat the ghee in the cleaned frying pan, add the onion, chilli, ginger, garlic and turmeric, and cook, stirring, over low heat until the onion is soft. Add the coriander, cumin, chilli powder, vinegar, meatballs and 350 ml (12 fl oz) water and stir gently. Cover and simmer for 30 minutes. Stir in the combined yoghurt and coconut milk and simmer for another 10 minutes with the pan partially covered. Serve with steamed rice.

Mix the mince with the other ingredients until well combined.

Cook the meatballs in two batches until browned all over.

Mix together the yoghurt and coconut milk and stir in.

# raitas & relishes

Add interest to your curries with one of these spicy, fresh relishes, then cool down with a chilled vegetable or herb yoghurt raita. All of these recipes serve four, as an accompaniment.

## cucumber raita

Mix 2 peeled, finely chopped Lebanese (short) cucumbers with 250 g (9 oz/1 cup) plain yoghurt. Fry 1 teaspoon each ground cumin and mustard seeds in a dry frying pan for 1 minute until aromatic. Add to the yoghurt mixture with ½ teaspoon grated fresh ginger. Season well with salt and pepper and garnish with paprika. Serve chilled.

## carrot raita

Place 35 g (1¼ oz/¼ cup) chopped pistachio nuts, 40 g (1½ oz/⅓ cup) sultanas (golden raisins) and 80 ml (2½ fl oz/⅓ cup) boiling water in a small bowl. Soak for 30 minutes, then drain and pat dry with paper towels. In another bowl, place 2 grated carrots, 185 g/6½ oz/¾ cup) plain yoghurt, 1 teaspoon crushed cardamom seeds, 1 teaspoon ground cumin and ¼ teaspoon chilli powder and mix well. Chill for 30 minutes. Stir the pistachio nut mixture into the yoghurt mixture, keeping a couple of tablespoons aside to garnish. Serve chilled.

## coriander chutney

Wash, dry and roughly chop 1 bunch (90 g/3¼ oz) coriander (cilantro), including the roots. Place in a food processor with 25 g (1 oz/¼ cup) desiccated coconut, 1 tablespoon soft brown sugar, 1 teaspoon salt, 1 tablespoon grated fresh ginger, 1 small chopped onion, 2 tablespoons lemon juice and 1–2 small green seeded chillies. Process for about 1 minute, or until finely chopped. Serve chilled.

## fresh mint relish

Finely chop 50 g (1¾ oz) mint, 2 spring onions (scallions) and 1 green chilli. Mix with 1 crushed garlic clove, 1 teaspoon caster (superfine) sugar, ½ teaspoon salt and 2 tablespoons lemon juice. Cover and chill for at least 1 hour. Garnish with fine slices of lemon and spring onion and serve.

## fresh tomato relish

Mix together 2 diced tomatoes, 3 finely sliced spring onions (scallions), 2 tablespoons finely chopped coriander (cilantro) leaves, 1 finely sliced green chilli, 1 tablespoon lemon juice and 1 teaspoon soft brown sugar. Season with salt and pepper. Serve chilled.

## coconut bananas

Peel 2 large bananas and cut into thick slices. Dip into 80 ml (2½ fl oz/⅓ cup) lemon juice, then toss in enough desiccated coconut to coat each piece. Serve at room temperature.

## yoghurt and mint raita

Combine 250 g (9 oz/1 cup) plain yoghurt, 20 g (¾ oz/⅓ cup) chopped mint and a pinch of cayenne pepper and mix well. Serve chilled.

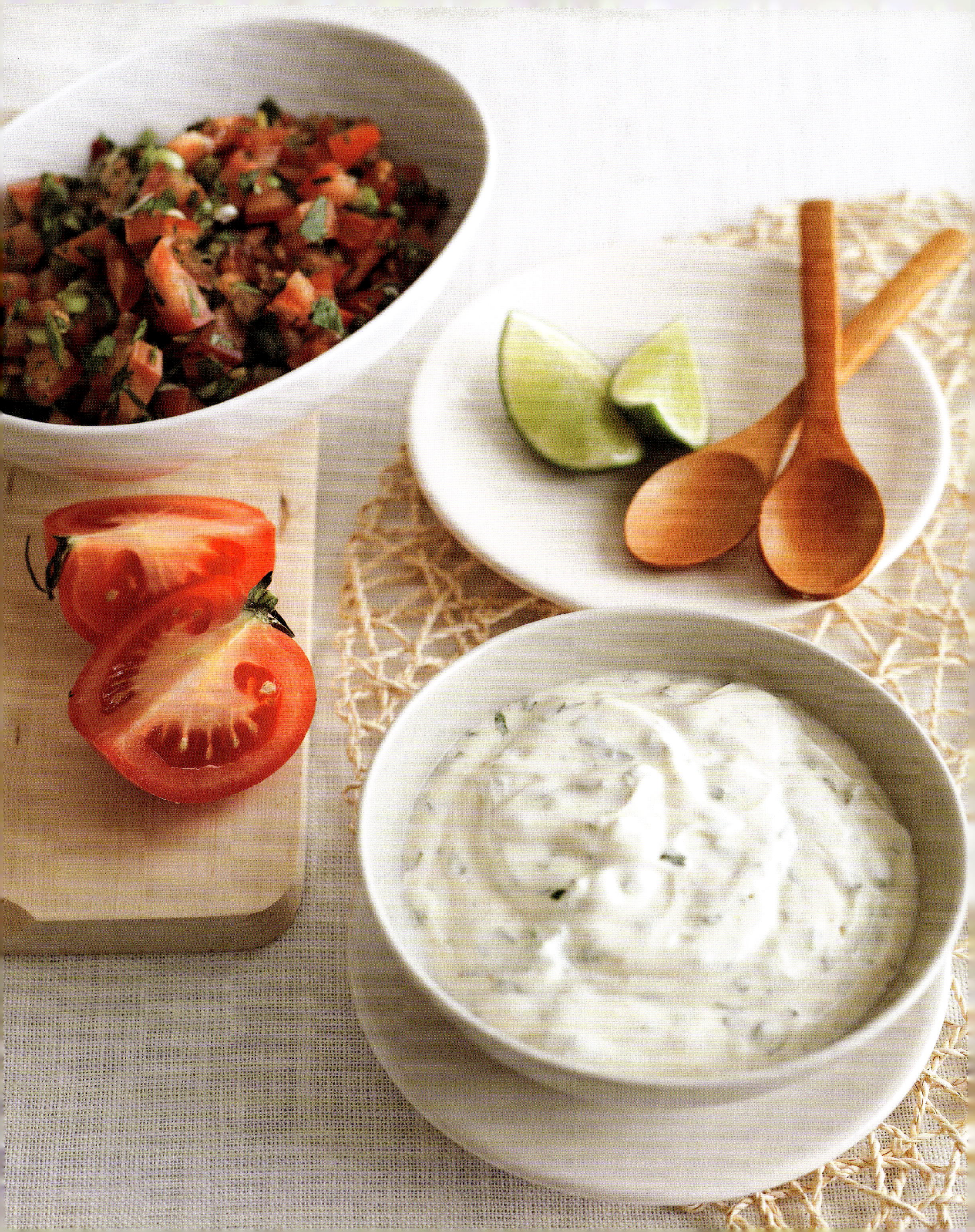

essential asian

## chicken mulligatawny

❋

Preparation time: 25 minutes + overnight chilling time
Cooking time: 4 hours
Serves 6

2 tomatoes, peeled
20 g (¾ oz) ghee
1 large onion, finely chopped
3 garlic cloves, crushed
8 curry leaves
55 g (2 oz/¼ cup) madras curry paste
250 g (9 oz/1 cup) red lentils, washed and drained
70 g (2½ oz/⅓ cup) short-grain rice
250 ml (9 fl oz/1 cup) coconut cream
2 tablespoons coriander (cilantro) leaves
mango chutney, to serve

STOCK
1.5 kg (3 lb 5 oz) whole chicken
1 carrot, chopped
2 celery stalks, chopped
4 spring onions (scallions), chopped
2 cm (¾ inch) piece of fresh ginger, sliced

**1** To make the stock, put all the ingredients and 4 litres (140 fl oz/16 cups) cold water in a large stockpot or saucepan. Bring to the boil, removing any scum that rises to the surface. Reduce the heat to low and simmer, partly covered, for 3 hours. Continue to remove any scum from the surface. Carefully remove the chicken and cool. Strain the stock into a bowl and cool. Cover and refrigerate overnight. Discard the skin and bones from the chicken and shred the flesh into small pieces. Cover and refrigerate overnight.

**2** Score a cross in the base of the tomatoes. Put in a heatproof bowl and cover with boiling water. Leave for 30 seconds then transfer to a bowl of cold water and peel the skin away from the cross. Cut the tomatoes in half, scoop out the seeds and chop the flesh.

**3** Melt the ghee in a large saucepan over medium heat. Cook the onion for 5 minutes, or until softened but not browned. Add the garlic and curry leaves and cook for 1 minute. Add the curry paste, cook for 1 minute, then stir in the lentils. Pour in the stock and bring to the boil over high heat, removing any scum from the surface. Reduce the heat, add the tomato and simmer for 30 minutes, or until the lentils are soft.

**4** Meanwhile, bring a large saucepan of water to the boil. Add the rice and cook for 12 minutes, stirring once or twice. Drain. Stir the rice into the soup with the chicken and coconut cream until warmed through — don't allow it to boil or it will curdle. Season. Sprinkle with the coriander and serve with the mango chutney.

## balti lamb

❋ ❋

Preparation time: 15 minutes
Cooking time: 1 hour 30 minutes
Serves 4

1 kg (2 lb 4 oz) lamb leg steaks
375 ml (13 fl oz/1½ cups) boiling water
1 tablespoon balti masala paste (page 114)
2 tablespoons ghee or oil
3 garlic cloves, crushed
1 tablespoon garam masala
1 large onion, finely chopped
4 tablespoons balti masala paste (page 114), extra
2 tablespoons chopped coriander (cilantro) leaves
coriander (cilantro) leaves, extra, to garnish
roti or naan bread, to serve

**1** Preheat the oven to 190°C (375°F/Gas 5).
**2** Cut the lamb into 3 cm (1¼ inch) cubes.
**3** Place the meat, boiling water and masala paste in a large casserole dish. Cover and cook for 30–40 minutes, or until slightly undercooked. Drain and reserve the stock.
**4** Heat the ghee in a balti pan or wok; stir-fry the garlic and garam masala for 1 minute. Add the onion and cook over medium heat until the onion is soft and golden brown. Increase the heat, add the extra masala paste and the lamb. Stir-fry for 5 minutes to brown the meat.

*chicken mulligatawny*

# india & pakistan

*pea, egg and ricotta curry*

## balti dishes

Balti is a type of curry originating in a region of northeastern Pakistan formerly known as Baltistan, and cooked in a traditional two-handled, cast-iron balti pan, karahi, which is similar to a wok. (Any lidded, heavy-based saucepan is a suitable replacement.) Traditional balti recipes are based on meat with subtle aromatic spices and only a small amount of chilli. The curry is slightly oily, contains fresh garlic, ginger and coriander, and is spiced with fennel, black mustard seeds, cloves, cardamom, coriander seeds, cumin, cassia bark and garam masala.

**5** Slowly add the reserved stock and simmer over low heat, stirring for 15 minutes.

**6** Add the coriander leaves and 250 ml (9 fl oz/1 cup) water. Simmer for 15 minutes or until the lamb is tender and the sauce is thickened slightly. Season to taste. Garnish with coriander leaves and serve with roti or naan bread.

## pea, egg and ricotta curry

Preparation time: 15 minutes
Cooking time: 30 minutes
Serves 4

4 hard-boiled eggs
½ teaspoon ground turmeric
2 small onions
125 g (4½ oz) baked ricotta cheese (see Note)
45 ml (1½ fl oz) melted ghee or oil
1 bay leaf
1 teaspoon finely chopped garlic
1½ teaspoons ground coriander
1½ teaspoons garam masala
½ teaspoon chilli powder (optional)
125 g (4½ oz/½ cup) tinned peeled, chopped tomatoes
1 tablespoon tomato paste (concentrated purée)
1 tablespoon plain yoghurt
80 g (2¾ oz/½ cup) frozen peas
2 tablespoons finely chopped coriander (cilantro) leaves

**1** Peel the eggs and coat them with the turmeric. Finely chop the onion and cut the ricotta into 1 cm (½ inch) cubes.
**2** Melt the ghee in a large saucepan and cook the eggs over moderate heat for 2 minutes until they are light brown, stirring constantly. Set aside.
**3** Add the bay leaf, onion and garlic to the pan and cook over moderately high heat, stirring frequently, until the mixture is well-reduced and pale gold. Lower the heat if the mixture is browning too quickly. Add the ground coriander, garam masala and chilli powder, if using, and cook until aromatic.
**4** Add the tomatoes, tomato paste and 125 ml (4 fl oz/½ cup) water. Cover and simmer for 5 minutes. Return the eggs to the pan with the ricotta, yoghurt, peas and ¼ teaspoon salt and cook for 5 minutes. Remove the bay leaf, sprinkle with the coriander and serve immediately.

NOTE: Baked ricotta cheese is available from delicatessens and some supermarkets, but it is easy enough to prepare your own. Preheat the oven to 160°C (315°F/Gas 2–3). Slice the required amount of fresh ricotta cheese (not cottage cheese or blended ricotta) into 3 cm (1¼ inch) thick slices. Place the ricotta on a lightly greased baking tray and bake for 25 minutes.

essential asian

## saffron

Saffron is prized for the fragrance, subtle flavour and the orange colour it imparts to foods. The wiry, vivid red-orange saffron threads are actually tiny stigmas of the saffron crocus flower — each delicate bloom must be plucked by hand and its three thread-like stigmas removed and dried. It takes more than 150 000 fresh flowers to produce 1 kg (2 lb 4 oz) saffron, which explains why it is the world's most expensive spice. Fortunately, only scant amounts are needed — ¼ teaspoon of loosely packed threads is sufficient to flavour and colour a dish to serve six people.

## saffron yoghurt chicken

❋

Preparation time: 30 minutes
Cooking time: 1 hour 15 minutes
Serves 4–6

1.5 kg (3 lb 5 oz) whole chicken
½ teaspoon saffron threads
2 tablespoons hot milk
3 garlic cloves, crushed
3 cm (1¼ inch) piece fresh ginger, finely grated
½ teaspoon ground turmeric
½ teaspoon ground cumin
¼ teaspoon ground cardamom
¼ teaspoon ground cloves
¼ teaspoon ground cinnamon
¼ teaspoon ground mace
90 g (3¼ oz/⅓ cup) plain yoghurt
1 tablespoon ghee or oil

1  Preheat the oven to 180°C (350°F/Gas 4).
2  Wash the chicken and pat dry. Remove any excess fat from inside the cavity.
3  Soak the saffron threads in the hot milk for 10 minutes, then squeeze the saffron to release the flavour and colour into the milk.
4  Transfer the saffron milk to a larger bowl; add the remaining ingredients and mix to combine.
5  Carefully lift the skin on the breast side of the chicken by working your fingers between the skin and the flesh. Pat half the spice mixture over the flesh. Rub the remaining spice mixture over the skin.
6  Place the chicken on a wire rack in a baking dish. Pour 250 ml (9 fl oz/1 cup) water into the dish; this will keep the chicken moist while it cooks. Roast the chicken for 1¼ hours or until browned and tender. Transfer the chicken to a serving dish, cover loosely with foil and allow to stand for 5 minutes before carving.

NOTE: Mace is a spice ground from the membrane which covers the nutmeg seed. It has a more subtle flavour than nutmeg.

# india & pakistan

## samosas and cucumber raita

Preparation time: 30 minutes
Cooking time: 25 minutes
Makes 24

1 tablespoon vegetable oil
1 onion, chopped
1 teaspoon finely grated fresh ginger
1 garlic clove, crushed
2 teaspoons ground coriander
2 teaspoons ground cumin
2 teaspoons garam masala
1½ teaspoons chilli powder
¼ teaspoon ground turmeric
300 g (10½ oz) potatoes, cut into 1 cm (½ inch) cubes and boiled
40 g (1½ oz/⅓ cup) frozen peas
2 tablespoons chopped coriander (cilantro) leaves
1 teaspoon lemon juice
6 sheets ready-rolled puff pastry
oil, for deep-frying

CUCUMBER RAITA
2 Lebanese (short) cucumbers, peeled, seeded and finely chopped
250 g (9 oz/1 cup) plain yoghurt
1 teaspoon cumin seeds
1 teaspoon mustard seeds
½ teaspoon finely grated fresh ginger

**1** To make the raita, put the cucumber and yoghurt in a bowl and mix together well.
**2** Dry-fry the cumin and mustard seeds in a small frying pan over medium heat for 1 minute, or until aromatic and lightly browned, then add to the yoghurt mixture. Stir in the ginger, season to taste with salt and pepper, and mix together well. Refrigerate until needed.
**3** Heat a wok over medium heat, add the oil and swirl to coat the base and side. Add the onion, ginger and garlic and cook for 2 minutes, or until softened. Add the spices, boiled potato, peas and 2 teaspoons water. Cook for 1 minute, or until all the moisture evaporates. Remove from the heat and stir in the coriander leaves and lemon juice.
**4** Cut out 12 rounds from the pastry sheets using a 12.5 cm (4¾ inch) cutter, then cut each round in half. Shape 1 semi-circle into a cone, wet the edges and seal the side seam, leaving an opening large enough for the filling. Spoon 3 teaspoons of the filling into the cone, then seal. Repeat to make 23 more samosas.
**5** Fill a wok or deep heavy-based saucepan one-third full of oil and heat to 180°C (350°F), or until a cube of bread dropped into the oil browns in 15 seconds. Cook the samosas in batches for 1–2 minutes, or until golden. Drain on crumpled paper towels and season. Serve with the chilled cucumber raita.

NOTE: Raita can be made ahead of time and stored in the refrigerator in an airtight container for up to 3 days.

Mix together the vegetables, currants, spices, lemon juice and soy sauce.

Fold the pastry over the filling to make a semicircle and press the edges together with a fork.

Cook the samosas two at a time until golden brown and puffed.

## saag paneer

✹ ✹

Preparation time: 20 minutes + 3 hours standing time
Cooking time: 30 minutes
Serves 4

2 litres (70 fl oz/8 cups) milk
80 ml (2½ fl oz/⅓ cup) lemon juice
100 g (3½ oz/⅓ cup) plain yoghurt
500 g (1 lb 2 oz) spinach
2 garlic cloves
2 cm (¾ inch) piece fresh ginger, finely grated
2 green chillies, chopped
1 onion, chopped
2 tablespoons ghee or oil
1 teaspoon ground cumin
½ teaspoon freshly grated nutmeg
125 ml (4 fl oz/½ cup) pouring (whipping) cream

1  Heat the milk in a large saucepan until just boiling. Reduce the heat, add the lemon juice and 2 tablespoons yoghurt, and stir until the mixture begins to curdle. Remove the pan from the heat and allow the milk mixture to stand for 5 minutes or until curds start to form.
2  Line a colander with muslin (cheesecloth). Pour the curd mixture into the colander and leave until most of the liquid drains away. Gather up the corners of the muslin, hold them together and squeeze as much moisture as possible from the curd. Return the muslin-wrapped curd to the colander and leave in a cool place for 3 hours until the curd is very firm and all the whey has drained away. Cut the cheese into 4 cm (1½ inch) cubes.
3  Steam the spinach over simmering water until tender. Squeeze out any excess moisture and chop finely. Place the garlic, ginger, chilli and onion in a food processor and process to form a paste.
4  Heat the ghee in a wok, add the paste and cook over medium heat for 5 minutes, or until the ghee begins to separate from the paste. Add the cumin, nutmeg, remaining yoghurt, 1 teaspoon salt and 250 ml (9 fl oz/1 cup) water and simmer for 5 minutes. Transfer the mixture to a food processor, add the steamed spinach and process until smooth. Return the mixture to the wok, add the chopped cheese and cream, and cook for 10 minutes or until the sauce is heated through.

## lamb dopiaza

✹ ✹

Preparation time: 20 minutes
Cooking time: 2 hours
Serves 4–6

1 kg (2 lb 4 oz) onions
5 garlic cloves
5 cm (2 inch) piece fresh ginger, finely grated
2 red chillies
1 teaspoon paprika
4 tablespoons chopped coriander (cilantro) leaves
2 tablespoons ground coriander
2 teaspoons black cumin seeds
4 tablespoons plain yoghurt
4 tablespoons ghee or oil
1 kg (2 lb 4 oz) diced lamb
6 cardamom pods, lightly crushed
1 teaspoon garam masala
steamed rice and naan bread, to serve

1  Slice half the onions and set aside; roughly chop the remaining onions.
2  Place the chopped onion, garlic, ginger, chilli, paprika, fresh and ground coriander, cumin seeds and yoghurt in a food processor and process until a smooth paste has formed.
3  Heat the ghee in a large saucepan; add the sliced onion and cook over medium heat for 10 minutes or until golden brown. Remove the onion from the pan using a slotted spoon and drain on paper towels.

# india & pakistan

**4** Add the lamb to the pan in batches and cook over high heat until browned. Remove from the pan and cover loosely with foil.

**5** Add the onion paste to the pan; cook for 5 minutes, or until the ghee starts to separate from the paste. Reduce the heat to low, return the meat to the pan with the cardamom pods, cover and cook for 1 hour or until the meat is tender.

**6** Add the fried onion and sprinkle the garam masala over the lamb; cover and continue cooking for 15 minutes. Serve with steamed rice and naan bread.

## butter chicken

✸ ✸

Preparation time: 30 minutes + 4 hours marinating time
Cooking time: 30 minutes
Serves 4

1 kg (2 lb 4 oz) boneless, skinless chicken thighs
60 ml (2 fl oz/¼ cup) lemon juice
250g (9 oz/1 cup) plain yoghurt
1 onion, chopped
2 garlic cloves, crushed
3 cm (1¼ inch) piece fresh ginger, finely grated
1 green chilli, chopped
2 teaspoons garam masala
2 teaspoons yellow food colouring
1 teaspoon red food colouring
125 g (4½ oz/½ cup) tomato paste (concentrated purée)
2 cm (¾ inch) piece fresh ginger, extra, finely grated
250 ml (9 fl oz/1 cup) pouring (whipping) cream
1 teaspoon garam masala, extra
2 teaspoons sugar
¼ teaspoon chilli powder
1 tablespoon lemon juice
1 teaspoon ground cumin
100 g (3½ oz) butter
steamed rice, to serve
kaffir lime (makrut) leaves, shredded, to serve

**1** Cut the chicken into strips 2 cm (¾ inch) thick. Sprinkle with 1 teaspoon salt and the lemon juice.

**2** Place the yoghurt, onion, garlic, ginger, chilli and garam masala in a food processor and process until smooth.

**3** Combine the food colourings in a small bowl, brush over the chicken and turn to coat. Add the yoghurt mixture and toss to combine. Cover and refrigerate for 4 hours. Remove the chicken from the marinade and allow to drain for 5 minutes.

**4** Preheat the oven to 220°C (425°F/ Gas 7). Bake the chicken in a shallow baking dish for 15 minutes, or until tender. Drain off any excess juice, cover loosely with foil and keep warm.

**5** Combine the tomato paste and 125 ml (4 fl oz/½ cup) water in a large bowl. Add the ginger, cream, extra garam masala, sugar, chilli powder, lemon juice and cumin and stir to combine.

**6** Melt the butter in a large saucepan over medium heat. Stir in the tomato mixture and bring to the boil. Cook for 2 minutes, then reduce the heat and add the chicken strips. Stir to coat the chicken in the sauce and simmer for 2 minutes longer or until heated through. Serve with steamed rice and shredded lime leaves.

### ghee

Ghee is clarified butter or pure butter fat. It gives a rich buttery taste to food and, because it has no milk solids, won't burn at high temperatures. Butter or a flavourless oil can be substituted for ghee. Alternatively, a mixture of half ghee and half extra light olive oil (which has little taste) has both the rich flavour of ghee and the health benefits of olive oil.

# breads

One of the surprises of northern Indian cuisine is the beautiful breads. From paper-thin parathas to puffed-up naan, they are traditionally cooked in a clay oven and torn apart to mop up curries.

### parathas
Place 280 g (10 oz/2¼ cups) atta flour and a pinch of salt in a large bowl. Rub in 40 g (1½ oz) ghee with your fingertips until fine and crumbly. Make a well in the centre and gradually add 185 ml (6 fl oz/¾ cup) cold water to form a firm dough. Turn onto a well-floured surface and knead until smooth. Cover with plastic wrap and set aside for 40 minutes. Divide into 10 portions. Roll each on a floured surface to a 13 cm (5 inch) circle. Brush lightly with melted ghee or oil. Cut through each round to the centre and roll tightly to form a cone shape, then press down on the pointed top. Re-roll into a 13 cm (5 inch) circle again. Cook one at a time in hot oil or ghee in a frying pan until puffed and lightly browned on both sides. Drain on paper towels. Makes 10.

### naan
Preheat the oven to 200°C (400°F/Gas 6). Sift together 500 g (1 lb 2 oz) plain (all-purpose) flour, 1 teaspoon baking powder, ½ teaspoon bicarbonate of soda (baking soda) and 1 teaspoon salt. Add 1 beaten egg, 1 tablespoon melted ghee or butter, 125g (4½ oz/½ cup) plain yoghurt and gradually add 250 ml (9 fl oz/1 cup) milk or enough to form a soft dough. Cover with a damp cloth and leave in a warm place for 2 hours. Knead on a well-floured surface for 2–3 minutes, or until smooth. Divide into eight portions and roll each one into an oval 15 cm (6 inches) long. Brush with water and place, wet side down, on greased baking trays. Brush with melted ghee or butter and bake for 8–10 minutes, or until golden brown. Makes 8.

### puris
Sift together 375 g (13 oz/2½ cups) wholemeal (wholewheat) flour and a pinch of salt. With your fingertips, rub in 1 tablespoon ghee or oil. Gradually add 250 ml (9 fl oz/1 cup) water to form a firm dough. Knead on a lightly floured surface until smooth. Cover with plastic wrap and set aside for 50 minutes. Divide into 18 portions and roll each into a 14 cm (5½ inch) circle. Heat 3 cm (1¼ inches) oil in a deep frying pan until moderately hot; fry one at a time, spooning oil over until they puff up and swell. Cook on each side until golden brown. Drain on paper towels. Serve immediately. Makes 18.

### chapattis
Place 280 g (10 oz/2¼ cups) atta flour and a pinch of salt in a large bowl. Gradually add 250 ml (9 fl oz/1 cup) water, or enough to form a firm dough. Knead on a lightly floured surface until smooth. Cover with plastic wrap and set aside for 50 minutes. Divide into 14 portions and roll into 14 cm (5½ inch) circles. Brush a heated frying pan with a little melted ghee or oil. Cook over medium heat, flattening the surface, until both sides are golden brown and bubbles appear. Makes 14.

### poppadoms
Poppadoms are thin wafers made of lentil, rice or potato flour. They can be found at Asian food stores. Use tongs to slide them one at a time into 2 cm (¾ inch) very hot oil — they should puff at once. Turn over, remove quickly and drain on paper towels.

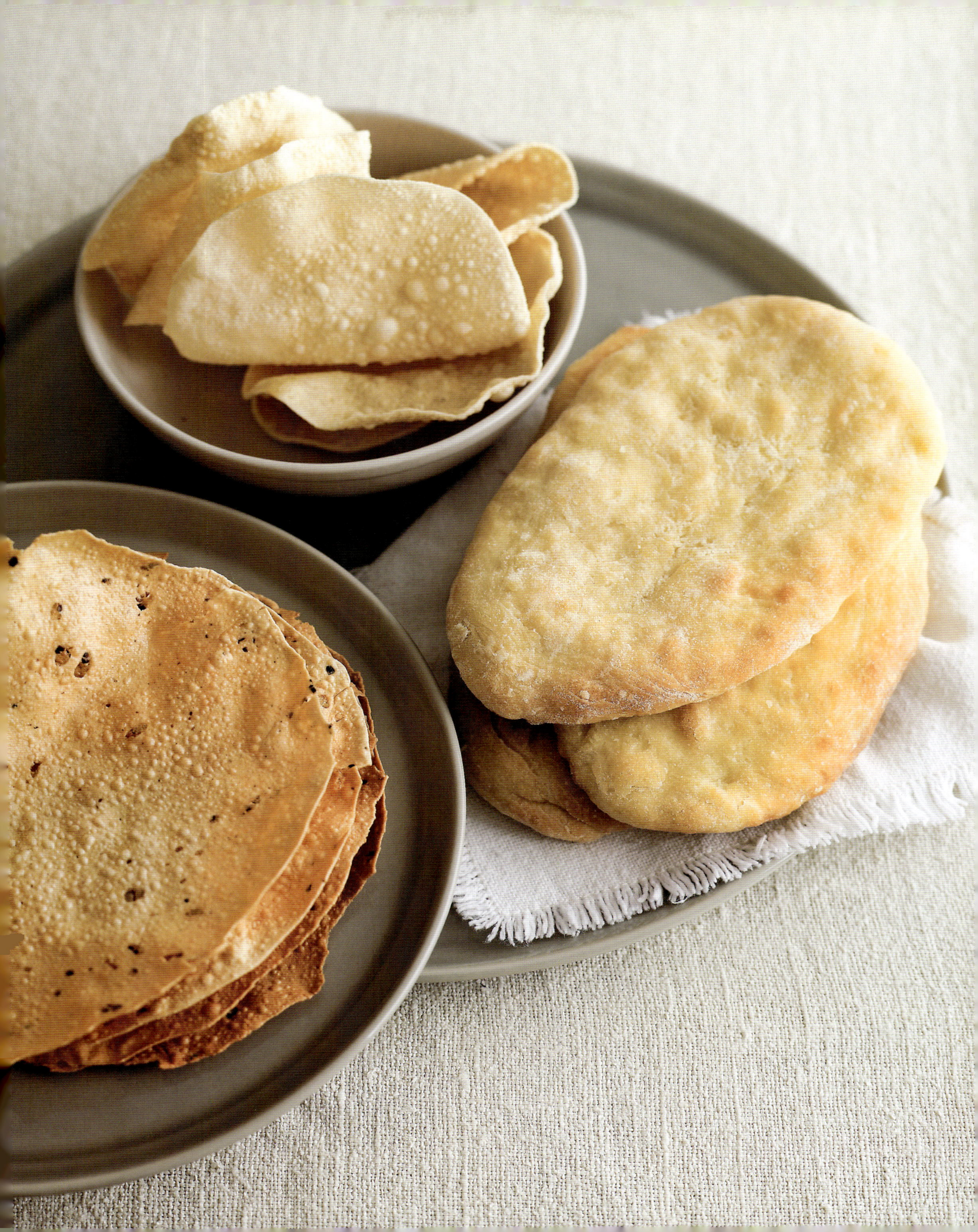

## dal

Preparation time: 15 minutes
Cooking time: 1 hour
Serves 4–6

250 g (9 oz/1 cup) red lentils
4 cm (1½ inch) piece fresh ginger, cut into 3 slices
½ teaspoon ground turmeric
3 tablespoons ghee or oil
2 garlic cloves, crushed
1 onion, finely chopped
pinch of asafoetida (optional, see Note)
1 teaspoon cumin seeds
1 teaspoon ground coriander
¼ teaspoon chilli powder
1 tablespoon chopped coriander (cilantro)

1  Place the lentils and 1 litre (35 fl oz/ 4 cups) water in a saucepan over medium heat and bring to the boil. Reduce the heat to low, add the ginger and turmeric, and simmer, covered, for 1 hour or until the lentils are tender. Stir every 5 minutes during the last 30 minutes to prevent the lentils sticking to the pan. Remove the ginger and stir in ½ teaspoon salt.

2  Meanwhile, heat the ghee in a frying pan. Add the garlic and onion, and cook over medium heat for 3 minutes, or until the onion is golden. Add the asafoetida, if using, cumin seeds, ground coriander and chilli powder, and cook for 2 minutes.

3  Add the onion mixture and fresh coriander to the lentils and stir gently to combine. Serve immediately.

NOTE: Asafoetida is a spice from the gum of a plant native to Afghanistan and Iran. When used sparingly, it has a subtle flavour.

## indian prawn fritters

Preparation time: 25 minutes + 30 minutes chilling time
Cooking time: 20 minutes
Makes 15

350 g (12 oz) raw prawns (shrimp)
1 onion, roughly chopped
2 garlic cloves, chopped
4 cm (1½ inch) piece fresh ginger, finely grated
1–2 tablespoons ready-made curry paste (see Note)
2 tablespoons lemon juice
15 g (½ oz/½ cup) coriander (cilantro) leaves
1 teaspoon ground turmeric
55 g (2 oz/½ cup) besan (chickpea flour)
oil, for shallow frying
plain yoghurt, to serve
lemon wedges, to serve

1  Peel the prawns and gently pull out the dark vein from each prawn back, starting at the head. Place the prawns, onion, garlic, ginger, curry paste, lemon juice, coriander, turmeric, ½ teaspoon salt and ¼ teaspoon pepper in a food processor and process for 20–30 seconds or until well combined. Cover and refrigerate for 30 minutes.

2  Roll tablespoons of the prawn mixture into round patties and lightly coat in besan flour. Heat about 2 cm (¾ inch) oil in a frying pan; add the fritters in batches,

and cook over medium heat for 3 minutes or until golden brown. Drain on paper towels and serve with plain yoghurt and lemon wedges.

NOTE: Curry pastes suitable to use with prawns are rogan josh, balti, tikka masala, vindaloo and tandoori.

## indian fried fish

Preparation time: 15 minutes
Cooking time: 20 minutes
Serves 4

500 g (1 lb 2 oz) firm white fish fillets
80 g (2¾ oz/¾ cup) besan (chickpea flour)
1 teaspoon garam masala
¼ teaspoon chilli powder
¼ teaspoon ground turmeric
2 tablespoons chopped coriander (cilantro) leaves
2 eggs, lightly beaten
oil, for shallow frying
steamed rice, to serve

**1** Wash the fish fillets, pat them dry with paper towels, and cut them in half lengthways.
**2** Sift the besan, 1 teaspoon salt, garam masala, chilli powder, turmeric and ¼ teaspoon pepper into a bowl. Add the coriander and stir to combine, then spread the mixture out on a plate.
**3** Dip each fish fillet into the egg, then into the spiced flour, shaking off any excess.
**4** Heat 2 cm (¾ inch) oil in a frying pan; fry the coated fish fillets in batches over high heat for 5 minutes or until crisp and golden. Serve with steamed rice and your choice of raitas (see page 202).

indian fried fish

essential asian

goan spiced mussels

## goan spiced mussels

Preparation time: 20 minutes
Cooking time: 20 minutes
Serves 4

1 kg (2 lb 4 oz) black mussels
3 tablespoons ghee or oil
5 garlic cloves, crushed
5 cm (2 inch) piece fresh ginger, finely grated
2 onions, finely chopped
3 red chillies, finely chopped
2 teaspoons ground cumin
2 teaspoons ground coriander
4 tomatoes, peeled, seeded and chopped
500 ml (17 fl oz/2 cups) fish stock
50 g (1¾ oz/1 cup) chopped coriander (cilantro) leaves
2 tablespoons lemon juice
steamed rice, to serve

**1** Remove the beards from the mussels and scrub them under cold water to remove any excess grit. Discard any which are already open.
**2** Heat the ghee in a wok, add the garlic, ginger and onion and cook over medium heat for 5 minutes, or until the onion is soft and golden. Add the chilli, cumin, coriander and tomato, and cook for 5 minutes.
**3** Add the mussels and stock and bring to the boil. Reduce the heat and simmer for 5 minutes. Discard any mussels that have not opened after this time.
**4** Remove the wok from the heat, stir through the chopped coriander and lemon juice, and serve with steamed rice.

## hyderabadi fish

Preparation time: 20 minutes
Cooking time: 30 minutes
Serves 4

3 tablespoons desiccated coconut
2 tablespoons cumin seeds

## india and the british

Colonial rule brought the British into contact with the rich cuisine of the Indian region. Many of the flavours were so much to their liking they became standard fare in Britain. Chutney, for example, now the traditional English accompaniment to cold meats, has its origin in the sweet-sour 'chatni' designed to partner fiery curries. Even Worcestershire sauce was originally an Indian recipe and owes its piquant flavour in large part to tamarind. The British breakfast dish kedgeree — curried rice with flaked smoked fish and garnished with hard-boiled eggs — comes from the Indian kadgeri, which is rice with onions, lentils and eggs. Mulligatawny soup is another British adaptation, this time of the southern Indian 'pepper water'. And while Indian teas helped establish the 'cuppa' as the British national drink, the returning colonials also brought back an enduring taste for lime with their gin.

# india & pakistan

3 tablespoons sesame seeds
1 tablespoon fenugreek seeds
2 onions, finely chopped
3 tablespoons oil
500 g (1 lb 2 oz) firm white fish fillets, cut into 5 cm (2 inch) pieces
1 tablespoon ground coriander
1 teaspoon ground ginger
1 teaspoon chilli powder
1 teaspoon ground turmeric
1 tomato, chopped
1 tablespoon tamarind concentrate
60 ml (2 fl oz/¼ cup) water

**1** Dry-fry the coconut, cumin, sesame seeds, fenugreek and onion in a frying pan for 10 minutes or until aromatic.
**2** Using a mortar and pestle or food processor, process the mixture until a paste is formed.
**3** Heat the oil in a large deep frying pan; add the fish and cook over medium heat for 5 minutes.
**4** Add the coconut mixture and the remaining ingredients and stir gently to combine. Cover and simmer for 5–10 minutes or until the fish is tender. Serve with steamed rice.

## cauliflower, tomato and green pea curry

Preparation time: 25 minutes
Cooking time: 20 minutes
Serves 4–6

1 small cauliflower
1 onion
2 large tomatoes
235 g (8½ oz/1½ cups) peas
60 ml (2 fl oz/¼ cup) ghee or oil
1 teaspoon crushed garlic
1 teaspoon finely grated fresh ginger
¾ teaspoon ground turmeric
1 tablespoon ground coriander
1 tablespoon ready-made vindaloo paste
2 teaspoons sugar
2 cardamom pods, lightly crushed
185 g (6½ oz/¾ cup) plain yoghurt

**1** Cut the cauliflower into small florets. Thinly slice the onion and cut the tomatoes into thin wedges. Steam the cauliflower and peas until tender.
**2** Heat the ghee in a large saucepan and cook the onion, garlic and ginger over medium heat until soft and golden. Add the turmeric, coriander, vindaloo paste, sugar, cardamom pods and yoghurt and cook for 3–4 minutes. Add the tomato and cook for 3–4 minutes.
**3** Add the cauliflower and peas and simmer for 3–4 minutes. Serve with steamed rice.

cauliflower, tomato and green pea curry

## vegetable pakoras

✹ ✹

Preparation time: 30 minutes
Cooking time: 20 minutes
Makes about 40

1 large potato
1 small cauliflower
1 small red capsicum (pepper)
1 onion
2 cabbage or 5 English spinach leaves
165 g (5¾ oz/1½ cups) besan (chickpea flour)
3 tablespoons plain (all-purpose) flour
2 teaspoons garam masala
2 teaspoons ground coriander
1 teaspoon bicarbonate of soda (baking soda)
1 teaspoon chilli powder
1 tablespoon lemon juice
½ cup frozen corn kernels, thawed
oil, for shallow frying
sweet mango chutney or tamarind sauce, to serve

**1** Boil the potato until just tender, then peel and chop finely.
**2** Finely chop the cauliflower, capsicum and onion. Shred the cabbage or spinach leaves.
**3** Sift the flours, garam masala, coriander, bicarbonate of soda and chilli powder into a bowl. Make a well in the centre, add 375 ml (13 fl oz/1½ cups) water and the lemon juice, and stir to make a smooth creamy batter, adding a little more water if necessary. Add the vegetables and mix in evenly.
**4** Heat about 2 cm (¾ inch) oil in a frying pan; place tablespoons of the mixture in the oil, about eight at a time, and fry over moderately high heat until golden; drain on paper towels. Serve hot with sweet mango chutney or tamarind sauce.

## battered chicken

✹ ✹

Preparation time: 30 minutes + 3 hours marinating time
Cooking time: 30 minutes
Serves 6

6 small chicken thighs, about 150 g (5½ oz) each
6 garlic cloves, crushed
5 cm (2 inch) piece fresh ginger, finely grated
3 tablespoons lime juice
125 g (4½ oz/½ cup) plain yoghurt
oil, for deep-frying

BATTER
80 g (2¾ oz/¾ cup) besan (chickpea flour)
1 teaspoon baking powder
1 teaspoon garam masala
¼ teaspoon ground turmeric
2 eggs, lightly beaten
2 tablespoons plain yoghurt

1 Remove the skin from the chicken and cut three deep incisions in each thigh.
2 Combine the garlic, ginger, ½ teaspoon salt, ½ teaspoon pepper, the lime juice and yoghurt in a large bowl. Add the chicken and toss to coat thoroughly. Cover and refrigerate for 3 hours.
3 To make the batter, sift the besan, baking powder, garam masala and turmeric into a bowl. Make a well in the centre, add the combined egg, yoghurt and 60 ml (2 fl oz/¼ cup) water, and stir until smooth.
4 Heat the oil in a wok or large frying pan. Dip each chicken thigh into the batter and deep-fry in batches for 8–10 minutes or until the chicken is crisp and tender. Serve with mango chutney.

## spiced roast leg of lamb

✻✻

Preparation time: 35 minutes
Cooking time: 2 hours
Serves 6

2 kg (4 lb 8 oz) leg of lamb
1 tablespoon lemon juice
1 garlic bulb, unpeeled
2 tablespoons ghee or oil
1½ tablespoons ground coriander
2 teaspoons ground cumin
2 cinnamon sticks
2 whole cloves
4 bay leaves
1 teaspoon chilli powder
4 cardamom pods, lightly crushed
125 g (4½ oz/½ cup) plain yoghurt
mint leaves, to garnish (optional)

1 Preheat the oven to 180°C (350°F/Gas 4).
2 Trim the excess fat from the lamb. Rub it all over with lemon juice and pepper, and place it in a roasting tin with the whole garlic and ghee. Bake for about 50 minutes, or until garlic cloves are soft.
3 Squeeze the soft cooked garlic pulp from the skins. Spread the garlic evenly over the lamb and sprinkle over the coriander and cumin. Add the cinnamon sticks, cloves, bay leaves, chilli powder and cardamom pods to the pan.
4 Roast the lamb for a further 50 minutes, or until cooked, basting it occasionally with the pan juices. Remove the lamb and set aside for 10–15 minutes before carving.
5 Add 375 ml (13 fl oz/1½ cups) water to the roasting tin and stir to combine the juices. Place the pan on the stovetop; cook over high heat until the liquid reduces and thickens. Remove the whole spices, and season with salt and pepper to taste. Stir in the yoghurt and heat through. Serve the sauce with the carved roast, garnished with mint leaves, if desired.

*spiced roast leg of lamb*

# burma

The food of Burma reflects the influences of her many neighbours, especially the two largest, China and India. China's influence can be seen in the use of noodles and soy sauce, while Burmese curries are Indian in origin, though not as highly spiced. They are flavoured with lots of garlic, ginger, turmeric, chilli, onion and shrimp paste and served with bowls of home-made chutneys and pickles. Bowls of piping-hot rice are served at every meal; though, unlike in other Asian countries, the rice is boiled until it is soft and moist, not steamed.

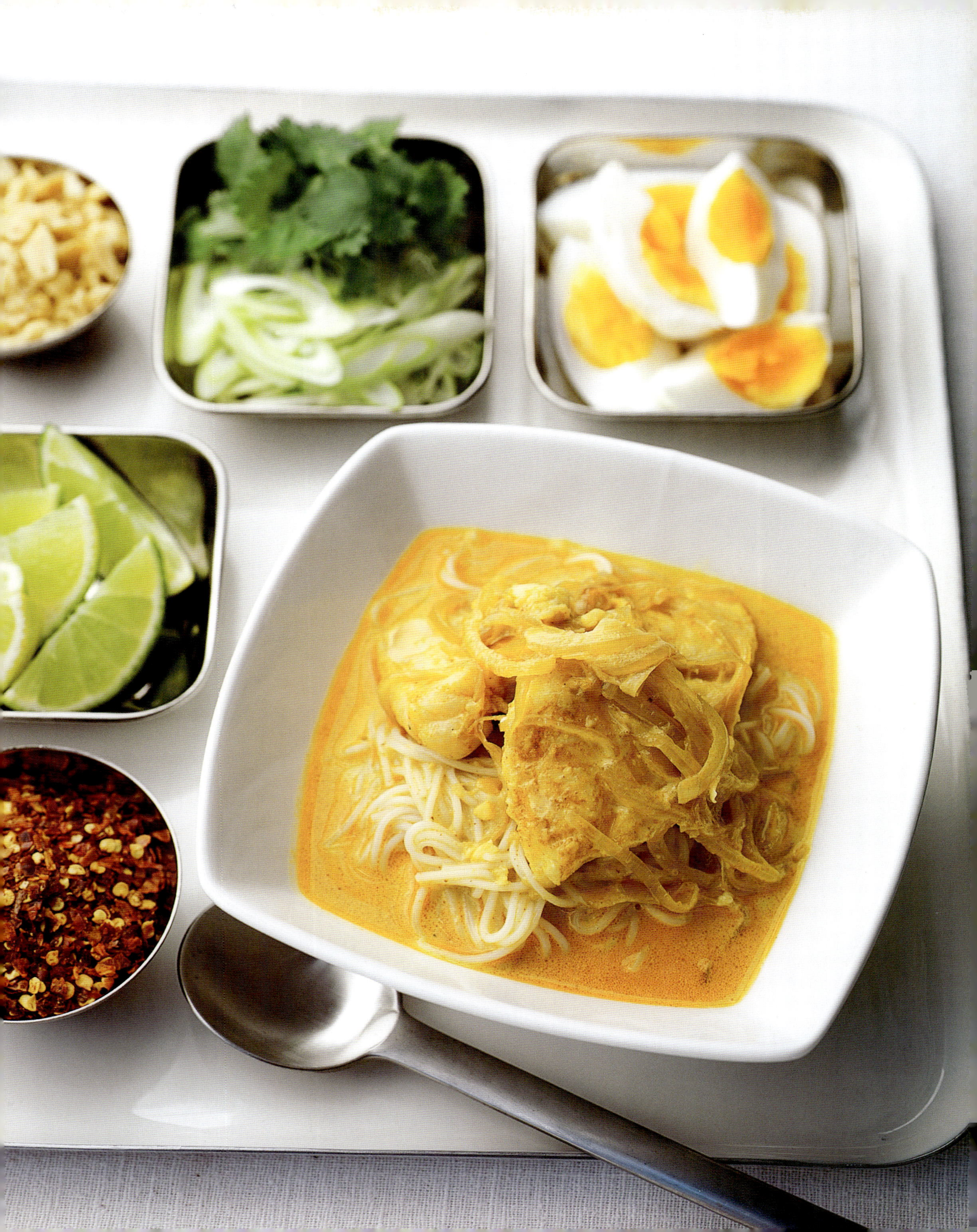

essential asian

# burma

## mixed vegetable salad

Preparation time: 25 minutes
Cooking time: 15 minutes
Serves 6

200 g (7 oz) green beans, trimmed, cut on the diagonal into 3 cm (1¼ inch) lengths
½ small cabbage, finely shredded
2 carrots, sliced
3 tablespoons white sesame seeds
125 ml (4 fl oz/½ cup) oil
2 onions, sliced
3 garlic cloves, thinly sliced
½ teaspoon ground turmeric
½ teaspoon paprika
125 g (4½ oz/1 cup) tinned bamboo shoots, sliced
90 g (3¼ oz/1 cup) bean sprouts, trimmed
1 Lebanese (short) cucumber, sliced
2 tablespoons lemon juice

**1** Place the beans, cabbage and carrot in separate heatproof bowls, cover with boiling water and leave for 1 minute, then drain. Plunge the vegetables into iced water, then drain again.
**2** Heat a wok; add the sesame seeds and cook, stirring, over a moderate heat until they turn golden brown. Set aside.
**3** Heat the oil in the wok; add the onion, and cook over a low heat until soft and golden. Add the garlic and cook for 2 more minutes. Add the turmeric and paprika and cook for a further 2 minutes. Drain on paper towels. Reserve the oil.
**4** Place the blanched vegetables and the bamboo shoots, bean sprouts and cucumber in a serving dish and drizzle over 2 tablespoons of the reserved cooking oil. Add the onion and garlic and toss through the vegetables along with ½ teaspoon salt and the lemon juice. Scatter the sesame seeds over the salad and serve as an accompaniment to a curry.

## fish in banana leaves

Preparation time: 30 minutes
Cooking time: 15 minutes
Serves 6

3 large banana leaves (see Note)
1 kg (2 lb 4 oz) firm white fish fillets
125 ml (4 fl oz/½ cup) coconut cream
2 garlic cloves, crushed
1 small onion, finely chopped
1 tablespoon finely chopped fresh ginger
2 teaspoons sesame oil
2 teaspoons salt
1 teaspoon ground turmeric
1 teaspoon paprika
¼ teaspoon chilli powder
2 teaspoons rice flour
2 tablespoons chopped coriander (cilantro) leaves
boiled rice, to serve

**1** Cut the banana leaves into six squares of about 25 cm (10 inches). Place the banana leaf pieces in a heatproof dish and pour boiling water over them. Leave for about 30 seconds, by which time the leaves should be pliable; drain.
**2** Cut the fish into 3 cm (1¼ inch) cubes. Place the fish in a large bowl and add the coconut cream, garlic, onion, ginger, sesame oil, salt, turmeric, paprika, chilli powder, rice flour and coriander. Use your hands to combine the ingredients well, making sure the fish is well covered with the mixture.
**3** Divide the fish mixture evenly and place each portion in the centre of a banana leaf piece. Fold in the sides of each piece to form a type of envelope. Hold the leaf in place with a toothpick or wooden skewer.
**4** Fill a large saucepan or steamer with 5 cm (2 inches) water. Place fish parcels on a steaming rack and cover and steam for 10–15 minutes, or until cooked. Open one parcel to check that the fish is cooked before serving. Serve with the boiled rice.

NOTE: If banana leaves are not available, cook the fish mixture in foil parcels.

Soak the banana leaf pieces in boiling water until they are pliable.

Use your hands to combine the fish mixture well.

## coconut prawn curry

Preparation time: **25 minutes**
Cooking time: **15 minutes**
Serves **4**

750 g (1 lb 10 oz) raw prawns (shrimp)
1 teaspoon ground turmeric
155 g (5½ oz/1 cup) roughly chopped onion
4 garlic cloves, crushed
½ teaspoon paprika
1 teaspoon seeded, finely chopped red chilli
pinch of ground cloves
¼ teaspoon ground cardamom
1 teaspoon finely chopped fresh ginger
3 tablespoons oil
2 tomatoes, diced
250 ml (9 fl oz/1 cup) coconut cream
2 tablespoons coriander (cilantro) leaves
boiled rice, to serve

**1** Peel the prawns, leaving the tails intact. Gently pull out the dark vein from each prawn back, starting at the head end. Toss the prawns with the turmeric.
**2** Place the onion, garlic, paprika, chilli, cloves, cardamom and ginger in a food processor and process until a paste forms.
**3** Heat the oil in a deep-sided frying pan; carefully add the spicy paste (it will splutter at this stage), stir it into the oil and cook over low heat for about 10 minutes. If the mixture starts to burn, add a little water. When the paste is cooked it should be a golden brown colour and will have oil around the edges.
**4** Stir in the prawns, tomato and coconut cream, and simmer for about 5 minutes or until the prawns are cooked. Stir in the coriander, season with salt and serve with the boiled rice.

## fried pork curry

Preparation time: **30 minutes**
Cooking time: **2 hours**
Serves **6**

310 g (11 oz/2 cups) roughly chopped onion
15 garlic cloves, crushed
4 tablespoons finely chopped fresh ginger
3 tablespoons peanut oil
1 tablespoon sesame oil
1½ teaspoons chilli powder
1 teaspoon ground turmeric
1.5 kg (3 lb 5 oz) boneless pork, cut into 3 cm (1¼ inch) cubes
1 tablespoon white vinegar
250 ml (9 fl oz/1 cup) water or chicken stock
2 tablespoons coriander (cilantro) leaves (optional)

**1** Place the onion, garlic and ginger in a food processor and process until a thick rough paste forms.
**2** Heat the peanut oil and sesame oil in a large frying pan; add the paste and cook over medium heat for about 15 minutes until it becomes a golden brown colour and has oil around the edges. Add the chilli powder, turmeric and pork, and stir well for a few minutes until the pork is well coated with the mixture.
**3** Add the vinegar and water, cover and simmer gently for 1½ hours or until the meat is tender. If necessary reduce the liquid by removing the lid and allowing the sauce to evaporate. Season with salt, to taste (the dish will need more if you use water rather than stock), and scatter over the coriander, if desired. Serve with boiled rice.

fried pork curry

# burma

## burma's national dish

Seafood, the product of the country's extensive coastline, features prominently in Burmese cuisine. The national dish is moh hin gha, a spicy fish soup with noodles. In Burmese cities, a 'take-away' family meal can be bought from street vendors who scoop steaming heaps of noodles into a supplied bowl, then ladle over the soup (which traditionally includes banana heart).

## fish soup with noodles

✹ ✹

Preparation time: 40 minutes
Cooking time: 25 minutes
Serves 8

750 g (1 lb 10 oz) firm white fish fillets, cut into 3 cm (1¼ inch) pieces
2 teaspoons ground turmeric
3 lemongrass stems
80 ml (2½ fl oz/⅓ cup) peanut oil
2 onions, thinly sliced
6 garlic cloves, crushed
2 teaspoons finely chopped fresh ginger
2 teaspoons paprika
1 tablespoon rice flour
500 ml (17 fl oz/2 cups) coconut milk
125 ml (4 fl oz/½ cup) fish sauce
500 g (1 lb 2 oz) somen noodles

GARNISHES
4 hard-boiled eggs, peeled and quartered
coriander (cilantro) leaves, chopped
spring onion (scallion), thinly sliced
4 limes, quartered
fish sauce, to taste
4 tablespoons chilli flakes
80 g (2¾ oz/½ cup) unsalted roasted peanuts, roughly chopped

1  Place the fish pieces on a plate and sprinkle with 1½ teaspoons salt and the turmeric. Set aside for 10 minutes.
2  Trim the lemongrass stems to about 18 cm (7 inches) long. Bruise the white fleshy ends so that the aroma will be released during cooking, and tie the stems into loops.
3  Heat the peanut oil in a large saucepan. Add the onion and cook over medium heat for 10 minutes, or until soft and lightly golden. Add the garlic and ginger and cook for 1 minute. Add the fish, paprika and rice flour and combine well. Pour in 1.5 litres (52 fl oz/6 cups) water, the coconut milk and fish sauce, and stir. Add the loops of lemongrass and simmer for 10 minutes, or until the fish is cooked.
4  Meanwhile, cook the noodles in a large saucepan of boiling water for 8–10 minutes, or until tender. Drain.
5  Place a mound of noodles in eight warm individual serving bowls and ladle over the fish soup. Offer the garnishes in separate small bowls so the diners can add them to their own taste.

essential asian

## mixed noodle and rice salad

Preparation time: **1 hour**
Cooking time: **40 minutes**
Serves **6**

300 g (10½ oz/1½ cups) long-grain rice
120 g (4¼ oz) fine dried egg noodles
60 g (2¼ oz) dried mung bean vermicelli
120 g (4¼ oz) dried rice vermicelli
90 g (3¼ oz/1 cup) bean sprouts, trimmed
2 potatoes, peeled and sliced
3 eggs
1 teaspoon oil
125 ml (4 fl oz/½ cup) peanut oil
4 large onions, quartered and thinly sliced
20 garlic cloves, thinly sliced
2 red chillies, seeded and sliced
25 g (1 oz/¾ cup) dried shrimps, ground to a powder
125 ml (4 fl oz/½ cup) fish sauce
185 ml (6 fl oz/¾ cup) tamarind concentrate
2 tablespoons chilli powder

**1** Fill two large saucepans with salted water and bring to the boil. To one, add the rice and cook for about 12 minutes or until tender. Drain, rinse and set aside. Add the egg noodles to the other pan and cook them for a couple of minutes until tender. Transfer the egg noodles to a colander, rinse under cold water and set aside. Place the mung bean vermicelli and rice vermicelli in separate heatproof bowls, cover them with boiling water and leave for 1–2 minutes until tender; rinse under cold water and drain. Place the bean sprouts in a heatproof bowl, cover them with boiling water and leave for 30 seconds; rinse under cold water and drain. Cook the potato in a large saucepan of boiling water until tender, drain, then rinse under cold water and set aside.
**2** Beat the eggs with ½ teaspoon salt and 1 tablespoon water. Heat the oil in a small frying pan; add the egg and cook over moderately low heat, gently drawing in the edges of the omelette to allow the uncooked egg to run to the outside. When the omelette is cooked through, flip it over and lightly brown the other side. Remove the omelette from the pan and allow it to cool before cutting it into thin strips.
**3** Heat the peanut oil in a large frying pan; cook the onion, garlic and chilli separately over a moderately high heat until crispy, adding more oil if necessary.
**4** Arrange the assorted noodles, rice, potato and bean sprouts on a large platter; place the omelette strips, chilli, onion, garlic, dried shrimp, fish sauce, tamarind and chilli powder in separate small dishes. The diners then serve themselves the salad ingredients and garnishes.

## burmese chicken

Preparation time: **15 minutes**
Cooking time: **1 hour**
Serves **4–6**

1.5 kg (3 lb 5 oz) whole chicken or chicken pieces (legs, thighs, wings, breasts)
2 tablespoons ghee or oil
2 onions, chopped
3 bay leaves
2 teaspoons ground turmeric
¼ teaspoon chilli powder
½ teaspoon ground cardamom
½ teaspoon ground cumin
½ teaspoon ground coriander
½ teaspoon ground ginger
1 cinnamon stick
2 lemongrass stems, white part only, chopped
6 garlic cloves, crushed
1 tablespoon grated fresh ginger
250 ml (9 fl oz/1 cup) chicken stock

*mixed noodle and rice salad*

# burma

**twelve varieties soup**

### rice burmese-style
In Burma, rice is not cooked by the absorption method. Instead, it is boiled in plenty of water, drained, then returned to the heat and covered to finish cooking.

1  If using a whole chicken, cut into pieces.
2  Heat the ghee in a large saucepan; add the onion and cook, stirring, until the onion is soft. Add the bay leaves, turmeric, chilli powder, cardamom, cumin, coriander, ground ginger, cinnamon stick, lemongrass, garlic and fresh ginger. Cook, stirring, for 1 minute or until aromatic.
3  Add the chicken pieces and stir to coat with the mixture. Stir in the stock and simmer, covered, for 45 minutes to 1 hour or until the chicken is tender.

## twelve varieties soup
✸

Preparation time: 45 minutes
Cooking time: 20 minutes
Serves 8

300 g (10½ oz) pork liver or lamb liver
200 g (7 oz) boneless, skinless chicken breast
30 g (1 oz) dried Chinese mushrooms
60 ml (2 fl oz/¼ cup) oil
3 onions, thinly sliced
4 garlic cloves, finely chopped
1 teaspoon finely chopped fresh ginger
2 tablespoons fish sauce
40 g (1½ oz/⅓ cup) sliced green beans, trimmed
40 g (1½ oz/⅓ cup) small cauliflower florets
30 g (1 oz/⅓ cup) sliced button mushrooms
15 g (½ oz/⅓ cup) shredded Chinese cabbage (wong bok)
20 g (¾ oz/⅓ cup) shredded spinach
30 g (1 oz/⅓ cup) bean sprouts, trimmed
3 spring onions (scallions), thinly sliced
1 tablespoon coriander (cilantro) leaves
3 eggs
1 tablespoon soy sauce
lime wedges (optional), to serve

1  Cook the liver in simmering water for 5 minutes. Remove from the heat, allow to cool and slice thinly. Cut the chicken into thin slices. Soak the mushrooms in hot water for 20 minutes. Drain, then squeeze to remove any excess liquid. Discard the stems and chop the caps finely.
2  Heat the oil in a wok, add the onion and cook over medium heat for 5 minutes, or until golden. Add the slices of liver and chicken and stir to combine. Add the garlic and ginger and cook for 1 minute, then pour in the fish sauce and cook for a further 2 minutes.
3  Put the Chinese mushrooms, beans, cauliflower, button mushrooms and onion mixture in a large saucepan. Add 2 litres (70 fl oz/8 cups) water, bring to the boil and cook until the vegetables are just tender. Add the cabbage, spinach and bean sprouts and cook for a further 5 minutes, or until just tender. Stir in the spring onion and coriander.
4  Break the eggs into the boiling soup and stir immediately. (The eggs will break up and cook.) Add the soy sauce and ¼ teaspoon pepper. Serve immediately with the lime wedges to squeeze into the soup, if desired.

## dry fish curry

✹ ✹

Preparation time: 20 minutes
Cooking time: 25 minutes
Serves 6

1 kg (2 lb 4 oz) firm white fish fillets, such as sea perch
2 tablespoons fish sauce
310 g (11 oz/2 cups) roughly chopped onion
4 garlic cloves, crushed
2 teaspoons finely chopped fresh ginger
2 teaspoons turmeric
1 red chilli, seeded and finely chopped
3 tablespoons oil
2 tablespoons chopped coriander (cilantro) leaves
boiled rice, to serve
lemon wedges, to serve

**1** Cut the fish into 4 cm (1½ inch) cubes. Place the fish pieces in a shallow dish and pour over the fish sauce.
**2** Place the onion, garlic, ginger, turmeric, chilli and 1 teaspoon salt into a food processor and process until a paste has formed.
**3** Heat the oil in a deep-sided frying pan; carefully add the spicy paste (at this stage it will splutter), stir it into the oil, lower the heat and cook gently for about 10 minutes. If the mixture starts to burn, add a little water. When the paste is cooked it should be a golden brown colour and have oil around the edges.
**4** Remove the fish pieces from the fish sauce and add them to the pan, stirring to cover them with the spicy paste. Raise the heat to medium and cook for about 5 minutes or until the fish is cooked through, turning it so it cooks evenly. Transfer the fish to a warm serving dish. If the remaining sauce is very liquid, reduce it over high heat until it thickens, then spoon it over the fish. Scatter the coriander over the fish and serve with the boiled rice and lemon wedges.

## beef, potato and okra curry

✹

Preparation time: 35 minutes
Cooking time: 2 hours 25 minutes
Serves 4

800 g (1 lb 12 oz) chuck or skirt steak
2 potatoes
200 g (7 oz) okra
155 g (5½ oz/1 cup) roughly chopped onion
4 garlic cloves, crushed
3 teaspoons finely chopped fresh ginger
1 teaspoon ground turmeric
½ teaspoon paprika
½ teaspoon chilli powder
4 tablespoons oil
1 tablespoon sesame oil
1 teaspoon ground cumin
375 ml (13 fl oz/1½ cups) water or beef stock
2 tablespoons garlic chives, finely snipped
1 lemon, cut into wedges
boiled rice, to serve

**1** Cut the beef into 3 cm (1¼ inch) cubes. Peel and cube the potatoes. Trim the okra; if large, halve them lengthways, otherwise leave whole.
**2** Place the onion, garlic, ginger, turmeric, paprika and chilli powder in a food processor and process until a thick paste forms.
**3** Heat the oils in a large heavy-based saucepan; add the onion mixture and cook over low heat for about 20 minutes, adding a little water if the mixture

starts to stick or burn. When the paste is cooked, it should be a golden brown colour with oil forming around the edges.
4  Add the beef and cook, stirring, for 5 minutes, until browned. Add the cumin and combine well. Pour in the water and simmer, covered, for about 2 hours or until the meat is tender. Add the potato and okra in the last 45 minutes of cooking; remove the lid for the final 10 minutes until the sauce reduces and thickens. Season with salt, to taste, sprinkle over the garlic chives, and serve with the lemon wedges and boiled rice.

## chicken curry

Preparation time: 45 minutes
Cooking time: 1 hour
Serves 6

1 kg (2 lb 4 oz) chicken thigh cutlets
2 large onions, roughly chopped
3 large garlic cloves, roughly chopped
5 cm (2 inch) piece fresh ginger, roughly chopped
2 tablespoons peanut oil
½ teaspoon shrimp paste
500 ml (17 fl oz/2 cups) coconut milk
1 teaspoon chilli powder (optional)
200 g (7 oz) dried rice vermicelli

ACCOMPANIMENTS
6 spring onions (scallions), sliced on the diagonal
10 g (¼ oz) chopped coriander (cilantro) leaves
2 tablespoons garlic flakes, lightly fried
2 tablespoons onion flakes, lightly fried
3 lemons, cut into wedges
12 dried chillies, fried in oil until crisp
fish sauce

1  Wash the chicken under cold water and pat dry with paper towels.
2  Place the onion, garlic and ginger in a food processor and process until smooth. Add a little water to help blend the mixture if necessary.
3  Heat the oil in a large saucepan; add the onion mixture and shrimp paste and cook, stirring, over high heat for 5 minutes. Add the chicken, and cook over medium heat, turning it until it browns. Add 1 teaspoon salt, the coconut milk and chilli powder, if using. Bring to the boil, reduce the heat and simmer, covered, for 30 minutes, stirring the mixture occasionally. Uncover the pan and cook for 15 minutes, or until the chicken is tender.
4  Place the noodles in a heatproof bowl, cover them with boiling water and leave them for 10 minutes. Drain the noodles and place them in a serving bowl.
5  Place the accompaniments in separate small bowls. The diners help themselves to a portion of the noodles, chicken curry and some, or all, of the accompaniments; the result will be as hot and tart as each person prefers.

chicken curry

# sri lanka

Despite its size, this tiny, beautiful island has an amazing variety of food and cooking styles. Traders and conquerors have left their gastronomic mark, but there is also a huge range of distinctive indigenous dishes. In most Sri Lankan households the main meal will be rice with one or two curries, soup, vegetables and a selection of sambols. Popular breakfast foods include crispy coconut and rice flour pancakes called 'hoppers'.

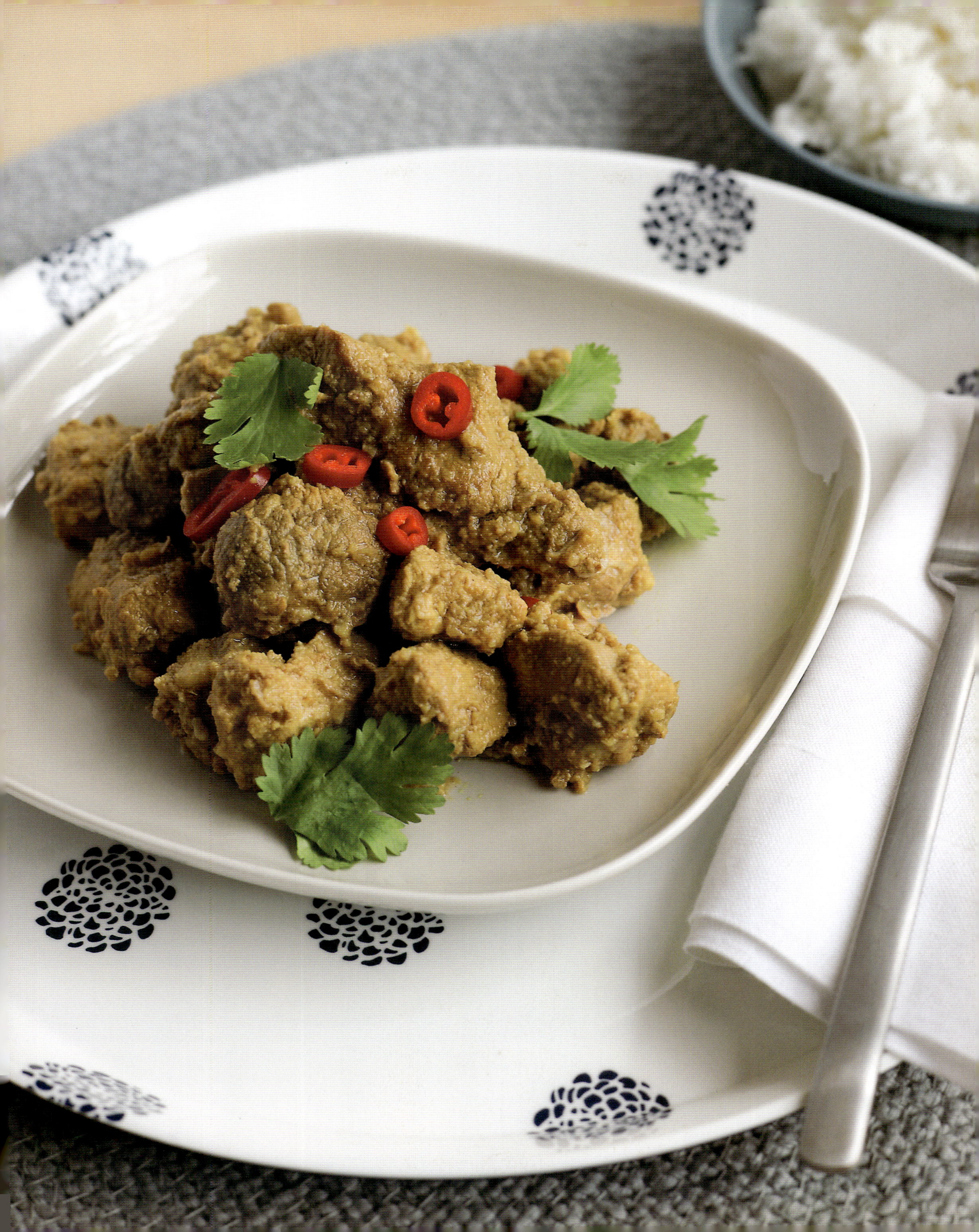

## lamb with palm sugar

Preparation time: 20 minutes
Cooking time: 1 hour 45 minutes
Serves 4

2 tablespoons oil
500 g (1 lb 2 oz) diced lamb
2 teaspoons chilli powder
1 tablespoon chopped lemongrass, white part only
1 tablespoon finely grated fresh ginger
300 g (10½ oz) sweet potato, peeled and sliced
2 tablespoons grated palm sugar (jaggery) or soft brown sugar
2 tablespoons lime juice
250 ml (9 fl oz/1 cup) water

**1** Heat the oil in a large heavy-based saucepan; add the lamb in batches and cook over high heat until browned. Drain on paper towels.
**2** Add the chilli powder, the lemongrass and the ginger to the pan, and cook for 1 minute.
**3** Return the meat to the pan with the sweet potato, palm sugar, lime juice and water; bring to the boil, reduce the heat and simmer, covered, for 1 hour. Remove the lid and simmer uncovered for 30 minutes or until the meat is tender.

lamb with palm sugar

## tamarind fish

Preparation time: 15 minutes + 1 hour marinating time
Cooking time: 15 minutes
Serves 6

2 garlic cloves, crushed
2 tablespoons tamarind concentrate
1 tablespoon Ceylon curry powder (pages 114–15)
½ teaspoon ground turmeric
1 tablespoon lemon juice
2 red chillies, finely chopped

### sri lankan food

Sri Lankan food reflects the cooking methods and flavours of the many countries which in the past have traded with or colonised the island. From the Portuguese, who ruled in the sixteenth and seventeenth centuries, come many of the sweetmeats served at festive occasions; frikkadels, a dish of fried meatballs, is a legacy of Dutch reign in the seventeenth and eighteenth centuries.

# sri lanka

6 fish steaks (such as swordfish, cod or warehou) about 150 g (5 oz) each
3 tablespoons oil
125 ml (4 fl oz/½ cup) coconut milk

**1** Combine the garlic, tamarind, curry powder, turmeric, lemon juice and chilli.
**2** Place the fish steaks in a shallow ovenproof dish. Brush the garlic mixture over both sides of the fish; cover and refrigerate for 1 hour.
**3** Heat the oil in a large frying pan over medium heat. Add the fish and cook for 2 minutes on each side. Stir in the coconut milk, reduce heat, cover and simmer gently for 10 minutes or until the fish flakes when tested with a fork.

# frikkadels

❋

Preparation time: **30 minutes**
Cooking time: **40 minutes**
Makes **about 25**

45 g (1¾ oz/½ cup) desiccated coconut
500 g (1 lb 2 oz) minced (ground) beef
1 garlic clove, crushed
1 onion, finely chopped
1 teaspoon ground cumin
¼ teaspoon ground cinnamon
½ teaspoon finely grated lime zest
1 tablespoon chopped dill
1 egg, lightly beaten
100 g (3½ oz/1 cup) dry breadcrumbs
oil, for deep-frying

YOGHURT DIPPING SAUCE
250 g (9 oz/1 cup) plain yoghurt
1 large handful mint, finely chopped
pinch of cayenne pepper

**1** Preheat the oven to 150°C (300°F/Gas 2). Spread the coconut on a baking tray and toast it in the oven for 10 minutes, or until dark golden, shaking the tray occasionally.
**2** Put the toasted coconut, beef, garlic, onion, cumin, cinnamon, lime zest and dill in a large bowl and mix to combine. Season with salt and pepper. Shape tablespoons of the mixture into balls. Dip the meatballs in the egg and then toss to coat in the breadcrumbs.
**3** Fill a deep heavy-based saucepan or deep-fryer one-third full of oil and heat to 180°C (350°F), or until a cube of bread dropped into the oil browns in 15 seconds. Add the meatballs in batches and cook for 5 minutes, or until deep golden brown and cooked through. Drain on paper towels.
**4** To make the yoghurt dipping sauce, combine the ingredients in a bowl and stir to combine. Serve the frikkadels with the dipping sauce.

Combine the coconut, beef, garlic, onion, spices, zest and dill.

Use your hands to roll tablespoons of the mixture into balls.

Deep-fry the balls until they are golden brown, then remove and drain on paper towels.

chicken omelette with coconut gravy

# sri lanka

## chicken omelette with coconut gravy

✹ ✹

Preparation time: 20 minutes
Cooking time: 25 minutes
Serves 4

½ barbecued chicken
1 large tomato, finely chopped
1 tablespoon chopped fresh dill
8 eggs
2 spring onions (scallions), chopped
lemon wedges, to serve

COCONUT GRAVY
410 ml (14¼ fl oz) coconut milk
½ teaspoon ground turmeric
2 cm (¾ inch) piece fresh ginger, finely grated
1 cinnamon stick
1 tablespoon lemon juice

1  Remove the bones from the chicken and shred the meat. Combine the chicken meat, tomato and dill in a bowl. Whisk the eggs and spring onion together in a large bowl.
2  Cook a quarter of the egg mixture in a lightly greased 25 cm (10 inch) non-stick frying pan. When the omelette is cooked, place a quarter of the chicken mixture in the centre, and fold in the four edges to form a parcel. Carefully transfer the omelette to a plate and repeat three times with the remaining mixture. Serve with the coconut gravy and lemon wedges.
3  To make the coconut gravy, place all the ingredients in a small saucepan and simmer for 15 minutes, or until the gravy thickens slightly.

## white vegetable curry

✹

Preparation time: 40 minutes
Cooking time: 35 minutes
Serves 4 as part of a meal

300 g (10½ oz) pumpkin (winter squash)
200 g (7 oz) potato
250 g (9 oz) okra
2 tablespoons oil
1 garlic clove, crushed
3 green chillies, seeded and very finely chopped
½ teaspoon ground turmeric
½ teaspoon fenugreek seeds
1 onion, chopped
8 curry leaves
1 cinnamon stick
500 ml (17 fl oz/2 cups) coconut milk
steamed rice, to serve

1  Peel the pumpkin and cut into 2 cm (¾ inch) cubes. Peel the potato and cut into 2 cm (¾ inch) cubes. Trim the stems from the okra.
2  Heat the oil in a large heavy-based saucepan; add the garlic, chilli, turmeric, fenugreek seeds and onion, and cook over medium heat for 5 minutes or until the onion is soft.
3  Add the pumpkin, potato, okra, curry leaves, cinnamon stick and coconut milk. Bring to the boil, reduce the heat and simmer, uncovered, for 25–30 minutes or until the vegetables are tender. Serve with the steamed rice.

## simmered beef in coconut gravy

✹

Preparation time: 30 minutes
Cooking time: 2 hours 20 minutes
Serves 4–6

2 kg (4 lb 8 oz) piece blade steak
2 tablespoons oil
3 tablespoons Ceylon curry powder (pages 114–15)
3 garlic cloves, crushed
2 tablespoons finely grated fresh ginger
3 tablespoons chopped lemongrass, white part only
2 onions, chopped
3 tablespoons tamarind concentrate
3 tablespoons vinegar
500 ml (17 fl oz/2 cups) beef stock
500 ml (17 fl oz/2 cups) coconut milk

1  Trim the meat of all fat and sinew and tie with kitchen string so that the meat holds its shape.
2  Heat the oil in a large heavy-based saucepan; add the meat and cook over high heat until it browns. Remove the meat from the pan and set aside.
3  Reduce the heat to medium; add the curry powder, garlic, ginger, lemongrass and onion, and cook for 5 minutes or until the oil begins to separate from the spices.
4  Return the meat to the pan; add the tamarind, vinegar, stock and coconut milk, and bring to the boil; reduce the heat, cover and simmer for 1 hour 45 minutes, or until the meat is tender.
5  Remove the meat from the pan and keep it warm. Bring the liquid to the boil and cook it, uncovered, for 10 minutes or until a thick gravy forms. Slice the meat and serve topped with the gravy.

NOTE: If Ceylon curry powder is not available or you do not have time to make your own, ask for a curry powder blend made for meat at an Asian food store.

## egghoppers with eggplant (aubergine) sambol

✸ ✸ ✸

Preparation time: 40 minutes +
 1 hour 10 minutes standing time
Cooking time: 2 hours 45 minutes
Makes 12–15

2 teaspoons dried yeast
125 ml (4 fl oz/½ cup) warm water
1 teaspoon caster (superfine) sugar
330 g (11 oz/1½ cups) medium-grain white rice
265 g (9 oz/1½ cups) rice flour
2 teaspoons salt
1.125 litres (39 fl oz/4½ cups) coconut milk
12–15 eggs

EGGPLANT SAMBOL
2 eggplants (aubergines), cut into 2 cm (¾ inch) cubes
60 ml (2 fl oz/¼ cup) oil
2 spring onions (scallions), finely chopped
1 teaspoon soft brown sugar
2 red chillies, finely chopped
2 green chillies, finely chopped
2 tablespoons chopped coriander (cilantro) leaves
1 tablespoon lemon juice

**1** Preheat the oven to 180°C (350°F/Gas 4). Place the yeast, warm water and sugar in a small bowl. Put the bowl in a warm, draught-free area for 10 minutes, or until foaming.
**2** Spread the rice on a baking tray and toast in the oven for about 15 minutes, until golden. Cool slightly, transfer to a food processor and process until finely ground.
**3** Combine the ground rice, rice flour and salt in a large bowl. Gradually whisk in the yeast mixture and coconut milk and mix to a smooth batter. Cover and set aside in a warm, draught-free area for 1 hour.
**4** To make the eggplant sambol, sprinkle the eggplant with salt and leave for 20 minutes; rinse and thoroughly pat dry with paper towels. Heat the oil in a large frying pan; add the eggplant, and cook over high heat for 10 minutes or until golden brown. Remove from the pan and toss through the spring onion, sugar, chilli, coriander and lemon juice. Set aside.
**5** Lightly grease a 23 cm (9 inch) non-stick frying pan. Pour 80 ml (2½ fl oz/⅓ cup) batter into the pan or enough to thinly coat the base of the pan; swirl the pan to cover the base. Crack 1 egg into the centre of the pan, and cook over low heat for 5–10 minutes — time will vary depending on the pan you use. When the edges are crisp and golden and the egghopper is cooked, gently remove it from the pan by sliding it out over the side of the pan. Cover the egghopper and keep it warm while cooking the remainder. Serve the egghoppers with the eggplant sambol.

# sri lanka

## cashew nut curry

Preparation time: 15 minutes
Cooking time: 55 minutes
Serves 6 as part of a shared meal

1 onion
2 green chillies
1 pandanus leaf (see Note)
750 ml (26 fl oz/3 cups) coconut milk
1 tablespoon finely grated fresh ginger
½ teaspoon ground turmeric
3 cm (1¼ inch) piece fresh galangal
8 curry leaves
1 cinnamon stick
250 g (9 oz) cashew nuts
2 tablespoons chopped coriander (cilantro) leaves

1  Chop the onion. Cut the chillies in half, remove the seeds and finely chop. Shred the pandanus leaf lengthways into about three sections, and tie into a large knot.
2  Combine the coconut milk, onion, ginger, turmeric, galangal, chilli, curry leaves, cinnamon stick and pandanus leaf in a saucepan and bring to the boil. Reduce the heat and simmer for 20 minutes. Add the cashew nuts, and cook for a further 30 minutes, or until the nuts are tender.
3  Remove from the heat and discard the galangal, cinnamon stick and pandanus leaf. Sprinkle over the coriander and serve with rice and a couple of other dishes.

NOTE: Popular in Southeast Asian cooking, pandanus leaves are most often used to flavour rice dishes. They are available from Asian food stores.

## red pork curry

Preparation time: 20 minutes + 1 hour marinating time
Cooking time: 20 minutes
Serves 4

4 dried red chillies
125 ml (4 fl oz/½ cup) boiling water
1 onion, chopped
2 garlic cloves, chopped
2 cm (¾ inch) piece fresh ginger, finely grated
1 tablespoon finely chopped lemongrass, white part only
500 g (1 lb 2 oz) pork fillet, cut into 2½ cm (1 inch) pieces
2 tablespoons tamarind concentrate
2 tablespoons ghee or oil
125 ml (4 fl oz/½ cup) coconut milk
red chillies, sliced, to garnish
coriander (cilantro) sprigs, to garnish

1  Place the chillies in a heatproof bowl, pour over the boiling water and soak for 10 minutes.
2  Process the chillies and soaking water, onion, garlic, ginger and lemongrass in a food processor until a paste has formed.
3  Place the pork in a shallow dish, add the chilli paste and tamarind, and mix to combine. Cover and refrigerate for 1 hour.
4  Heat the ghee in a wok, then add the pork in batches, and cook over high heat for 5 minutes. Return all meat to the pan with any leftover marinade, stir in the coconut milk, and simmer for 5 minutes. Garnish with chilli and coriander.

## spicy seafood

Preparation time: **20 minutes**
Cooking time: **15 minutes**
Serves **4**

500 g (1 lb 2 oz) raw prawns (shrimp)
2 squid tubes
250 g (9 oz) mussels
3 tablespoons oil
2 onions, sliced
2 garlic cloves, crushed
1 tablespoon finely grated fresh ginger
½ teaspoon ground turmeric
1 teaspoon chilli powder
1 teaspoon paprika
60 ml (2 fl oz/¼ cup) tomato passata (puréed tomatoes)
1 teaspoon grated palm sugar (jaggery) or soft brown sugar
steamed rice, to serve

**1** Peel the prawns. Gently pull out the dark vein from each prawn back, starting at the head end. Cut the squid tubes into 6 cm (2½ inch) squares and score a criss-cross pattern lightly into the flesh with a small sharp knife. Scrub the mussels and remove the hairy beards.
**2** Heat the oil in a large heavy-based saucepan or wok; add the onion, garlic and ginger, and cook over medium heat for 3–5 minutes or until the onion is soft.
**3** Add the turmeric, chilli powder and paprika, and cook for 2 minutes or until the oil begins to separate from the spices.
**4** Add the seafood to the pan and cook over high heat for 3–5 minutes or until the prawns are pink. Stir in the tomato passata and sugar and stir-fry for 3 minutes or until the sauce is heated through. Serve with the steamed rice.

## sri lankan lentils

Preparation time: **15 minutes**
Cooking time: **1 hour**
Serves **4**

spicy seafood

2 tablespoons oil
2 onions, thinly sliced
2 small red chillies, finely chopped
2 teaspoons dried shrimp
1 teaspoon ground turmeric
500 g (1 lb 2 oz/2 cups) red lentils
4 curry leaves
500 ml (17 fl oz/2 cups) coconut milk
250 ml (9 fl oz/1 cup) vegetable stock
1 cinnamon stick
10 cm (4 inch) lemongrass stem

**1** Heat the oil in a medium saucepan over medium heat. Cook the onion for 10 minutes, or until it is a deep golden brown. Remove half the onion and set aside to use as a garnish.
**2** Add the chilli, dried shrimp and turmeric, and cook for 2 minutes. Stir in lentils, curry leaves, coconut milk, stock, cinnamon stick and lemongrass; bring to the boil, reduce heat and simmer, uncovered, for 45 minutes. Remove the cinnamon stick and lemongrass. Garnish with reserved onion.

# sri lanka

## fish with flaked coconut

✹ ✹

Preparation time: 20 minutes
Cooking time: 50 minutes
Serves 4

45 g (1¾ oz/½ cup) desiccated coconut
110 g (3¾ oz/2 cups) flaked coconut
500 g (1 lb 2 oz) firm white fish fillets
½ teaspoon freshly ground black pepper
1 teaspoon ground turmeric
1 tablespoon lime juice
1 whole star anise
1 cinnamon stick
2 teaspoons cumin seeds
1 dried chilli
2 tablespoons oil
3 garlic cloves, crushed
3 onions, thinly sliced
steamed rice, to serve

1  Spread the desiccated and flaked coconut on a baking tray and toast it in a 150°C (300°F/Gas 2) oven for 10 minutes or until it is dark golden, shaking the tray occasionally.
2  Place the fish, pepper, turmeric and lime juice in a frying pan, cover with water and simmer gently for 15 minutes or until the fish flakes when tested with a fork. Remove the fish fillets from the liquid and allow to cool slightly before flaking it into pieces.
3  Dry-roast the star anise, cinnamon stick, cumin seeds and chilli in a frying pan over medium heat for 5 minutes. Transfer to a food processor or use a mortar and pestle and grind to a fine powder.
4  Heat the oil in a wok; add the garlic, onion and spice powder, and stir-fry over medium–high heat for 10 minutes or until the onion is soft.
5  Add the fish and coconut to the wok. Use two wooden spoons to toss the fish in the pan for 5 minutes or until heated through. Serve with the steamed rice.

## sri lankan curries

Unlike the curry powders of India, the spices that go into Ceylon curry powder — used in the black or brown curries that are characteristic of Sri Lanka — are roasted until dark, giving the mixture a completely different flavour and aroma. Dishes made with Ceylon curry powder have a distinctive deep colour. Chillies, ground or powdered, give red curries both colour and heat, which can be scorching! White curries, on the other hand, are based on coconut milk and are usually mild.

# desserts

A burst of cooling sweetness is the perfect end to an Asian meal. Most Asian desserts make use of the natural sweetness of tropical fruits — coconuts, bananas and mangoes. Sticky rice, black or white, pancakes and semolina are often included to balance the tartness of the fruit, while ice creams and chilled custards refresh the palate.

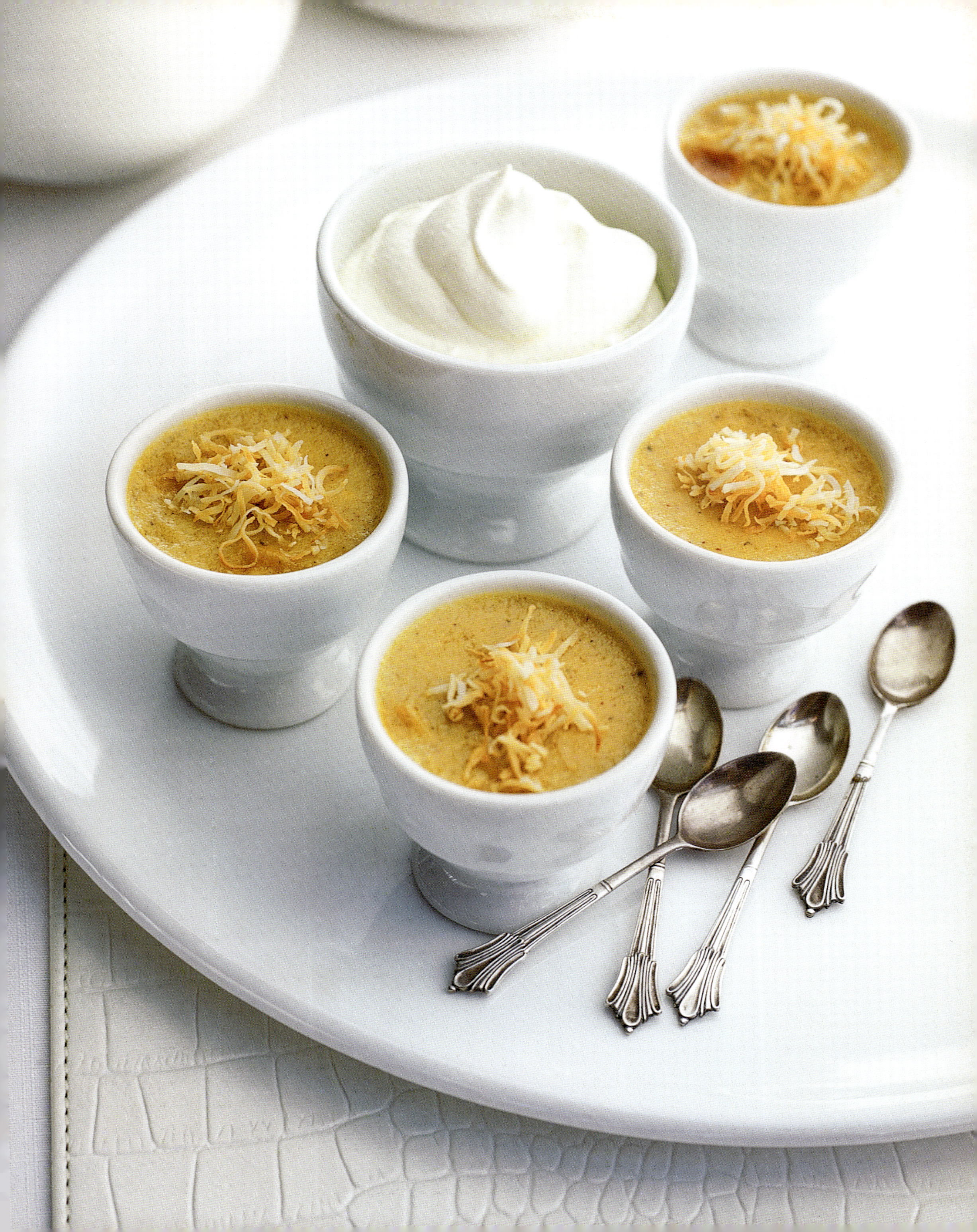

# coconut semolina slice

Preparation time: **20 minutes**
Cooking time: **1 hour**
Serves **8–10**

50 g (1¾ oz) sesame seeds
125 g (4½ oz/1 cup) fine semolina
230 g (8 oz/1 cup) caster (superfine) sugar
750 ml (26 fl oz/3 cups) coconut cream
2 tablespoons ghee or oil
2 eggs, separated
¼ teaspoon ground cardamom
fresh fruit, to serve

**1** Preheat the oven to 160°C (315°F/Gas 2–3). Lightly grease an 18 x 28 cm (7 x 11¼ inch) shallow tin.
**2** Toast the sesame seeds in a dry frying pan over medium heat for 3–4 minutes, shaking the pan gently, until the seeds are golden brown; remove from the pan at once to prevent burning.
**3** Put the semolina, sugar and coconut cream in a large saucepan and stir over medium heat for 5 minutes, or until boiling. Add the ghee and continue stirring until the mixture comes away from the sides of the pan. Set aside to cool.
**4** Whisk the egg whites until stiff peaks form. Fold the egg whites, egg yolks and cardamom into the cooled semolina mixture. Spoon the mixture into the prepared tin and sprinkle with the sesame seeds. Bake for 45 minutes, or until pale brown. Cut into diamond shapes and serve with fresh fruit.

## sago pudding

Preparation time: 20 minutes + 1 hour soaking and 2 hours chilling time
Cooking time: 20 minutes
Serves 6

200 g (7 oz/1 cup) sago
185 g (6½ oz/1 cup) lightly packed soft brown sugar
250 ml (9 fl oz/1 cup) coconut cream, well chilled

1  Soak the sago in 750 ml (26 fl oz/3 cups) water for 1 hour. Pour into a saucepan, add 2 tablespoons of the sugar and bring to the boil over low heat, stirring constantly. Reduce the heat and simmer, stirring occasionally, for 8 minutes. Cover and cook for 2–3 minutes, until the mixture is thick and the sago grains are translucent.
2  Half-fill six wet 125 ml (4 fl oz/½ cup) moulds with the sago mixture. Refrigerate for 2 hours, or until set.
3  Combine the remaining sugar with 250 ml (9 fl oz/1 cup) water in a small saucepan and cook over low heat until the sugar has dissolved. Simmer for 5–7 minutes, or until the syrup thickens. Remove from the heat and cool.
4  To serve, unmould the sago by wiping a cloth dipped in hot water over the mould and turn out onto a plate. Top with the sugar syrup and coconut cream.

## banana and coconut pancakes

Preparation time: 10 minutes
Cooking time: 30 minutes
Serves 4–6

1 tablespoon shredded coconut
40 g (1½ oz/⅓ cup) plain (all-purpose) flour
2 tablespoons rice flour
55 g (2 oz/¼ cup) caster (superfine) sugar
25 g (1 oz/¼ cup) desiccated coconut
250 ml (9 fl oz/1 cup) coconut milk
1 egg, lightly beaten
butter, for frying
60 g (2¼ oz) butter, extra
4 large bananas, cut on the diagonal into thick slices
60 g (2¼ oz/⅓ cup) lightly packed soft brown sugar
80 ml (2½ fl oz/⅓ cup) lime juice
finely shredded lime zest, to serve

1  Spread the shredded coconut on a baking tray and toast it in a 150°C (300°F/Gas 2) oven for 10 minutes, or until it is dark golden, shaking the tray occasionally. Remove from the tray and set aside. Sift the flours into a bowl. Add the sugar and desiccated coconut and mix. Make a well in the centre, pour in the combined coconut milk and egg, and beat until smooth.
2  Melt a little butter in a non-stick frying pan. Pour 60 ml (2 fl oz/¼ cup) of the pancake mixture into the pan and cook over medium heat until the underside is golden. Turn the pancake over and cook the other side. Transfer to a plate and cover with a tea towel (dish towel) to keep warm. Repeat with the remaining pancake batter, buttering the pan when necessary.
3  Heat the extra butter in the pan, add the banana, toss until coated, and cook over medium heat until the banana starts to soften and brown. Sprinkle with the brown sugar and shake the pan gently until the sugar melts. Stir in the lime juice. Divide the banana among the pancakes and fold over to enclose. Sprinkle with the toasted coconut and shredded lime zest.

*banana and coconut pancakes*

essential asian

## sticky rice

Sticky rice is also known as glutinous rice, though it does not contain gluten but a large amount of starch. It needs to be soaked before steaming. It is usually served as a dessert, but some Asian countries (for example, Laos) use it as an accompaniment to savoury dishes instead of white long grain.

## sticky rice with mangoes

✸ ✸

Preparation time: 40 minutes + overnight soaking time
Cooking time: 1 hour
Serves 4

400 g (14 oz/2 cups) glutinous white rice
1 tablespoon white sesame seeds
250 ml (9 fl oz/1 cup) coconut milk
70 g (2½ oz/½ cup) grated palm sugar (jaggery) or soft brown sugar
2–3 mangoes, peeled, stoned and sliced
60 ml (2 fl oz/¼ cup) coconut cream
mint leaves, to garnish

**1** Put the rice in a sieve and wash it under cold running water until the water runs clear. Put the rice in a glass or ceramic bowl, cover it with water and leave it to soak overnight, or for a minimum of 12 hours. Drain the rice.
**2** Line a metal or bamboo steamer with muslin (cheesecloth). Place the rice on top of the muslin and cover the steamer with a tight-fitting lid. Place the steamer over a saucepan of boiling water and steam over low–medium heat for 50 minutes, or until the rice is cooked. Transfer the rice to a large bowl and fluff it up with a fork.
**3** Toast the sesame seeds in a dry frying pan over medium heat for 3–4 minutes, shaking the pan gently, until the seeds are golden brown. Remove from the pan at once to prevent burning.
**4** Pour the coconut milk into a small saucepan, then add the palm sugar and ¼ teaspoon salt. Slowly bring the mixture to the boil, stirring constantly until the sugar has dissolved. Reduce the heat and simmer for 5 minutes, or until the mixture thickens slightly. Stir the mixture often while it is simmering, and take care that it does not stick to the bottom of the pan.
**5** Slowly pour the coconut milk mixture over the top of the rice. Use a fork to lift and fluff the rice. Do not stir the liquid through, otherwise the rice will become too gluggy. Let the rice mixture rest for 20 minutes before carefully spooning it into the centre of four warmed serving plates. Arrange the mango slices around the rice mounds. Spoon a little coconut cream over the rice, sprinkle with the sesame seeds, and garnish with the mint.

# desserts

## chinese fortune cookies

✹ ✹

Preparation time: 55 minutes
Cooking time: 50 minutes
Makes about 30

3 egg whites
60 g (2¼ oz/½ cup) icing (confectioners') sugar, sifted
45 g (1¾ oz) unsalted butter, melted
60 g (2¼ oz/½ cup) plain (all-purpose) flour

**1** Preheat the oven to 180°C (350°F/Gas 4). Line a baking tray with baking paper. Draw three circles with 8 cm (3¼ inch) diameters on the paper.
**2** Put the egg whites in a bowl and whisk until just frothy. Add the icing sugar and butter and stir until smooth. Add the flour and mix until smooth. Allow to stand for 15 minutes.
**3** Use a flat-bladed knife to spread 1½ level teaspoons of the mixture over each circle. Bake for 5 minutes, or until slightly brown around the edges. Working quickly, remove the cookies from the tray by sliding a flat-bladed knife under each. Place a written fortune message on each cookie. Fold the cookie in half to form a semi-circle, then fold again over a blunt-edged object like the rim of a glass. Allow to cool on a wire rack. Repeat with the remaining mixture.

NOTE: Cook no more than two or three cookies at a time, otherwise they will harden too quickly and break when folding.

## spicy coconut custard

✹ ✹

Preparation time: 20 minutes
Cooking time: 1 hour
Makes 8

2 cinnamon sticks
1 teaspoon freshly grated nutmeg
2 teaspoons whole cloves
310 ml (10¾ fl oz/1¼ cups) pouring (whipping) cream
90 g (3¼ oz) chopped palm sugar (jaggery) or soft brown sugar
270 ml (9½ fl oz) tin coconut milk
3 eggs, lightly beaten
2 egg yolks, lightly beaten
whipped cream, to serve
toasted shredded coconut, to serve

**1** Preheat the oven to 160°C (315°F/Gas 2–3). Combine the cinnamon, nutmeg, cloves, cream and 250 ml (9 fl oz/1 cup) water in a saucepan. Bring to simmering point, reduce the heat to very low and leave for 5 minutes to allow the spices to infuse the liquid. Add the palm sugar and coconut milk, return to low heat and stir until the sugar has dissolved.
**2** Whisk the eggs and egg yolks in a bowl until combined. Stir in the spiced mixture, then strain, discarding the whole spices. Pour into eight 125 ml (4 fl oz/½ cup) ramekins or dariole moulds. Place in a baking dish and pour in enough hot water to come halfway up the sides of the ramekins. Bake for 40–45 minutes until set. The custards should wobble slightly when the dish is shaken lightly. Remove the custards from the baking dish. Serve hot or chilled with whipped cream and the toasted shredded coconut sprinkled over the top.

spicy coconut custard

essential asian

## mango ice cream
✺

Preparation time: 20 minutes + freezing time
Cooking time: nil
Serves 6

400 g (14 oz) fresh mango flesh (see Note)
125 g (4½ oz/½ cup) caster (superfine) sugar
3 tablespoons mango or apricot nectar
250 ml (9 fl oz/1 cup) pouring (whipping) cream
extra mango slices

1  Place the mango in a food processor and process until smooth. Transfer the mango purée to a bowl and add the sugar and nectar. Stir until the sugar has dissolved.
2  Whisk the cream in a small bowl until stiff peaks form and then gently fold it through the mango mixture.
3  Spoon the mixture into a shallow cake tin, cover and freeze for 1½ hours or until half-frozen.
4  Quickly spoon the mixture into a food processor and process for 30 seconds, or until smooth. Return the mixture to the tin or a plastic container, cover and freeze completely.
5  Remove the ice cream from the freezer 15 minutes before serving to allow it to soften a little. Serve the ice cream in scoops with some extra mango.

NOTE: Frozen or tinned mango can be used if fresh mango is not available.

mango ice cream

## sticky black rice
✺ ✺

Preparation time: 10 minutes + 8 hours soaking time
Cooking time: 40 minutes
Serves 6–8

400 g (14 oz/2 cups) black rice
500 ml (17 fl oz/2 cups) coconut milk
90 g (3¼ oz/½ cup) grated palm sugar (jaggery) or soft brown sugar
3 tablespoons caster (superfine) sugar
3 fresh pandanus leaves, shredded and knotted
3 tablespoons coconut cream
3 tablespoons creamed corn

1  Place the rice in a large glass or ceramic bowl and add enough water to cover it. Soak the rice for at least 8 hours or overnight. Drain the rice and transfer it to a medium saucepan with 1 litre (35 fl oz/4 cups) water. Slowly bring to the boil, stirring frequently, then simmer for 20 minutes, or until tender. Drain.
2  In a large heavy-based saucepan, heat the coconut milk until almost boiling. Add the palm sugar, caster sugar and pandanus leaves, and stir until the sugars dissolve. Add the rice and stir for 3–4 minutes without boiling.
3  Turn off the heat, cover the pan and let it stand for 15 minutes to allow

# desserts

## pandanus leaves

Also known as screwpine, these long, flat, aromatic leaves add colour and a distinct flavour to both savoury and sweet dishes in Thailand, Sri Lanka, Malaysia and Indonesia. Before adding to the dish, partly shred the leaf or cut it into sections — this helps to release the flavour — then tie the leaf in a knot to hold the sections together. A short strip can be added when cooking rice. Available fresh or frozen from some Asian food stores, but more widely available dried.

the flavours to be absorbed. Remove the pandanus leaves. Serve the rice warm with the coconut cream and creamed corn.

## almond jelly

✹

Preparation time: 5 minutes + 1 hour chilling time
Cooking time: 5 minutes
Serves 4–6

80 g (2¾ oz/⅓ cup) caster (superfine) sugar
2 teaspoons agar-agar (see Note)
170 ml (5½ fl oz/⅔ cup) evaporated milk
½ teaspoon natural almond extract
3 mandarins, peeled and segmented, or 300 g (10½ oz) cherries, pitted and chilled

1  Put 500 ml (17 fl oz/2 cups) cold water and the sugar in a small saucepan. Sprinkle over the agar-agar. Bring the mixture to the boil and simmer for about 1 minute. Remove from the heat and add the evaporated milk and natural almond extract.
2  Pour the mixture into a shallow 18 x 28 cm (7 x 11¼ inch) cake tin to set. Chill for at least 1 hour. Cut the jelly into diamond shapes, and serve with the fruit.

NOTE: Agar-agar is similar to gelatin but does not need refrigeration to help it set. If it is unavailable, use 3 teaspoons of powdered gelatin sprinkled over 125 ml (4 fl oz/½ cup) cold water to soften. Stir the gelatin mixture into the water and sugar mixture, bring to the boil, then remove it from the heat — there is no need to simmer. Proceed with the method as described but refrigerate the jelly for 5 hours instead.

# egg tarts

☼ ☼ ☼

Preparation time: 45 minutes + 30 minutes chilling time
Cooking time: 15 minutes
Makes 18

OUTER DOUGH
165 g (5¾ oz/1⅓ cups) plain (all-purpose) flour
2 tablespoons icing (confectioners') sugar
2 tablespoons oil

INNER DOUGH
125 g (4½ oz/1 cup) plain (all-purpose) flour
100 g (3½ oz) lard, chopped

CUSTARD
55 g (2 oz/¼ cup) caster (superfine) sugar
2 eggs

1  To make the outer dough, sift the flour and icing sugar into a bowl. Make a well in the centre. Combine the oil with 80 ml (2½ fl oz/⅓ cup) water and pour into the dry ingredients. Mix with a flat-bladed knife, using a cutting action, to form a rough dough. (If the flour is very dry, add a little water.) Turn out onto a lightly floured surface and gather together in a smooth ball. Cover and set aside for 15 minutes.

2  To make the inner dough, sift flour into a bowl. Using your fingertips, rub the lard into the flour until the mixture resembles breadcrumbs. Press the dough together into a ball, cover and set aside for 15 minutes.

3  On a lightly floured surface, roll the outer dough into a rectangle about 10 x 20 cm (4 x 8 inches). On a lightly floured surface, roll the inner dough into a smaller rectangle, one-third the size of the outer dough. Place the inner dough in the centre of the outer dough. Fold the outer dough over the inner dough so the short edges overlap and the inner dough is enclosed. Pinch the edges together to seal. Roll the dough away from you in one direction into a long rectangle, until it is about half as thick as it was previously. Fold the pastry into three layers by taking the left-hand edge over first, and then folding the right-hand edge on top. Wrap the dough in plastic wrap and refrigerate for 30 minutes. Preheat the oven to 210°C (415°F/Gas 6–7). Brush two 12-hole round-based patty pans with melted butter or oil.

4  To make the custard, place 80 ml (2½ fl oz/⅓ cup) water and the sugar in a saucepan and stir, without boiling, until sugar has dissolved. Bring to the boil and simmer, without stirring, for 1 minute. Cool the mixture for 5 minutes. Put the eggs in a bowl and whisk lightly with a fork. Whisk the sugar syrup into the eggs until just combined. Strain.

5  Place the pastry on a lightly floured surface. With one open end towards you, roll out to a rectangle about 3 mm (⅛ inch) thick. Cut out rounds of pastry using a 7 cm (2¾ inch) fluted cutter. Carefully place the pastry rounds into the prepared patty pans. Fill each pastry case two-thirds full with the egg custard mixture. Bake for 15 minutes, or until just set. Be careful not to overcook. Leave the egg tarts to cool for 3 minutes before removing from the tin. Cool the tarts on a wire rack, and serve warm or cold.

egg tarts

Fold the outer dough over the inner dough so the short edges of the outer dough overlap.

Roll the dough in one direction into a long rectangle until it is about half as thick as it was before.

Cut out the rounds of pastry using a fluted cutter and carefully place the rounds into the patty pans.

# desserts

## sweet won tons

✹ ✹

Preparation time: **15 minutes**
Cooking time: **30 minutes**
Makes **30**

125 g (4½ oz) fresh dates, pitted and chopped
2 bananas, finely chopped
45 g (1¾ oz/½ cup) flaked almonds, lightly crushed
½ teaspoon ground cinnamon
60 won ton wrappers
oil, for deep-frying
icing (confectioners') sugar, to dust

**1** Mix together the dates, banana, almonds and cinnamon. Put 2 teaspoons of the fruit mixture into the centre of a won ton wrapper, and brush the edges lightly with water. Place another won ton wrapper on top at an angle so the wrappers make a star shape. Place the won tons on a baking tray lined with baking paper. Repeat with the remaining ingredients (do not stack the won tons on top of each other).
**2** Fill a deep-fryer or large heavy-based saucepan one-third full of oil and heat to 180ºC (350ºF), or until a cube of bread dropped into the oil browns in 15 seconds. Deep-fry the won tons, in small batches for 2 minutes, or until crisp and golden. Drain on paper towels. Dust lightly with the icing sugar before serving.

# index

Page numbers in *italics* refer to photographs. Page numbers in **bold** refer to margin notes.

almond jelly  245, *245*
annatto seeds  **93**
Asian greens  12, *12*
Asian rice flour  15
Assam tea  180
atta flour  15
aubergines  *see* eggplants

bagoong  18, *18*, **88**
bai horapha  12, *12*
bai kaphrao  13, *13*
bai manglaek  *12*, 12–13
baked fish with spices  57, *57*
baked spiced fish cutlets  52–53
Bali, feasts in  **61**
Balinese chilli squid  63, *63*
Balinese fried fish  60–61, *61*
Balinese fried rice  60, *60*
balti dishes  **205**
  balti lamb  204–5
  balti masala paste  114
bamboo shoots  12, *12*
banana leaves  12, *12*
  fish in banana leaves  *220*, 221
  prawns steamed in banana leaves  131, *131*
  steamed fish in banana leaves  105, *105*
bananas
  banana and coconut pancakes  241, *241*
  coconut bananas  202
barbecued food
  barbecued beef  *160*, 160–61
  barbecued Chinese pork  12
  barbecued fish  *140*, 141
  barbecued seafood  *78*, 79
basil  12–13, *12–13*
  fried rice with coriander and basil  124–25
  steamed mussels with lemon grass, basil and wine  112, *112*
basmati rice  94

batter  37, 190, 216
battered chicken  216–17
bean curd  *see* tofu
bean sprouts  **49**
beans  *see* black beans; green beans; snake beans
beef
  barbecued beef  *160*, 160–61
  beef, potato and okra curry  226–27
  beef fillet in coconut  46
  beef fondue with rice paper wrappers and salad  157, *157*
  beef pho (beef soup), 141, *141*
  beef soup with rice noodles  50, *50*
  beef with capsicum and oyster sauce  38
  beef with mandarin  24, *24*
  fried rice noodle pancake with garlic beef  150, *150*
  frikkadels  231, *231*
  Indonesian rendang  59, *59*
  kofta on skewers  54
  Laotian beef salad  132–33
  Laotian dried beef with green papaya salad  133, *133*
  lemon grass beef skewers  135, *135*
  Madras curry  194, *194*
  Malaysian rendang  80–81
  meat dumpling soup, 165, *165*
  rotis with spicy meat filling  *74*, 74–75
  simmered beef in coconut gravy  233
  skewers of beef, capsicum and spring onion  191, *191*
  sour beef soup  96–97
  spicy beef curry  121
  steak in roasted sesame seed marinade  178
  stir-fried beef and snow peas  28
  stir-fried hot beef  62–63
  stock  10
  sukiyaki  175
  teriyaki steak kebabs  54
  Thai beef salad  125, *125*
  vermicelli with stir-fried beef and vegetables, 168–69
  warm beef and watercress salad  145
besan  15
bird's eye chillies  13, *13*
blachan  *see* shrimp paste

black beans  13, *13*
  eggplant slices in black bean sauce  *142*, 142–43
black fungus  13, *13*
  ginger chicken with black fungus  122–23
black satin chicken  36–37
black tea  180
blended tea  180
bok choy  12, *12*
braised duck with mushrooms  146, *146*
breads  210
Burma  218–27
  national dish  **223**
Burmese chicken  224–25
butter chicken  209, *209*

Cambodia  126–35
Cambodian mint  19, *19*
candlenuts  13, *13*
Cantonese lemon chicken  23, *23*
capsicums
  beef with capsicum and oyster sauce  38
  skewers of beef, capsicum and spring onion  191, *191*
  stuffed capsicums  34
caramel sauce  139
caramelised prawns  139, *139*
cardamom  13, *13*
carrot raita  202
cashews
  cashew nut curry  235, *235*
  chicken with pineapple and cashews  151, *151*
cauliflower
  cauliflower, tomato and green pea curry  215, *215*
  stir-fried cauliflower and snake beans  109
celery cabbage  *see* Chinese cabbage
cellophane noodles  *see* mung bean vermicelli
Ceylon curry powder  114
Ceylon tea  180
cha siew  12, *12*
chapatti  15
chapattis  210
chestnuts, water  19, *19*

# index

chicken
- battered chicken 216–17
- black satin chicken 36–37
- Burmese chicken 224–25
- butter chicken 209, *209*
- Cantonese lemon chicken 23, *23*
- chicken adobo 93, *93*
- chicken and peanut panang curry 107, *107*
- chicken and pumpkin stew 129, *129*
- chicken and sweet corn soup 25
- chicken and vegetable salad 116, *116*
- chicken curry 227, *227*
- chicken domburi 183
- chicken kapitan 81, *81*
- chicken mince with herbs and spices 132, *132*
- chicken moneybags 34, *35*
- chicken mulligatawny 204, *204*
- chicken omelette with coconut gravy *232*, 233
- chicken satays 54
- chicken soup with vermicelli and vegetables *48*, 49
- chicken stew 169, *169*
- chicken tikka 198–99
- chicken with pineapple and cashews 151, *151*
- chopping 11, *11*
- clay pot chicken and vegetables 31, *31*
- crispy skin chicken 39, *39*
- curried rice noodles with chicken 116–17
- empanadas 97, *97*
- ginger chicken with black fungus 122–23
- green chicken curry 103, *103*
- green pawpaw, chicken and fresh herb salad 150–51
- Malaysian coconut chicken 74
- nonya lime chicken 83, *83*
- rice with chicken and mushrooms 190–91
- rice with chicken and seafood 89, *89*
- saffron yoghurt chicken 206, *206*
- savoury egg custard 176, *176*
- smoked five-spice chicken 41, *41*
- spicy roast chicken 50, *51*

*chicken, contd...*
- steamed sake chicken 172–73
- steamed spicy chicken *130*, 130–31
- stir-fried chicken with lemon grass, ginger and chilli 138, *138*
- stock 10
- tamarind chicken 57
- tandoori chicken 196, *196*
- teriyaki chicken 186
- tom kha gai 100, *100*
- Vietnamese chicken salad 142
- Vietnamese coleslaw 146–47
- yakitori (skewered chicken) 188–89

chickpea curry 200, *200*

chillies 13, *13*
- Balinese chilli squid 63, *63*
- chilli bean paste **29**, *29*
- chilli crab 68, *69*
- chilli flakes 13, *13*
- chilli paste 114
- chilli pork kebabs 54
- chilli powder 13, *13*
- chilli prawn and snake bean stir-fry 152
- chilli sauce 82
- chilli spare ribs 28, *28*
- cucumber salad with peanuts and chilli 123, *123*
- dried 13, *13*
- fresh 13, *13*
- garlic prawns in chilli sauce 70
- handling 11, *11*
- steamed fish cutlets with ginger and chilli 110, *110*
- stir-fried chicken with lemon grass, ginger and chilli 138, *138*
- sweet chilli sauce 148

China 20–43

Chinese barbecued pork 12, *38*, 38–39

Chinese broccoli 12, *12*

Chinese cabbage 12, *12*
- kim chi 161, *161*
- Vietnamese coleslaw 146–47

Chinese chard 12, *12*

Chinese chives 15

Chinese mushrooms, dried 16, *16*

Chinese flowering cabbage 12, *12*

Chinese fortune cookies 243

Chinese fried rice 30

Chinese green vegetables 43

Chinese kale 12, *12*

Chinese rice wine 17

Chinese vegetables 42, *42*, 43

Chinese white cabbage 12, *12*

chorizo, combination noodles with 90, *90*

choy sum 12, *12*

chutneys **214**
- coriander chutney 202
- sweet mango chutney 162, *163*

cilantro *see* coriander

clay pot chicken and vegetables 31, *31*

cleavers 8

cloud ear *see* black fungus

coconut
- banana and coconut pancakes 241, *241*
- beef fillet in coconut 46
- coconut bananas 202
- coconut gravy 233
- coconut prawn curry 222
- coconut semolina slice 240, *240*
- festive coconut rice *64*, 64–65
- fish with flaked coconut 237, *237*
- grating coconut **58**
- Malaysian coconut chicken 74
- prawns in coconut 91, *91*
- Siamese noodles in spicy coconut sauce 70–71, *71*
- spicy coconut custard 243, *243*
- vegetable coconut curry 58, *58*

coconut cream 14, *14*

coconut milk 14
- fish fillets in coconut milk 104

coffee grinder 8

combination noodles with chorizo 90, *90*

coriander 14, *14*
- coriander chutney 202
- coriander pork with fresh pineapple 111, *111*
- crisp fried whole fish with sour pepper and coriander sauce 108–9, *109*
- fried rice with coriander and basil 124–25
- storing fresh coriander 117

corn
- chicken and sweet corn soup 25
- fresh corn sambal 65

cornflour, adding 42

crab
- chilli crab  68, 69
- crab, prawn and potato fritters  138–39
- crab meat  **143**
- crabmeat dim sims  34
- crispy fried crab  27, 27
- vermicelli and crab meat stir-fry  143, 143

crepes, prawn  96, 96
crisp fried whole fish with sour pepper and coriander sauce  108–9, 109
crispy fried crab  27, 27
crispy skin chicken  39, 39
crunchy stuffed tofu puffs  82–83
crystal prawns  26–27
cucumber
- cucumber raita  202
- cucumber salad with peanuts and chilli  123, 123
- samosas and cucumber raita  207, 207

cumin  14, 14
curries
- beef, potato and okra curry  226–27
- cashew nut curry  235
- cauliflower, tomato and green pea curry  215, 215
- chicken and peanut panang  107, 107
- chicken curry  227, 227
- chickpea curry  200, 200
- coconut prawn curry  222
- curried rice noodles with chicken  116–17
- curry paste  83
- dry fish curry  226, 226
- dry potato and pea curry  195, 195
- fiery prawn curry  52, 52
- fried pork curry  222, 222
- green chicken curry  103, 103
- green curry with sweet potato and eggplant  124, 124
- hot pork curry with pumpkin  106
- Madras curry  194, 194
- Malaysian fish curry  80, 80
- pea, egg and ricotta curry  205, 205
- red pork curry  235, 235
- red vegetable curry  102, 102
- spicy beef curry  121
- Sri Lankan  **237**
- vegetable coconut curry  58, 58
- white vegetable curry  233

curry leaves  14, 14
curry pastes  9–10, 114
- balti masala paste  114
- chilli paste  114
- green curry paste  110–11
- Indonesian sambal paste  114
- red curry paste  102–3
- Thai curry pastes  **111**

curry powders
- Ceylon curry powder  114
- fish curry powder  **80**
- garam masala  114

custard
- savoury egg custard  176, 176
- spicy coconut custard  243, 243

cutting  8

daikon  14, 14
Darjeeling tea  180
dashi  14, 14
dashi stock  **174**
deep-fried spiced tofu  46, 47
deep-frying tips  9
desserts  238–47
- almond jelly  245, 245
- banana and coconut pancakes  241, 241
- Chinese fortune cookies  243
- coconut semolina slice  240, 240
- egg tarts  246, 246
- mango ice cream  244, 244
- sago pudding  241
- spicy coconut custard  243, 243
- sticky black rice  244–45
- sticky rice with mangoes  242, 242
- sweet won tons  246, 247

dhal  212, 212
dim sims, crabmeat  34
dipping sauces  see sauces
dressings  56, 56, 84, 142, 155
duck
- braised duck with mushrooms  146, 146
- chopping  11, 11
- peking duck with mandarin pancakes  32, 33
- watercress and duck salad with lychees  120, 120

dumpling soup, meat  165, 165

earl grey tea  180
egg noodles  16, 16
eggplants  14, 14
- egghoppers with eggplant (aubergine) sambol  234, 234
- eggplant kebabs with miso  187, 187
- eggplant pickle  162
- eggplant slices in black bean sauce  142, 142–43
- green curry with sweet potato and eggplant  124, 124
- spicy eggplant and fish purée in salad leaves  134–35
- spicy roasted eggplant with tofu  117, 117
- sweet garlic eggplant  43

eggs
- egg strip bundles  160
- egg tarts  246, 246
- egghoppers with eggplant (aubergine) sambol  234, 234
- eggs scrambled with prawns and peas  183
- pea, egg and ricotta curry  205, 205
- savoury egg custard  176, 176
- son-in-law eggs  121, 121
- spicy eggs and snake beans  82, 82

empanadas  97, 97
English breakfast tea  180

fenugreek  14, 14
festive coconut rice  64, 64–65
fiery prawn curry  52, 52
finger food  72, 73
fish see also seafood
- baked fish cakes  59
- baked fish with spices  57, 57
- baked spiced fish cutlets  52–53
- Balinese fried fish  60–61, 61
- crisp fried whole fish with sour pepper and coriander sauce  108–9, 109
- dry fish curry  226, 226
- fish and herb salad  84, 84
- fish and noodle soup  130
- fish balls  **77**
- fish curry powder  **80**
- fish fillets in coconut milk  104
- fish in banana leaves  220, 221

# index

*fish, contd...*
    fish soup with noodles  223, *223*
    fish with flaked coconut  237, *237*
    fish with ginger and black pepper  92–93
    grilled fish steaks  186, *186*
    hand-shaped tuna sushi  184, *185*
    Hyderabadi fish  214–15
    Indian fried fish  213, *213*
    Laotian fish balls  128–29
    Malaysian fish curry  80, *80*
    marinated salmon strips  184
    salmon nabe  189, *189*
    salmon sushi roll  172, *172*
    smoked salmon rice balls  174
    spicy eggplant and fish purée in salad leaves  134–35
    spicy grilled fish pieces  154, *154*
    steamed fish cutlets with ginger and chilli  110, *110*
    steamed fish in banana leaves  105, *105*
    stock  10
    tamarind fish  230–31
    Thai fish cakes  122, *122*
    whole barbecued fish  140, *141*
    whole steamed fish with crisp finish  40, *40*
    fish sauce  14, *14*
five-spice powder  15
five-spice salt  39
flours  15
fondue, beef, with rice paper wrappers and salad  157, *157*
Formosa tea  180
fortune cookies, Chinese  243
fried and steamed scallops with ginger  26, *26*
fried pork curry  222, *222*
fried rice noodle pancake with garlic beef  150, *150*
fried rice noodles  76, *76*
fried rice with coriander and basil  124–25
frikkadels  231, *231*
fritters
    crab, prawn and potato fritters  138–39
    Indian prawn fritters  212
    prawn fritters  88, *88*
frying tips  9
fukkien noodles  16, *16*

gado gado (vegetables with peanut sauce)  49
gai larn  12, *12*
galangal  15, *15*, **100**
garam masala  15, 114, **200**
garlic  15
    crisp fried  14, *14*
    fried rice noodle pancake with garlic beef  150, *150*
    garlic prawns in chilli sauce  70
    lemon and garlic dipping sauce  145, 148
    sweet garlic eggplant  43
garlic chives  15
genmai-cha  180
ghee  **209**
ginger  15, *15*
    fish with ginger and black pepper  92–93
    fried and steamed scallops with ginger  26, *26*
    ginger chicken with black fungus  122–23
    pickled ginger  162
    preparing  11, *11*
    soy and ginger sauce  148, 190
    steamed fish cutlets with ginger and chilli  110, *110*
    stir-fried chicken with lemon grass, ginger and chilli  138, *138*
glass noodles  *see* mung bean vermicelli
glutinous rice  94, 242
Goan spiced mussels  214, *214*
golden mountain sauce  15
golden prawn puffs  100–101
gow gee wrappers  19, *19*
green beans in sesame seed sauce  188, *188*
green chicken curry  103, *103*
green curry paste  110–11
green curry with sweet potato and eggplant  124, *124*
green onions  18, *18*
green papayas
    green papaya and peanut salad  118, *118*
    green papaya salad  133, *133*
green pawpaws  17, *17*
    green pawpaw, chicken and fresh herb salad  150–51

green tea  180
grilled fish steaks  186, *186*
grilled pork  134, *134*
grinding apparatus  8
gunpowder tea  180

hand-shaped tuna sushi  184, *185*
harusame noodles  16
hoisin sauce  15
hokkien noodles  16, *16*
holy basil  13, *13*
honey prawns  37, *37*
Hyderabadi fish  214–15

ice cream, mango  244, *244*
inari  19
inari sushi  184, *184*
India  192–217
    and the British  **214**
Indian fried fish  213, *213*
Indian prawn fritters  212
Indonesia  44–65
Indonesian rendang  59, *59*
Indonesian sambal paste  114
Irish breakfast tea  180

Japan  170–91
Japanese horseradish  19, *19*
Japanese soy sauce  18
jasmine rice  94
jasmine tea  180

kaffir lime (makrut) leaves  15
kaffir limes  15
kebabs
    chilli pork kebabs  54
    eggplant kebabs with miso  187, *187*
    teriyaki steak kebabs  54
kecap manis  15
kimchi  161, *161*
knives  8
kofta on skewers  54
Korea  158–69
Korean pasta  *see* potato starch noodles
Korean vermicelli  *see* potato starch noodles

ladies' finger  *see* okra
laksa leaf  19, *19*

251

lamb
    balti lamb 204–5
    lamb dopiaza 208–9
    lamb kofta 201, *201*
    lamb with palm sugar 230, *230*
    Malaysian lamb satays 54
    rotis with spicy meat filling *74,* 74–75
    spiced roast leg of lamb 217, *217*
Laos 126–35
Laotian beef salad 132–33
Laotian dried beef with green papaya salad 133, *133*
Laotian fish balls 128–29
lapsang souchong 180
larb (spicy pork salad) 104, *104*
leeks, stir-fried prawns with 30, *30*
lemon basil *12,* 12–13
lemon grass 15, *15,* **138**
    lemon grass beef skewers 135, *135*
    preparing 11, *11*
    steamed mussels with lemon grass, basil and wine 112, *112*
    stir-fried chicken with lemon grass, ginger and chilli 138, *138*
lemons
    Cantonese lemon chicken 23, *23*
    lemon and garlic dipping sauce 145, 148
    lemon sauce 23
lentils
    dhal 212, *212*
    hot lentil soup 195
    lentil bhuja casserole 199, *199*
    Sri Lankan lentils 236
lettuce
    pork and lettuce parcels *144,* 145
    Vietnamese lettuce-wrapped spring rolls 147, *147*
    Vietnamese pancakes in lettuce parcels 153, *153*
limes
    lime oil pickle 162, *163*
    nonya lime chicken 83, *83*
    prawns in lime coconut sauce *106,* 106–7
long beans  *see* snake beans
long-grain rice 94
lychees, watercress and duck salad with 120, *120*

Madras curry 194, *194*
Malaysia 66–85
Malaysian coconut chicken 74
Malaysian fish curry 80, *80*
Malaysian lamb satays 54
Malaysian rendang 80–81
mandarin
    beef with mandarin 24, *24*
    dried mandarin peel **24**
    peking duck with mandarin pancakes 32, *33*
mangoes
    mango ice cream 244, *244*
    sticky rice with mangoes 242, *242*
    sweet mango chutney 162, *163*
marinated salmon strips 184
marinating **132**
meat *see also* beef; lamb; pork
    meat dumpling soup 165, *165*
    preparing 11, *11*
mee goreng (fried noodles) 53, *53*
mee grob 112–13
mint
    fresh mint relish 202
    Vietnamese 19, *19*
    yoghurt and mint raita 202
mirin 17
miso 15, *15*
    eggplant kebabs with miso 187, *187*
    tofu miso soup 174, *174*
mixed sashimi 173, *173*
mortar and pestle 8, *10*
mung bean vermicelli 16, *16,* **150**
    vermicelli and crab meat stir-fry 143, *143*
    vermicelli with stir-fried beef and vegetables 168–69
    vermicelli with stir-fried squid and tomatoes 154–55
mushrooms 16, *16*
    braised duck with mushrooms 146, *146*
    rice with chicken and mushrooms 190–91
mussels
    Goan spiced mussels 214, *214*
    steamed mussels with lemon grass, basil and wine 112, *112*

naan 210
napa cabbage  *see* Chinese cabbage
nasi goreng (fried rice) 46
nonya food **83**
nonya lime chicken 83, *83*
noodle-coated prawns 190, *190*
noodles 16–17, *16–17 see also* rice noodles; udon noodles
    combination noodles with chorizo 90, *90*
    etiquette for eating **183**
    fish and noodle soup 130
    fish soup with noodles 223, *223*
    mee goreng 53, *53*
    mixed noodle and rice salad 224, *224*
    noodles with prawns and pork 29, *29*
    pork ball soup with noodles 156, *156*
    prawn and noodle soup 75, *75*
    Siamese noodles in spicy coconut sauce 70–71, *71*
nori 17, *17*

okra 17, *17*
    beef, potato and okra curry 226–27
omelettes
    chicken omelette with coconut gravy *232,* 233
    prawn omelette with oyster sauce 22, *22*
    stuffed prawn omelettes 108, *108*
onions
    crisp fried 14, *14*
    onion bhaji 197
oolong tea 180
oxtail and vegetable stew 92, *92*
oyster sauce 17

pad thai 113, *113*
Pakistan 192–217
palm sugar 17, *17*
pancakes
    banana and coconut pancakes 241, *241*
    fried rice noodle pancake with garlic beef 150, *150*
    peking duck with mandarin pancakes 32, *33*
    shredded potato pancakes 164, *164*
    split pea and rice pancakes 168, *168*
    Vietnamese pancakes in lettuce parcels 153, *153*

# index

pandanus leaves **245**
papayas *see* green papayas
parathas 210
pastry 97, *97*
pawpaws, green *see* green pawpaws
peanuts
   chicken and peanut panang curry 107, *107*
   cucumber salad with peanuts and chilli 123, *123*
   green papaya and peanut salad 118, *118*
peanut satay sauce 148
   peanut sauce 49
peas
   cauliflower, tomato and green pea curry 215, *215*
   dry potato and pea curry 195, *195*
   eggs scrambled with prawns and peas 183
   pea, egg and ricotta curry 205, *205*
peking duck with mandarin pancakes 32, *33*
peppery pork with vegetables 156–57
Phillipines 86–97
   Spanish influence **91**
pickles 162, *163*
   eggplant pickle 162
   lime oil pickle 162, *163*
   pickled ginger 162
pickled vegetables 162
pineapples
   chicken with pineapple and cashews 151, *151*
   coriander pork with fresh pineapple 111, *111*
plum sauce 17
poppadoms 210
pork
   barbecued Chinese 12, *38*, 38–39
   chilli pork kebabs 54
   chilli spare ribs 28, *28*
   chopping pork mince 153
   coriander pork with fresh pineapple 111, *111*
   empanadas 97, *97*
   fried pork curry 222, *222*
   grilled pork 134, *134*
   hot pork curry with pumpkin 106

*pork, contd...*
   larb (spicy pork salad) 104, *104*
   meat dumpling soup 165, *165*
   noodles with prawns and pork 29, *29*
   pad thai 113, *113*
   peppery pork with vegetables 156–57
   pork and lettuce parcels *144*, 145
   pork ball soup with noodles 156, *156*
   pork sambalan 56
   pork vindaloo 197, *197*
   pork with plum sauce 42–43
   pork with spinach 164–65
   red pork curry 235, *235*
   seared pork skewers 145
   Singapore spare ribs 84–85, *85*
   spareribs with sesame seeds 167, *167*
   sweet and sour pork 40–41
   sweet kecap pork 62, *62*
   tonkatsu *178*, 178–79
   Vietnamese pancakes in lettuce parcels 153, *153*
   Vietnamese pork and prawn salad 155, *155*
potato starch noodles 16
   potato noodles with vegetables 166, *166*
potatoes
   beef, potato and okra curry 226–27
   crab, prawn and potato fritters 138–39
   dry potato and pea curry 195, *195*
   shredded potato pancakes 164, *164*
prawns
   caramelised prawns 139, *139*
   chilli prawn and snake bean stir-fry 152
   coconut prawn curry 222
   crystal prawns 26–27
   eggs scrambled with prawns and peas 183
   fiery prawn curry 52, *52*
   garlic prawns in chilli sauce 70
   golden prawn puffs 100–101
   honey prawns 37, *37*
   Indian prawn fritters 212
   mee goreng (fried noodles) 53, *53*
   mee grob 112–13
   noodle-coated prawns 190, *190*
   noodles with prawns and pork 29, *29*
   peeling 11, *11*

*prawns, contd...*
   prawn and noodle soup 75, *75*
   prawn and vegetable tempura 176, *177*
   prawn crepes 96, *96*
   prawn filling 96, *96*
   prawn fritters 88, *88*
   prawn gow gees 34
   prawn laksa 76–77, *77*
   prawn omelette with oyster sauce 22, *22*
   prawn toasts 72, *73*
   prawns in coconut 91, *91*
   prawns in lime coconut sauce *106*, 106–7
   prawns steamed in banana leaves 131, *131*
   spicy prawns in sarongs 79, *79*
   stir-fried prawns with leeks 30, *30*
   stuffed prawn omelettes 108, *108*
   tom yum goong 101, *101*
   Vietnamese pancakes in lettuce parcels 153, *153*
   Vietnamese pork and prawn salad 155, *155*
preparation techniques 11, *11*
pumpkin
   chicken and pumpkin stew 129, *129*
   hot pork curry with pumpkin 106
   sweet braised pumpkin 152, *152*
purées
   Laotian **135**
   spicy eggplant and fish purée in salad leaves 134–35
puris 210
purple basil 13, *13*

raitas
   carrot raita 202
   cucumber raita 202
   samosas and cucumber raita 207, *207*
   yoghurt and mint raita 202
red curry paste 102–3
red pork curry 235, *235*
red vegetable curry 102, *102*
relishes
   fresh mint relish 202
   fresh tomato relish 202

rice
   Balinese fried rice  60, *60*
   Burmese-style  **225**
   Chinese fried rice  30
   cooking methods  94
   festive coconut rice  *64,* 64–65
   fried rice with coriander and basil  124–25
   mixed noodle and rice salad  224, *224*
   nasi goreng  46
   rice with chicken and mushrooms  190–91
   rice with chicken and seafood  89, *89*
   smoked salmon rice balls  174
   split pea and rice pancakes with vegetables  168, *168*
   sticky  **242**
   sticky black rice  244–45
   sticky rice with mangoes  242, *242*
   types of  94
rice flour, Asian  15
rice noodles  16, *16*
   beef soup with rice noodles  50, *50*
   curried rice noodles with chicken  116–17
   fried rice noodle pancake with garlic beef  150, *150*
   fried rice noodles  76, *76*
   rice stick noodles  16, *16*
rice paper wrappers  19, *19*
   beef fondue with rice paper wrappers and salad  157, *157*
rice vermicelli  16, *16*
rice vinegar  17
rice wine  17, **23**
ricotta
   pea, egg and ricotta curry  205, *205*
rogan josh  198, *198*
rotis with spicy meat filling  *74,* 74–75
russian caravan tea  180

saag paneer  208, *208*
saffron  17, *17,* **206**
   saffron yoghurt chicken  206, *206*
sago pudding  241
sake  17

salads
   beef fondue with rice paper wrappers and salad  157, *157*
   chicken and vegetable salad  116, *116*
   cold vegetable salad with spice dressing  56, *56*
   cucumber salad with peanuts and chilli  123, *123*
   fish and herb salad  84, *84*
   green papaya and peanut salad  118, *118*
   green papaya salad  133, *133*
   green pawpaw, chicken and fresh herb salad  150–51
   Laotian beef salad  132–33
   larb (spicy pork salad)  104, *104*
   mixed noodle and rice salad  224, *224*
   mixed vegetable salad  70, *70,* 221
   Thai  **125**
   Thai beef salad  125, *125*
   Vietnamese chicken salad  142
   Vietnamese coleslaw  146–47
   Vietnamese pork and prawn salad  155, *155*
   warm beef and watercress salad  145
   watercress and duck salad with lychees  120, *120*
salmon
   marinated salmon strips  184
   salmon nabe  189, *189*
   salmon sushi roll  172, *172*
   smoked salmon rice balls  174
salt, five-spice  39
sambal oelek  18, *18*
sambol, eggplant (aubergine)  234, *234*
samosas and cucumber raita  207, *207*
sashimi  **173**
   mixed sashimi  173, *173*
satays
   chicken satays  54
   Malaysian lamb satays  54
   peanut satay sauce  148
sauces
   caramel sauce  139
   chilli sauce  82
   dipping sauce  118, 148, 153, *153,* 164, 178, 179
   lemon and garlic dipping sauce  145, 148
   lemon sauce  23

*sauces, contd...*
   peanut satay sauce  148
   peanut sauce  49
   sesame seed sauce  148, 189
   soy and ginger sauce  148, 190
   sweet chilli sauce  148
   Thai dipping sauce  148
   Vietnamese dipping sauce  147, 148
   yoghurt dipping sauce  231
savoury egg custard  176, *176*
scallions  18, *18*
scallops, fried and steamed with ginger  26, *26*
seafood *see also* fish
   Balinese chilli squid  63, *63*
   barbecued seafood  *78,* 79
   caramelised prawns  139, *139*
   chilli crab  *68,* 69
   chilli prawn and snake bean stir-fry  152
   coconut prawn curry  222
   crab, prawn and potato fritters  138–39
   crispy fried crab  27, *27*
   crystal prawns  26–27
   eggs scrambled with prawns and peas  183
   fiery prawn curry  52, *52*
   fried and steamed scallops with ginger  26, *26*
   garlic prawns in chilli sauce  70
   Goan spiced mussels  214, *214*
   golden prawn puffs  100–101
   honey prawns  37, *37*
   Indian prawn fritters  212
   mee goreng (fried noodles)  53, *53*
   mee grob  112–13
   noodle-coated prawns  190, *190*
   noodles with prawns and pork  29, *29*
   prawn and vegetable tempura  176, *177*
   prawn crepes  96, *96*
   prawn fritters  88, *88*
   prawn gow gees  34
   prawn laksa  76–77, *77*
   prawn omelette with oyster sauce  22, *22*
   prawn toasts  72, *73*
   prawns in coconut  91, *91*
   prawns in lime coconut sauce  *106,* 106–7
   prawns steamed in banana leaves  131, *131*

# index

*seafood, contd...*
   rice with chicken and seafood  89, *89*
   seafood soup  128, *128*
   seafood won tons  72
   spicy prawns in sarongs  79, *79*
   spicy seafood  236, *236*
   steamed mussels with lemon grass, basil and wine  112, *112*
   stir-fried prawns with leeks  30, *30*
   stuffed prawn omelettes  108, *108*
   tom yum goong  101, *101*
   vermicelli and crab meat stir-fry  143, *143*
   vermicelli with stir-fried squid and tomatoes  154–55
   Vietnamese pork and prawn salad  155, *155*
seared pork skewers  145
seasoning mix  27
seaweed
   sesame and seaweed sprinkle  **167**
sencha tea  180
sesame oil  18
sesame seeds  18, *18*
   green beans in sesame seed sauce  188, *188*
   sesame and seaweed sprinkle  **167**
   sesame seed sauce  148, 189
   spareribs with sesame seeds  167, *167*
   steak in roasted sesame seed marinade  178
shallots, red Asian  18, *18*
shanghai noodles  17, *17*
shaosing  17
shaoxing rice wine  **23**
shichimi togarashi  **179**
shiitake mushrooms  16, *16*
shirataki noodles  17, *17*
short-grain rice  94
shoshoyu  18
shredded potato pancakes  164, *164*
shrimp paste  18, *18*, **64, 88**
shrimp sauce  *see* bagoong
Siamese noodles in spicy coconut sauce  70–71, *71*
Sichuan cooking  **37**
Sichuan soup  36, *36*
Singapore  66–85

Singapore noodles  16, *16*, 69, *69*
Singapore spare ribs  84–85, *85*
skewers *see also* kebabs; satays
   kofta on skewers  54
   lemon grass beef skewers  135, *135*
   seared pork skewers  145
   skewers of beef, capsicum and spring onion  191, *191*
   yakitori (skewered chicken)  188–89
smoked five-spice chicken  41, *41*
smoked salmon rice balls  174
snake beans  18, *18*
   chilli prawn and snake bean stir-fry  152
   spicy eggs and snake beans  82, *82*
   stir-fried cauliflower and snake beans  109
snow peas, stir-fried beef and  28
soba (buckwheat) noodles  16, *16*
   chilled soba noodles  179, *179*
somen noodles  17, *17*
son-in-law eggs  121, *121*
soups
   beef pho  141, *141*
   beef soup with rice noodles  50, *50*
   chicken and sweet corn soup  25
   chicken soup with vermicelli and vegetables  48, *49*
   fish and noodle soup  130
   fish soup with noodles  223, *223*
   hot lentil soup  195
   meat dumpling soup  165, *165*
   pork ball soup with noodles  156, *156*
   prawn and noodle soup  75, *75*
   seafood soup  128, *128*
   sichuan soup  36, *36*
   sour beef soup  96–97
   tofu miso soup  174, *174*
   twelve varieties soup  225, *225*
   udon noodle soup  *182*, 183
   won ton soup  25, *25*
sour beef soup  96–97
soy and ginger sauce  148, 190
soy sauce  18, **31**
spare ribs
   chilli spare ribs  28, *28*
   Singapore spare ribs  84–85, *85*
   spareribs with sesame seeds  167, *167*
spice dressing  56, *56*

spice paste  52, 62, 63, 70–71, 79, 80, 130
spiced roast leg of lamb  217, *217*
spices
   dry-roasting  10, *10*
   grinding  8
spicy beef curry  121
spicy coconut custard  243, *243*
spicy eggplant and fish purée in salad leaves  134–35
spicy eggs and snake beans  82, *82*
spicy grilled fish pieces  154, *154*
spicy prawns in sarongs  79, *79*
spicy roast chicken  50, *51*
spicy roasted eggplant with tofu  117, *117*
spicy seafood  236, *236*
spinach, pork with  164–65
split pea and rice pancakes with vegetables  168, *168*
spring onions  18, *18*
   skewers of beef, capsicum and spring onion  191, *191*
spring rolls  **71**
   fresh spring rolls  118, *119*
   spring roll wrappers  19, *19*
   Thai spring rolls  72, *73*
   Vietnamese lettuce-wrapped spring rolls  147, *147*
squid
   Balinese chilli squid  63, *63*
   vermicelli with stir-fried squid and tomatoes  154–55
Sri Lanka  228–37
Sri Lankan lentils  236
star anise  18, *18*
steak in roasted sesame seed marinade  178
steamed food
   steamed fish cutlets with ginger and chilli  110, *110*
   steamed fish in banana leaves  105, *105*
   steamed fish with crisp finish  40, *40*
   steamed mussels with lemon grass, basil and wine  112, *112*
   steamed sake chicken  172–73
   steamed spicy chicken  *130*, 130–31
   steaming tips  9

stews
   chicken and pumpkin stew 129, *129*
   chicken stew 169, *169*
   oxtail and vegetable stew 92, *92*
sticky black rice 244–45
sticky rice with mangoes 242, *242*
stir fries
   chilli prawn and snake bean stir-fry 152
   stir-fried beef and snow peas 28
   stir-fried cauliflower and snake beans 109
   stir-fried chicken with lemon grass, ginger and chilli 138, *138*
   stir-fried hot beef 62–63
   stir-fried prawns with leeks 30, *30*
   stir-fried vegetables 43
   stir-frying tips 9
   vermicelli with stir-fried beef and vegetables 168–69
   vermicelli with stir-fried squid and tomatoes 154–55
stocks 10, **174**
straw mushrooms 16, *16*
stuffed prawn omelettes 108, *108*
sukiyaki 175
sushi **173**
   hand-shaped tuna sushi 184, *185*
   inari sushi 184, *184*
   salmon sushi roll 172, *172*
sweet and sour pork 40–41
sweet braised pumpkin 152, *152*
sweet chilli sauce 148
sweet corn  *see* corn
sweet garlic eggplant 43
sweet kecap pork 62, *62*
sweet mango chutney 162, *163*
sweet potato and eggplant, green curry with 124, *124*
sweet soy sauce 15
sweet won tons 246, *247*

tamarind 19, *19*, **101**
   mixed vegetables with tamarind 65, *65*
   tamarind chicken 57
   tamarind fish 230–31
tandoor oven **196**
tandoori 196
   tandoori chicken 196, *196*
tangerine, dried peel 24

teas 180
   brewing 180
techniques, preparation 11, *11*
tempura, prawn and vegetable 176, *177*
teriyaki chicken 186
teriyaki steak kebabs 54
Thai basil 12, *12*
Thai beef salad 125, *125*
Thai curry pastes **111**
Thai dipping sauce 148
Thai fish cakes 122, *122*
Thai meals **123**
Thai salads **125**
Thai spring rolls 72, *73*
Thailand 98–125
tofu 19, *19,* **46**
   crunchy stuffed tofu puffs 82–83
   deep-fried spiced tofu 46, *47*
   spicy roasted eggplant with tofu 117, *117*
   tofu miso soup 174, *174*
   tofu pouches 19
tom kha gai 100, *100*
tom yum goong 101, *101*
tomatoes
   cauliflower, tomato and green pea curry 215, *215*
   fresh tomato relish 202
   vermicelli with stir-fried squid and tomatoes 154–55
tonkatsu *178,* 178–79
tuna sushi, hand-shaped 184, *185*
turmeric 19, *19*

udon noodles 17, *17*
   udon noodle soup 182, *183*

vegetables
   chicken and vegetable salad 116, *116*
   Chinese vegetables 42, *42,* 43
   cold vegetable salad with spice dressing 56, *56*
   gado gado (vegetables with peanut sauce) 49
   mixed vegetable salad 70, *70,* 221
   mixed vegetables with tamarind 65, *65*
   oxtail and vegetable stew 92, *92*
   peppery pork with vegetables 156–57
   pickled vegetables 162

*vegetables, contd...*
   preparing 11, *11*
   red vegetable curry 102, *102*
   stir-fried vegetables 43
   vegetable coconut curry 58, *58*
   vegetable korma 200–201
   vegetable pakoras 216, *216*
   vegetarian won tons 72
   white vegetable curry 233
vermicelli and crab meat stir-fry 143, *143*
vermicelli with stir-fried beef and vegetables 168–69
vermicelli with stir-fried squid and tomatoes 154–55
Vietnam 136–57
Vietnamese chicken salad 142
Vietnamese coleslaw 146–47
Vietnamese dipping sauce 147, 148
Vietnamese lettuce-wrapped spring rolls 147, *147*
Vietnamese mint 19, *19*
Vietnamese pancakes in lettuce parcels 153, *153*
Vietnamese pork and prawn salad 155, *155*
vinegar, rice 17

wasabi 19, *19*
water chestnuts 19, *19*
watercress 19
   warm beef and watercress salad 145
   watercress and duck salad with lychees 120, *120*
woks 8
won ton soup 25, *25*
won tons
   seafood won tons 72
   sweet won tons 246, *247*
   vegetarian won tons 72
   won ton wrappers 19, *19*

yakitori (skewered chicken) 188–89
yard-long beans  *see* snake beans
yoghurt **198**
   saffron yoghurt chicken 206, *206*
   yoghurt and mint raita 202
   yoghurt dipping sauce 231
yum cha 34–35, *34–35*
yunnan tea 180